Born in 1926, Sir Ronald Waterhouse, GBE grew up in a Liberal family in North Wales. Wartime service in the RAF led to study of Law at Cambridge and he was called to the Bar at Middle Temple in 1952. His long and distinguished legal career encompassed a diverse practice as barrister and silk before becoming a High Court judge in 1978. He was married to Lady Sarah Waterhouse and had three children. He died shortly after completing this memoir in 2011 at the age of 85.

CHILD OF ANOTHER CENTURY

Recollections of a High Court Judge

RONALD WATERHOUSE

THE RADCLIFFE PRESS
LONDON • NEW YORK

For Sarah, Thomas, Sophie and Laura,
the most important of all

Published in 2013 by The Radcliffe Press
An imprint of I.B.Tauris & Co Ltd
6 Salem Road, London W2 4BU
175 Fifth Avenue, New York NY 10010
www.ibtauris.com

Distributed in the United States and Canada Exclusively by Palgrave Macmillan
175 Fifth Avenue, New York NY 10010

ISBN: 978 1 78076 499 3

A full CIP record for this book is available from the British Library
A full CIP record is available from the Library of Congress

Library of Congress Catalog Card Number: available

Typeset by JCS Publishing Services Ltd, www.jcs-publishing.co.uk
Printed and bound by CPI Group (UK) Ltd, Croydon, CR0 4YY

CONTENTS

List of Illustrations   vii
Preface   ix

1   Roots   1
2   Background   8
3   Beginnings   14
4   County Schoolboy   19
5   Bird without Wings   31
6   Cambridge Proper   45
7   Apprentice Barrister   59
8   The Welsh Bar in the 1950s   70
9   Barrister's Devil   84
10   Spreading my Wings   99
11   Settling Down   110
12   Some Notable Trials in the 1960s   124
13   In the Front Row   140
14   The Perils of Libel Litigation   151
15   Forays to Singapore   166
16   Some Public Diversions   182
17   Farewell to the Bar   191
18   Judicial Springtime   203
19   Presiding Judge for Wales and Cheshire   218
20   Soldiering on in the Family Division   233
21   Queen's Bench Judge   245
22   Family Events and More Extra-judicial Activity   261
23   Middle Temple Treasurer   268

24 Winding up to the North Wales Tribunal   276
25 Winding Down   287

Index   299

ILLUSTRATIONS

1   Portrait of the author, Sir Ronald Waterhouse, in evening dress, wearing the insignia of the honour of Knight Grand Cross of the British Empire (GBE)

2   The author in the garden of the Middle Temple in the year that he was Treasurer, 1995

3   The author in his robe as GBE at the service of dedication to the Order

4   Cambridge Union Society, Michaelmas term, 1950, when the author was president

5   Robin Day and Norman St John Stevas at the Oxford and Cambridge Union Boat Race

6   The author on his graduation day, 1951

7   Portrait of Sir William Mars-Jones wearing the clothes of a Queen's Counsel

8   Sarah Ingram, engagement picture, 1960

9   Wedding of the author and Sarah Ingram at the Temple Church, London on 16 July 1960

10   The author dressed as a Queen's Counsel on the day he took silk, 1969

11   At the baptism of Alexander Day, June 1974

12   The author as QC leading Leon Brittan in a libel case at Sheffield, 1976

13   The author at the House of Lords on the day he was sworn in as a High Court judge by the Lord Chancellor, 9 January 1978

14   The author with daughter Laura and Orlando in Regent's Park, early 1980s

15 The author as president of the Llangollen International Eisteddfod

16 The author at a holiday house in L'Isle-sur-la-Sorgue, Provence, relaxing after a very busy summer, 1995

17 The author with his wife Sarah at Buckingham Palace to receive his GBE from the Prince of Wales, 17 April 2002

18 The author with Sarah at the Middle Temple Hall for a dinner in honour of Gavin Arthur, November 2002

19 Laura Waterhouse's wedding in May 2003

20 The countryside near the author's home in Herefordshire

21 The author in his garden in Herefordshire with daughter Sophie and their beloved Labrador, Benjy

22 Thomas Waterhouse in New York in the 1980s

23 The author's grandsons: David, James and Mark

24 Sophie Waterhouse in an olive grove in Rhodes, 1993

25 Sophie in Lindos, 1993

26 The author and Sarah in Herefordshire, early 2000s

27 Breakfast in Herefordshire in 2009 with the author, Laura and Andrew Shakeshaft

28 The author at one of his favourite restaurants in Venasque, in Provence, in October 2007

PREFACE

Unless one is an important person or a celebrity, there is no really acceptable excuse now for writing one's autobiography, still less for publishing it, and I fall far short of either requirement. Like most children, however, I failed to ask my parents a host of questions about their pasts and have lived on to regret the omission deeply. I began writing these memoirs, therefore, mainly for my wife and children and for anyone else in my family who cares to read them. It was convenient also to do so because I had accumulated throughout my life vast mounds of paper associated with my activities and there was a pressing need to reduce them drastically, a process that involved reliving my life rather self-indulgently anyway.

The result has emerged over many months and it has slowly dawned upon me that most of the institutions and patterns of existence that dominated my life have disappeared with the century that shaped me. I was reared in Nonconformist North Wales, attended a Welsh county (later grammar) school and went on to a male-dominated and largely segregated university. I chose the Bar as a profession when Assizes and Quarter Sessions still convened to administer justice in the shires and large cities, and they continued to do so for another 20 years. I joined the Wales and Chester Circuit, which only existed as such for just over 50 years, during almost the whole of which period I was a member, albeit in an honorary capacity latterly. Then, as a High Court judge, I sat all over England and Wales under the aegis of real Lord Chancellors, who were effective independent heads of the judiciary before the ill-thought-out changes under Tony Blair and before judicial work became bedevilled by artificial human rights issues and political (or at least quasi-political) decisions. It may, therefore, be of some historical interest to record a lawyer's life in the second half of the twentieth century in some detail.

One other aspect of my life is worth mentioning, namely, my extraordinary good fortune in knowing and becoming friends with truly outstanding individuals in every phase of my life. It began at school with my French teacher Sarah Grace Cooke, the Miss Moffat of Emlyn Williams' *The Corn is Green*. At Cambridge, there was the star of my generation, Percy Cradock, who became our ambassador to China and then adviser to Prime Minister Margaret Thatcher. It is invidious to name only a few of the many, but, when I was a Bar student there was Robin Day, who became a lifelong friend, and my exceptional mentor and pupil master Bill Mars-Jones, who never forgot his roots in Llansannan. There were other great figures in the University of Wales: Edmund Davies, Cledwyn Hughes, Elwyn Jones and Gareth Williams, as well as my friend from schooldays, Professor J. Gwynn Williams of Bangor, who became president of the National Library of Wales. Above all, perhaps, the brave and modest Tasker Watkins VC on the one hand and the charming polymath Solly Zuckerman OM on the other. They have enriched my life and I would like to play a part in keeping memories of them alive.

The reader will not find much bitterness or character assassination in these pages, even though most of my contemporaries are now dead. I regret to say that I am now as grumpy as most old men about the twenty-first-century scene, but life has been exceptionally kind to me and I am deeply grateful to everyone who has contributed to that, most especially my dear wife and children, to whom this book is dedicated.

1

ROOTS

I was born in a large redbrick house overlooking the river Dee estuary to Liverpool and beyond on 8 May 1926, in the middle of the General Strike. That date in the year was to assume much greater significance 19 years later when it became VE Day, but on my birthday *The Times* newspaper (price two pence) was limited to a mere four pages because of the strike, and its main report was of a speech by Sir John Simon to the House of Commons denouncing the strike as illegal. As for the view, which extended to Blackpool Tower on the brightest days, it suffused the first 18 years of my life and probably induced in me, at least temporarily, a rather exaggerated idea of my place in the world.

The house, called Highfield, was a mile or so east of the town of Holywell in Flintshire, on the main highway from Chester into North Wales. Holywell then, like Flintshire, was a rather uneasy amalgam of English and Welsh, urban and rural. It was said to be in decline in my time because earlier, by the end of the seventeenth century, it had been the largest town in north-east Wales. Much of its importance was attributable to St Winifred's Well, a Roman Catholic shrine and focus of pilgrimage, and Basingwerk Abbey, dating from the twelfth century, which was responsible for the well and various mills, malt-houses, markets and fairs under royal charter. From those beginnings, large-scale development followed in the eighteenth century in the course of the Industrial Revolution, making use of the considerable volume of water draining from limestone hills above and to the south of Holywell. Thus, by the end of that century, copperworking factories and cotton mills were firmly established in the Greenfield valley, immediately below Holywell, as well as lead mines in the higher surrounding area. The later decline was evidenced by census figures of 13,342 in 1851, compared with 9,809 in 1911.

My own family presence in Holywell dated from 1874, the year in which my paternal grandfather, Thomas Holmes Waterhouse, a Yorkshireman, was appointed secretary of the Welsh Flannel Manufacturing Company, which was formed that year by Urias Bromley, who had the necessary technical knowledge, and William Brown, of the well-known department store Browns of Chester (now owned by Debenhams). The new company with Bromley as manager operated two mills, the Crescent (or Lower) Mill, a former cotton mill, and the Upper Mill spinning and weaving flannel, which were operations that had been carried on there by earlier owners for about a quarter of a century and provided about 200 jobs, some of the workers being housed opposite the factory in a terrace called 'the barracks'. The six-storey Upper Mill was destroyed by fire in 1883 but it was replaced the following year by a three-storey mill; the factory survived another fire in 1898, which necessitated further rebuilding.

My grandfather was only 26 years old when he became secretary of this company. He had been born in Bradford on 22 May 1848, one of seven children of another Thomas, born 40 years earlier, who became a bookseller and estate agent in Bradford after a period as a schoolmaster in Eccleshill, the suburb of Bradford in which he was born. Grandfather Thomas was brought up in Northgate, Bradford, near the Lord Nelson Inn, and was apprenticed as a wool stapler for four or five years before being employed (I know not in what role) in Chester for another five years. He remained secretary of the flannel manufacturing company at Holywell for 25 years until he succeeded Urias Bromley as manager, only three years before his untimely death from pneumonia on 23 February 1902, at the age of 53. His wife, my paternal grandmother, had already died in 1895; she was Eliza Sarah Sanders, who had been born in Totnes in Devon in 1846 and married my grandfather in March 1876, quite soon after his move to Holywell. Her death also was attributed to pneumonia, said to have been contributed to by rheumatic fever that she had contracted as a child when she fell into the river Dart.

The result of these early deaths was that my father, also named Thomas but always called Tom, the second of eight children of my grandparents, found himself responsible for six younger siblings, aged between 13 and 22, when he himself was just a month short of his twenty-fourth birthday. He had to shoulder this responsibility because his eldest brother, Sidney, then 25 years old, was already married to a Totnes cousin and committed to training for the Congregational ministry at Lancashire Independent College in Whalley Range, Manchester, having graduated from the University College of Wales, Aberystwyth. He was ordained in October 1903 and remained in that ministry, latterly at Hemel Hempstead and then Rayleigh in Essex, until his retirement about 50 years later.

Faced with this daunting prospect, my father's first major decision was to bicycle the 17 miles to Chester to see the controlling shareholder of the flannel manufacturing company, Harry Brown, a son of the company's founder. My father's bold request was to be appointed manager forthwith in succession to his father, and it required extraordinary faith on Mr Brown's part to accede to this. My father had joined the company's staff after attending Oswestry High School for Boys (founded in 1407) as a weekly boarder with his brother Harold but his general experience was obviously very limited. Nevertheless, after taking a weekend to consider the matter, Mr Brown agreed to my father's request, with the result that my father remained with the company, latterly as chairman and managing director, for another 55 years until the company was sold.

Despite the difficulties facing them, my father's brothers and sisters were dispersed quite successfully. Harold, the third eldest, went to Bradford to join his uncle David, who had taken over the estate agency started by my great-grandfather in 1844 and which was continued by David under the name of David Waterhouse and Nephews at Britannia House, Bradford. Harold prospered there: he was a prominent Rotarian and Freemason and became Deputy Lord Mayor during the Second World War but he died, aged 67, on 10 July 1947.

My father's youngest sister, Minnie, born on 16 March 1886, went to Bradford with Harold. She was said to have been very artistic and vivacious and shortly before the First World War she married William (Billy) Ogden, the eldest son of the founder of Ogdens of Harrogate, jewellers and diamond merchants, who opened their first shop in that attractive Yorkshire spa in 1893 and a branch in Duke Street, St James's in London, at the end of that war. In 1925 Billy left the company to set up his own business in London, and later his charming and philanthropic son, my cousin Richard, established the highly successful jewellery business at 28 Burlington Arcade that bears his own name and continues to thrive. Richard died on 14 October 2005, leaving his eldest son Robert to run the business. Sadly, Minnie's marriage to Billy was unhappy, despite the birth of Richard and two attractive sisters, Lorna and Jean: Billy was said to be fond of rich living and fast cars and Minnie died tragically at my parents' home in 1922, aged only 36.

My father's other brothers and sisters, with the exception of Beatrice Maud (Bea), all survived into their eighties. Bea, who had a good contralto voice, as does her daughter Barbara, married a Wesleyan Methodist minister, Christopher Dawson, who became a missionary in India for several years.

They returned to the UK at the end of the First World War and lived for seven years in Holywell, where two sons, Robert and Peter, were born and Christopher, who had left the ministry, was employed as secretary of the Welsh Textile Manufacturers' Association. He then resumed his ministry, serving successively in the East Midlands, Portsmouth, Dorset and finally Portsmouth again. Bea died on 7 December 1948, shortly before her sixty-fourth birthday, and Christopher, who was a few months younger than her, survived her by only 15 months.

Ethel was the only sibling of my father to remain single. She was born on 17 November 1881 and eventually became a pastry cook, working as such for Kettles in Finchley Road, Hampstead. She lived in a flat in Mapesbury Road, Brondesbury, where I stayed with her for a time during my Royal Air Force (RAF) service, before she retired to Holywell to live with her brother Horace. The proprietor of Kettles may now be remembered only as the father of Professor Arnold Kettle, a lifelong communist, who was a member of the party's executive committee. Arnold was otherwise a distinguished literary critic and the first professor of literature at the Open University: my aunt greatly admired him despite (rather than because of) his political views.

My youngest paternal uncle was Edgar, who was orphaned at the age of only 13 years and went to live with his cousins in Totnes, later training as an electrical engineer at Bradford Technical College, apparently at the expense of his eldest brother, Sidney. He became a great friend of Billy Ogden and volunteered with him for army service on the day when the First World War began, being commissioned later in the Royal Army Service Corps and serving in Egypt. He was employed by GEC at Witton from 1936 and lived latterly at Sutton Coldfield with his unmarried daughter Joyce, after the death of his wife late in the Second World War; he himself died on 2 February 1973, aged 83.

Thus it was that my father and his brother Horace, who was born in 1884, were left to carry the Waterhouse flag in Holywell, and they remained prominent in town and county affairs for the next 60 years. Horace was young enough to be educated at the new Holywell County School, which opened in 1895, and he married a local girl, Gladys Hughes, who unhappily succumbed to dementia at quite an early age, possibly as the result of an accidental fall from a first-floor window when cleaning it. Horace's main business career was as manager of the Gwalia Shirt (Manufacturing) Company Limited in the Greenfield valley, but he was also a partner with my father in T. and H. Waterhouse, wool merchants, a firm that bought wool directly from farmers – one of only three such firms permitted to do so in North Wales under the wool rationing scheme that operated during the Second World War. Major other interests in Horace's life were the English Congregational (Tabernacle) Church in Holywell and the Urban District Council. He was a deacon and secretary of that church, as well as superintendent of its Sunday school, for over 50 years: he served on the council for a similar period, for which service he received the MBE in 1958. In the end he outlived my father by nearly three years, dying on 22 April 1964 and bringing to an end the residence of Waterhouses in Holywell after 90 years.

I have included rather a lengthy account of my father's generation of the family because it gives an accurate picture of our modest social background and explains how a large and young alien family in North Wales coped when orphaned early in the twentieth century. My father himself remained a bachelor until 1915, living with Horace at Blodwen Villas, which became the latter's first matrimonial home, and being looked after by an admirable spinster, Mary Griffiths, always known to us children as Auntie Griff, who remained a family friend throughout her life. Tom led a very busy life. He was a good sportsman, played hockey for North Wales in 1899 and was selected as a reserve for Wales against Ireland. He played golf quite competently, using enviable wooden clubs with exotic names such as mashie niblick, and he had a handicap of 14 when captain of the local golf club. In the woollen mill he saw through major modernisation before the First World War and, like his own father, was very active as a deacon of the Tabernacle Church and as a member of the Holywell Urban District Council. A postcard printed in 1910 shows my father in May of that year reading, as chairman of the council, the proclamation of the succession of King George V, following a formal procession in which the flannel mills band took part.

My father's bachelordom ended at the late age of 37 when he married my mother, Doris Helena Gough, on 4 September 1915 at Olton Parish Church, Solihull. They had met two years earlier when Billy and Minnie Ogden had taken Tom on a cruise to the Canary Islands, on which William and Ellen Gough, my maternal grandparents, had taken their daughter. It was an unlikely match because Tom was over twice her age when they met but it proved to be very successful, lasting 46 years: Doris was an exemplary wife and mother who lived on for 32 years after my father's death, dying at the age of 97 in London on 17 December 1993.

The Goughs were based in Birmingham because William Gough had become joint managing director of the largest department store there, known then as Newbury's Limited of Old Square, later Lewis's, and subsequently the site of Birmingham County Court. He was employed by

Newbury's for 36 years from 1886 and became a director in 1903. He had been born on 24 September 1864 at Bishop's Castle in Shropshire, the son of a builder, Thomas Gough, who built the church there, and Mary Ann, née Cole, formerly of Abergavenny. He left school at 16 and worked first for ironwork manufacturers in Birmingham for five years before visiting Australia in 1885 and working for short periods in Brisbane and Sydney. He married my grandmother, Ellen (Nell) Sylvester, on 8 July 1890, and my mother was brought up in a large comfortable house known as Ivy Lodge in St Bernard's Road, Olton. She had an elder brother Harold, born on 16 October 1891, and a younger sister Lorna, born on a 9 June 1902, who was a talented pianist but who died all too young of acute pulmonary tuberculosis on 10 September 1921, just a couple of months after her father retired. William was a very cultivated man who ran a book club for himself and his friends and whose own library included complete editions of most of the major novelists of his era. Ill-health brought about his retirement and he died in the same year as Lorna, shortly after her.

My mother's brother Harold was a familiar and popular member of our family, whom we saw at least annually during our summer holidays with my maternal grandmother, who lived as a widow at 9 Elgin Road, Sutton in Surrey, with her older spinster sister, Mary, quite close to Harold and his wife and son. Harold joined the Royal Horse Artillery as a member of the Territorial Army as early as 1908 and he was commissioned in the Royal Warwickshire Regiment in December 1914. He was awarded the Military Cross as a lieutenant on 6 September 1916 for his courage in leading patrols behind the enemy lines on the Western Front (the award had been established only eight months earlier, on 28 December 1915). Most of his working life after the war was spent with British Celanese at their head office in Hanover Square and I did not envy his daily commute between his nearest underground station at Morden and Oxford Circus. He and his wife May (Dixon) provided a very warm and comfortable haven for me at Sutton during numerous weekends while I was serving in the RAF. Like his father, Harold's main diversion was in books and he used *The Times* Book Club in Wigmore Street to supplement his own extensive library. His wife belonged to a large family; one brother, Bert, was a housemaster and mathematics teacher at Dulwich College as well as being an Anglican priest; another brother, Jack, was for many years headmaster of King's College School, Wimbledon.

The Goughs were quite a talented family. William's brother Tom was a noted headmaster of Retford Grammar School and his daughters were accomplished musicians. Muriel, whose obituary in *The Times* was written by the respected writer on music Professor E.J. Dent, was a leading figure in the Old Vic opera company in the 1920s. Before the First World War she was a member of the Court Opera at Weimar, where she sang light soprano parts in all the standard operas. At the Old Vic she was a leader in the Mozart revival, appearing as Susanna, the Queen of the Night and Zerlina among many roles, and Professor Dent described her as 'the most trusted adviser' of theatrical producer Lilian Baylis on operatic affairs. She retired soon after the opening of Sadler's Wells in 1921 but remained a governor of the theatre for many years. Her sister Helen, with whom she lived in London, was a violinist who played with the Queen's Hall Orchestra.

The transition from Birmingham to Holywell in wartime must have been quite a shock for my mother but she never mentioned this to her children, as far as I am aware. She was barely out of school, having been educated conventionally and well at the Anglican Convent in Olton, and her background was essentially conservative, quite sophisticated and metropolitan. Nevertheless, she seems to have settled down quickly to a very different way of life in the newly built house (Highfield) that was to be her home for nearly 50 years.

I should interpose here that my father was already 36 years old when war was declared in 1914 and thus beyond the normal call-up age for military service. More importantly, he was in a reserved occupation as the manager of a factory that produced army uniforms throughout the war. He did, however, enrol as a volunteer under the 'Derby scheme' initiated by Prime Minister Herbert Asquith in May 1915 with Lord Edward Derby as Director-General of Recruitment. This scheme encouraged men to register voluntarily on the basis that, once they had done so, they would be called up for service only when necessary. In the event, the scheme was short lived because of the scale of losses on the Western Front, and Lloyd George introduced military conscription to replace it in January 1916.

My father and mother started a family with the birth of my brother Stuart on 30 April 1918. There followed, in almost arithmetic progression, Thomas in September 1920, Neil on 19 March 1923, myself on 8 May 1926 and, at last, a daughter Sylvia (now known mostly as Sally) on 5 August 1928. Sadly, Thomas died on 15 February 1923 of an internal complaint that would now be regarded as remediable and my mother had the very great misfortune of losing a son, her father and her sister, all within the space of 18 months.

2

BACKGROUND

Although the tentacles of my extended family were eventually spread quite far and wide, as I have shown, Holywell itself was quite a snug and compact little town as I remember it; it did not change very much between the wars. Major industrial activity in the Greenfield valley had long subsided by then but Flintshire, particularly Deeside, had played host to important new industries. The first of these was the major steelworks of John Summers and Sons at Hawarden Bridge, which employed up to 30,000 and grew from 1896 onwards. More critically from my father's point of view, Courtaulds Limited established four factories manufacturing artificial textiles at Flint and Greenfield, employing 10,000 people at their peak; a large aircraft factory followed at Broughton, near Hawarden. The latter remains an important employer in the county, part of the Airbus enterprise, but production at Courtaulds declined from 1950, and the last of its Flintshire factories closed in 1989. 'Heavy end' iron and steel-making operations at Hawarden Bridge ended in March 1980 with the loss of 6,500 jobs, and manufacturing activity generally there has been very greatly reduced. In my childhood, however, these industries were thriving and the impact of the industrial depression elsewhere was muted.

Insensitive and unimaginative planning decisions since the Second World War have destroyed the character of the centre of Holywell, which I regard now as an ugly mess, which may be irremediable despite some recent improvements. When I was young, though, it had the atmosphere of a large village. The shopkeepers were tradesmen of long standing, typified by James Ayer, a tall and handsome draper, who would stand outside his shop, smoking slowly one of his daily ration of seven cigars. He lived not far away in the town with his diminutive Scots wife in a substantial house with a grass tennis court, the scene of many excellent summer parties in the garden. Multiple retail shops had begun to appear elsewhere in England, and to a much lesser extent in Wales, but they had certainly not reached Holywell; nightmares about the threat of supermarkets did not afflict our prosperous butchers, grocers, greengrocers and chemists for another generation.

As in many other parts of Wales, there was no very visible or influential squirearchy. We did have the amiable fourth Baron Mostyn of Mostyn Hall, whose son and heir, Roger, won the Military Cross in the Second World War and whose family owned large parts of Llandudno. Lord Mostyn's main interest, however, was in sheepdog trials and he did not otherwise seek to play a role in local life. From a historical point of view, the Pennant family of Downing Hall, Whitford, were of greater interest. Their ancestor, Thomas Pennant, was an admired historian whose account of his tour in Scotland and his voyage to the Hebrides in 1772 can still be purchased, now in paperback, and who was a correspondent of the naturalist Gilbert White of Selborne. Pennant himself has been described as one of the most eminent naturalists of the eighteenth century and was elected a Fellow of the Royal Society in 1767. The Pennant descendants no longer occupied Downing Hall in my time and were known as the Pennants of Bodfari, but Arthur, the oldest living in Flintshire, was a magistrate and lived in St Asaph. His much-loved brother David, who was a major in the Royal Signals during the Second World War, became (in effect) the leader of the practising Bar in Cardiff and then a distinguished County Court (later Circuit) judge in Mid-Wales and eventually Bournemouth. He maintained a link with his native county by serving as a deputy chairman of Flintshire Quarter Sessions.

Holywell had some modest claims to literary fame in England rather than Wales. Its most notorious resident in my father's time was Frederick Rolfe, the self-styled Baron Corvo, about whom A.J.A. Symons wrote so felicitously in *The Quest for Corvo* and whose novel *Hadrian the Seventh* was to become a highly successful play when adapted by Peter Luke. Chapter 7 of Symons' book gives an account of Rolfe's stays in Holywell in 1895 and 1898. After a brief visit to the nearby Franciscan monastery at Pantasaph – to which Francis Thompson had retreated earlier for three years when fighting his drug addiction and where he is said to have written *The Hound of Heaven* – Rolfe was engaged (at his own suggestion) by the Reverend Father Sidney de Vere Beauclerk, SJ, the priest in charge of St Winifred's Well, to paint a set of banners for the well in return for free lodgings and the use of a schoolroom as a studio. Rolfe called himself Father Austin during this stay and alleged that Father Beauclerk had agreed to pay him for each banner. He became increasingly vituperative and pursued his vendetta against the priest in the columns of a local paper, the *Holywell Record*, of which he became editor. But it was to no avail: the journal died and Rolfe ended in the local workhouse before departing for Oxford after the unfortunate Father Beauclerk had been posted by his church elsewhere. In a later short story based on his experiences at Holywell, Rolfe referred to it very unkindly as 'Sewer's End'.

A less close, but more or less contemporaneous, literary connection was with David Jones, the Welsh writer and artist, born in London in 1895, who was made a Companion of Honour in 1974 and who was the author of *In Parenthesis* and *Anathemata*. His father James was born in Holywell in 1860 and apprenticed there as a printer to another local newspaper, the *Flintshire Observer*. After a period in Liverpool, James moved to London to work for the Christian Herald Publishing Company, of which he eventually became production manager.

These peripheral connections were transcended in my time by a much closer and more celebrated local hero, Emlyn Williams, who became the most famous alumnus of my school, Holywell County School (from 1945, Holywell Grammar School). Emlyn was always very loyal to his roots and I had the great good fortune to be taught French by his mentor, Sarah Grace Cooke, whom Emlyn took as the model for the heroine (Miss Moffat) of his great play and film *The Corn is Green*. In the play this role was taken by Dame Sybil Thorndike, who spent some time studying Miss Cooke beforehand; in the film the role was played by Bette Davis.

Emlyn Williams was born in 1905 at Rhewl Mostyn, a village just above Mostyn in the Dee estuary, and soon moved with his parents about a mile to the White Lion Inn, Glanrafon, which his father took over as licensee, after having spent many years, from the age of 12, as a sailor stoker. Emlyn's lyrical and moving account of his own childhood and schooldays is the first section of his autobiographical volume, *George*, and conjures up for me powerful nostalgic memories of my own rather different childhood and the countryside around Holywell, with which I became very familiar. He attended the county school, where he excelled, from 1916 to 1923 and walked five miles to school and five miles back daily for the first 18 months until his school report was so good that his father bought a second-hand bicycle for him. Ultimately, with great encouragement from Miss Cooke, Emlyn's work was crowned with an open scholarship to Christ Church, Oxford, in July 1923.

Those who wish to know more about this exceptional man must seek out *George* and its sequel, *Emlyn*, for his beguiling account of his life to the age of 30. I must record that his aura enveloped us still throughout my youth, and his success, particularly as a playwright, was celebrated with great pride throughout Holywell and district.

By the time that I was born, my father's interests and activities had broadened well beyond Holywell. He had become a county councillor and had given up the urban district council, on which my uncle Horace had, in effect, replaced him. My father was also becoming an increasingly prominent member of the Liberal Party, which remained the largest party on the county council, against the national trend, for about 40 years. Tom had been taken as a young man by his own father to Hawarden Castle to hear William Gladstone address a large crowd and remained a staunch Liberal throughout his life. Despite being brought up in North Wales, however, he was not an uncritical fan of David Lloyd George and had many disagreements with him over the years. My father tended to prefer the cast of mind of Herbert Asquith and was strongly opposed to Lloyd George's decision to fight the 1918 general election as a national government; the election became known as the 'coupon' election because candidates supporting the government were endorsed with a piece of paper verifying their status.

Opposition to Lloyd George for forsaking the Liberal Party in this way was quite strong in Wales, and the opponents were dubbed 'Wee Frees', after dissident members of the Free Church of Scotland who refused to accept union with the United Presbyterian Church. My father was a leader of this opposition in North Wales; in Mid-Wales the charismatic Professor Thomas Levi, head of the law department at the University College of Wales, Aberystwyth, was prominent; in South Wales there was the barrister Rhys Hopkin Morris (later a KC and a knight), who secured the Cardiganshire parliamentary seat in December 1923 in a surprise victory over Lloyd George's candidate, the recently elected member Ernest Evans. The latter had won the seat at a famous by-election in February 1921 and later became the member for the University of Wales until being appointed as the North Wales County Court judge in 1942. Hopkin Morris held Cardiganshire for nine years until he went on to achieve many other distinctions, returning to Parliament for Carmarthen West in 1945.

Lloyd George sought reconciliation with the Wee Frees after leaving 10 Downing Street, and this was given formal effect at a great meeting in Llandrindod Wells on 14 June 1924, at which the only discordant note was struck by Hopkin Morris. My father proposed the second resolution, to adopt as policy a joint manifesto agreed by Lloyd George and Asquith, which was carried unanimously. In the succeeding years an uneasy truce was maintained between Lloyd George and Asquith and their respective supporters. My father served in the late 1920s on a Liberal Party committee chaired by Sir Arthur Hobhouse, which was intended to secure fair selection of parliamentary candidates between the rivals. However, Lloyd George always had the advantage of controlling what was called 'the Lloyd George fund', allegedly collected earlier by Liberal Party whips in anticipation of future needs and about which controversy continues to this day.

These activities were a distraction for my father in a difficult period for the declining woollen industry. Wartime prosperity had been succeeded by much harder times. The Holywell factory was now Holywell Textile Mills Limited and Tom had advanced to managing director from 1909, becoming chairman in 1930. He was also president of the Welsh Textile Manufacturers' Association, embracing about 35 smaller mills dotted about the principality, from 1920. The market for goods manufactured from natural fibres was shrinking. Tom was not willing to tie the factory to the whims of a major retailer, but seeking sales elsewhere for the blankets and heavy tweeds that were then being produced was hard and anxious work.

These financial worries must have haunted my father throughout the 1920s and 1930s and he paid himself a modest salary after comparative affluence during the war years, but he was a strong man with considerable self-belief and he did not allow his anxieties to impinge upon his children. We were aware of the difficulties of the woollen trade in the inter-war years but we believed that they would be overcome, so our recollections of childhood are of largely uninterrupted and secure happiness.

One other important aspect of our upbringing must be mentioned because it was central to our way of life: total abstinence from alcohol. The family explanation, probably true, is that my great-grandfather Thomas had joined Bradford Temperance Society in 1835. He was a staunch Methodist, like his father, and the immediate spur to his teetotalism is said to have been the death of his older brother David (born on 2 June 1798), who fell off a horse into the Bradford canal and drowned on 25 January 1832 when allegedly drunk. In any event, it was a time when drunkenness was a great social evil in the north of England following the Industrial Revolution, and that itself may have been sufficient to prompt my great-grandfather's decision.

The result was that my father and his brothers and sisters all observed the family rule and we had at home from the mid-1930s a large framed certificate attesting to our century of total abstinence. My mother did not have any similar background but she willingly adopted teetotalism, and both my parents remained faithful to it. My own generation has regrettably broken the chain but we were fortunate to have that inheritance, and my parents' descendants have so far avoided any outbreak of alcoholism. A consequence of the abstinence for my father and mother was that their social life was more restricted than it would otherwise have been but they never seemed to be oppressed by this and it did not seem to mar their enjoyment of life. Nor did we as children feel that we were being brought up in an unduly strait-laced fashion. To counteract any accusation of narrow mindedness, my father decided at the age of 40 to take up smoking both cigarettes and a pipe as well as the occasional cigar. That was long before the dire medical warnings of later years and he encouraged his sons to smoke from the age of 18 years as a calming pastime.

3

BEGINNINGS

I was largely shielded from the outside world until 1933 because my parents arranged for me to have tuition at home from the daughter of a retired Nonconformist minister. She was a comfortably shaped matter-of-fact spinster called Wyn Brynford Jones, who proved to be a kindly and efficient governess. The result was that when I joined the local primary school, Holywell Council School, in September 1930 I was able to keep up with my peers. I am rather ashamed to say that I still have all my council school reports and that for Christmas 1933 shows that I was second in a class of 21 'scholars'. I remember that the boy who surpassed me then and several times later was from a very deprived home, and I often wonder what happened to him in later life. I am sure that he would have progressed to the county school and beyond if he had had more favourable home circumstances.

My recollections of that period, apart from my family and teachers, are very vague and do not begin to have real clarity until 1935. One public event did impinge upon me, however, and that was the mining disaster at Gresford Colliery near Wrexham on 22 September 1934 in which 266 men lost their lives. At that time, 1,850 of the 2,200 employees at the colliery worked underground and the impact of the event in North Wales cannot be overstated. Hartley Shawcross first came to prominence as a barrister when he appeared for the mine owners at the subsequent inquest. The politician and barrister Stafford Cripps represented the families of the deceased and the mineworkers without charging a fee.

The year 1935 was exciting for me, a kind of dawn, for several reasons. At home it was notable for the arrival of electricity: before then we had existed on gaslights. I remember also my first visit to the local cinema at Holywell, the Prince of Wales, to see a film called *Jungle Hell*, which (my parents hoped) would not include any contaminating material. Even more excitingly, my father took me to a test match for the first time during our annual August holiday with my maternal grandmother in Sutton. It was at the Oval cricket ground and the visitors were a great South African team under H.F. Wade, with A.D. Nourse and Bruce Mitchell in the side. The England captain was the highly respected R.E.S. (Bob) Wyatt, whose nephew Woodrow was to become a neighbour and friend 35 years later; England lost the series.

The final test match the following year was even more exciting. England, under Gubby Allen, declared at 471 for 8 wickets, with help from Wally Hammond and Maurice Leyland, and I saw All India, captained by the Maharajah of Vizianagaram, bowled out for 222 by Voce, Allen, Verity and Sims. Equally thrilling for me was to be taken to the White City Stadium on 15 August 1936 to see the contest between the USA and the British Empire immediately after the Berlin Olympic Games. Jesse Owens ran in the 4 x 100 yards relay and the USA dominated the match, but the vast crowd rose as one when, at last, A.G.K. Brown breasted the tape in front at the end of the last lap of the mile relay. I do not know what happened to him in later life but his brother Alan Kilner Brown, an able but lesser athlete, became a High Court judge and lived into his nineties.

My father owned four acres of land surrounding Highfield, and much later this was extended to 30 acres by the purchase of Pistyll Hall next door. Our own land was let from time to time for grazing and, more importantly, there was a dairy farm opposite the drive leading to our house. I became a friend of one of the farmer's sons, who was roughly my own age, and it was particularly exciting to be allowed into the shippons (not then parlours) at milking time. Numerous milkmaids tried to teach me how to milk the herd without getting kicked but I never achieved any real success at it and was glad when the arrival of electricity eventually led to the introduction of milking machines at the farm.

Memories of one part of the farming calendar, haymaking, will remain with me always and it is sad that technical progress has robbed modern children (and their elders) of its joys. Each stage in the process had its particular pleasures, culminating in the collective effort of loading the hay with pitchforks onto lorries drawn by splendidly strong shire horses. The sun always seemed to be shining on warm summer evenings, and the sandwiches we ate and the dandelion and burdock we drank never tasted as good elsewhere.

One feature of my childhood must seem quite bizarre to the vast majority of modern children. Sunday observance was taken seriously in our household and no Sunday papers were taken. My father was the senior deacon of the

Tabernacle Church and we attended morning service on Sundays and
Sunday school almost invariably. We would also attend the evening service
quite often, especially if there was an eloquent visiting preacher, such as the
Reverend Gordon Lang of Chepstow, who would stay with us on his annual
visits and continued to do so after he returned to the House of Commons
as Labour MP for Stalybridge and Hyde in 1945. His sermons were always
stimulating and refreshing, in contrast to our usual more pedestrian fare,
and he was adept at teasing my sister. At Sunday school we were under the
watchful eye of Uncle Horace, who was the superintendent, and we had to
undergo annual scripture examinations under the auspices of the county
Sunday school union.

Sabbath observance was only part of what was expected of us. My sister
and I particularly were expected to perform: singing solo, reciting and
acting in short religious plays were all skills rightly or wrongly attributed
to us and I have ever since been ashamed of my rather brazen readiness
to perform in public. A sideline involved competing in the annual Band of
Hope eisteddfod in the main public hall (the Assembly Hall) at Holywell.
The modern English reader will find this event very mysterious, but
eisteddfodau are common throughout Wales as competitions in poetry,
recitation and music especially; the Band of Hope was a junior branch of the
temperance movement, supported by all the Nonconformist churches but
evidenced in Holywell and district only by its annual eisteddfod. The poems
to be recited all had a temperance theme and were often of a cringe-making
kind. However, a much freer rein was allowed to singers and my greatest
triumph as a boy soprano was singing Schubert's *Heidenroslein* in English
after prolonged and very good coaching by my mother.

One other aspect of my rather unusual early childhood needs to be
mentioned and that is, inevitably, politics. My awareness grew in pace with
the rise of Nazi Germany while Britain was ruled by a coalition government
under Ramsey Macdonald and then Stanley Baldwin. My father was
no supporter of the Peace Pledge Union and the talk at our family table
was of the abject and successive failures of the League of Nations and the
British government to take any effective action about the reoccupation of
the Rhineland, the invasion of Abyssinia by Italy, the Spanish Civil War, the
invasion of Austria by Germany and so on. As for the coalition itself, my
father was strongly opposed to the action of those Liberals who agreed in
1931 to take part in it.

It tends to be forgotten that one of the most important Liberal waverers
in the early stages was Herbert Samuel; I have a copy of a letter to my father
dated 23 January 1933 from David Lloyd George, which reads as follows:

My dear Waterhouse,

The 'Guardian' and 'Post' gave the North Wales Federation proceedings an extraordinarily good show on Saturday. However, I have no doubt at all that the action for which you were largely responsible is already having a very great effect. I have heard just now – confidentially – that the idea of a manifesto which emanated from Ramsey Muir has already been abandoned. It is very likely that Samuel cld. not agree to Ramsey Muir's draft. But I am also told that Samuel will attend the mtg. of the Executive on Friday next to expound his views as to the attitude which ought to be adopted, or rather persisted in, by official Liberalism. This makes the Friday mtg. an occasion of first importance. I do hope you really will be able to attend. I fear you are the only one who will put up a fight for Radicalism with the doughty help of your Welsh colleague Edmunds.

If the NLF [National Liberal Federation] are committed by some resolution taken at the Friday mtg. to the Samuelite attitude, Liberalism, in my opinion, is finally doomed Perhaps you will let me know immediately after the mtg. on Friday what has happened, and if you and Edmunds care to come down here, with anyone else you like to bring along with you on Friday or Saturday, I shall be delighted to put you up.

Ever sincerely,

D. Lloyd George

I do not have any record of what happened at the meeting on 27 January 1933 but, in the end, Viscount Samuel, as he later became, rejected further flirtation with the coalition and remained within the fold of true Liberals.

In 1937 it became my turn to move on to Holywell County School, from which Stuart had departed for the London School of Economics (LSE) in 1936 and where Neil had taken his place three years before me. My father was not opposed to private education, from which he himself had benefited, and I believe that he would have sent his sons to Shrewsbury if he had been able to afford to do so. With the inter-war state of the woollen industry that was out of the question. Another factor was that he had been chairman of Flintshire education committee from 1925 to 1934 and felt under a duty to uphold the merits of the county's schools. However, he did send my sister at the age of 13 to Howell's School, Denbigh, a Drapers' Company school.

In the event I have never seriously regretted being educated in the state system, as it is then was. On the down side, I missed sound training in the Classics. Greek was not taught at all and, although I enjoyed Latin to the School Certificate stage, it was not taught in an inspiring way, and much of its literature remains a closed book to me. The other minus factor was the absence of first-class playing fields: in particular, there were very few good cricket pitches in North Wales as a whole and almost none in state schools, partly because of the terrain. How fortunate our son Thomas was in this respect when he attended Uppingham School! The compensations far outweighed these considerations, as will become apparent in the next chapter. Above all, state education enabled me to live at home until the age of 18 and to benefit from the daily company, stimulation and encouragement of my parents, for which I will always be grateful.

4

COUNTY SCHOOLBOY

I spent seven happy and rewarding years at Holywell County School from 1937 to 1944, despite the rigours of wartime from 1939. It was one of five similar schools in the small county of Flint established under the Welsh Intermediate Education Act 1889, enacted the year after the Local Government Act 1888, under which county councils succeeded county Quarter Sessions as the main administrators of the counties. The new councils took over effective responsibility for schools when the Balfour Act of 1902 came into force. In my time, each of the Flintshire county schools had 500 to 600 pupils, so that up to about 3,000 out of a potential school population of the relevant age bracket, estimated to be 19,000, had the benefit of a 'grammar school' education. Those who did not surmount the hurdle of the 11-plus examination usually had the opportunity to go to one of five central schools, as they were called, in which the curriculum was less academic and was intended to lead to further technical education or to a job at the age of 15 or over. Otherwise, pupils were likely to remain at their council school until leaving for employment at 14 or over, although there were two senior schools on Deeside catering for some of them.

For the first 60 years or so of the twentieth century this county school structure, which was similar throughout Wales, was a highly successful feature of Welsh education and produced a very high percentage of its leaders in all walks of life. There was, of course, a comparatively small number of Welsh children who went to the very few public schools in Wales and some, particularly from affluent families in South Wales, to English public schools. But, in the main, the teachers, preachers, scientists, politicians, businessmen and administrators in Wales for most of the twentieth century were county school educated and they served the principality well.

Although I was a member of the Labour Party for many years from 1952 onwards, I remain convinced that the destruction of this core framework of Welsh education through the replacement of the county grammar schools, as they had become known under the Butler Education Act 1945, by comprehensive schools was an arrogant and unforgivable act of vandalism for which we will continue to pay a heavy price. It was, of course, propagated by many trades unionists and other members of the Labour Party who considered that they had been unfairly robbed of opportunities because of failing the 11-plus examination. I accept fully that the system needed radical reform to provide wider flexibility, encouragement and opportunities from the age of 11 years, but it was grievously wrong to destroy the part of the structure that provided children from the poorest backgrounds with a realistic chance of rising to the top. Labour ministers who had no personal knowledge of the state system and had benefited from elitist education themselves should have approached educational reorganisation with much greater humility and taken the trouble to assess dispassionately the great contribution made by the county grammar schools in the course of over half a century instead of embracing the populist idea of 'comprehensive' education uncritically.

What is particularly sad is that the impact of the change is especially noticeable in Wales for reasons that are implicit in what I have already said. More recent educational and social studies continue to confirm that access to the very best higher education (and with it the top career opportunities) is now more difficult for children who are financially poor. Comprehensive schools do not, in general, provide them with the essential ladder to overcome their initial disadvantage, whereas county grammar schools did do so for very many of them. There must be an educational elite if the United Kingdom is to survive in the modern competitive world, and the challenge is to provide access to membership of that elite for as wide a cross-section of the population as possible.

The quality of teaching at Holywell County School varied quite widely but the general standard was reasonably good and the turnover of staff was remarkably low, despite wartime demands on manpower (and, to a lesser extent, womanpower). Of the 19 members of the staff in 1939, including the domestic science teacher and the visiting violin teacher, 14 were still listed in 1945, two of them being on active service, and another having left only to marry a continuing staff member.

The headmaster throughout my time and from the early 1920s was Rhys T. Davies, as he always signed himself. Born in Llanfyllin in the lovely county of Montgomery, he was a history graduate of the University of Wales and an idealist with great reverence for scholarship. He was also a strong supporter of the Welsh Wesleyan Methodist Church, in which he was a lay preacher. He dressed always in a flannel shirt with a stiff white collar, and we thought that he was very absent-minded and incapable of disciplining a substantial school population, but he was remembered and greatly liked by the vast majority of pupils who passed through the school during his reign. Moreover, he was given firm, outstanding support by the deputy head teacher, Sarah Grace Cooke, who had done so much to encourage and help Emlyn Williams. Above all, Rhys Davies managed to convey to all of us his genuine love of learning, even though he was probably not very widely read himself, and many of us were glad in later years to have spent time under his influence.

Miss Cooke, as we knew her, was a very different personality who commanded the respect and admiration of everyone and was a doughty champion of the school staff. She was a forceful, straight-talking Yorkshirewoman who eventually retired in the Michaelmas term 1943 on reaching the age of 60. The last years of her life were spent in Leeds with her lifelong companion, Miss Swallow, and she died there on 1 May 1964. Although a strong character, she was an exceptionally generous woman and, unlike many teachers, a voracious reader who aimed to read (or at least peruse) five books every week. To mark her retirement a special school ceremony was held, at which I as head boy had to speak; there was great excitement because Emlyn Williams himself attended it and spoke later at an evening ceremony.

My memories of the county school are mainly of the later wartime years but I do remember two special holiday events in 1938 and 1939 when I attended summer camps of what was called the Welsh Schoolboys' Camp. King George VI, as Duke of York, had taken an initiative in the 1920s to organise summer camps at Southwold for young people to give them an opportunity to mix with each other and to see the countryside. This idea was copied in Wales to the extent that county school boys were invited to meet in Mid-Wales and camp together for a fortnight under the leadership of T.I. Ellis, the headmaster of Rhyl County School, who was the son of the well-known former Welsh Liberal MP, sometimes described as 'the forerunner' of David Lloyd George. The first camp that I attended, in August 1938, was on the banks of the river Wye at Llanfaredd, a short distance south-east of Builth Wells; the following year it was held on the cliffs at Morfa Bychan, Llanfarian, immediately south of the beach at Aberystwyth. The camps were very well attended, particularly by boys from South Wales, and it was very refreshing for me to meet them because they were much more outgoing and hedonistic than their North Wales contemporaries. The most memorable teacher who attended was Phil Burton (the legendary uncle and father-substitute of Richard Burton, the actor), one of whose many talents was telling ghost stories by lamplight to a spellbound audience of schoolboys.

There was very good news for our immediate family early in that summer of 1939, despite the gathering war clouds. Stuart had had a successful time at the London School of Economics, playing a full part in its life, despite having to commute a substantial distance daily from my grandmother's house in Sutton, where he stayed throughout his years at the university. He played cricket for LSE and was very active in Liberal politics, making a lifelong friend of Arthur Seldon, who later founded the Institute of Economic Affairs with Lord Harris of High Cross, which was to provide key ideas and support for Margaret Thatcher. Stuart also managed to work hard at the same time under Professor Sir Arnold Plant, graduating with first-class honours in the bachelor of commerce degree in June 1939 and winning a Cassel Scholarship, which he was able to take up after the war when he spent nine months in the USA studying American marketing methods. Partly as a reward for these achievements and partly because war was so obviously imminent by then, my father took Stuart on holiday in August 1939 to Dinard and St Malo, which was a poignant experience for both of them.

The outbreak of war deprived me of my own first chance of a visit to France in 1940. One of Miss Cooke's many kindnesses was to organise exchanges with French students. Stuart had stayed earlier in Arras with the family of a French boy, who had spent some weeks with us in turn, and in 1939 we played host to another boy, also of Arras, a remarkably sophisticated young man who was slightly older than me. I remember that he routed me at tennis and was generally rather bored so that he stayed with us for a shorter time than had been arranged; it seems that he then went on to Blackpool, which was even less congenial and whence he had to be rescued by Miss Cooke. Needless to say, my projected visit to Arras in 1940 never materialised and, sadly, we do not know whether either of the French families we had had contact with survived the Nazi occupation.

In North Wales our military allegiance was to the Royal Welsh Fusiliers, who had their headquarters in Wrexham, and the outbreak of war saw the local members of the Territorial Army parading reassuringly through the streets of Holywell, but any misconceived complacency was shattered by the time that we greeted the survivors on their return from the Dunkirk beaches less than nine months later. Stuart was called up in February 1940, after helping my father at the textile mill for a few months while waiting for his papers, and he was enlisted in the Royal Army Service Corps, undergoing his initial training near Bournemouth. He was commissioned in due course and ended up as a very young lieutenant-colonel on the staff of Field Marshal Montgomery at 21 Army Group in north-west Europe. My brother Neil had decided to train as a civil engineer and had left school, after a rather indifferent performance in the School Certificate examination, to become articled to the county surveyor at Mold. He enjoyed the work and remained there until he decided to follow his friend Eric Brook to Liverpool University in the autumn of 1942 to read civil engineering. Neil was called up to serve in the army in November 1943; he was later commissioned in the Royal Warwickshire Regiment and served in East Africa.

The 'phoney war' gave way to much grimmer reality and one of the stray pictures that sticks in my mind is of lying in the sunshine on the grass at school after the fall of France, looking at the blue sky and wondering what our fate would be. As it turned out, we were to remain in comparative safety, despite Flintshire's industrial base. Our greatest excitement and alarm occurred later when Liverpool was attacked persistently by German bombers. From Highfield we had a grandstand view across the Dee estuary to Heswall and thence to Liverpool, where the Anglican cathedral, still under construction, was the clearest of landmarks; the whole city seemed to be ablaze during air raids. The only danger to us was from returning aircraft, which occasionally dropped any unused bombs, incendiary and otherwise (and even land mines), on the countryside.

My small response to these events was to serve as an air raid messenger, the most junior position in the Air Raid Precautions (ARP) service, from January 1940 to July 1942. This involved attending from time to time at the town hall in the middle of the night and keeping company there with Lilian Kerfoot-Roberts, the delightful and amusing spinster daughter of Holywell's senior solicitor, who was, in effect, at the controls of the organisation. I had already begun to smoke cigarettes illicitly, in spite of my father's attempts to sabotage this activity, and Lilian, herself a dedicated smoker, proved to be a tolerant companion. All in all, therefore, I was not displeased when I was called out on duty, and this was long before warnings about lung cancer and heart disease became a daily ritual. I was very sad indeed years later to learn that Lilian had suffered the cruel fate of dying in a fire that she had started accidentally at home with a cigarette.

My service in the ARP ended because on 12 February 1942 I joined our school branch or flight of the Air Training Corps (ATC) with the ambition of becoming a pilot. Various science and mathematics teachers became our officers and it is remarkable how well organised the corps as a whole became in a very short time. I enjoyed its wide range of activities, including competitive athletics on a North Wales scale. Having lived now through an era when competitive sport has been frowned upon by the politically correct and acres of playing fields have been lost to commercial development, I am amazed at the generous support my contemporaries and I were given in a whole range of sporting and other activities by members of the school staff, who gave up hours of their leisure time during evenings and on Saturdays to do so without any financial reward.

The ATC certainly whetted my appetite for flying and provided early instruction in such subjects as navigation, meteorology, principles of flight and engines, as well as aircraft recognition. This stood me in good stead when a wing commander visited the school in March 1943 to interview potential trainee aircrew. The result was that I was accepted for a short university course under RAF auspices at St John's College, Cambridge, beginning in the autumn after I left school, and I remained in the ATC until that course began in October 1944.

Although wartime brought with it many restrictions, I am surprised, on looking back at programmes that I have kept, at the number and variety of entertainments that a small town such as Holywell enjoyed in those years. There was a very determined attempt to ensure that 'culture' was brought to the people, and celebrity concerts, as they were called, were particularly popular. Perhaps most surprising of all, the Old Vic company visited Holywell twice in the course of tours of North Wales. In February 1941 they brought *Macbeth* with Lewis Casson and his wife Sybil Thorndike in the leading roles and Abraham Sofaer as Macduff. The Cassons' daughter, Ann, had a small part in the production and stayed with us. The following year, again for two nights in February, they performed Gilbert Murray's English version of *Medea* with the same principals and Paul Scofield as the messenger. Ann Casson very kindly returned in April 1943 to play Mary Magdalene in an ambitious Passion Festival at Flint, in which I was cast in the lowly role of Annas, a high priest.

The hero of the celebrity concerts, when he had leave from the Welsh Guards, was David Lloyd, our most distinguished local tenor. One of seven children of a coalminer, he had been a carpenter at Ffynnongroew on the river Dee but quickly made a name for himself as an amateur soloist, with the result that my father was asked to take him to Hawarden Castle to sing to Sir Walford Davies, who stayed there on a visit in the early 1930s. Sir Walford was impressed and arranged for David to enter the Guildhall School of Music, where he won a major scholarship to add to an award from the Flintshire education committee. David won several prestigious prizes at the Guildhall School and, as early as 1938, he joined the Glyndebourne opera company under Fritz Busch. He was principal tenor at Sadler's Wells when the war interrupted his blossoming career in opera and he resumed it only briefly in 1946, preferring a less demanding life on the concert platform. He had, however, a fine lyric tenor voice that was greatly admired, especially in Wales. Later, in 1958, I appeared as junior counsel to William Mars-Jones QC for David Lloyd when he sued the BBC unsuccessfully for damages for injuries that he suffered in June 1954 when he tripped over a television cable, but I will defer an account of that until later.

There were many other notable singers who visited Holywell in those wartime years. I remember particularly Isobel Baillie, Mary Hamlin and Mary Jarred and tenors such as Trefor Jones, Jan van der Gucht, Walter Glynne and the Yorkshireman Walter Widdup, all of whom inspired in me a love of vocal music that has given me lifelong pleasure.

Opportunities to hear instrumental music were much less frequent but I did learn, in rather an odd way, to play the piano for my own pleasure, if no one else's. My mother had begun to teach me to play when I was still at the council school because there was no obviously suitable teacher available locally and she herself had been well taught. But I did not buckle down to the necessary preliminary discipline, hoping for results pleasing to myself much too quickly. Eventually, my home lessons petered out and I did not play again until I started tinkering with the piano in my early teens. It was fairly easy to teach myself to play a small number of easy pieces such as the English national anthem; then, using the basic major chords from these pieces, I strummed away at other tunes, organising chords below the melodic line. The results were not always very pleasing to other ears but my fingers responded fairly well and over the years I learnt to play more or less accurately from sheet music. My competence has never matched my taste, so I remain a mere 'honky-tonk' pianist addicted to *The Great American Song Book*, but it gives me great continuing pleasure to play, and I would welcome a second career as a bar pianist with a white piano. In retrospect, I regret that my mother did not persuade the excellent local organist to teach me because the end result might have been much better.

The pace of life inevitably increased as I became more senior but I am mildly surprised at the range of our activities. The first priority, of course, was preparation for the School Certificate examination in the version administered by the Central Welsh Board. I sat 14 papers altogether in the summer term of 1941, covering nine subjects, including French and Spanish. I had rather assumed that I would take conventional arts subjects for the Higher School Certificate, as it was then called, but I had a facility for mathematics and it was eventually decided that I should move into the science division of the sixth form and read physics, pure mathematics and applied mathematics, each as a main subject. I was sensibly advised also that it would be wise to take Latin and German at School Certificate level because of their general importance. The result was that in 1942 I sat these additional subjects successfully.

Despite this extra work, I had a rather easier time academically in the sixth form than I would have had if I had opted for arts subjects. I found mathematics very satisfying at Higher Certificate level and enjoyed calculus particularly. Applied mathematics was also very attractive as the basis of much civil engineering. It was the era of Lancelot Hogben's two bestsellers, *Mathematics for the Million* and *Science for the Citizen*, and I felt that I was preparing myself realistically for the modern world academically, even though I lacked a strong practical bent.

I have always doubted how far I could have pursued mathematics successfully at university, not least because I found solid geometry a particularly difficult subject. There was some loose talk of putting me in for a Cambridge scholarship in mathematics but my teachers made it clear that they did not have the range and experience to justify such a forlorn exercise. Equally importantly, my very tentative idea that I might become an actuary via mathematics was challenged when I was about 16 years old by the suggestion, made by an inspector of schools who heard me make a speech, that I should become a barrister. At that point I had not even heard of the profession but I quickly became attracted to the idea, which remained with me ever afterwards.

My last two years at the school were very busy and enjoyable, although my academic achievements were less than they should have been. I had an early opportunity to see a little of the practice of the law because my father became High Sheriff of Flintshire for a year from Easter 1942 and I went to the county Assizes at Mold in June of that year and again in February 1943. On the first occasion he attended upon Mr Justice MacNaughten and on the second Mr Justice Stable, whose elder son Philip later became a lifelong friend of mine. There were only a few cases to be dealt with because crime was not rife during the war years, and there were few barristers still practising in North Wales because so many were serving in the forces. As a result, I found the standard of advocacy disappointing, but this encouraged rather than discouraged me.

I was awarded a Flintshire county exhibition of £60 per annum for three years in both 1943 and 1944 on the basis of my Higher School Certificate results but I was not top of my school on either occasion.

The most prized award in those days for county school pupils was a state scholarship of £100 a year. In 1943 my clever and amusing school contemporary Paul Neale achieved this and went on to become a lecturer in the leading veterinary school at Liverpool University; in 1944, rather to my irritation, the winner was an able former girlfriend of mine, Sadie Stubbs, who later gained first-class honours in history at Bedford College in London University and then taught for many years at a well-known county grammar school for girls.

For me the results had become slightly less important because I had been accepted for the RAF university short course at St John's College, Cambridge mentioned earlier. The follow-up to that interview in March 1943 was that I was enlisted in the Royal Air Force Volunteer Reserves (RAFVR) a year later after a medical examination that revealed that I was slightly colour blind. This meant that I was fit for pilot duties except those of a night fighter. I was then called in August 1944 to RAF Station Padgate, near Warrington, for more extensive testing, partly on a Link trainer, and interviewing. I was given the grade that I wanted, namely, PNB, which meant that I was suitable for training as a pilot, navigator or bomb aimer. About three years later an unkind RAF friend of mine, having access to my personal records, informed me that the interviewing board had described my appearance as 'clean but tired' and my manner as 'sententious'. On reflection, I think that these assessments were remarkably accurate: my defence to the latter is that I was asked a tempting question about what General Eisenhower ought to do in some current crisis and immodestly answered it instead of dissembling.

Throughout this period at school my obsession with most forms of ball games persisted, with the result that I was captain of both cricket and soccer as well as head prefect and a house captain. This combination of activities was not particularly unusual but I was certainly allowed a wider range of responsibilities than I would have been at a more competitive public (i.e. private) school. The standard of cricket was pretty low because of the scarcity of good pitches in the area. We rarely made 100 runs in an innings and my recollection is that my top score for the school as an opening batsman was 34 runs. Soccer was a different matter, however, because most pupils played and the general standard was quite high. From time to time even first division (as it then was) scouts showed interest in a player, although no one in my time was tempted by a career as a professional, whose weekly wage was only £10 with a bonus of £2 for a win and £1 for a draw. As a result of my Holywell training I was able to win my colours for St John's College First XI in the 1944/45 season, when we were champions of the inter-collegiate league.

Two other matters need to be mentioned before I leave my school days. The first is that Holywell County School was, of course, co-educational, and there were roughly as many girl pupils as boys. We were as conscious then as any teenager is today of our tumultuous pubescence but we remained astonishingly innocent or perhaps, more accurately, restrained. Middle-class morality prevailed. The girls' physical education teacher started voluntary ballroom dancing classes when I was about 14 years old and these attracted a very enthusiastic following, which in turn led to a great deal of 'walking out', particularly on Saturday evenings if the boys' and girls' teams were playing in the same town. There were intense romances of this kind but very, very few illicit liaisons. The girls preserved their virginity as far as I am aware and only one couple, who subsequently married very happily, were thought to have been a possible exception to the general rule. The boys' general pleasure was considerably enhanced early in the war when Liverpool's Aigburth Vale High School for Girls was evacuated to us, bringing a touch of sophistication; two of the most popular girls stayed on with us after their school returned to Liverpool.

I am not clear that co-education equipped me to deal better with the competition for girls later at Cambridge, where the historical imbalance between the sexes was temporarily alleviated by the presence of Queen Mary's College, London, but it certainly provided more fun at school, outweighing any distracting effect that it had on one's studies. Moreover, homosexuality never cropped up at school as far as I was aware.

School did not provide me with lifelong friends, which I regret, but that was only because I became more or less permanently detached from Holywell once I left school. Nevertheless, it has always been a great, if rare, pleasure to meet up with school contemporaries. Many of them went on to achieve distinction in a variety of fields, particularly in the academic world. My closest friend at school has, however, remained an important friend of mine, and has never ceased to amuse and entertain me whenever we meet. He is now Emeritus Professor J. Gwynn Williams CBE, DLitt (Hon), who became vice-principal of the University of Wales, Bangor, as well as professor of Welsh history there. His publications include histories of both the Bangor college and of the University of Wales generally to 1939, and he served both as chairman of the University of Wales Press and president of the National Library of Wales. I learnt a great deal from him as an adolescent in the course of long walks that we undertook together and he prevented me from becoming a narrow science student.

A bizarre consequence of this friendship was that I was invited by Gwynn's father, who was the supervising minister of the (Welsh) Wesleyan

Methodist Church circuit of chapels centred on Holywell, to become a lay preacher when I was 17 years old. I would have been wiser to have declined this kind invitation but I was urged to accept, despite my lack of Welsh, because of the severe shortage of preachers in those wartime years. In the event I preached on only two or three occasions but I have an all too vivid memory of addressing a small, mystified congregation one Sunday afternoon in the village of Ysceifiog on the doctrine of our redemption, a sermon based entirely on the Archbishop of Canterbury's Lent Book for 1943 by the Reverend Nathaniel Micklem. Gwynn has never since ceased to remind me of this *folie de grandeur* on my part.

Another odd excursion into public speaking occurred in January 1944 when I attended, with about 2,000 others, a conference for 'Tomorrow's Citizens' at the Central Hall, Westminster, organised by the Council for Education in World Citizenship. The galaxy of speakers included Gilbert Murray, Professor E.H. Carr, Sir William Beveridge, Philip Noel-Baker and J.B. Priestley. Each afternoon there were discussion groups (no doubt they would be called workshops now, for reasons unknown to me) and I was required to act as rapporteur for one of these groups. This led to my selection, with a headmaster and two other pupils, to take part in a broadcast on the BBC Home Service on the Wednesday following the conference. As a result I had the pleasure of making a second trip to London that vacation and my task was easy because I merely had to read a script that I had helped to prepare. My fee for this was 3 guineas, and I received also £2.9s.8d. for my travel.

I have dwelt on my schooldays at rather great length, partly as self-indulgence on looking at the papers that I have retained but, more excusably, because they shaped and influenced me for many years to come. I reaped the inestimable advantage of a secure, loving home and was given every possible encouragement to develop myself on the basis that I would never know whether I could succeed at any particular thing if I did not try to do it, whether or not others were prepared to have a go.

Living at home, I also had the chance to meet and talk with a variety of interesting visitors. Some were politicians such as Lord Davies of Llandinam, who had been a Liberal MP and, as a strong supporter of the League of Nations, had given the Temple of Peace in Cardiff to Wales. He had written a large tome entitled *The Problem of the Twentieth Century*, which (I regret to say) many possessed but few seemed to have read. Lord Davies' two sisters acquired an astonishing collection of impressionist and post-impressionist pictures at their Montgomeryshire home, Gregynog, which they ultimately gave to the National Museum of Wales. Other visiting politicians were the lawyer and politician Dingle Foot, Wilfrid Roberts MP and, latterly, Clement Davies, who succeeded Sir Archibald Sinclair as leader of the Liberal Party in 1945. Those who were forewarned would sometimes bring a bottle of whisky with them in their suitcase in order to fortify themselves surreptitiously in our temperance household, but one who would have nothing to do with such a subterfuge was Lieutenant-General Sir William Dobbie. He had been Governor of Malta from 1940 to 1942, at the height of its peril. As a member of the Plymouth Brethren he stayed with us when he spoke at a religious meeting in Holywell organised by the Evangelical Church Council and Christian Fellowship.

5

BIRD WITHOUT WINGS

I was remarkably lucky to be introduced to service life in October 1944 via an RAF short course at Cambridge University. The practical reality was that, instead of sharing a dull Nissen hut on a benighted RAF station with a dozen or so other conscripts, I found myself sharing generous rooms in the famous New Court of St John's College with a delightful, amusing man who was to become a firm friend.

That man was Bob Sloman, the son of a respected rugby league international who skippered the Lions on two tours and also led Oldham. Bob was something of a mystery figure at first because he disappeared for about two days: he was fulfilling his immediate ambition to read the unexpurgated version of Boccaccio's *Decameron* in the university library. But he proved to be a warm companion, and my great regret was that he did not return to St John's on demobilisation, only because of his own administrative inefficiency, and went instead to Exeter University to read English. He was a true free spirit, a generation ahead of his time. While the rest of us duly became middle-class mortgage slaves, he never considered that a conventional professional or business career was either necessary or appropriate for him. At various times he was an actor in a travelling repertory company, a cinema usher, the circulation manager of the *Sunday Times* and then holder of the wholesale franchise at Brighton for a number of Sunday papers. His real passion was for writing, and two of his plays, *The Golden Rivet* and *The Tinker* (filmed as *The Wild and the Willing*), had West End runs; he also wrote a number of episodes of *Dr Who* for television with Barry Letts. Meanwhile, he managed to play rugby (union) until he was 40 years old, representing Devon 20 times in the 1950s, and to qualify as a pilot, despite having his aircrew training brought to an abrupt halt, like nearly all of us on the same short course, in August 1945.

My home for the next five months was to be number 19 in New Court, the neo-Gothic part of St John's College known irreverently as 'the wedding cake'. This was on the third floor and the sitting room faced the length of the Backs, with the river Cam on the left, so that the view from it was as spectacular as any in Cambridge. I was never as fortunate again and the memory of that lovely panorama in autumn sunshine remains with me to this day.

Cambridge did not feel entirely benign, however, because there were many wartime restrictions and I felt a homesickness that many of my contemporaries had overcome much earlier when they entered boarding schools. We were also subject to service discipline as well as university regulations that were much less liberal than they are now. Half of each week was spent on aircrew training in subjects such as air navigation, meteorology, theory of flight, engines, signals, armaments and so forth. The rest of my working time was devoted to conventional university instruction in economics, which I was permitted to read despite not having read arts subjects for the Higher School Certificate. This was an exception to the general rule and I found essay writing for my supervisors quite a challenge without the benefit of similar experience in the sixth form at school.

I had chosen to read economics on the understanding that it would prove to be a useful supplement to law in practice at the Bar later, and I would have liked to continue reading the subject on my return to Cambridge if that had been a practicable choice. But I am sure that my later grounding in law at Cambridge was a very necessary foundation in my case for successful practice. As it was, the short course in economics was most stimulating, covering all the subjects studied in Part I of the Tripos (as the Cambridge undergraduate course is known) and the examination at the end of the course was granted, rather generously, a status equivalent to Part I. The economics school at Cambridge enjoyed a very high reputation at the time, despite the absence of John Maynard Keynes, perhaps its most eminent professor, and I remember particularly the pleasure of listening to lecturers such as Gerald Shove and Maurice Dobbs (the latter a communist, lecturing on wages). My only regret was that Joan Robinson was regarded as too advanced for Part I students.

It was difficult to take academic studies as seriously as they deserved with war service looming, but we all seemed to work sufficiently hard to get by. My life at Cambridge then was much more intense than it was when I returned later and I played soccer quite strenuously for the college first XI as well so there was not a lot of time for self-indulgence. I did, however, break the chain of family teetotalism modestly and was urged to see how much beer I could drink: my recollection is that my capacity did not exceed five pints and I have never since attempted to check this. I had not then become aware of the astounding greater capacity of coalminers, steelworkers and even rugger players.

As aircrew trainees we became members of the Cambridge University Air Squadron (CUAS), the headquarters of which were in Fen Causeway, opposite the Leys School, and our elegant commanding officer, Wing Commander Lewis, had been a member of the teaching staff at the school. There were about 120 of us, divided into eight flights. The flight commander of my flight, Flight 5, S.F. Everiss, was a particularly brave officer, by profession a schoolteacher; he looked quite frail but was said to have undertaken many hazardous operations in France. On the whole we were treated remarkably kindly as potential officers and I remain proud to wear my CUAS tie. As you would expect, we were quite an interesting lot and had widely varied careers after the war. My especial friends in the same flight were Hamish Maxwell, the son of the tobacco controller, Sir Alexander Maxwell, and Louis Marshall, who had a Belgian mother, and became the European legal director of Colgate Palmolive. Hamish had a highly successful career in the USA, becoming chairman and chief executive of Philip Morris and then for a short time chairman of the advertising and marketing company WPP on his retirement from Philip Morris. He was awarded an honorary LLD (higher doctorate in law) by Cambridge University for his work in raising financial support for the university in the USA.

Other members of the same small flight were Dennis Lannigan, who became chairman of the marketing giant J. Walter Thompson in Europe; David Kinnersley, who became chief executive of the North-West Water Authority and later founded Water Aid; and John Wait, who became a notable fast bowler for Surrey after winning a blue at Cambridge. The other flights had similarly able members such as Charles Whitby, later a leading Queen's Counsel and a member of the Criminal Injuries Compensation Board after taking a first in history at Peterhouse, and Huw Thomas, who became an ITN newscaster after starting to practise at the Bar. In parallel, there were potential aircrew undergoing training in air squadrons at other universities and we all met up at Torquay after our short courses ended in March 1945. I came to know particularly well several members of the Oxford University Air Squadron such as Godfrey Smith, later of the *Sunday Times*, and Peter Emery, who became the long-serving Conservative MP for Honiton and a joint founder of the Bow Group, the Conservative Party think tank.

University life at Cambridge was as normal as it could be in wartime during my blissful interlude there. Very soon after I arrived Professor

C.E.M. Joad of the BBC *Brains Trust* programme addressed a packed audience on the future of civilisation, without referring much to the future. Soon after he finished speaking there was a riot between his fans and his critics. The police were called in and tear gas and thunderbolts were used in the course of the fracas, which was described by the *Daily Express* as the worst rag since the war began. It was overshadowed, however, by a further rag on Sunday 5 November, reviving a Cambridge tradition, in which 700 undergraduates took part and which provoked strong criticism on predictable lines in many newspapers. The volatility of the students probably sprang from growing optimism about the war, despite the continuing German V-bomb campaign. De Gaulle was already installed in Paris and the Allied landings in the south of France had been successfully accomplished in August 1944.

Although the wartime political truce continued, political life was beginning to stir again. I dutifully joined the newly revived university Liberal Society and went on to attend the Union Society in the Lent term, where a chairman of debates presided in lieu of a president for the duration of the war. In the Michaelmas term 1944 the holder of that office was Peter Goldman, later unfairly notorious as the defeated Conservative candidate in the 1962 Orpington by-election won by the Liberal, Eric Lubbock (now Lord Avebury), whose constituency party president at the time was my brother Stuart. Of closer interest was the Lent term chairman of debates in 1945, Stanley Clement Davies, whose father became Liberal leader that year. Clement Davies senior spoke in one of the debates and I also heard in the Union Society the politicians Arthur Greenwood, James Griffiths and Beverley Baxter.

There were many other pleasing distractions, not least in music. Herbert Howells was still the organist at St John's College, and the indefatigable Myra Hess played two Mozart concertos with the New London Orchestra conducted by Alec Sherman at the Guildhall in a concert that I described to my parents as 'the most marvellous concert I have been to'. There was also a succession of excellent films to see, such as *Rebecca*, *Pimpernel Smith*, *Sanders of the River* and *Henry V*, which seemed to be much better than anything on offer in North Wales. My recollection of all these things after over 60 years may seem odd but I have cheated by re-reading the letters that I wrote to my parents fairly assiduously during this, my first absence from home. What is much more remarkable by contemporary standards is that my mother wrote just over 50 letters to me during the five and a half months of the short course, despite having to write also to my two brothers in the army in Belgium and East Africa and my sister at Howell's School, Denbigh.

I received also 19 letters from my faithful friend Gwynn Williams, who was serving as a writer in the Royal Navy.

The most memorable event of my leave at the end of the short course was the funeral of David Lloyd George at Llanystumdwy in the Lleyn Peninsula, to which I drove my father. Lloyd George died at Criccieth on 26 March 1945, aged 82, and was buried on the banks of the river Dwyfor after his coffin had been brought to the graveside by horse and farm lorry. The scene and the singing of 10,000 men and women who had gathered in the open air to pay their last respects to him were unforgettable. I have no other particular recollection of that leave except for a trip to the Royal Court Theatre in Liverpool to see the legendary Jack Buchanan and Coral Browne with Athene Seyler in Frederick Lonsdale's *The Last of Mrs Cheyney*, produced by Tyrone Guthrie.

The Liberals were excited because Sir William Beveridge, the former director of the London School of Economics and author of the great report on social welfare that bears his name, had joined them. My parents were particularly anxious to find a suitable parliamentary candidate for Flintshire to replace the well-meaning but unworldly son of a former Liberal MP for the county, who had been compelled to resign as candidate because of dissatisfaction with his performance. My own concern, however, was to get on with my RAF career as soon as possible and I was glad to become fully enlisted when I reported for duty at Torquay on 19 April 1945. I think it is fair to say that we were all relieved when the war against Germany ended in victory 19 days later.

My introduction to the realities of service life was not very harsh. On arriving in Torquay I found that I was allocated to the Windermere Hotel, which had been taken over, along with several other hotels, by the RAF, and that I was a member of Flight 3 in C Squadron, together with 40 others, most of whom were already well known to me. We spent most of those spring days undergoing the drilling of one kind or another that formed the main part of the Initial Training Wing (ITW) course. It was our first encounter with real discipline but it was not severe and we were young and eventually quite fit physically. We had reason to be very grateful also to the gallant ladies of the Women's Voluntary Service, formed during the Second World War to help civilians initially but who provided us with very welcome tea and cakes at strategic points in the town to relieve our labours.

Spit and polish do not lend themselves to interesting recollections but I was fortunate that two of my friends had accessible safe havens. Bob Sloman's parents were running a public house at Paignton, and Louis Marshall's mother and step-father lived at Sandbanks on the edge of Poole harbour; they were all very welcoming. I have two main memories of the period. The first is of the victory celebrations on VE night, which was my nineteenth birthday and which I spent in a public house called The Hole in the Wall, drinking draught Devonshire cider. It is not an experience that I would voluntarily repeat and I tottered back to the Windermere Hotel very much the worse for wear. The second is of a squadron parade to bid farewell to our commanding officer, who was retiring from the RAF. He was understandably moved by the occasion, telling us that we were a fine body of men (the cream of the country) who would soon be hazarding our lives over the Burmese jungle, which did not sound particularly inviting at the time.

There was a short leave at home in June 1945 at the end of our ITW course and for me it was dominated by the general election set for 5 July, for which campaigning began a month earlier. I spent several hours driving the Liberal candidate around but my enthusiasm for this was abruptly ended when he had the impertinence and stupidity to make an unambiguous homosexual advance to me as I was driving and he was in the front passenger seat. I decided reluctantly not to inform my father because he would have insisted on disowning this newly appointed candidate. Fortunately, the seat was won again by the Conservatives represented by Nigel Birch, son of a general, who became a government minister later and defeated me soundly in the 1959 general election after the constituency had been divided. I learnt much later that our candidate's proclivities were quite well known when he stood again for Parliament, this time in Anglesey against the popular Cledwyn Hughes.

In the course of my leave Sir William Beveridge, who toured the whole country on behalf of the Liberals, visited Flintshire and stayed overnight with us. I remember walking in the garden with him before breakfast when he expressed confidence that the Liberals would win at least 300 seats, essentially on the strength of his own appeal. In the event, however, they received a meagre 9 per cent of the vote and won only 12 seats against 393 for Labour and 208 for the Conservatives.

Nevertheless the year was a memorable one for my father because his appointment as a commander of the Order of the British Empire was announced in the birthday honours list and he was one of nine CBEs invested by King George VI at Holyrood Palace in September 1945. Another appointment in July of that year, which gave him particular pleasure, was to be the sole vice-chairman of Flintshire Quarter Sessions, a post he held until he reached retirement.

The next stage in training for cadet pilots was called Grading School, and in 1945 there were two centres for this: at Burnaston in Derbyshire and

Brough in Yorkshire. I was allocated to RAF Station Burnaston, between Derby and Nottingham, which occupied what had been Derby airfield with an associated flying club. There at last we began to fly in earnest. The grading process involved 12 hours flying in a dual-control Tiger Moth with tests after five and a half, eight and a half, and eleven and a half hours. There was also the possibility of flying solo in the course of the 12 hours. One was not given time to brood about this in advance: to my surprise the instructor told me to take the aircraft up alone for 'a circuit and bump' as soon as I finished my five and half hours' test and so I got over my first important hurdle quite quickly without any fuss.

We were at Burnaston for about five weeks and, on achieving the necessary standard, expected to move on to Rhodesia or Canada under the Empire Training Scheme to undergo the major part of our training at Elementary Flying Training School (EFTS) and then Advanced Flying School (AFS). The prospect of escape for a time from wartime rationing and other restrictions was undoubtedly exciting but our hopes were very soon to be dashed, even before the end of our next leave. The dropping of atom bombs on Hiroshima and Nagasaki on 6 and 9 August 1945 led very rapidly to the end of the war against Japan on 15 August, which meant that further large-scale training of aircrew was no longer necessary. The result was that when we reported back from leave to the aircrew cadet holding centre at Heaton Park, Salford, we were told that we would be re-mustered to ground duties unless we chose to sign on for three years with a view to training for a short service commission as aircrew at the RAF College at Cranwell. Although this alternative did have some attractions, most of us were not prepared to defer our civilian careers for such a long period and opted reluctantly for ground duties, without realising that in the end we would be required to serve in that capacity until 1948.

Our low spirits at Heaton Park were raised when we were told that any of us who had private accommodation available in London could be transferred there for clerical duties pending decisions about our longer-term postings. Few of us did have such accommodation but the prospect of being in London rather than in some remote RAF station was not to be missed and a large number of us disobeyed the service maxim of never volunteering for anything – but without any subsequent regrets.

My own rather tenuous hope was to take refuge with my brother Neil's closest friend, Eric Brook. His father had been a mill manager under my father before transferring to a similar post with Courtaulds and he himself had achieved first-class honours in civil engineering at Liverpool University and a master's degree before joining the Ministry of Aircraft Production for war work. He was posted to London and was living in modest lodgings in Ealing, where I hoped I might be able to join him.

Rather surprisingly my hope was fulfilled and I became a boarder in Miss Parsons' lodging house at 4 Gordon Road in September 1945, where I was to remain for the next 14 months. Even more surprisingly, Miss Parsons was able to take in Louis Marshall at 4 Gordon Road and to arrange a room for Hamish Maxwell and his friend Guy Neale in a nearby house on the basis that they breakfasted and dined with her. Guy was another amusing and talented man. His father, Sir Walter Neale, was a recently retired Indian civil servant who had been ADC to the secretary of state for India for several years. Guy himself was an excellent cartoonist and his ambition was to be involved in film production as an artist (he was a cousin of the actor Robert Morley). He had been educated at Stowe with his friend George Melly – later well known as a jazz musician – who was very camp in his manner in 1945 and stationed in the Royal Navy at Chatham. George enlivened us from time to time by calling to collect Guy for a night out on the town. I believe that Guy did achieve his ambition later in Paris but I lost track of him and it seems that he died when still young.

Miss Parsons proved to be a charming and tolerant landlady but the household as a whole seemed to be living in a time warp and would have formed a very suitable background for a stage play. There was a quiet Scottish sixth baronet, whose wife had just died and whose hand was bitten by Miss Parsons' dog; the sister of a well-known High Court judge and her husband, who rejoiced in his brother-in-law's eminence; and an able but testy bachelor civil servant whose only diversion was to drink four large whiskies nightly in a local pub after dinner. Eric left soon after our arrival to work for the construction company McAlpine in Cheshire and Louis and I were then able to share his old room. We were not troubled by our fellow lodgers, and Miss Parsons was a good plain cook with the limited materials available in that immediate post-war era. The only shock to my system that I remember was having bloater for breakfast, which no one elsewhere has offered me since.

The work to which my group of volunteers was assigned was very splendidly located on the top floor of Harvey Nichols' Knightsbridge store. There a section of the Air Ministry accounts department dealing with officers who were being demobilised was posted. Our clerical duties were not very demanding and a major preoccupation was giving the appearance of working, whether or not one's particular task had been completed, To do the work quickly and then to read a book or a newspaper was considered in the civil service to be at least very bad manners and was expressly vetoed by our head of section, a short-tempered Irishman of higher executive officer status. I survived this regime for seven or eight months until the beginning of May 1946, at which point my diary entries read:

3 Fri.
   News of posting to Hallam Street. Appalling.

4 Sat.
   Pleasant rows with head of section. No hope of averting my fate.

The background to these rather cryptic entries was that four of us had adopted the agreeable practice of taking a tea break in the afternoon at a nearby Kardomah Café. Eventually, our head of section had become aware of this despite our ingenious subterfuges and had forbidden us from continuing to absent ourselves in this way, on the ground that it was contrary to good order and air force discipline. We regarded this ruling as unreasonable and inconvenient and so continued to visit the café, albeit with greater circumspection. The head was not to be fooled and was rightly incensed by our intellectual arrogance. The denouement came when he followed us in order to catch us red handed and was only prevented from doing so by a kindly waitress, who helped us to escape via the kitchen and a back door into Basil Street.

I am not certain what disciplinary action was taken against my fellow conspirators but I was regarded as a ringleader and retribution was swift. I duly reported the following Monday at Hallam Street, expecting a reprimand and an uncomfortable posting, but was told to report the next day, 7 May 1946, the eve of my twentieth birthday, at the India Office, where I found myself to be personal assistant or secretary to the air liaison officer to the Royal Indian Air Force, a most comfortable assignment that I was happy to retain for nearly two years until my own demobilisation.

I was extraordinarily lucky to end up at the India Office, working for pleasant and relaxed wing commanders (later group captains), particularly the elegant R.A.R. Coote-Robinson from 29 July 1946. The main work then of the air liaison officer was to look after the welfare of numerous officers of the Royal Indian Air Force who came to the UK for further training. Most of these officers were quite senior and only required administrative help with ration books, travel and so on. Later, when India was partitioned in mid-August 1947, we had to deal with two separate air forces. The India Office had been merged with the Dominions Office to become the Commonwealth Relations Office six weeks earlier. But, for the most part, our basic work was unchanged and we remained comfortably ensconced on the first floor, conveniently close to the entrance to the India Office at the top of Clive Steps, with St James's Park a stone's throw away.

One the many advantages of my closeness to Wing Commander Coote-Robinson was that I was soon able to persuade him that it was demeaning for him to have as his secretary a mere aircraftman second class. Within two months of his arrival, therefore, it was arranged that I should sit the qualifying examination for leading aircraftman, a necessary pre-condition of my indecently rapid promotion to acting corporal and then acting sergeant with effect from 23 September 1946, just as Gwynn Williams was being demobilised after sailing to the Far East in the same ship as George Melly, having undergone fruitless training in Japanese. Both my brothers had also been demobilised. Stuart had returned from the British Army of the Rhine (BAOR) in Germany in May 1946 and was about to take up his Cassel Scholarship from the LSE by visiting the USA for nine months to study American methods of marketing, starting with Proctor and Gamble. Neil was about to resume the second year of his civil engineering degree course at Liverpool, having passed the intermediate examination before he was called up.

My settled position at the India Office enabled me to contemplate attending evening lectures in law at London University as a gentle introduction to the subject and I was encouraged to do so by Dewi Seaborne Davies, who had lectured Stuart in legal topics at the LSE. He had then succeeded David Lloyd George briefly as Liberal MP for Caernarfon Boroughs before being defeated by a Conservative solicitor in the 1945 general election. I was able to talk to him in August the following year because I holidayed with my family at the Vaynol Hotel, Abersoch, and Seaborne Davies came over from his home in Pwllheli to dine with us. He was a particularly able and witty man, much sought after as an after-dinner speaker, one of a line of brilliant Welsh lawyers who graduated from the University College of Wales, Aberystwyth, as it was known formerly, under Professor Levi, and who went on to Cambridge University, many to my own college. In the year that I talked to him at Abersoch he was appointed professor of common law and dean of the faculty at Liverpool University. Shortly afterwards he became warden of Derby Hall, where my brother Neil was to live, and he served later both as pro vice-chancellor of the university and as a prominent member of the Home Office Criminal Law Revision Committee.

I have a recollection (but no record) of visiting Dr Harold Potter, the dean of law at King's College, London, and father of the recently retired president of the Family Division of the Supreme Court, with a view to enrolling as a part-time student there, but the main lectures that I attended were at the LSE. On constitutional law there was the renowned Glanville Williams, another product of Pwllheli, Aberystwyth and St John's College, Cambridge, who later became Rouse Ball professor of English law at Cambridge and achieved international fame. His innovative book *Learning the Law* was read by every serious student and was an invaluable guide, but his expertise was wide ranging and, when I attended his lectures, he had just been awarded his doctorate by Cambridge University. I also attended lectures on contract by yet another outstanding Welshman, Professor Sir David Hughes-Parry, who had read economics at Aberystwyth and then law at Peterhouse, Cambridge. It was a particular privilege to be lectured by him because he was vice-chancellor of London University from 1945 to 1948.

Attending university lectures in the evenings made commuting from Ealing Broadway much less practical and comfortable. Fortunately, I found a comfortable ground-floor bed-sitting room at 44 Kendal Street, off the Edgware Road, into which I moved at the end of November 1946 and where I celebrated my twenty-first birthday on 8 May 1947. My father continued to make frequent visits to London throughout the time I was stationed there, either to attend meetings of the County Councils' Association, of which he later became vice-president and chairman of its police committee, or on Textile Mills' business. On these visits he was a splendid fount of hospitality at dinner and the theatre. Food was still, of course, rationed and restaurants were subject to strict regulations. The maximum permitted basic charge for a meal when lunching or dining in a restaurant was five shillings, but grander places such as the Savoy or the Ritz hotels were allowed to impose a surcharge of eight shillings and sixpence on top of this; and lesser surcharges by others were permitted according to their status. The cost of teetotal dining was, therefore, quite modest. My father usually stayed at the Waldorf Hotel in the Aldwych and a favourite restaurant was Kettners in Soho but we would also dine at the Savoy or Simpson's in the Strand, with the result that I acquired a knowledge of London cuisine beyond my years.

At the same time I saw more plays and other entertainments than during any other similar period of my life. I still had 42 programmes for theatrical productions seen by me during those two and a half years, until I gave them to the Garrick Club. There were programmes for performances by the New London Opera Company at the Cambridge Theatre (including *Don Pasquale* with Mariano Stabile) and I saw Sir Thomas Beecham conducting the London Philharmonic Orchestra at the Stoll Theatre in Kingsway; at other concerts I heard both Pablo Casals and Benno Moiseiwitsch playing with the short-lived National Symphony Orchestra. However gloomy the country as a whole seemed to be in the midst of immediate post-war restrictions, London's Theatreland was booming, with actors such as Noel Coward, John Gielgud, Laurence Olivier, Ralph Richardson, Edith Evans, Sybil Thorndike, Vivien Leigh, John Clements, Kay Hammond, Robert Morley, Wendy Hiller and Alastair Sim all on show from time to time. Moreover, there were wonderful entertainers such as the Crazy Gang, Robertson Hare, Alfred Drayton, Jack Buchanan, Joyce Grenfell, Hermione Gingold, Henry Kendall, Beatrice Lillie and even Laurel and Hardy, all of whom I saw with other now-famous stars.

A pleasing adventure while I was living at 44 Kendal Street was my first visit abroad, at the suggestion of Hamish Maxwell. The object was a fortnight's skiing in Switzerland at Engelberg, about 20 miles from Lucerne, courtesy of Sir Henry Lunn Limited, at the height of the season in February 1947. We travelled by boat and train, staying at the Bellevue Hotel, which provided excellent food and a dance band, and Lunns' bill, excluding the hire of skis and so on, was £38.8s.10d. There were, of course, currency restrictions and I took with me the equivalent of £25 spending money. This was the small cost of escaping wartime restrictions for a moment and the first sight of the fruit and confectionery counters as we passed through Basle station was unforgettable. The skiing itself was a delight and I shall always regret that it did not become a regular feature of my life.

I moved on from 44 Kendal Street in or about June 1947 because my aunt Ethel became ill and went to Holywell to convalesce at the home of my uncle Horace before moving to a flat in Worthing. It was convenient, therefore, that I should replace her in her flat at 5 Teignmouth Road, Brondesbury. Although I attended law lectures at London University until the end of the academic year, I did not have to sit any examinations then. It seemed sensible, however, to join an Inn of Court and to start reading for the Bar when it became clear that I would not be demobilised until 1948. It was permissible to take Part 1 examinations, of which there were five, one or more at a time, and so I opted in July 1947 for the Roman law and criminal law examinations to be taken early in December of that year. At the same time I made inquiries about the Inns of Court and eventually chose the Middle Temple because it seemed to offer more valuable scholarships than the other Inns. A major advantage of joining an Inn early was that one could begin 'keeping terms' without eating qualifying dinners while the latter were suspended because of post-war rationing; the usual requirement was that one had to 'keep' 12 terms by eating three dinners each term before one could be called to the Bar. That requirement was not reimposed until Michaelmas 1950, after a year in which lunches would qualify for the dining terms. I was admitted as a student member of the Middle Temple on 4 November 1947, at a cost of £83.13s.0d. (including £50 deposit).

The correspondence course for the Part 1 exams was quite intense and involved answering model questions with short essays after reading the prescribed texts (Leage on Roman law, Maine on ancient law and Kenny on criminal law). The tutors were highly experienced, so one could be confident that one had covered the course and that one was prepared for the type of question that would be set. If proof were to be required of that, the results provided it. I was awarded a first in Roman law, but was brought down to earth in criminal law, in which I gained only a third. The latter paper was more difficult than I had expected and I am not pleased (but unsurprised) to record that a later judicial friend of mine, Charles Pitchford, who had been a prisoner of war in Germany after being shot down in the RAF, was awarded one of the six firsts in the same examination (out of 489 who sat it).

I did then embark on Gibson and Weldon's course for the paper in contract and tort with a view to sitting it in April 1948 but became distracted with preparations for my release from the RAF, which eventually occurred on 10 March 1948, almost three years after I had entered full-time service. My father was not too pleased that I had fallen by the wayside but I did pull myself together by June and start the course in constitutional law and English legal history, which had been my intention earlier. I sat the examination in September before returning to Cambridge and was reasonably satisfied with a second class (there were five firsts).

Although I have referred earlier with confidence to my prospect of returning to St John's College, it was not until October 1947 that I was assured of a place the following autumn to read law. Even when I was certain of a place (I suspect as the result of an intervention by Seaborne Davies), the tutor for law students was hoping that I would attend a long vacation term in 1948 and then take Part II of the law Tripos and my law degree (LLB) in June 1949 because there was such a large number of students as a result of demobilisation. However, I made successful objections to this with the result that it was agreed in April 1948 that I should sit Part II in June 1950 and that attendance for a long vacation term would be unnecessary. Happily also, I was reassigned to Mr Wordie's benevolent care as my tutor and in the end I remained at Cambridge until June 1951, taking the LLB examination after Part II of the law Tripos.

Meanwhile, the release arrangements for my demobilisation group, 66, were first announced in October 1947 and came to fruition about two months later than originally announced. Meanwhile, we moved from the old India Office to a warmer and more comfortable office in Clarence House,

Matthew Parker Street; and in the end I had to dismantle everything because the Air Liaison Section was to cease to be a part of the Commonwealth Relations Office at the end of March 1948, when its functions were to be taken over by the respective high commissioners for India and Pakistan.

6

CAMBRIDGE PROPER

Six months at home passed quickly and fairly uneventfully before I was back in Cambridge and ready to embrace the law full time. My main concerns were that I felt very poor financially and short of respectable civilian clothes but these problems gradually resolved themselves. I was also rather unfit physically, because the posting of Louis Marshall away from London had robbed me of my regular tennis opponent. I went a little way to remedying this by turning out for the village cricket team at Gorsedd, two or three miles from Holywell, and playing golf fairly regularly with Stuart at Holywell golf club. To aid my studies in constitutional law and legal history I obtained a ticket to read at St Deiniol's Library in Hawarden, founded in 1902 by William Gladstone with 32,000 volumes that he had collected and now greatly expanded. It was intended to be a 'good working library', in the words of his daughter, and it provided a very helpful sanctuary for me.

Then it was back to Cambridge very thankfully in October 1948, not to the luxury of 19 New Court at St John's this time but to modest lodgings at 20 Milton Road, off Chesterton Road, for my year out of college. Modest they were but very comfortable also and I was well looked after by my landlady, Mrs Wisbey. For most of my working life I regarded autumn as my spring, a time of cool fresh days, of hopes and resolutions and a degree of self-delusion. This may help to explain how I came to tell my parents in my first letter home on 17 October that I proposed to do 51 hours work each week – 10 hours of lectures, 3 hours' supervisions, 12 hours' preparation for supervisions and 26 hours' further reading. If only I had been able to keep to such a regime, what academic distinction might I have achieved!

St John's was, and probably still is, the second largest college in Cambridge and it catered for a wide range of academic disciplines. It was not strictly a 'law college' but it still basked in the reputation of Professor Sir Percy Winfield, 70 years old in 1948, the recently retired Rouse Ball professor of English law, after whom the college law society was subsequently named and whose textbook on the law of tort was the standard work for students in my time. Although the college was said to have cold-shouldered its former law fellow Glanville Williams quite unjustly because of his pacifist views, with the result that he pursued his distinguished career elsewhere, it still had a strong law teaching staff headed by Stanley Bailey, its director of studies in law, who himself became the Rouse Ball professor in 1950 in succession to H.A. Hollond. Stanley Bailey was a genial man and a witty lecturer on trusts and real property who wrote an excellent textbook on wills. He was also a keen follower of cricket and admirer of his namesake Trevor Bailey, the England all-rounder who had graduated in history and English from St John's in 1948.

The pattern of training in all subjects was that the university was responsible for lectures but one's college supplied a personal supervisor (tutor) in each subject that one was reading for the annual examination, although the supervisor was not necessarily a member of one's own college. Returning ex-servicemen who had been at the college previously on a service short course were regarded as having passed one part of a Tripos, and those who were to read law on their return were expected to sit the Law Qualifying II examination in their first year back and then Part II of the law Tripos in the following year. However, it was decided that I should sit the full Part I in law in my first year because I had passed two of the subjects for it (constitutional law and Roman law) already in the Bar examinations. This would earn me a BA degree after one year when coupled with my second class in economics on the RAF short course.

All my supervisors in that first year were very able men of distinction. In addition to Mr Bailey, then a university reader in law, there were R.M. Jackson (later Downing professor) in constitutional law, whose book on the machinery of justice in England was a bestseller; Kenneth Scott, the editor of *Chitty on Contract*; Sydney Templeman, a Johnian (i.e. former student of St John's) practising at the Chancery Bar, who was to progress to the House of Lords as a Lord of Appeal for 12 years; and Kurt Lipstein, who had arrived as a refugee from Germany in 1934 at the age of 25 and became a pillar of the law faculty at Cambridge and the Squire Law Library, succeeding to the chair of comparative law in 1973. The last named was my only non-Johnian supervisor (he was then a member of Trinity College and became a fellow of Clare College in 1956). I was very fortunate to come under the wing of this gifted man, whom I saw quite regularly in later years when he became an honorary bencher of the Middle Temple and who retained his vivacity and acute intelligence until his death in 2006 at the age of 97. Altogether, one could not have asked for a more civilised and knowledgeable team of instructors.

The university lecturers for Part I of the law Tripos were also formidable. They were led by the great Sir Hersch Lauterpacht, Whewell professor of international law from 1937 and one of the leading international lawyers of the century, who succeeded Sir Arnold McNair (as he then was) as a judge of the International Court of Justice in 1954 but died much too early, in 1960, when he was only 63 years old. Other lecturers included Professor E.C.S. Wade, co-author with George Phillips of the text book on constitutional law, and Professor P.W. Duff and David Daube, yet another outstanding refugee who later became Regius professor at Oxford, in Roman law.

The result for me of all this expert guidance was a 2(1) in the Tripos examination in June 1949, a classification granted only to two others, Norman St John-Stevas (later Lord St John of Fawley) and the able and delightful Poppy Stanley, who married Professor Tony Jolowicz of Trinity College, another distinguished lawyer, and who herself reigned very successfully for many years as bursar of Girton College. My director of studies, Mr Bailey, was kind about my efforts, stressing the importance of completing the required number of questions in each examination, which I had failed to do; he thought that I might manage a first in Part II, not knowing of the distractions that I would expose myself to in my second year. My college was equally kind and awarded me a McMahon studentship of £200 a year for four years, which gave me vital financial assistance into my first couple of years as a barrister.

The other recipient of a McMahon studentship in 1949 was Percy Cradock, in my judgement the most brilliant of all my generation at Cambridge. He became the British ambassador to the Republic of China, then special adviser to Prime Minister Thatcher and finally chairman of the Joint Intelligence Committee for seven years. I met him first as a fellow Johnian student attending on Dr Lipstein in his room in the Squire Law Library for a supervision in international law. He had already achieved a starred first (i.e. with special distinction) in Part I of the English Tripos and was starting to read law by preparing for the Law Qualifying II examination. In the end he achieved a first in Part II law and went on to a starred first in the LLB examination in 1951. All this was achieved without any visible effort on his part. He was known throughout the university as the most accomplished Union speaker and commanded a large attendance whenever it was known that he would speak.

I doubt very much whether I would have become president of the Union Society if I had not met Percy early on and been befriended by him. It was he who encouraged me to speak frequently in Union debates and it was through him that I came to know all the leading figures in undergraduate politics quite soon. My initial inclination had been to pay more attention to the university Liberal Club, and I did so in my first few terms, but gradually the emphasis shifted and my main preoccupation from the beginning of 1950 was with the Union Society.

The president of the Liberal Club in my first term was a well-known North Walian, Glyn Tegai Hughes, the son of a Wesleyan Methodist minister and recently demobilised from the army in the rank of major. He was engaged in research for his PhD after graduating in modern languages at Corpus Christi. He was later a prominent Liberal candidate in Denbighshire and then warden for many years of Gregynog, the house and estate in Montgomeryshire bequeathed by the famous sisters of Lord Davies of Llandinam to the University of Wales as a conference and teaching centre. The Liberal Club was fortunate to have Glyn's mature guidance, and its membership was surprisingly strong. I quickly became involved in its management, progressing to secretary in the Easter (summer) term of 1949 and then vice-president in the following term under the presidency of Martin McCormack, who was reading economics and had come into residence a year ahead of my return.

My role in the Union Society in my first year back at Cambridge was limited to occasional speeches from the floor of little consequence. However, the debates were faithfully reported in both the *Varsity* newspaper, read by undergraduates, and the more academic *Cambridge Review*, so that one was able to indulge in modest self-advertising if the reporter (invariably an active Union member) was kindly disposed. Liberalism was still a greater preoccupation for me and, as the term was ending, I attended a meeting of the Liberal Party Council in London, where I met for the first time Emlyn Hooson, who was to become a lifelong friend. This was followed less than a fortnight later by the annual party assembly, which was held that year in Hastings and which I attended with my brother Stuart.

The Liberal Party was anxious to field as many candidates as possible in the looming general election. Stuart was already the candidate for the new constituency of East Flintshire and I considered, but sensibly rejected, the possibility of standing for Chester against the sitting Conservative member, then Basil Nield KC of the Northern Circuit. The election took place in the Lent term 1950, by which time I had become president of the Liberal Club and secretary of the Union Society. Five members of the Liberal Club stood as candidates in that election, of whom Glyn Tegai Hughes in West Denbigh was the most serious contender.

The high point of the Liberal Club term was a visit by Viscount Samuel, then leader of the Liberal Party in the House of Lords, who addressed a packed audience of 600 to 700 in the Union Society debating chamber (the largest Liberal Club meeting within living memory). It was a thrill to walk over to the Master's Lodge at Trinity, where the Viscount was staying with G.M. Trevelyan, and then to preside for him at the meeting. In his address he spoke vehemently against an alliance with the Conservatives, saying that it would extinguish the Liberal Party. I did not have the temerity to remind him that that was precisely the view of David Lloyd George when he, as Herbert Samuel, was flirting with the idea of supporting the Conservatives in the early 1930s.

Other notable speakers at the Liberal Club were Graham Hutton, Professor Denis Brogan, Shaw Desmond and, at the annual dinner at the Dorothy Café, Sir Andrew McFadyean, then president of the party. But we ourselves were active outside Cambridge also, speaking particularly for our candidates in East Anglia; and I spoke at least twice in West Denbighshire, where Glyn Tegai Hughes failed by only 1,200 votes. My brother Stuart was less successful in neighbouring East Flintshire, coming third with 8,010 votes to Eirene White (21,529) and the Conservative, George Currie (14,832), after being adopted as candidate late in 1949.

By this time I had been elected chairman of the Union of University Liberal Societies (UULS) in June 1949 and I served as such until I felt obliged to resign because of the pressure of other work after the 1950 election. While I held that office I was an ex-officio member of both the Liberal Party Council and the National Executive Committee. The UULS was quite a strong organisation in those days, with members at over 20 universities; it even produced two issues of its own magazine, edited by Tom Houston of University College, Oxford, during my year of office. It was in this context that I first met Jeremy Thorpe, who was the Oxford representative on the Liberal Party Council, and corresponded with him quite frequently. Most of his attributes now known to a wider public through his leadership of the party in the 1960s and 1970s were manifest even then: he was an elegant old Etonian who played the violin and had already developed his considerable talent as a mimic. He had the advantage of a formidable mother, who wore a monocle, and a family connection with the Lloyd George clan. His manner was flamboyant and he invariably addressed me as 'old world courtesy' because of my very different languid demeanour and something I must have said to him.

My own participation in Liberal Party affairs culminated in a speech at the annual party assembly held at Scarborough in September 1950. By then I had progressed to the presidency of the Union Society and my friend Godfrey Smith, also a Liberal, had been elected to the same office at Oxford for the same Michaelmas term. We were invited, therefore, to speak from the platform on the opening day in support of an Executive Committee motion headed 'The Liberal Party – why we fight on' to be moved by Dingle Foot, who himself joined the Labour Party later at much the same time as Lady Megan Lloyd George and re-entered Parliament in 1957 as a Labour MP. Godfrey spoke much more elegantly than I did and he has since firmly established his reputation as a novelist, editor and journalist, not least as a long-time columnist in the *Sunday Times*.

My allegiance to the Liberal Party did not, I regret to say, survive for many months after the 1951 general election. My attendance at party council meetings and assemblies had brought me face to face with the pious smugness of many active Liberals and the virulent hatred of differing factions within the party. I found the atmosphere quite suffocating. It seemed to me that the Attlee government had pursued an honest course in the interests of a majority of the people and deserved support, even though the party inevitably had a lunatic fringe.

These criticisms did not apply, however, to my fellow members of the university Liberal Club, who were generally good fun and some of whom became long-standing friends. I must confess also that my middle-of-the-road political position at Cambridge undoubtedly helped me to gain office in the Union Society. My good luck in that respect began when the president Denzil Freeth kindly invited me to make my first 'paper speech' (i.e. from the dispatch box) in the Michaelmas term 1949 by proposing the motion 'The artist is of more value to the community than the politician'. My opponent in the debate was Philip Goodhart, who had the double distinction of being one of three sons of famous professor of law A.L. Goodhart – who was to become Master of University College, Oxford in 1951 – and a member of the extended family of ex-Governor Lehman of United States political and banking fame. The debate went well from my point of view and my speech was favourably reported by my friend Donald Macmillan and by Norman St John-Stevas, who always wrote kindly of me. The occasion was, therefore, a helpful showcase for me and followed my first essay as a *Varsity* reporter when I gave an account of a debate in which the comedian Gillie Potter, famous for his 'Heard at Hogsnorton' radio broadcasts, had starred.

This mild success emboldened me to stand for the secretaryship of the Union at the end of that term but without much prospect of success. My major opponent happened to be Philip Goodhart, who had not been on his best form when espousing the politician against the artist; but there were four other prominent Conservatives ranged against me as well. To my considerable surprise, I emerged as victor over Goodhart by 363 votes to 282 after the final transfer of votes, although I believe that I was well down in the earlier stages. The absence of a Labour candidate certainly helped me. Jack Ashley led the committee list with 393 votes but was defeated by David Hirst for the vice-presidency and Percy Cradock was elected president in a contest with St John-Stevas.

From then on, progress was much easier for me because I was thrust into prominence as an office holder in each of the academic terms of 1950. It was a special pleasure to serve under the brilliant Percy Cradock, and his term as president ended with a motion despairing the decline in the art of public speaking proposed by Percy and opposed by Duncan Macrae, one of my favourite undergraduate speakers of that generation. Percy assembled a constellation of guest speakers for that debate, including two outstanding legal ex-presidents, Lord Justice Birkett and Mr Justice Devlin (as he then was), as well as the Marquess of Reading KC (son of lawyer and politician Rufus Isaacs) and Dingle Foot, brother of an ex-president, Hugh Foot, and himself a former president of the Oxford Union Society. The debate lived up to its cast: it was the most memorable in my time at Cambridge and I am glad to have an autographed copy of the printed notice of it as a memento.

That Lent term of 1950 I opposed the motion 'This House is devoted to useless knowledge' and the following term I spoke for the motion 'This House prefers Madame du Barry to Mrs Pankhurst' with the distinguished help of Brian (later Professor) Abel-Smith, Miss C.A. Lejeune, Geoffrey Howe and Julian Williams (later Vice Lord Lieutenant for Cornwall) among others. Thus, I again avoided being involved in the more obviously party political debates. I note also with some pleasure that all three main speakers in the Easter term against the immediate reimposition of corporal punishment for crimes of violence were Conservatives and then or ultimately peers, namely, Hurd of Westwell, Lloyd of Berwick and the second Lord Mancroft, although Lloyd naturally ceased being an active Conservative on becoming a judge.

Other than Percy Cradock, the speaker who made the greatest impression in debate in that first half of 1950 was undoubtedly Keith Kyle of Magdalen College, Oxford, who later became a close friend and remained a most eloquent and literate speaker throughout his life. He was notoriously absent minded and ill organised in practical matters, with the result that he arrived as a guest speaker in a debate about atomic energy well after it had begun: he had had to hitch-hike from Oxford after missing his train. Nevertheless, he strode confidently, if somewhat bedraggled, into the debating chamber and was soon haranguing the attentive audience passionately and persuasively without a note. Even Percy Cradock, in the chair, could scarce forbear from cheering. Keith went on to demonstrate his brilliance as a reporter and historian on television, as the Washington correspondent of *The Economist* and with his definitive book on the Suez disaster, to mention only some of his many activities.

Two special events during this period need to be mentioned. One was the first televised Union debate on 2 June 1950. Television was still very much in its infancy then and many people did not acquire a set until the coronation of Queen Elizabeth II three years later. The BBC considered that it would be too expensive to televise a debate on the spot in Cambridge and so the necessary furnishings, including the president's chair, were transported to Alexandra Palace. Our selected opponents were from Birmingham University, and Julian Williams and I were required to oppose the motion 'That this House wishes that it had a television set' in a half-hour programme at 9:30 p.m., which was introduced by Tony Benn, who was then employed by the BBC. Fortunately, after we had rehearsed intensively from 2 p.m., the debate went off without a hitch. Reading my speech over 50 years later, I confess that I am rather pleased with it and C.A. Lejeune was good enough to say in the *Observer* newspaper, 'The debate between Cambridge and Birmingham Universities turned out to be fine fun. Cambridge's RJ [sic] Waterhouse in particular, with an act suggestive of a graft between Winston Churchill and Naunton Wayne, is a stylist who could give points to many professional entertainers.'

No doubt this event helped to ensure my election as president three days later. I had hoped to be unopposed but Charles Pickthorn, the son and heir of the Cambridge University MP Sir Henry, decided to stand against me. I defeated him by 394 votes to 99, so my honour was satisfied. Jack Ashley was duly elected vice-president and Gautam Mathur from Lahore, a leading figure in the university Majlis (a debating society for Indian students), beat Julian Williams for the secretaryship.

The other and more widely publicised event was unique: a boat race between the officers and committees of the Cambridge and Oxford Unions on the river Cam after the May races, on 10 June. The Oxford president that term, who needs no introduction, was Robin Day. He and Norman St John-Stevas were already highly developed self-publicists and the race, attended by a full complement of the paparazzi, was their joint idea. Photographs of the dinner-jacketed crews were often resurrected by the press during Robin's lifetime and I do so again as a salute to him. My recollection is that the result was a deliberate tie and that we threw our cox, Norman, in full evening dress, into the river.

The examination for Part II of the law Tripos had begun on 25 May 1950 and I noted in my diary four days later that I was feeling like death as the result of lack of sleep. My preparation for the criminal law paper had been particularly cursory because I was foolishly relying on my very modest achievement in the subject in Part 1 of the Bar examinations two years earlier. I was told after the examination that my leisurely efforts to deal with the paper gave some comfort to my fellow examinees. However, my friends on the board of examiners saved the day for me and I was fortunate to emerge with a 2(2) overall.

That vacation was busy, but not with legal reading. My main responsibility was to arrange the programme of eight Union debates for the following term, which was particularly important because the Michaelmas term was the main recruiting term. It was necessary also for me to find some gainful employment to justify my existence to a limited extent financially. It seems that I declined work at the De Havilland aircraft factory near Hawarden, because it was rather far away, but the kindly and influential manager of Courtaulds' large Greenfield factory, on the outskirts of Holywell, agreed to employ me and I started on 12 July at the fair wage of £6 per week. After visiting several departments I was employed by the laboratory as a checker until mid-August.

The work of arranging the programme of debates for the Michaelmas term proved to be much more demanding than I had expected and it continued almost to the end of my term of office because I had to deal with a disappointing number of last-minute withdrawals. I was particularly incensed by being let down on the day of the opening debate by Kenneth Tynan, then only a rising, if outrageous, star in the limited Oxford firmament. He had agreed to oppose the motion 'This House prefers the cap and bells to the cap and gown', which was to be proposed by the very popular old Johnian 'Professor' Jimmy Edwards. I had reserved two rooms, at Tynan's request, at the University Arms Hotel for himself and a 'lady guest' but received this telegram at about midday:

> Urgent sharp sudden and sickening attack of intestinal 'flu makes it impossible for me to attend tonight's debate. I am furious having prepared an alarming yet gay rigmarole concerning such beguiling kickshaws as these [sic] collected letters of Morse to Marconi, life and times of well known French epistemologist Louis Darnsse together with a plea for the society of disused positives especially peccable arc and ert the heartbreaking story of the Transylvanian vowel ship and finally survey of two books, Robert Newton's autobiography entitled a Bill for Edana and new novel by Nancy Mitford entitled Nine months is not enough. However please accept deepest regrets. I hope you will ask me again when I stop vomiting. Sincerely Ken Tynan.

It will not surprise you that I was not amused and the incident still rankles because independent reports from Oxford cast some doubt on the extent of Tynan's incapacity. However, if the telegram is a fair indication of what he might have said in his speech, we may have been fortunate not to hear it.

My face was saved by the distinguished Cambridge professor of political science, Denis Brogan (later knighted), who was already a household name as a broadcaster and an authority on all things American. With extreme generosity he agreed to stand in for the relatively unknown Tynan at almost the twelfth hour and ensured the debate's success: at the end of it 632 votes were cast, mainly (of course) in favour of the motion.

Presidency of the Union was my first (and probably last) experience of power without any accompanying grave responsibility and I enjoyed that Michaelmas term enormously. It would be wearisome for the reader if I were to give an account of the seven other debates but I will refer to some of them briefly.

The second debate was on the conventional motion of no confidence in the government, which was carried by a handsome majority. Again, I was let down by the announced guest speaker against the motion, the Minister of Works, R.R. Stokes, but his very able substitute was the future Chancellor of the Exchequer and later Prime Minister, Jim Callaghan, whose speech was a tour de force. The motion was supported by another future Chancellor, Peter Thorneycroft, and by yet another, Geoffrey Howe, from the floor.

In the fourth debate Brigadier Anthony Head defaulted. To my great delight, however, Brigadier Head's replacement against Dick Crossman on the subject of German rearmament was Bob Boothby, Crossman's regular sparring partner and friend. I had to postpone the debate from Tuesday to Wednesday, but that was a minor inconvenience when the debate was bound to be both amusing and of high quality. A bonus for me was that Boothby produced an outstandingly good-looking lady guest, who sat in the gallery opposite me throughout the debate; he won the argument in favour of rearmament by a small majority with the assistance of a speech from the floor by Douglas Hurd, a future president of the Union and later foreign secretary. It is a reflection on the Cambridge democratic system, however, that both Hurd and Howe had failed in the election for the Union committee that term!

The other guest speakers for my presidential term all turned up and lived up to expectations. They included the novelist Nigel Balchin, Compton Mackenzie, Victor Gollancz, Hopkin Morris KC, MP, and my own MP and future election opponent Nigel Birch. For the final debate, when I handed over to my successor Jack Ashley, I elected to propose the motion 'This House cherishes its illusions' and the Oxford Union president, Godfrey Smith, agreed to oppose it. The guest speakers were two very skilled performers at the Bar, Vincent (later Mr Justice) Lloyd-Jones KC and Richard O'Sullivan KC, the Recorder of Derby. It was by no means a great debate but the motion was carried by acclamation and the *Cambridge Review* reporter, Edward Greenfield (later an authority on recorded music) let us down fairly lightly.

Three outings with my fellow president Godfrey were especially interesting. One was to the Insurance Debating Society in the library at Lloyd's, under the chairmanship of Sir Philip D'Ambrumenil, when I proposed the motion 'This House has no faith in human progress'. The high point of the occasion for me was a sumptuous dinner after the debate, beginning with oysters, in eating which I received my first lesson. Godfrey and I clashed again three weeks later in a televised debate on 13 December from the Old Hall, Lincoln's Inn, as guests of the Hardwicke Society. The motion proposed by Godfrey and opposed by me with the help of Jack Ashley was 'This House deplores the decline of the middle classes'. For me, apart from the excitement of being televised, the main interest was hearing Ivan Yates, then Treasurer elect of the Oxford Union, speak in support of the motion. His speech, as a committed member of the Labour Party, was brilliantly witty and, when delivered later in the Union itself, won him the presidency. He became a dear friend who was best man at my wedding and a very successful journalist on the *Observer*. It was a cruel blow when he died much too young on 12 February 1975 at the age of only 48, struck by a motor vehicle in St John's Wood.

The other joint venture in London with Godfrey was bizarre. It happened that Queen Juliana of the Netherlands paid a state visit to the UK in November and she decided that she would like to meet a representative group of British youth. Neither Godfrey nor I felt that we were very representative but we were summoned to meet Her Majesty at the Netherlands embassy and duly took tea with her at 4.20 p.m. precisely on 23 November. I was invited to sit on a sofa with the Queen as Godfrey and I conversed with her briefly and I have kept the rather absurd photographs taken of us with our umbrellas as we left, looking like very green young diplomats.

And so a busy term for me ended with the unopposed return of Jack Ashley as president for the Lent term 1951 and Donald Macmillan and Julian Williams, the heir to Caerhays Castle in Cornwall, elected vice-president and secretary, respectively. After a very social vacation, mainly at home, and much snow, I returned to Cambridge full of good intentions to try to improve my academic record when sitting the LLB examination on 24 and 25 May. I had chosen the conventional mixed bag of private law subjects, namely, sale of goods, transfer of moveables in Roman and English law, trusts and conflict of laws, all of which required serious attention, and I did my best early in the year to catch up with much that I had missed during the previous term.

My aspirations were in vain, however, because I succumbed to the irresistible temptation presented by an invitation from the United States' Institute of International Education to take part in a debating tour of American universities and colleges during the Easter vacation. The invitation was for two representatives of the Cambridge Union Society to visit 26 of these institutions from the east to west coasts in the space of 30 days, returning to England on 26 April, exactly four weeks before the LLB examination was due to begin. Jack and I had little difficulty in selecting ourselves as the most suitable representatives and, to our great delight, this was accepted without audible demur.

These debating tours were by then an established feature of Union activity. An early team from Cambridge in 1924, had comprised R.A. Butler, A.P. (later Mr Justice) Marshall and J.G.W. Sparrow, who became a KC and wrote a book about the Moors murder trial. The 1925 Cambridge team was even more formidable with Patrick (later Lord) Devlin, Geoffrey Lloyd (later a Cabinet minister) and the future Archbishop of Canterbury, Michael Ramsey. More recently, there had been favourable publicity about the tours because Kenneth Harris of the *Observer* had written *Travelling Tongues*, giving a detailed account of his own tour from Oxford in 1947 with Sir Edward (later Lord) Boyle and Tony Benn.

Jack proved to be the best of travelling companions and he has given his own amusing recollections of the tour in his autobiography. He was in fine entertaining form throughout the tour and caused numerous women students' hearts to throb unavailingly. We travelled out by the *Queen Mary* and returned, in the company of the victorious Cambridge boat race crew, by the *Queen Elizabeth*. Our sponsors could only afford tourist class fares for us but this was greatly mitigated by the kindness of Brian Russell, a contemporary in the Union Society, whose father was general manager of the Cunard Line and who arranged for us to be given the freedom of the cabin class on both liners. The experience of transatlantic crossing by liner was unforgettable but much more punishing on the return journey because we lost an hour's sleep each night for five consecutive nights, which I found to be quite as taxing as jet lag in later years.

After a night in New York, we began our tour in earnest at St Joseph's College, Philadelphia, the only college in the States to provide us with whisky as refreshment, and found ourselves debating before at least 3,000 students in the basketball stadium. We had provided in advance six topics on which we were prepared to debate, having tried rather ineffectually to gather our thoughts on the journey out. Our main aim, however, was to demonstrate Cambridge wit and light-heartedness, which was not always well received by the academic staff responsible for teaching 'speech'. But, as always, American audiences were very warm and generous and the colleges wrote very tolerantly about us to our sponsors in New York.

Our topics for debate were as controversial as you would expect. The three most popular were: 'This House regrets the American way of life', 'This House deplores the banning of Communism in free democratic states' and 'Democratic Socialism is the most effective barrier to Soviet Communism'. More or less armed with these, we travelled from coast to coast and back again by rail, air and Greyhound bus. Our journey took us from Pennsylvania via Ohio, Illinois and Kansas to Texas; then we had a peep at the Grand Canyon en route to Los Angeles, where we spent Easter. Our return journey took us north to San Francisco (for Berkeley) and Seattle before turning east and flitting through Idaho, Oregon, Utah, Colorado, South Dakota and Ohio to New York, where we debated at the delightful (women's) Wells College in Aurora and finally at Columbia University. A particular memory on the way back is of arriving at Chicago station on 17 April to hear all the factory hooters sounding off in protest at the dismissal of General Douglas MacArthur by President Truman and marking the moment when the General landed in San Francisco on his return from Japan.

For me there followed a painful and anxious month reading, rather than revising, for the LLB examination, which was all over in two days at the end of May. As in the previous year, I survived with a 2(2) classification and a bowed head; my shame was not alleviated in April 1985 when it was converted by university decree to an LLM without any further academic effort on my part.

I have taken up a lot of space in recounting what I did at Cambridge because it influenced fundamentally so many aspects of my later life. Above all, it gave me confidence to compete in the wider world and provided me with a galaxy of able, amusing and reliable friends. Most of my friends were in their mid-twenties and we did not take ourselves very seriously: laughter was always echoing in my ears. What astonishes me in retrospect 60 years later is how fully our characters and personalities were already formed then and how little all of us, from the prominent to the obscure, have changed in the intervening years. One feels great nostalgia inevitably for one's undergraduate days but I have never subsequently wanted to relive the past. Cambridge is and was such an entrancing place with so many opportunities that my wish would be to return there as an undergraduate at least twice in order to pursue entirely different student careers of academic and sporting endeavour to make up for my omissions between 1948 and 1951.

7

APPRENTICE BARRISTER

In 1951 the Bar final examination was very different from what it is now. Then it was just another academic hurdle to overcome before one could practise, whereas now the course is intended to provide a much wider practical training for the profession. Another important difference was that in 1951 it was necessary to go to London to take the training course, unless one was brave enough to do it from home by correspondence with the law tutorial firm Gibson and Weldon; there are now several approved centres ranged around the country where one can take what is called the Bar vocational course.

In London there were two main choices of training for me: either a full academic year's course at the Inns of Court School of Law with many of the lectures given by Oxbridge and London university staff or the more popular (and lazier) option of three months' expert cramming by Gibson and Weldon at their premises in Chancery Lane. At the age of 25 I was naturally anxious to start my career as soon as possible and had no hesitation in opting for Gibson and Weldon, to whom I reported on 21 August 1951 for my first lecture, with a view to sitting the Bar final in the week of 5 December. To my delight, Robin Day was taking the same course but he was in a separate group that included Paul Sieghart (later chairman of Justice) and two other fellow sufferers who became friends, Michael Dillon (later a Midland QC and Circuit judge) and Graham Routledge, brother of the fine actress Patricia and ultimately a canon of St Paul's Cathedral.

Before starting the course I had the extreme good luck to find a flat in the basement of 39 Cadogan Place, SW1, with a separate entrance in Cadogan Lane. It was a location well above my modest status but the rent was reasonable and I was helped greatly by my parents' wish that my sister Sylvia and I should share accommodation in London. She had just come down from Edinburgh University and, like so many of her female contemporaries then, was about to take a secretarial course as a preliminary to a professional career. However, during the summer she had entered a competition run by *Vogue* magazine to attract potential journalists and had received an honourable mention. She was told that employment might be found for her if a suitable vacancy occurred and she was duly offered work six months later as a journalist on the *Vogue Export Book* at the princely salary of £7 per week, which (of course) she accepted. Meanwhile, Sylvia had joined me at 39 Cadogan Place on 4 October 1951 and we shared the flat there for nearly three hectic years.

It was good to be alive in London that autumn despite the pressures of the Bar final course. Very many of my friends were there, as were several of Sylvia's attractive girlfriends from Edinburgh, so there was a good basis for social life. A major distraction was a further general election, following Labour's narrow victory in February 1950, and there was a mood of disaffection with austerity (exemplified in the personality of Sir Stafford Cripps) so that the uneasy stalemate could not be prolonged indefinitely. Robin Day had installed himself in a bed-sitting room in a barrister's house in Walton Street, on the other side of Sloane Street, and he was very ready to lead me off to the hustings in Kensington and Chelsea while the campaign raged. At the same time, King George VI underwent an operation that was a prelude to his death in February 1952. As expected, the election on 25 October resulted in the defeat of Labour and the return of Winston Churchill with a Conservative overall majority of 17.

The election over, we could at last concentrate on work, with Gibson and Weldon's frequent test papers to keep us up to the mark. The teaching was highly skilled and there could be no acceptable excuse for failure. Competition for library space in which to work was intense, particularly so in the Middle Temple because its war-damaged library had not yet been rebuilt and was housed temporarily in a pre-fabricated building in Brick Court. On Robin's initiative we solved the problem by joining for a short period the Royal Empire (now Commonwealth) Society in Northumberland Avenue, which had an admirable and under-used library. We would work away there until the mid-evening and then emerge hungrily to enter the nearby Lyons' Corner House in the Strand to the stately music of a palm court orchestra. I remember that the food there was always reliable and the bread rolls of superior quality. How sad it is that the Corner Houses have long since ceased to exist! The regime that I have described proved adequate for our needs and we managed to negotiate the Bar final examination with places in the third class, like the vast majority of those who sat it.

And so an eventful year ended with Christmas at home in Holywell after Robin Day and I had completed our obligatory dinners in Middle Temple hall to qualify for call to the Bar and I had bought my first 'hard hat' (bowler) at Lock's in St James's Street. It had been a very social Michaelmas term for Sylvia and me and we had seen much of my father and Stuart on their frequent business visits as well as our friends.

Then, as now, an embryo barrister was expected to undergo 12 months' pupillage with an experienced junior barrister or two consecutive periods of six months, changing pupil master midway through the year. The code of conduct about this was much less formal then than it has since become and one could accept legal work and appear in court as soon as one was called. But the wise advice was not to do so until one had spent a reasonable time learning the ropes. The fee to be paid to the barrister, which was sometimes waived, was 50 guineas for six months plus three guineas to the barrister's clerk.

I was exceptionally fortunate in the selection of my pupil masters, who were both graduates of St John's College, Cambridge. My supervisors there, or one or two of them, thought that I might have some aptitude for Chancery law (land, conveyancing, trusts and company work) and arranged for me to meet John Brightman, a very successful junior, who was in the same chambers at 2 New Square, Lincoln's Inn, as my degree supervisor Sydney Templeman. I would have been even more nervous than I was if I had been able to foresee that both Brightman and Templeman would become Lords of Appeal and that a recent pupil of Brightman's, Margaret Thatcher, would become prime minister. However, Brightman did agree to take me on as a pupil and, as his room was filled with instructions from solicitors who were seeking his advice, he arranged that I should share a room with the very congenial Templeman.

Lord Brightman, who died in 2006 at the age of 94, was an attractive, upright man of supreme integrity. After practising for a few years, he served with distinction in the RNVR throughout the Second World War, married a beautiful Greek girl when he was naval attaché in Ankara and then returned to very successful practice, culminating in his appointment to the Lords in 1982. I could not have had a better tutor in all aspects of work at the Bar, and to be able to read and work at his papers under his guidance was a splendid introduction.

Call night for both Robin and me as well as many of our university contemporaries was on 5 February 1952. In the Middle Temple that year the Treasurer, who performed the ceremony, was the very recently retired Lord Chancellor, Earl Jowitt. A fine-looking man with a sonorous voice, he addressed us appropriately and we were left in no doubt about the gravity of the step that we were taking. Unfortunately, my father was unwell with bronchitis that evening, but my mother came to London for the occasion and stayed the night with us at the flat.

That night assumed national importance for a very different reason because King George VI died and the new Queen flew back from Kenya with the Duke of Edinburgh the next day. Thus, on my first appearance in court robed as a barrister with my pupil master, I wore the traditional mourning bands, worn only during rare periods of official court mourning.

My promising pupillage in Chancery was interrupted all too soon because a Cambridge Liberal friend of mine, Hugh Corrie, had performed a stint as a marshal for one of the most senior judges of the Queen's Bench Division, Sir Reginald (the Honourable Mr Justice) Croom-Johnson, a former Conservative MP, and suggested that I would both enjoy a similar experience and profit from it. He did not mean profit from it financially because the remuneration was two guineas per day and remains the same, as far as I am aware, to this day. However, the idea appealed to me, despite the judge's rather fearsome reputation, and he very kindly agreed to take me as his marshal for the northern part of the Wales and Chester Circuit and treated me gently and courteously throughout.

In those much happier legal days High Court judges still went out on Assize from London to try criminal cases (general gaol delivery) and civil suits (oyer and terminer), as they had done continuously from the reign of Henry II. By the twentieth century this was essentially the work of the Queen's Bench Division judges, who would spend half their judicial time visiting Assize towns on the seven circuits into which England and Wales were divided. A judge's opportunity to choose which circuit to visit depended on his seniority until a fairer system was devised by Sir John Donaldson when Lord Widgery was Lord Chief Justice. Thus, in 1952 the less demanding and more rural circuits (the Western, Oxford, Wales and Chester) were still usually chosen by the more senior judges for obvious reasons.

The result of this was that I was very privileged to join Mr Justice Croom-Johnson at his room in the Royal Courts of Justice on 30 April 1952 to travel with him to Paddington station and thence in a reserved first-class compartment of the old kind to Welshpool, where we were met by the top-hatted station master in full morning dress and greeted by the high sheriff and under sheriff en route to the judges' lodgings at Llanerchyddol Hall.

Sir Basil Nield wrote a nostalgic book in 1972 entitled *Farewell to the Assizes* on his retirement as a High Court judge and it contains an interesting account of the 61 towns within the circuit system, all of which he visited, and of the judges' lodgings where he stayed. By that time, when he visited Welshpool, Montgomeryshire had acquired its own house for use by the judges, whereas in 1952 the practice was to hire a stately mansion to accommodate the judge and his immediate personal staff during the Assize. All this was, of course, changed on 1 January 1972 when the recommendations of the Royal Commission on Assizes and Quarter Sessions presided over by Lord Beeching were implemented. The Assize system was then abolished; the Crown Court in its many manifestations was born; and Welshpool, along with many other towns, including county towns, ceased to be on a High Court judge's itinerary in normal circumstances.

Llanerchyddol Hall was certainly an eye-opener for me, standing as it does in lovely landscaped grounds at the end of a mile-long drive. The house itself, built in 1820, is a forbidding castellated structure but had in 1952 a beautifully furnished drawing room. Its owners, who were required to be away during our visit, were three Vernon sisters, nieces of the former Judge Parfitt (a Warwickshire cricketer in his time), who formed an amateur but skilled trio on piano, violin and cello. They have long since departed, but the house and grounds remain in private hands and the present owners offer bed and breakfast accommodation in a four-room suite.

My sense of unreality about my role and position was heightened by the absence of any gas or electricity supply. Lighting was still by oil lamps and candles, although there was an Aga cooker. Most appropriately, the travelling butler assigned to the judge was very old and unsteady and, as I dined in semi-darkness at the opposite end of the table from the judge, I was reminded irresistibly of Thomas Love Peacock's *Nightmare Abbey*, of which I had seen an excellent production only two months earlier at the Westminster Theatre.

The demands made of a marshal were light indeed and our journey through North Wales in fine early summer weather was gentle and most enjoyable. My tour as a marshal lasted until 16 June, ending with two weeks at Chester in the company of another Queen's Bench judge, Mr Justice Ormerod, who later became the first former County Court judge to be appointed to the Court of Appeal. Our route had taken us briefly to Dolgellau, for a week to Caernarfon and then in swift succession to Beaumaris, Ruthin and Mold before Chester.

The lodgings at Dolgellau were in a private hotel, Caerynwch, on the road out to Machynlleth and in the shadow of Cader Idris with the river

Mawddach flowing through the grounds. The Elizabethan house was of special interest because it was the former home of Baron Richards in the mid-eighteenth century, and he became Lord Chief Baron of the Exchequer after a period as Lord Chief Justice of Chester. The list of cases at the Assize was short, but the newly elected MP for Lloyd George's former parliamentary seat, Peter Thomas, later secretary of state for Wales, appeared as counsel for the prosecution.

Our stay at Caernarfon was particularly important for me because the stars of the Wales and Chester Circuit were appearing in a civil action there. Glyn Jones, William Arthian Davies, Edmund Davies and Vincent Lloyd-Jones were all QCs already and each became a High Court judge within the following eight years, starting with Arthian Davies that autumn. William Mars-Jones, another Johnian, who had been born and brought up at Llansannan in Denbighshire, was also in the case. It was he who persuaded me that I ought to try my luck at the common law Bar and join the Wales and Chester Circuit in view of my background. We had another link because Mars-Jones' father had been a successful woollen merchant, as well as a general agricultural merchant, who had shared the privilege of buying fleeces from North Wales farmers with my father and uncle and one other merchant throughout the Second World War.

Glyn Jones, the acting leader of the circuit, and Edmund Davies, who both came to lunch at the lodgings, were equally firm in their advice, so that I did not hesitate long before accepting Mars-Jones' kind offer to take me as his first pupil. I was influenced also by the fact that it was unlikely that I would be offered a tenancy in Brightman's chambers because a new tenant had been taken on there quite recently and needed time to make his way before another member of chambers was recruited.

Beaumaris was memorable for a brief sitting in the oldest courthouse in Britain, built in 1614, then still in use. The most remarkable feature was the elevated (and cramped) jury box, and the building is now a museum. However, Ruthin was much more instructive for me because I heard my first murder trial there. Leading for the defence was Rose Heilbron QC, the first woman barrister to practise as a silk (Helena Normanton, her predecessor in silk, did not do so), and Vincent Lloyd-Jones QC led for the prosecution. The case was very well conducted on both sides but the defendant, Harry Huxley, had no real defence and was sentenced to death on the second day of the trial.

The High Sheriff of Denbighshire was the Hon. John McLaren, a son of Lord Aberconway and a particularly elegant Old Etonian. His wife was Lady Rose McLaren, a sister of the Marquis of Anglesey and rightly renowned for her beauty. They lived in a cottage on the Bodnant estate and it was a unique experience to lunch with them, Lord Aberconway and the Angleseys on the Sunday of our visit and then to see Bodnant in sunshine at its spectacular full-blossomed best. It was a great sadness that John McLaren died less than a year later. At Mold the work was unremarkable but we stayed at Sychdyn (or Soughton) Hall, now a luxury hotel but then the home of Wynne Bankes, who had been for 10 years private secretary to successive Lord Chancellors. He was a son of Lord Justice Bankes, who had often sat in a famous division of the Court of Appeal comprising Thomas Edward Scrutton, James Atkin and himself. The latter, who lived into his nineties, had always been especially kind to my father and sponsored his appointment as vice-chairman of Quarter Sessions. It was particularly interesting, therefore, to be in the great man's house, which was built as a bishop's palace in 1714 and amended by Sir Charles Barry in the 1820s on the instructions of William John Bankes, the great traveller. While we were there the judge was good enough to visit my parents for tea at Highfield before we moved on to the Chester lodgings at Upton Heyes, next to Chester Zoo.

My social obligations at Chester were lightened by the welcome presence not only of Mr Justice Ormerod but also of his marshal, Huw Thomas, who had been a friend since RAF short course days. The judge had great charm and was a talented musician. He had played the big drum in the Blackburn Symphony Orchestra and had become a patron of Kathleen Ferrier, whom he had known since her days as an amateur singer in Blackburn. This was of particular interest to me because I had heard her moving recital with Gerald Moore in Lincoln's Inn Hall only six weeks earlier; and, very sadly, the judge was to preside at a memorial concert for her 20 months later in the same hall when Sir John Barbirolli conducted a string section of the Halle Orchestra and Evelyn Rothwell and Denis Matthews played.

The remainder of my pupillage with John Brightman passed in something of a haze because I was preoccupied with thoughts of common law practice and intended to make my first real court appearance at Flintshire Quarter Sessions to be held at Mold on 3 July. Courts of Quarter Sessions exercised jurisdiction broadly parallel to that of Assizes but dealt, in general, with lesser offences. The presiding chairman would be a qualified lawyer, who would conduct trials in the same manner as a judge, but who would sit with justices of the peace who were fellow members of the court with an equal say, particularly in matters of sentence. In Flintshire, the chairman was a High Court judge, Sir Austin Jones, son of a former local vicar, and his deputy then was Sir Ernest Goodman-Roberts QC, son of a former

Mold solicitor. Sir Ernest had been Conservative MP for Flintshire for five years in the 1920s and then Chief Justice of Burma from 1936 for about 10 years. However, in the 1950s he usually sat as a commissioner at the Central Criminal Court (the Old Bailey), where he was known irreverently as 'Bamboo Bill'.

My own task in July 1952 was to appear before Sir Austin and various justices of the peace, including my father. It was unusual for a barrister to appear before a member of his own family and it was frowned upon by bench and Bar alike but, on this occasion, Sir Austin insisted that my father should not leave the bench during the hearing of my cases because he knew that it was my first appearance and that they involved three pleas of guilty, in two of which I appeared for the prosecution and was not therefore concerned with the severity of the sentences.

Having taken the plunge in this way, I hurried off the same afternoon to Swansea to attend Bar mess that evening on the first day of Swansea Assizes in order to complete the procedure necessary for my election as a member of the Wales and Chester Circuit, which I had begun at Chester. It seems that no one objected and so I was duly sworn in, enabling me to collect a PPD (poor person's defence) as part of the largesse of Mr Justice Croom-Johnson the following morning. This required me to defend a young man charged with unlawful carnal knowledge of a girl aged under 16 years (but over 12 years); the available defence was that he had believed at the time of the offence on reasonable grounds that she was at least 16 years old. In the event the case was not heard until mid-July, when it came on before Mr Justice Ormerod and a jury and, to my relieved surprise, the defendant was acquitted.

My pupillage with Mars-Jones at Farrar's Building, in the Temple, adjacent to the round part of Temple Church, began on 22 July and his practice was to be a major preoccupation of mine for the next five years until he took silk. Mars-Jones was a very forceful personality, quite different from John Brightman, and a considerable entertainer as a guitarist and talented mimic. At St John's College, Cambridge, in the late 1930s, after attaining first-class honours at the University College of Wales, Aberystwyth, he had run several dance bands to the detriment of his academic progress. He had then served in the RNVR throughout the war, sailing in Russian and Maltese convoys as a radar direction officer on aircraft carriers, and had emerged as a lieutenant-commander with a military MBE when he stood as Labour candidate for West Denbighshire in the 1945 general election. His subsequent progress at the Bar was very rapid and he was arguably already the most successful junior barrister on the circuit by the time that I became his pupil.

Despite his natural gregariousness and love of the good life, Mars-Jones was an exceptionally hard worker and I could not have had a better mentor in the fields in which he practised. As a junior barrister, a major component of his work was personal-injuries litigation but he appeared regularly also in major criminal cases and, as was the custom then, he accepted divorce work on circuit when he was not otherwise engaged. Whatever the nature of the case might be, Mars-Jones' preparation was meticulous and the many solicitors who sent work to him were always confident that he would have mastered the material sent to him fully before they met.

Mars-Jones had married a fellow barrister, Sheila Cobon, before I met him and they were installed in a flat in Gray's Inn, where they lived for the rest of their lives, changing flat only once. They were integral parts of the life of the Inn for about 40 years, and their second son, Adam, the well-known writer and critic, gave touching and very accurate accounts of both of them in his essay in the compilation *Sons and Mothers* edited by Matthew and Victoria Glendinning. Sheila served for many years as a law reporter for *The Times* and the *Weekly Law Reports* and was also a successful chairman of London rent tribunals. My wife and I had special reason to be grateful to her because she proved to be an excellent godmother to our younger daughter Laura.

The advice to young barristers in those days was to hang around chambers during vacations because opportunities to appear in court as a replacement for a more experienced barrister might well occur. In my case a separate reason was that I was expected to 'devil' paperwork for my pupil master. There were always numerous sets of papers awaiting his attention in relation to which an advice (opinion) and/or a pleading (statement of the case) was required urgently. As his pupil, I was expected to read these papers and to attempt to deal with them as Mars-Jones would have done. This was an essential part of my apprenticeship and a mixed blessing for Mars-Jones: it could make his task easier if one was broadly correct but it could also be a quite punishing chore for him to read one's efforts if one was not.

In the event August 1952 was not a rewarding month for me financially. My only appearance in court was at Bow Street Magistrates' Court for a Johnian contemporary who was training as a doctor at Westminster Hospital. Flushed with a certain amount of alcohol, he had foolishly entered a nurses' hostel at the hospital, hoping to meet up with a nurse of his acquaintance for an obvious purpose. His presence was discovered all too soon and, because a purse or two had gone missing previously in the hostel, the police decided to charge my student friend with burglary, that is, breaking and entering the hostel with intent to steal, although there was no evidence at all that he had had a larcenous intention. His case was not reached on the first occasion when it was listed and on the second occasion I managed (with the assistance of the dean of the medical school) to persuade the prosecution to drop the charge, so I did not have to raise my voice in court.

My movements for the rest of that year were largely dictated by Mars-Jones' court commitments. Most of these were in North Wales at that time so that I was able to stay quite often at home with my parents, but Mars-Jones was a generous man and he spent a considerable amount of money entertaining me at dinner and in other ways. He was a very amusing companion, and pupillage with him was great fun as well as highly instructive. It provided me also with a wide range of introductions to solicitors in a short period of time, thus easing the development of my own practice later.

Our journeys took me all over North Wales again, starting with a rare arbitration in Denbigh in which Arthian Davies QC made one of his last appearances as a barrister before becoming a judge. It was during this period that I tackled my first substantial jury trial alone through the kindness of the well-known Holywell solicitor J. Kerfoot-Roberts. The case was heard at Chester Assizes before the very experienced and able Mr Justice Streatfield, who handled me with velvet gloves, realising how inexperienced I was. I have kept my brief, marked eight and two guineas, for sentimental reasons and because the defendant was acquitted of all charges on two indictments alleging conspiracy to contravene the food-rationing regulations and numerous breaches of those regulations. The judge ruled at the end of the prosecution case that there was no case to go to the jury on four counts and the jury acquitted the defendant on three other counts, with the result that the prosecution decided not to offer any evidence on the remaining charges. Thus I was able to feel the incomparable glow of self-satisfaction that follows a job successfully completed!

My underlying anxiety as my pupillage year approached its end was that of every other apprentice barrister, namely, whether I would be accepted as a tenant in my pupil master's chambers. My prospects at Farrar's Building were by no means clear cut because another young Welsh barrister, Esyr Lewis, had been taken on as a tenant in July 1952, and Arthian Davies QC had been replaced by another Wales and Chester Circuit member, John Marnan, a former Irish Guards officer who was intending to apply for silk soon. Although I did not know it at the time, there was also a strong outside contender for a place in the chambers. He is now His Honour George Dobry CBE, QC; he did a great deal in later years to assist the establishment of the legal profession in Poland after that country's traumatic years of fascism and communism. However, my pupil master proved to be a persuasive advocate for me and, to my great relief, I was accepted as a tenant from January 1953 on the basis that Esyr and I would act as 'devils' for Mars-Jones in order to enable him to keep pace with his voluminous paperwork.

You may well wonder how on earth I survived financially. That is a reasonable question and I am not confident about the answer. It was certainly not on my earnings from the Bar, which totalled 166 guineas (£174.40) in the whole year and which barely covered my chambers expenses, quite apart from travelling and hotel expenses. I must point out, however, that the third-class (now standard) return fare from Euston to Holywell was only about £3.30 and I was often able to stay at my parents' home overnight, as I have already said.

My assured annual income was only £200 from the McMahon studentship until the autumn of 1953, when I began to receive an additional £200 per year for three years from a Middle Temple Harmsworth Scholarship, which was awarded to me, at the second time of asking, at the end of September that year. I was fortunate to have a modest supplement as an ex-serviceman in the form of a Further Education and Training (FET) grant as a result of the kind intervention of Sir Walter Monckton, then KC, who had become the new Minister of Labour and National Service. The Ministry was understandably reluctant to fund my training further and refused me a grant for pupillage, but I was encouraged to write directly to Sir Walter as a fellow barrister: he followed the accepted etiquette of the Bar by replying to me personally and promptly in his own handwriting. What he said was that the decision against me had been correct but that he had given instructions that the rule should be waived for me because I was a deserving case!

My impecuniosity was such that I had to beg for a subsidy from my maternal grandmother to meet the cost of a holiday trip to Spain (£10 passage with Robin Jenks' car and £25 travel allowance). She and her older sister, Mary Sylvester, who predeceased her early in 1940, aged 82, had lived with us at Highfield from the outbreak of the Second World War. She died on 23 October 1952, at the age of 85, only two months after this final generosity on her part. For the rest of my outgoings I had to rely upon my father, who was already 74 years old. It was not until the summer of 1956 that I was able to supplement my income from the law by a regular payment for quasi-journalism from the BBC, which freed me from dependency on my father and helped me to start repaying my parents with a modest annuity for the rest of their lives. My bank overdraft at the end of 1952 was £370, having risen from £100 when I was called to the Bar, and I remained overdrawn continuously until just after I took silk in 1969.

8

THE WELSH BAR IN THE 1950s

Farrar's Building, which was my practising home for a quarter of a century, was rebuilt after its predecessor was destroyed in 1679 by a great fire that started in Pump Court. The new building was named after the Treasurer of the Inner Temple for that year, Thomas Farrer (the second 'a' resulted from popular usage). James Boswell lived there briefly in 1763 and first entertained Dr Johnson to dinner there. It was later pulled down in 1876 and replaced by the present, uglier building at a cost of about £6,000. This building was fortunate to survive the devastating bombing in the Second World War that laid low many of the neighbouring buildings. The first tenant of part of the new building was Sir William Harcourt, later Gladstone's Chancellor of the Exchequer, who probably ought to have succeeded him as prime minister instead of Queen Victoria's choice, Lord Rosebery.

When I became a tenant in February 1953, the relevant history of chambers extended back only to 1922, but they are still going strong. The building has four floors and a basement that was used for storage but is now an integral part of chambers; it has also been equipped with a lift, which was almost unthinkable in my time. For the first 30 years of its modern existence there were three and then two separate sets of barristers in the building, but the surviving two amalgamated very early in my pupillage when Arthian Davies became a judge. In due course, my chambers took over the tenancy of the whole building from the Inner Temple and we were lucky not to have to seek annexes elsewhere, as so many other chambers had to when the Bar expanded.

Arthian Davies' successor as head of the chambers was a strange, able man called Gerald Thesiger QC, a descendant of Lord Chelmsford, the Lord Chancellor for two periods in the 1860s, who himself became a

Queen's Bench judge in 1958. If I say that his cousins included Wilfred, the explorer and writer, and Ernest, the actor famed for playing the role of a butler, it may give some idea of the complexity of his personality. I was to share a room with him for five years, and he was always courteous to me but distant. He did not have a conventional civil practice but was much in demand in parliamentary private bill work and local authority work generally. His other main activities were as chairman of West Kent Quarter Sessions and Recorder successively of Hastings and Southend, so that he was very familiar with criminal law and, unusually, tended to view problems of civil law in the light of criminal law principles.

Farrar's Building was not regarded as one of the top chambers in the Temple but it was a good middle-tier set with a wide range of work. Chambers then were very much smaller than they are now and there were no more than about 14 active tenants in mine when I started. The ancestry of the general common law part of the chambers went back to Lord Merriman, who had taken the second floor in January 1922, adding the first floor later; he was still president of the Probate Divorce and Admiralty Division in 1953, having served earlier as Solicitor-General. His successor as head of the chambers for 12 years was Lord Morris of Borth-y-Gest, who continued to be a very loyal attender at chambers events. As for the ground floor, the tenants had specialised in parliamentary work for a long time and Jeremy Thorpe's father had been a member for the last three years before his early death in 1943. The head of the set when amalgamation took place was Harold Willis, a highly respected practitioner who took silk in 1952 and served as Treasurer of the Middle Temple in 1969; it was he who took over the headship of chambers in 1958 when Thesiger became a judge.

The amalgamation worked well because we had two very experienced clerks. The senior of the two, Joseph Smee, was a small man with a large, attractive personality and he had entered the Temple in 1904 at the age of 14. It was he who took care of all the civil and criminal work while Frank Crane, who had started in 1911 and had won the DCM in the First World War, came to us as clerk to the ground-floor set. Frank continued to look after the parliamentary and allied work, taking on much of Gerald Thesiger's work in the process. This arrangement continued for nearly 10 years until both clerks retired; it was very sad that Frank died in 1962, a very few months into his retirement, and he was rightly described as 'a gentle, kindly man'.

Although Farrar's Building has understandably been regarded at times since 1953 as Welsh circuit chambers, that is really a misnomer. When I became a tenant only four of us were members of the Wales and Chester Circuit and the number of juniors practising on the circuit has always been small, even as the chambers has expanded. We did, however, recruit over the years a number of silks who had practised at the local Bar in Wales as juniors and we maintained a strong link by having several Cardiff, Swansea and Chester barristers as 'door tenants', who used our chambers as a second home when they had work, usually appeals, in London. At least four of these recruits became head of the chambers after I had left, and all four (Lord Justice Roch, Lord Williams of Mostyn QC, Gerard Elias QC and Patrick Harrington QC) have had very successful careers in differing ways.

The senior junior in the chambers, with an entirely civil practice, was a quiet impressive man called H.J. Baxter, who had been a lieutenant-colonel in the Intelligence Corps during the war and became a respected County Court judge. He was one of the select few who had achieved a first in the Bar final examination and he shared a room with another clever man, Anthony Barrowclough, who was appointed to be the first parliamentary ombudsman in 1985. But it was Mars-Jones who dominated the chambers while still a junior barrister, and it was to him that Esyr and I owed allegiance as his 'devils'. We were later joined by W.L. Monro Davies, after he had done his pupillage elsewhere. The arrangement was that we would wade into Mars-Jones' outstanding paperwork and draft it for him; he would consider our drafts and, if was able to accept them to a substantial extent, they would be typed with his amendments and, in due course, he would pay us half his fee for the work (a process in which he was both fair and honest).

This arrangement was, of course, extremely beneficial to each of us because it provided vital additional income and, equally importantly, it introduced us to a wide range of work that we would not otherwise have seen. Mars-Jones was not exactly a slave driver but he certainly expected us to put his work before our pleasure. In those days it was customary for chambers to open for the morning on Saturdays, and we would meet Bill then, often on his return from a heavy week's work on circuit, and review both the work accomplished and that yet to be done. But we would then repair to a local hostelry with him for suitable refreshment before going our separate ways.

At a later stage, certainly by the 1960s, starting at the Bar became much less financially hazardous. The problem was to secure a tenancy in reasonably successful chambers but, if that was overcome, there was a good prospect of earning a living income quite soon. That was not the position in the 1950s, however, and many of my contemporaries who had intended to practise left the Bar early on. Friends and colleagues who did this but later became very well known in other spheres included Robin Day, Jeremy Thorpe, Norman St John-Stevas, Patrick Jenkin, Peter Gibbins, Michael Summerskill and Percy Cradock. In summary, the short-term prospects were not good, except

perhaps at some country centres, even though the long-term future proved
to be excellent for those who clung on at the Bar.

In 1953 there were about 2,000 practising barristers in England and
Wales but the number dipped well below that figure in the course of the
decade before it began to grow steadily to its present level of over 12,000.
The reason for this early decline was that legal aid had not yet become a really
valuable source of income, as it did later for the large majority of barristers.
The Legal Aid and Advice Act 1949, making provision for legal aid for
litigants in civil and divorce actions, was still in its infancy, and poor persons'
defences (PPDs) in the criminal courts earned a junior barrister only three
guineas (£3.15) for a plea in mitigation when the defendant pleaded guilty
or if a trial lasted less than five hours. For a dock brief, when counsel was
selected and paid for by the defendant himself, without the intervention of a
solicitor, the only fee was two guineas, however long the proceedings lasted.
In civil work, if the client had a legal aid certificate under the new Act, one
received 85 per cent of what was assessed by a court official (a taxing master
or district registrar) as a fair fee, but one usually had to wait many months
(at best) for the assessment to be made.

As time went by, the volume of litigation, particularly for personal
injuries sustained in road or industrial accidents, mushroomed so that
many barristers (including me) earned substantial incomes from the work.
A typical fee for a trial would be between 30 and 50 guineas with 'refresh-
ers' to be added for each additional day that the trial lasted. In criminal
cases the fees for poor persons' defences were increased by 50 per cent in
the autumn of 1953 but it was not until 1960 that they were assessed as
a fair fee for the work done (without a 15 per cent reduction), by which
time my practice was mainly in civil cases. The other main source of
income for a general common law barrister was divorce work. Although
there was already a specialist divorce Bar in London, most common law
barristers would accept divorce work because it was usually comparatively
undemanding. The fee for appearing in an undefended divorce suit rose
gradually from five and two guineas (the two being for a conference with
the client) to ten or twelve and two guineas; and one received 85 per cent
of this fee if the client was 'legally aided'. A local barrister might well have
half a dozen or more such cases listed in a morning so that the work was a
very profitable sideline and remained so throughout the 1950s and 1960s
while I was a junior barrister.

As I have said earlier, barristers' assessed fees were invariably stated in
guineas and a small amount, of the order of 5 per cent, was added as a fee
for the clerk. Most barristers' clerks were more generously remunerated,

however, and a common arrangement, which was adopted in Farrar's Building, was to pay one's clerk 10 per cent of the total amount received as a fee for a case (including the added fee for the clerk). Thus, the senior clerk in successful chambers received a very substantial income. The arrangement was tolerated until barristers' earnings escalated from 1979 onwards, following the substantial reductions in income tax, which made high fees much more worthwhile. After 1979 more realistic arrangements began to be made, but it must be remembered that, when I was at the Bar, a barrister was usually required to pay an additional 10 per cent of his gross earnings as such to the head of chambers as a contribution to the rent of chambers from an Inn of Court and general office expenses, including the wages of junior clerks and a typist.

This was the financial framework of the profession that I entered with great hopes but guarded optimism in 1953. My one major advantage was that I was unmarried, and remained so until 1960, because I could not possibly have supported a wife much earlier. A lesser, but relevant, advantage was that, because of national service, I was three or four years older than many when they start at the Bar. I had therefore a thin veneer of maturity, which did not fool solicitors but was slightly reassuring to lay clients.

Although the prospects for a young barrister seemed to be rather daunting when I started to practise, as they always had been in the past, the long-term prospects proved to be excellent, if one was able to survive the first five or ten years. The contemporaries I mentioned who left the Bar did so for a variety of reasons, but not for want of the necessary ability. Several were bent on political careers and two opted for the Foreign Office. Robin Day was probably the keenest of them to practise at the Bar and had an excellent pupillage with a star of the junior criminal bar, Fred (later Lord Justice) Lawton, but both his parents were dead and he did not have the financial means to support himself through the early years. I was lucky to have my father to support me, albeit with some difficulty, and political temptation only came several years later and then fruitlessly.

The reason why, unknown to us, long-term prospects were to be so good was that both the Bar and the bench were to expand dramatically in the last four decades of the twentieth century. The 2,000 barristers in practice in 1953 (480 of whom were in provincial centres) reduced in number to 1,925 by the end of 1959 but then substantial growth began with the result that, by the time that I was sworn in as a judge in January 1978 the practising Bar had more than doubled in size. On 1 October 1977 there were 4,076, of whom 336 were women, and 1,182 practised provincially. A year later the comparable figures were 4,263, 370 and 1,273.

Increases in the ranks of the Supreme Court judges had matched this expansion of the Bar. The Court of Appeal, excluding heads of division, had risen from 8 to 17, Queen's Bench judges from 23 to 45, Chancery judges from 7 to 11 and Family (previously Probate Divorce and Admiralty) judges from 8 to 16. Equally importantly, the recommendations of the Beeching Commission had been implemented in January 1972 with a vast increase in the full-time judiciary at Circuit judge (previously County Court and Quarter Sessions) level. The opportunities for preferment available to the relatively small number of barristers in successful practice from the 1950s were therefore considerable by the mid-1970s.

Since then the Bar has continued to expand rapidly, as I said earlier, and the judiciary has grown further, although not as dramatically. These further increases have given rise to major problems, including huge increases in the size of barristers' chambers and a loss of professional intimacy, so that starting at the Bar now seems to me to be even more daunting than it was for me, even if one is able to secure a good pupillage with a tenancy to follow.

I was fortunate in another major respect in joining what was then the Wales and Chester Circuit of barristers at its zenith. A pedant might counter that the circuit only existed as such for 62 years and so the word 'zenith' is inappropriate but I have in mind a much longer history of the practising Bar in Wales, extending over at least four and a half centuries. Without going into unnecessary detail, the laws of England were not fully applied to Wales until the reign of Henry VIII, when statutes enacted in 1535/36 and 1542 sought to establish order in place of the previous chaos. It was in the latter year that the King's Court of Great Session in Wales was created, and it remained in being for nearly three centuries until it was abolished in 1830, in the teeth of fierce opposition, and replaced by the English circuit system. During that long period there were four circuits covering Wales, two in the south and two in the north, each with two judges latterly, who were practising barristers; in 1785, for example, about 50 counsel were listed as practising on one or other of these four circuits. From 1830 onwards, under the English system, there were two circuits, the South Wales (excluding Monmouthshire) and Chester and the North Wales and Chester with about 34 practising barristers divided almost equally between the two.

The reason why Chester was annexed to the name of both these circuits was that Queen's Counsel belonging to either were permitted to appear in Cheshire without having to charge a special additional fee for doing so, which would otherwise have been required for trespassing on an alien circuit. When the Second World War started, however, the ranks of barristers in North Wales were severely depleted because so many of them joined the services and it was decided in 1940 that the right of audience in North Wales should be extended to members of the South Wales and Chester Circuit. Thus, *de facto*, an almost full union of the two circuits occurred and it was completed *de jure* in the autumn of 1945 when delegations were appointed to meet the Bar Council to give effect to the amalgamation.

The Wales and Chester Circuit came into being officially with about 120 members and with local practising centres at Cardiff, Swansea, Chester and, from time to time, Carmarthen. It included the whole of Cheshire but not Monmouthshire until January 1972, when the latter county, later called Gwent, was transferred to it on the demise of the Oxford Circuit. The local Bar at Newport under Charles Pitchford opted then to join the Wales and Chester Circuit and moved to Cardiff, where they set up very successful separate chambers. Henceforth, there were to be six barristers' circuits instead of seven. The only relevant further change was that we lost Cheshire, to the great distress of many of us, in April 2007 as a consequence of administrative changes imposed by the Lord Chancellor and (it is said) of devolution.

By the time that I joined the circuit in July 1952 the circuit system generally was about to become less rigid because of improvements in transport and a general reaction against anti-competitive rules. The requirement of special fees for 'trespassing' to which I referred was regarded as anachronistic and was soon replaced by a system of much smaller daily penalty payments that were payable by counsel rather than the lay client; even those payments were dispensed with in the 1970s. It thus became unnecessary eventually for a barrister to join a circuit in order to appear in the provinces (it had never been necessary to do so to appear in the central London courts) but circuit loyalty remained strong in those who did join and the system as a whole continues to be very beneficial in helping to secure the maintenance of high professional standards, imposing the necessary discipline and aiding the continuing education of the Bar.

This was the background of the circuit that provided me with a substantial part of my earnings throughout my 25 years of practice at the Bar. Its leader when I joined was still Ralph Sutton QC, mainly remembered as the co-author of the student textbook *Sutton and Shannon* on the law of contract, which went through many editions. He was a distinguished common lawyer but was semi-retired by 1952 and the *de facto* leader of the circuit was Glyn Jones QC, who was appointed a judge of the Queen's Bench Division the following year, after impressing Lord Goddard when he visited the circuit as Lord Chief Justice. On Glyn Jones' elevation, Edmund Davies QC became the leader for the next five years until he too was appointed a Queen's Bench judge and was succeeded by Vincent Lloyd-Jones QC, a brother of the well-known Congregational minister and former physician, Dr Martin Lloyd-Jones of Westminster Chapel in Buckingham Gate. These three QCs with Arthian Davies QC formed a particularly strong quartet at the head of the circuit when I joined and were excellent models for a young aspiring barrister to follow. Vincent in turn became a High Court judge in 1960 but was less happy in that role because he was assigned to the Probate Divorce and Admiralty Division in which the work was spiritually uncongenial to him. His consolation in later life was the success of his son David as an orchestral conductor and the first music director of English Opera North.

Despite what I have just written, the major strength of the circuit when I began lay in the formidable membership of the junior Bar, most of whom had returned from war service and two of whom had endured long periods of confinement as prisoners of war (another was Charles Pitchford, who joined from Newport later). Outstanding among them was Elwyn Jones, already Labour MP for West Ham South, who took silk in 1953, joining in that rank another MP, Roderic Bowen, who preceded him by a year and who represented Cardiganshire as a Liberal until he became a national insurance commissioner in 1966. Elwyn, of course, served as Attorney-General from 1964 to 1970 and then as Lord Chancellor for five years from 1974, the first member of a Welsh circuit to hold that office since Lord Sankey in the early 1930s, who began practice at the Bar in Cardiff.

Other prominent junior members of the circuit were Norman Richards, later the senior official referee; Geraint Rees (brother of the better-known Goronwy Rees, friend of the spy Burgess and sometime principal of University College Wales, Aberystwyth), who became a Metropolitan magistrate and then a judge of the Central Criminal Court (the Old Bailey); Ewan Wallis-Jones, eventually the senior judge of Cardiff County Court; Peter (later Lord) Thomas, then the recently elected Conservative MP for Conway, who was to be appointed secretary of state for Wales in the Heath government and chairman of the Conservative Party; and Bill Mars-Jones, my pupil master, who was appointed a Queen's Bench judge in 1969. All of these juniors practised from London chambers but the amount of work available on circuit was already sufficient to support strong local junior Bars at Cardiff, Swansea and Chester, and the balance of convenience was very much in favour of local practice, eliminating repetitive long rail and road journeys to and from London. It was only QCs who were required to have their chambers in London, and even that rule was annulled by the end of the 1960s.

Cardiff was a particularly strong centre and had David Pennant and Meurig Evans as two of its most prominent juniors, followed by a galaxy of eminent people that included Phillip Wien, Norman Francis, John Rutter and, most distinguished of all, Tasker Watkins VC, who had won his magnificent award for bravery in the battle of the Falaise Gap in August 1944. I must mention also another brave man, Tommy Rhys-Roberts, who won the George Medal in the Italian campaign and whose splendid eccentricities and generosity delighted (most of the time) a generation of his fellow members of the circuit. All of these, except Tommy, became in due course able High Court or circuit judges and Tasker ended up as Deputy Chief Justice as well as a Lord Justice of Appeal. As for Tommy, he was the son of a well-known Welsh diva and a London solicitor who was for a number of years a partner of David Lloyd George. It was fitting, therefore, that he should lead us at every Bar mess in singing the anthem 'Lloyd George Knew my Father' to the tune of 'Onward Christian Soldiers'. He took silk in 1972 and I shall never forget appearing against him for two defendants in his last case, when he conducted the prosecution of several defendants for conspiracy to rob a Cardiff bank most effectively only three weeks before he died of cancer in 1975.

Swansea, where Edmund Davies had practised before the war, was less strong in numbers than Cardiff for obvious reasons but had a number of prominent characters in its two sets of chambers. Several County Court judges had practised there in the past and at least two were still on the bench. The major set in St Helen's Road (the landlord of which was Norman Richards) was headed by Rowe Harding, a sporting hero who had been a notable rugby wing three-quarter and captain of Cambridge University and Wales in the 1920s. Joint head with him was Alun Talfan Davies, later knighted, who became a legendary figure as a barrister and an entrepreneur. The son of a Presbyterian minister with a well-known brother and a nephew who became controller of the BBC in Wales, Alun built up a huge practice in West Wales as a junior barrister and, after taking silk in 1961, was heavily involved in a wide spectrum of activities in Wales from the National Eisteddfod and Harlech Television to the Commercial Bank of Wales. He managed also, while still practising, to serve as Recorder of Cardiff, an appellate judge of Jersey and Guernsey and a member of the Criminal Injuries Compensation Board. In the same chambers also, already building up a large practice, was the much admired Breuan Rees, who became the most effective junior on the circuit and might well have been appointed junior counsel to the Treasury in London in 1967 but for his untimely death that year from a heart complaint.

There were only three or four barristers practising in Chester chambers before the end of the Second World War but the Bar grew rapidly there after the war under the leadership of two outstanding men, Emlyn later Lord Hooson QC and Sir Robin David QC. I had met Emlyn Hooson in university days when he was a prominent Liberal at the University College of Wales, Aberystwyth. After a pupillage in Liverpool, he very bravely moved to Chester, taking over the experienced clerk, Bill Jones, to a senior junior barrister who had just died and, in effect, reopening the latter's chambers. Emlyn made rapid progress and continued to do so after taking silk in 1960, despite being elected Liberal MP for Montgomeryshire in 1962 in succession to Clement Davies QC. His chambers too have flourished, having provided a practising base for two peers, Lord Thomas QC of Gresford and Lord Carlile QC of Berriew, as well as several circuit judges; by the time that I retired in 1996 it had 20 members.

The other set of chambers in Chester, at 40 King Street, was quite firmly established with Francis Williams QC, of long North Wales ancestry, as its head. In 1952, the year in which he took silk, he was already mainly a part-time judicial figure, holding office in many county Quarter Sessions and the recordership of Birkenhead. He succeeded his brother as the eighth baronet in 1971. Two of the senior juniors in the chambers, Gerry Lind-Smith and John Seys-Llewellyn, had been called to the Bar before the war and progressed to the County Court bench before the Beeching changes occurred. The driving force was provided by Robin David, who had started off as a rather nervous advocate in 1949 but had shaken this off rapidly and had acquired a dominant criminal practice and a growing civil practice by 1952. He was appointed a deputy chairman of Cheshire Quarter Sessions as early as 1962 and took silk in 1968, but his likely progress to the High Court bench was arrested then because he agreed to accept the newly created full-time office of chairman of Cheshire Quarter Sessions. This became a circuit judgeship in 1972, and Robin remained the senior judge of the Crown Court in Cheshire until his retirement in 1997, having been knighted in 1995. He earned widespread admiration as a judge and, like Judge Francis in Cardiff, declined advancement to the High Court bench, in his case because he wished to look after his wife, who was very disabled for many years until her death in 1999. By the time that I retired there were 23 barristers in 40 King Street and 18 in a third set of chambers in Chester, so that the total Bar there had increased from 4 to 61 in the half-century following the end of the war.

I have given this detailed picture of the Wales and Chester Circuit in 1952 because it was the pool into which I plunged when I began to practise.

At that time Mars-Jones' own practice was mainly in the north because his family roots were in Denbighshire and it was natural for me to follow in his footsteps, not only as his pupil but also because my father was well known in North Wales.

Looking back now, I am very glad that for the whole of the period when I was in junior practice, that is, from 1953 to 1969, the old system of Assizes and Quarter Sessions still reigned. It was clear that it could not continue indefinitely because of the rate of increase in the volume of cases to be dealt with on indictment, committals for sentence from magistrates' courts and appeals from those courts. But it was comforting to a novice to be following procedures that had been in force for many years and to appear in courts with a long tradition in the administration of justice.

A particularly attractive feature of the system, of which one became aware very soon, was the friendship and intimacy of the Bar, unlike any other profession that I know, but which has now been diluted to some extent by the explosive increase in its numbers. The procedures at Assizes and Quarter Sessions encouraged this comradeship of the profession. In earlier eras the Bar would, for example, follow the High Court judge and the circuit officers from one Assize town to another so that the Bar mess was a nightly affair. Even in my time there would be great assemblies of the junior Bar on the first day of major Assizes and Quarter Sessions when anticipated pleas of guilty were listed for hearing and disposal so that a well-attended dinner could be convened at the Bar hotel. Moreover, it was the practice at virtually all Assizes for the high sheriff to invite local worthies and the Bar and solicitors to luncheon on the first day, providing an influential captive audience for the most junior barrister, whose duty it was to propose a witty vote of thanks. Unhappily, most of that has now been lost with the establishment of the Crown Court in almost continuous session throughout the year in all the main regional centres. Bar mess is still held according to patterns that vary from circuit to circuit, but it is often mainly an assembly for dinner of local barristers after a formal meeting to discuss circuit matters; visiting judges are usually invited to one of these dinners during a tour of duty at a major centre.

My own experience as a junior barrister can be conveniently divided into two periods: the first was from 1953 to Easter 1957, when my 'devilling' work ceased because Mars-Jones became a QC; the second was from then until Easter 1969, when I myself took silk, Mars-Jones having been appointed a Queen's Bench judge on St David's Day that year.

In my first post-pupillage year at the Bar from 6 February 1953 I earned fees from my own practice totalling £640 (double my earnings in the previous year), but about 85 per cent of the total was for work in criminal and divorce cases and it was almost wholly earned from solicitors in the northern part of my circuit. Moreover, only a substantial part of these fees (mainly those in criminal cases) was paid within the year. My highest fee was 50 guineas for defending a man at Flintshire Assizes, for which I had to miss the wedding of a very close friend, Kenneth James, and my lowest fee was one guinea each for three poor persons' (servicemen's) divorces heard at one sitting in Chester. On top of these earnings I was paid by Mars-Jones about £150 for 'devilling', which was a very important bonus and helped me to keep my head just above water financially.

Socially, life was about as pleasant as it could be for a young bachelor in London. Sylvia and I were surrounded by friends, and Chelsea was just around the corner: we did not have to wait for the so-called 'Swinging Sixties' to enjoy the King's Road to the full, contrary to the impression of modern journalists who were not even born then. We began 1953 with a lively 'at home' party including budding politicians such as Geoffrey Howe, Norman St John-Stevas, Philip Goodhart and Jack Ashley, the producer Anthony Besch, a range of journalists including Eve Perrick and Doone Beale, some barristers, of course, and a sprinkling of diplomats whom I had met with and through Kenneth James.

This helped to set the tone for the year but our numbers were seriously affected by the separate departures of Kenneth James, Robin Day and Keith Kyle. The former flew off to Tokyo by Comet on 14 August to take up his first overseas posting in the Foreign Office and, more regretfully, Robin Day left for Washington on 23 August, travelling by the SS *Queen Elizabeth*, to work as a press officer for the British Information Services. As I have said earlier, he had excellent prospects for success at the Bar but, already aged 29, he did not have the financial support necessary to carry him through the difficult early years of practice. I can still picture the small gloomy party that saw him off at Waterloo station, including Ivan Yates, Meg Gratey, my sister and me. We did not realise then that he would be back in about a year and ready to take the plunge into broadcasting and journalism. Robin was fortunate also to be joined in Washington within a couple of months by his great Oxford friend, Keith Kyle, on the latter's appointment as the Washington correspondent of *The Economist*.

There was much to please a young man in London then with time to enjoy himself. I remember particularly the review *Airs on a Shoestring* at the Royal Court Theatre with Max Adrian and Moyra Frazer, *A Woman of No Importance* at the Savoy, *The Apple Cart* with Noel Coward as King Magnus at the Theatre Royal, Haymarket, and Terence Rattigan's *Sleeping Prince* with the Oliviers at the Phoenix. Irmgard Seefried was rivalling Elisabeth Schwarzkopf in recital with Gerald Moore at the Royal Festival Hall and there were concerts by the newly formed Leppard Chamber Orchestra (later to become the English Chamber Orchestra) at the Wigmore Hall, sponsored by Kenneth James' close friend from Cambridge days, Leopold de Rothschild. I also attended memorial recitals for Kathleen Ferrier and Dylan Thomas, both of whom died in 1953. The moving recital for the former on 14 December in Lincoln's Inn, in which Denis Matthews played a Bach concerto, has already been mentioned; there was a grander commemoration of Dylan Thomas two months later at the Royal Festival Hall with a glittering cast, including Emlyn Williams.

While I sauntered along as a complacent bachelor, matrimony was very much in the air for my contemporaries in 1953. Most importantly, my eldest brother Stuart married Margaret Elinor Owen on 17 June at Flint Parish Church and I acted as his best man. Their marriage proved to be very happy and lasted for nearly 40 years until Margaret's untimely death from the cruel motor neurone disease on 4 June 1993. Their son Michael, whose main occupation is that of an independent television producer, wrote a very moving book, *Staying Close*, published by Constable in 2003, in which he spells out a positive approach to dying and bereavement in the light of this sad experience.

Concentrating on my legal work meant that I eschewed politics for the time being with some relief and I was glad not to have to make many public speeches outside court. I did accept an invitation from another Johnian, Ian McIntyre, to speak in his change of officers debate on 4 June 1953, when he retired as president of the Union Society. He was to have a very successful career in the BBC, rising to controller of Radio Four and then Radio Three and later spending a year as an associate editor of *The Times*. However, his choice of motion on this occasion, which I had to oppose, was the not very inspiring statement 'Too many people talk too much'. It is difficult enough to speak effectively to a sophisticated Union Society audience on returning after one's own time unless one has already achieved distinction in the outside world or, at least, the subject is to one's taste. In the event I would have been wiser to decline the president's kind invitation because I was not at all happy with my performance on that occasion. Otherwise, I seem to have kept myself free from extramural performances, apart from a couple of short broadcasts on the BBC's North American service at the invitation of Ivan Yates, who had become a talks producer on the service.

Thus, at the age of 27, I was more or less fully launched on what was to become my lifetime career. It was to prove extremely demanding, to an extent that I did not then fully understand; but, years later, I do not regret the decision that I made and I am very grateful that, unlike many who started out much later, I did not have to cope with several career changes during my working life.

9

BARRISTER'S DEVIL

Bill Mars-Jones had by far the broadest junior practice on the Wales and Chester Circuit during the period when I devilled for him and a great advantage for me was that, on occasions, I was briefed as his junior: he became used to working with me and found my notes for him reasonably legible. His cases were usually, of course, much more interesting and often more dramatic than anything that came my way in those early years. A striking example was provided early on by a trial at Carmarthen Assizes in March 1954 in which a 25-year-old farm worker (and son of a butcher) called Ronald Harries was convicted of murdering a smallholder and agricultural contractor, John Harries, and his wife, who were described as second cousins of the accused man.

Leading counsel for the prosecution was Edmund Davies QC with Mars-Jones as his junior and I was given a noting brief, which meant that I had to record the evidence as accurately as I could, mainly for the benefit of my leader, whilst Mars-Jones was able to concentrate on giving him wider assistance (my own fee was 12 guineas per day). The case attracted national publicity because of the callousness of the crime and the difficulty that had been encountered in discovering what had happened to the deceased couple after they had last been seen alive, other than by the accused, at the end of a harvest thanksgiving service on 16 October 1953. The death penalty was still in force for murder and Ronald Harries, who was defended by Vincent Lloyd-Jones QC and Elwyn Jones, was later hanged because there were no meaningful mitigating circumstances.

The accused had been interviewed by the police following the disappearance of the two deceased and had said that he had driven them to Carmarthen railway station during the morning of Saturday 17 October, where they were to catch a train to London for a holiday, an explanation that he had given to two associates of the deceased, which they had not believed and which had resulted in a report to the police. Detective Superintendent Capstick of Scotland Yard was called in to lead the investigation and he organised large-scale search parties in which 400 local farmers took part over an area of about 80 square miles in the quest for the bodies, which were eventually found on 16 November in part of a field where kale had been replanted upside down.

Ronald Harries protested his innocence throughout his trial before Mr Justice Havers, which lasted seven days. A crowd of 5,000, mostly women, who awaited the verdict of the jury in the square outside the Old Shire Hall, cheered the outcome and booed Harries as he was driven away to Swansea prison. He had been very pert and self-confident when Edmund Davies first cross-examined him the previous Friday afternoon and Edmund had been rather taken aback by his performance then; but meticulous preparation by my leader, who remained in Carmathen over the weekend, produced very different results the following Monday, when Harries had some difficulty in remembering his earlier extempore lies. His appeal was heard by the Court of Criminal Appeal two months later but it was virtually unarguable and I prize the copy of Capstick's excellent report of his investigation, which accompanied my brief.

Otherwise, my practice continued much as before but it increased reasonably steadily. My gross earnings for the second post-pupillage year were £1,080, so I had nearly doubled the previous year, which was regarded as a desirable objective in one's early years; and devilling continued to bring in about £200 a year. In court my activities were almost wholly in Cheshire and North Wales, apart from my one foray into South Wales in the Harries case. Mars-Jones had another notorious murder case at Carmarthen Assizes the following year, in which the Polish accused, Onufrejczyk, was thought to have fed the body of his business partner into a pig food machine and was convicted of murder without any trace of the body being found; my fellow devil, Esyr Lewis, was deservedly awarded the noting brief for the prosecution in that case.

I remained in the flat at 39 Cadogan Place with Sylvia until the end of July 1954. Altogether, it was a pleasing time and during this period Sylvia met her future husband John Thompson, later director of radio at the Independent Broadcasting Authority, whom she married in December 1957, shortly before he became New York correspondent of the *Daily Express*.

On leaving 39 Cadogan Place I was able to move in the autumn of 1954 to 98 Beaufort Mansions in Beaufort Street, Chelsea, to share a flat with

Robin Day and Ivan Yates, while Mrs Yates, Ivan's mother, who was the tenant, visited South Africa for several months. Robin had returned from Washington and had started to freelance for a short period, giving Workers' Education Association (WEA) lectures, among other activities, before he was appointed as a talks producer for BBC radio. My main recollection of our joint sub-tenancy is of highly sophisticated arguments every fortnight or so about the apportionment of the household expenses, bearing in mind our different busy and irregular lives as well as our impecuniosity! However, we managed to remain good friends and I was lucky enough to be able to help Robin in a positive way immediately after our very convenient and comfortable stay together came to an end on 2 June 1955.

Eleven days later, I lunched at Gray's Inn with Esyr Lewis and saw on the noticeboard an advertisement for newscasters posted by Independent Television News. The new television channel, ITV, was due to start that autumn and the advertisement indicated that a new type of newsreader with wider responsibilities and strong personality was being sought: a barrister, for example, might have the necessary qualities to fulfil the role. It struck me immediately that Robin could be an ideal candidate for this opening and I telephoned him at once at the BBC to tell him about it. Such was the need for discretion that he left his office to go to a public call box to continue the conversation, but it proved to be a decisive moment for him, as he always acknowledged in his writings. He duly entered the selection process, which was under the direction of Aidan Crawley, the former MP who was the first editor of ITN. Robin was eventually chosen, against very tough competition, as one of the first three intended newscasters. The other two chosen were Tony Crosland and Christopher Chataway, but the former withdrew because he wanted to write a book (later published with the title *The Conservative Enemy*); and Ludovic Kennedy became the third newscaster in the late spring of 1956. Robin began working for ITN on 22 August 1955 and rapidly became one of the best-known public faces when commercial television was launched exactly a month later (he presented the news for the first time the following evening).

Sylvia had herself joined the BBC as a talks producer by this time and was working on *Woman's Hour* under Janet Quigley. She had moved from *Vogue Export Book* to the *Daily Express* and from there to *Time and Tide*, a weekly political magazine owned and edited by Lady Rhondda. Sylvia remained with the BBC intermittently until she retired, leaving first to join her husband in the USA and later to care for their three children.

Soon after leaving Beaufort Mansions I was able, at the beginning of July 1955, to move to the top floor of 131 Old Church Street, Chelsea, a house owned by a Millington-Synge, opposite the famous houses at 64 and 66, one by Gropius and Maxwell Fry (occupied then by Benn Levy and Fay Compton) and the other by Mendelsohn and Chermayeff. It was a delightful location, close to the Chelsea Arts Club, and I was sorry to leave at the end of April 1956 for more spacious accommodation at 39 Roland Gardens, SW7, now part of a rather expensive hotel.

I kept alive my inevitable continuing interest in politics by joining, at the invitation of Ivan Yates, an informal group of contemporaries, almost wholly made up of Labour Party members, who met irregularly at each other's houses or flats to hear a prominent politician's views on a current issue. We called ourselves, rather discreetly, 'The Group', not wishing to rival the Conservative Bow Group, which was achieving great prominence at the time under friends such as Geoffrey Howe, Patrick Jenkin and Peter Emery. A history of our more modest group was edited and published much later by Michael Summerskill (son of Dr Edith) and Brian Bivett (then deputy director of the Institute of British Contemporary History) under the title *The Group, 1954–1960: A Time of Hope.*

Two of the main moving spirits were Bill Rodgers and Dick Taverne, who were anxious to move away from old ideologies and to lead more moderate thinking. It is not surprising that some members of the group became the nucleus, or part of it, of the Campaign for Democratic Socialism, supporting Hugh Gaitskell and contesting the campaign for unilateral nuclear disarmament, which gained momentum within the Labour Party from 1957 onwards and achieved its greatest victory at the Scarborough annual party conference on 5 October 1960. We called ourselves for this purpose the 'Labour Manifesto Group', 26 of us having signed a manifesto addressed to the Labour movement, which was written by Tony Crosland and Philip Williams, a fellow of Nuffield College, Oxford, and published on 29 October 1960.

Before we became embroiled in the nuclear disarmament debate, however, there was a more urgent and controversial subject on which to focus our attention, namely, the ill-starred Suez adventure, of which Keith Kyle later provided the definitive history, *Suez*. It may be difficult for younger people to understand the extent to which the British government's actions in the autumn of 1956 divided opinion in this country, but there were close parallels nearly 50 years later in relation to the invasion of Iraq, of which Keith was acutely aware. A major difference, however, was that the British action in 1956 was firmly opposed by the United States government. Then, very many British lawyers, including Sir Walter Monckton QC in the Cabinet, who moved sideways from minister for defence to paymaster-general on 18 October as the crisis loomed, questioned the legality of the British invasion; and there were, of course, very strong suspicions (later proved to be justified) of collusion between Britain, France and Israel.

Like many of my contemporaries at the Bar, I was firmly opposed to the invasion and I attended a few meetings with like-minded persons, not limited to members of the Bar. We called ourselves the 'Suez Protest Group' and we joined in a great demonstration in Trafalgar Square on Sunday, 4 November, at which Aneurin Bevan was in sparkling form, repairing damage caused by Edith Summerskill in a misjudged earlier speech. Prominent at our meetings were Peter Webster, later chairman of the Bar and a High Court judge, Paul Johnson, the well-known journalist and historian who was then decidedly left wing, and Geoffrey Howe. The one positive action that three of us did take was to write a letter to Monckton, urging him to use his influence to save the peace and looking to him with 'sympathy and hope'. This letter was seen by Keith Kyle when he was revising his book for reissue in 2003 in the light of further disclosed government papers: it was dated 4 November 1956 and the signatories were Peter Webster, Dick Taverne and myself. Keith records that Sir Walter replied warmly but non-committally to Dick Taverne; a memorandum that he wrote for the record at the same time contained the sentence 'I have never been able to convince myself that armed intervention was right but I have not been prepared to resign.' He had been assured that such a step would bring the government down. As for our protest group, it was agreed on 15 November that we should disband because our main purpose, the ending of the war, had been achieved.

An unusual event in 1956 was an invitation from Ivan Yates to spend the weekend at Randolph Churchill's house at East Bergholt in Suffolk, in the latter's absence but with his permission. This was at the end of January when Ivan was helping Randolph to write the biography of his father that Martin Gilbert was to complete after Randolph's death. Ivan was one of a succession of distinguished helpers and his main job was to assemble the vast material available in date order so that Randolph could then work on it. I had met Randolph previously at dinner at the Cambridge Union and had not warmed to him, but it was fascinating to explore his lovely house close to the river Stour, to admire the many excellent paintings by Sir Winston that filled the walls and even to stare guiltily at the address book on his desk, filled with the names of almost everyone who mattered.

The Conservative Party annual conference that year was held, rather unusually, at Llandudno, quite near my parents' home. Robin Day, who was reporting it for ITN, invited me to join him there and I sat with him and the cameras viewing the scene from the highest benches before mingling with leading politicians on the promenade and having tea with Christopher Chataway at the Imperial Hotel. This was in mid-October 1956, at the height of the Suez crisis (the canal was nationalised by Nasser on 26 July), a fortnight before Israel's attack on Egypt. My main recollection is of Harold Macmillan, then Chancellor of the Exchequer, shuffling along as he walked, like an old man; it was reported that Dr Charles Hill (then Postmaster-General and later chairman of the BBC) unkindly described him as pretending to be an elder statesman but he was to be prime minister three months later.

Another important act of kindness to me by Ivan Yates, who had become a talks producer for the BBC overseas service by 1955, was to invite me to deputise for Bernard Levin by writing the script on 3 June 1955 for a programme called 'Round Up of the London Weeklies'. This was a weekly programme for North America that was recorded late on Friday afternoons by a journalist (Sam Pollock) as narrator and actors who read extracts from the numerous political weeklies then published in the UK. My task was to choose the extracts and to write the linking narration for a fee of 10 guineas, which was a very welcome additional income for a struggling barrister. Just over a year later Bernard Levin decided to end his contract and I took over the weekly stint in July 1956. It was not always easy to fit the commitment in with my practice at the Bar but I was allowed to supply a deputy and my future brother-in-law, John Thompson, and later Dick Taverne were very acceptable in that role. In the event I was able to continue this work for about three years, latterly with John Danvers as my producer, until it became impracticable for me to do so in the final run-up to the 1959 general election, in which I was a Labour candidate.

My work for the BBC at Bush House was highly congenial and rewarding in many ways other than merely financial. The establishment of talks producers was very impressive and included, from time to time, Tony and David Wedgwood Benn and Jack Ashley as well as Ivan and John Danvers, both of whom died much too young; one of the programme organisers was John Terraine, the distinguished historian of the First World War and defender of the reputation of Field Marshal Earl Haig. The readers on my programme included the actors Robert Rietty and John Glenn. The latter subsequently ran successful restaurants with a partner in Old Church Street, Chelsea, and at Chichester Festival Theatre: it was at the first of these that my wife and I had the bizarre experience of dining next to and very close to Laurence Olivier and Stewart Granger as they discussed in detail the shortcomings of their former wives!

My income from the BBC was a great boon after my scholarship income came to an end. By the time that Mars-Jones took silk at Easter 1957 my fees earned from the Bar had risen to about £1,900 a year, having increased by £300 to £400 each year since I began; but that was well short of the utopian target of doubling each year. It must be stressed also that the figures quoted were my gross earnings. My deductible expenses for tax purposes were always about one-third of gross earnings, the main components being the tenth to my clerk, a further tenth towards chambers expenses and the cost of travel and accommodation.

In order to achieve this income after five years I was in one court or another most days. Crime and divorce still formed a substantial part of my work and most of this was in Cheshire or North Wales, so I spent a great deal of time travelling between London and circuit, but I was beginning to acquire civil work involving the drafting of pleadings (statement of a party's case) and advising by written opinions. This latter work was very important as the foundation of a broad practice and was more demanding, in my view, than most criminal work; a disadvantage was that one usually had to wait until the civil action had been tried or settled to receive payment for one's work and the delay might be for many months or even several years. The emphasis on work in the northern part of my circuit in my earlier years at the Bar suggests that I might have joined one of the two major chambers in Chester but this would have been at the expense of the long-term advantage of being already established in London on eventually taking silk.

It is very sound advice to aspiring young barristers that they should never rely upon friends to get going. One's friends tend to have too critical or sceptical a view of one's capabilities to entrust one with any really challenging legal case. I must say, however, that I was shown great kindness from the beginning by Holywell solicitors, especially the ebullient Kerfoot-Roberts, and a host of North Wales solicitors led by the distinguished Cyril Jones, then approaching 90 years old, who were supporters of Mars-Jones and who took me under their wing. This patronage extended as far as Pwllheli and I owed a great deal to John Roberts and Gwyndaf Williams of that town as well as David Lloyd George's nephew, William George (Wyl bach), later the Archdruid of Wales. In London, too, I was fortunate to have the support of a very able friend, Ben Hooberman, whom I met through Ivan Yates and who soon married a university friend of my sister, Ellen Rosenthal. Very early in his practising career Ben decided to found his own firm under the name of Lawford and Co. in Gray's Inn and it became increasingly powerful after winning Frank Chapple's case against Frank Foulkes and others in 1961 about vote rigging in the Electrical Trades Union elections. Yet another friend and supporter was Jim Storey, whom I had met at Cambridge and who became a partner in Russell Jones and Walker (as well as an Anglican priest), acting for the steelworkers' union and the Police Federation.

My legal work in those early years was not exciting enough to justify detailed recall here but I do remember one town-planning appeal in which I was involved as junior to Edmund Davies QC. Town and country planning was really a specialist field at the Bar following the comprehensive Act of 1947 but it was still quite usual for the common law Bar to appear in some planning appeals on circuit and so I appeared from time to time for Flintshire County Council, instructed by their well-known deputy clerk (shortly to become clerk), Haydn Rees.

The appellant in this case was George Brookes, a senior member of a prosperous Rhyl family, who was himself a successful farmer with an outstanding herd of Ayrshire cattle on the outskirts of the town. Like many another, he wanted to have a caravan camp, his choice of site being the whole of a large field adjoining the main road from St Asaph to Rhyl, and he asserted that he had established this as a caravan site before the Act of 1947 came into force and so he did not require planning permission. The County Council rejected this claim on the ground that any earlier siting of caravans there had been limited to short holiday periods, which had not had the effect of altering the agricultural use of the land within the meaning of the Act. Enforcement notices were duly served on Brookes requiring removal of the caravans and he joined battle by appealing to the local magistrates' court.

A great deal of money was at stake for the appellant, who was a strong Conservative supporter, and his first thought was to instruct Sir David Maxwell Fyfe QC, a former secretary of state for Wales, known affectionately as 'Dai Bananas', to appear for him. On learning that Sir David had been transformed into Viscount Kilmuir as Lord Chancellor, he decided to make do with Viscount Hailsham QC, who had by then succeeded his father and had not yet disclaimed his hereditary peerage. He was soon to be appointed First Lord of the Admiralty in the Macmillan government but was still in full practice as a silk. Faced with this star, the council sensibly decided to instruct Edmund Davies QC to lead for them and I was lucky to be briefed as his junior, thus receiving my highest fee for a single case up to then and further reward when Brookes appealed to the Queen's Bench Divisional Court, and there was yet another hearing before magistrates when neither Lord Hailsham nor Edmund Davies was available.

I remember particularly how intimidating the case must have been for the St Asaph magistrates who heard it in July 1955 but they were equal to the task. The chairman was the brother of Judge (David) Pennant and a descendant of Thomas Pennant, to both of whom I have referred earlier. He was well able to understand the issues and control the proceedings, and Lord Goddard, who presided over the subsequent appeal, complimented the bench on the way in which they had dealt with the matter. The demands on me were very light because I had such an able and experienced leader but I did have to summon up some courage on the second day, when Edmund Davies had left to keep another appointment and I had to protest about some inaccuracy, as I saw it, in Hailsham's final speech.

The council emerged victorious and the Divisional Court hearing took place the following April. Lord Hailsham argued that the justices had got the facts wrong, a difficult argument to sustain as a point of law, but the court approved the justices' finding that the use had been limited to 15 caravans and that it had been appropriate to define the area of the field where that had occurred. The saga ended with another hearing, I think before a planning inspector, in September 1957. Hailsham was by then a member of the Cabinet and so Brookes instructed the formidable Ted Megarry QC, later vice-chancellor and *de facto* head of the Chancery Division, who had taken silk the previous year and who was the author of several student books that had been part of my diet as a law student and novice barrister. As Edmund Davies was engaged elsewhere, Haydn Rees decided that a leader was not needed for the council and I was fortunate, therefore, that Megarry proved to be a very courteous opponent and not at all condescending. We disposed of the case this time in two much shorter days.

It was in relation to this case and another Divisional Court appeal heard later in 1956 that I received my 'red bag' from Edmund Davies in January 1957. The practice was, and presumably continues to be, for a Queen's Counsel to be permitted to present to a junior who was not a novice and who had given him special help in a case a red bag to hold his wig and robes in place of the blue bag with which all barristers start out. This practice does give rise to transient jealousies from time to time and a limitation is placed on the number that can be given by any one silk because standards in the matter tend to vary but, for the recipient, it is a pleasant custom and a visible mark of progress. The other case before the Divisional Court related to conditions that had been imposed by a local licensing committee at Rhyl when granting a licence to the Queen's Theatre. We acted for the theatre and failed in the Divisional Court but triumphed before a strong Court of Appeal made up of Lords Justices Singleton, Jenkins and Parker.

Visits to the Divisional Court were a special challenge for a young barrister and quite often enabled one to get one's name in an official law report, which had a certain kudos. In the Divisional Court of the Probate,

Divorce and Admiralty Division, the president, Lord Merriman, almost invariably presided and sat with one other judge (described as a 'consenting adult' by Mr Justice Melford Stephenson). It was well known that Lord Merriman disagreed profoundly with the views of Lord Justice Denning (as he then was) on the requirements of 'constructive desertion' in divorce cases, that is, conduct having the effect of driving out a spouse from the matrimonial home and thus amounting to desertion by the person who remained. It was very unwise, therefore, to cite a Denning judgment to the president, except (perhaps) to criticise it cautiously. A great deal of quiet amusement was to be had in this area but, on the whole, the law emerged eventually without too much damage.

Appearances in the Queen's Bench Divisional Court were rather more intimidating. This was partly because of the venue, which was usually the Lord Chief Justice's very large court, and partly because the court was often crowded with lawyers, litigants, the press and observers. There were always three judges then, dressed very elegantly in black and ermine, and it was rather unusual if the Lord Chief Justice himself did not preside. Lord Goddard was the Lord Chief Justice for my first six years at the Bar (he was 81 years old when he retired, having seen out many of his potential successors), and appearing before him was a legal education in itself. He had a very strong personality but he was no bully: he was apt to take a fairly firm view of a case early on but would still listen to any good argument by counsel and was willing to change his mind, unlike some weaker men. It was always exciting to be before him and I remember him with affection, as do many of my contemporaries at the Bar.

Lord Goddard was the last Lord Chief Justice to undertake lengthy visits to the circuits like other Assize judges. He did this on the northern part of the Wales and Chester Circuit in May 1956, starting at Welshpool and accompanied by Michael Turner (later Mr Justice Turner) as his very elegant marshal. I have two special memories of that visit. At Welshpool he dealt very kindly with my old client who had the annoying and apparently incurable habit of stealing overcoats in public houses. More significantly from my point of view, I had to defend at Mold Assizes a young woman who pleaded not guilty to bigamy with an already-married soldier. After she had been convicted, Lord Goddard justifiably referred to the brazenness of her defence but then noticed that I looked rather downcast at the criticism, whereupon he went out of his way to say that this bad defence had been well presented by me. The result was that nearly everyone present thought that I had earned special praise at the highest level and only the judge and I knew that he had merely let down a young barrister as lightly as possible.

Divisional Court appearances were more stimulating in Lord Goddard's time and also in the time of his courteous and highly experienced successor, Lord Parker, who had been Treasury counsel in common law matters before becoming a judge. It was particularly instructive when one was led before this court by prominent counsel such as Edmund Davies QC or Daniel Brabin QC. The latter was the star of the Northern Circuit: a teetotaller with a champagne personality, who was probably the most effective cross-examiner that I ever heard, although he would disarmingly and misleadingly claim not to know any specialist law. A helpful provider of work in the Divisional Court at that time was one Gubay senior, who liked to trade on the promenade at Rhyl, despite being prosecuted for it, but later turned to much more profitable trading within the law by founding Kwik Save, which enabled him to retire in great comfort to the Isle of Man.

Although these forays were interesting and provided good publicity, the best training undoubtedly for a novice barrister was in jury trials, whether for the defence or the prosecution. There was no Crown Prosecution Service in those days and only a limited number of county or borough prosecuting solicitors. In rural counties particularly, the allocation of prosecution work to counsel was often influenced by the chief constable or someone on his staff who would instruct counsel through a local firm of solicitors. On the whole, the work was shared out reasonably fairly, although there were some justified complaints from time to time, and the great advantage for competent barristers was that they gained valuable experience on both sides of the fence. I should add that I have an innate distrust of barristers who customarily do criminal work but who refuse to appear for the prosecution, and there are too many of them.

A useful vehicle for young barristers on circuit was the defence of men under the age of 24 when charged with unlawful sexual intercourse (called 'carnal knowledge' by statute until 1956) with a girl under the age of 16 but over the age of 12. As I have said earlier, a statutory defence was provided for such a man if he had not previously been charged with a like offence and could prove that he had believed the girl to be of the age of 16 or over, with reasonable cause for that belief. There were a number of promising issues, therefore, to be explored at a trial, and the risk of a catastrophic error in advancing the defence case was fairly low, as I had demonstrated at Swansea Assizes in July 1952, very shortly after marshalling.

Such cases had to be tried then by a High Court judge but much of my own experience was at Quarter Sessions before a bewildering variety of chairmen. At the summit, so to speak, was Lord Morris of Borth-y-Gest, a Lord of Appeal, as chairman in Caernarvonshire; at base, in terms of legal experience, was Lord Aberconway, the second baron and owner of beautiful Bodnant, in Denbighshire. The latter was the chairman of numerous companies, including the shipbuilders John Brown and Co., and had been parliamentary private secretary to David Lloyd George early in the century, but his experience of legal practice after his call to the Bar at Lincoln's Inn in 1903 was very limited indeed. It was touching to appear before him because he would often weep sympathetically as one made one's plea in mitigation but he was not a particularly 'soft touch'. In trials his summing-up had to be prepared for him by the clerk of the peace as the case progressed and then handed up to him at the appropriate moment.

Other chairmen were well able to compose their own summings-up but it was many years since some of them had been in active practice. Lord Goddard was said to be unhappy that the chairman in Montgomeryshire was the local MP and Liberal leader, Clement Davies QC; in Cheshire the chairman was currently registrar of the Privy Council, having been private secretary to the Lord Chancellor earlier (there were times when he addressed bemused young criminals before him in the tone and language of a public school headmaster).

Adjusting one's style and presentation to these varied tribunals was certainly a challenge and I hope that we benefited from the experience. It certainly added great interest to circuit practice, which I much preferred at that stage to its London equivalent, and I do not think that the system produced any great injustice. The appointments became increasingly professional, however, with the return of so many barristers from the armed services and few 'amateurs' survived in office at Quarter Sessions by the time that the Beeching Commission was appointed to review the whole procedure.

A staple diet at Quarter Sessions before the introduction of the breathalyser test in 1967 was provided by trials for driving while under the influence of alcohol, of which there were usually two or three in the list at any busy Quarter Sessions. These trials tended to follow a certain ritual and some junior barristers became specialists in the technique of presenting a successful defence. One began with the alleged bad driving, followed by the police officer's approach to the defendant, the alleged smell of alcohol and glassy eyes, the request to get out of the vehicle and so on to the eventual examination by a general medical practitioner, usually one retained by the police for the purpose. Each phase of this process gave wide scope for sarcastic cross-examination and most juries were ready to be sympathetic with the defendant unless there had been a collision: the percentage of acquittals was so great that more stringent legislation was inevitable and the criminal Bar lost a valuable source of income because there were few ways in which one could attack breathalyser evidence successfully once the initial technical problems had been overcome by the police.

A recurring difficulty facing defending advocates in criminal trials in the 1950s and 1960s (and, of course, before that) was the reliance by the prosecution in most cases on what were given the slang name of 'verbals', that is, alleged oral admissions by a person accused, usually very soon after arrest. A classic but trite and incredible example would be 'It's a fair cop, guv'. There were judge-made rules intended to ensure that only truly voluntary statements by a defendant were introduced in evidence but such statements did not have to be in writing. It was customary for an accused person to be interviewed by one police officer in the presence of another without any note being taken. Eventually a statement might be made by the accused and signed by him but a jury would often hear details of a long preceding interview recorded by the police officers in their notebooks at least an hour or so after the event but said by them to be totally accurate. Unless one's client had strong intelligence as well as a good memory, it was very difficult to attack these 'verbals' successfully; a further but similar problem was that it was equally difficult to establish that any improper inducement to confess or threat had been made by a police officer in the absence of a reliable contemporaneous record.

These difficulties were undoubtedly oppressive until the enactment of the Police and Criminal Evidence Act 1972 and the regulations made under it, which radically altered police procedures and led to the recording of interviews contemporaneously. Before that, there was undoubtedly a predisposition on the part of most senior judges and magistrates to accept police evidence as accurate, unless a really compelling challenge to it could be put forward: detailed recollection by one's client of how an interview had progressed was usually an essential foundation for such a challenge.

This lesson was brought home to me very clearly in a conspiracy trial at Ruthin Assizes in May 1955 before Mr Justice (later Lord Justice) Sellers, who had practised in commercial law and on the Northern Circuit. Three men were charged with conspiracy and six offences of corruption in relation to the supply of timber to a Wrexham colliery. The prosecution, led by Edmund Davies QC, relied heavily on admissions alleged to have been made by the accused to the police. The admissibility of these statements was challenged by two of them so that there had to be a 'trial within a trial' before the judge in the absence of the jury on this issue. Both had supplied very full details to their counsel, Mars-Jones and Philip Owen, of their conversations with the police, which had included improper inducements, false statements by the police and other breaches of proper procedure; they both gave evidence on those lines after the police officers had been cross-examined. The result was that a real doubt was created in the judge's mind as to the credibility of the police officers and he ruled that the alleged admissions should not be put in evidence. This meant that there was insufficient evidence against the two defendants to go to the jury, who were directed by the judge to acquit them. I had no similar instructions from my client to enable me to challenge his alleged statements successfully but, to my great delight, Mr Justice Sellers took the view that it would be unjust in the particular circumstances of the case for it to proceed against my client alone and the judge directed that he too should be acquitted. Thus, the outcome was very unusual as the result of the actions of a strong and fair-minded judge but it would probably not have ended in this way if two of the defendants had not supplied their solicitors and counsel with convincing accounts of what the police had said and done.

While the emphasis in my circuit practice in the early years was on criminal cases, my clerk rightly warned me against getting involved similarly in London because the intention was that I should acquire a mainly civil practice. The major criminal work in London, at the Old Bailey and London and Middlesex sessions, went usually to chambers that specialised in such work. For the general civil lawyer there was plenty of work in the London County Courts before a wide range of judges, of varying temperament and ability. There was a great deal of litigation about rent-controlled premises under the Rent Acts and, of course, about accidents of all kinds involving personal injuries. I was glad to take on this work whenever it was offered to me because it provided excellent training in advocacy and was often interesting in itself to a newcomer to the law.

The year 1956 was the year of *Rebel without a Cause* with James Dean in the cinema and the theatre scene in London was as lively as ever. *Look back in Anger* was first performed by the English Stage Company at the Royal Court Theatre on my birthday (8 May) that year, *Waltz of the Toreadors* by Anouilh drew full houses at the Criterion Theatre and I attended the premiere of *Guys and Dolls* at the Coliseum on 19 September. With a modest income I did not aspire to be seen in expensive restaurants but there were plenty of good restaurants in Kensington and Chelsea where one could dine and drink reasonably good French wine at a cost closer to £5 than £10. French rather than Italian cuisine was dominant but I remember with particular affection and nostalgia the elegant La Speranza, at the junction of Brompton Road and Beauchamp Place. It is sad that, 50 years later, none of such favoured and intimate eating places as Le Reve, the Blue Cockatoo,

the Ox on the Roof, Mathesons and 19 Mossop Street remains. And what
has happened to unpretentious clubs where one could dine and dance such
as the Pheasantry, the Jacaranda, the Blue Angel, Esmerelda's Barn (once
owned briefly by inheritance by Cyril Jones' son) and the Royal Court
Theatre Club, where Clement Freud was the witty host? Life was certainly
not dull, even if we were less opulent than our successors.

Away from London, the dark cloud was the continuing need to find a
buyer for the Holywell Textile Mills. It can be imagined how severe a blow
this was for my father after over 85 years of family association with the
company and when he had hoped to hand on responsibility for its future
to my brothers Stuart and Neil. In the circumstances he withstood the
pressures extraordinarily well, at least on the surface, and eventually an
appropriate buyer was found. Barclays Bank had appointed a receiver in the
autumn of 1956 and a sale was then agreed, with effect from 12 February
1957, to a partnership comprising two sons, Edward and Islwyn, of Lord
Davies of Llandinam, who were concerned about the future of the Welsh
woollen industry, and an electrical trader from Wrexham called Wellum,
who had made substantial profits from the sale of television sets. The
result was that Wellum took over control effectively from 1 January 1957;
my father retired, Stuart left Holywell for Kent in pursuit of employment
and Neil agreed to stay on at least temporarily but eventually resigned with
effect from 30 September 1957 to work for Laidlaw and Fairgrieve Limited,
a well-known company of woollen yarn spinners in Galashiels. One of that
company's directors, Russell Fairgrieve, was a friend of Neil and a prominent
Scottish Conservative MP for several years. Stuart, on the other hand, found
work with W.F. Stanley and Co., scientific-instrument makers, of Holborn,
and bought a house in Orpington, into which he moved in November 1957
with his wife Margaret and son Michael.

10

SPREADING MY WINGS

Easter 1957 was very important for Bill Mars-Jones because this was when he achieved the rank of Queen's Counsel. The procedure for appointment has changed over the years but I doubt very much whether it has been improved. The custom then was for applications to be made early in the calendar year and for each applicant to seek the support of at least two High Court judges or other senior judicial figures, who agreed to have their names mentioned in the application to the Lord Chancellor. Another requirement was that the applicant had to inform every practising junior member of his circuit who was senior in call to him of his application; this was to enable those more senior to consider before the closing date whether they ought not to apply themselves in order not to be outranked. The Lord Chancellor would then engage in widespread consultations personally and through his senior staff before making his decisions. My understanding is that the applicants would be divided into three suggested categories – never, sometime perhaps and now – whereupon the final list of successful candidates would be settled at a meeting between the Lord Chancellor and the heads of the divisions and published on Maundy Thursday.

The guiding principle for many years had been that there should be about one QC for every 10 barristers in active practice, so that in the 1950s there were usually about 20 appointed each year. Leading work was quite scarce and hence some successful juniors were very hesitant about applying for silk and the number of applications at any one time was limited so that a busy junior of 10 years or more seniority could be reasonably confident that his application would succeed first time. Now, however, success is much more of a lottery following the resumption of annual appointments after the lapse of two or three years. With over

12,000 practising barristers and a backlog to be made up, there are several hundred applications to be dealt with at a time and very many worthy candidates may well be disappointed. The difficulties have been so great that the Lord Chancellor had to ask Baroness Butler-Sloss, after she had retired from the presidency of the Family Division, to take charge of winnowing the applications.

Mars-Jones' application for silk, at the age of 41, was very timely in the light of his large practice, which involved an inescapable load of paperwork to be dealt with mainly outside court sitting hours, and his status on the Wales and Chester Circuit. Arthian Davies and Glyn Jones were already on the High Court bench and Edmund Davies and Vincent Lloyd-Jones were expected to follow them soon, as they did in 1958 and 1960, respectively. Moreover, other silks such as Roderic Bowen and particularly Elwyn Jones were MPs whose availability on circuit could not always be relied upon because of the demands of parliamentary business. There were good prospects, therefore, for a new generation of silks and it was appropriate that Mars-Jones should lead the way in the wake of Norman Richards, who was 10 years older than him and later became an official referee.

For Mars-Jones' devils this was also a very important moment. On the one hand it meant that we lost our steady income from his paperwork but, on the other, we had the opportunity to succeed to at least part of his work in our own names. Of the three of us, I was probably best placed in terms of circuit work in Cheshire and North Wales because my link with Mars-Jones was well known and I had carried out quite a lot of work there myself. But there was wider work, particularly for trades unions and insurance companies, for which the succession was very uncertain and the most I could hope for was a small share.

Developments of this kind do not occur overnight and my income in the year from February 1957 increased only marginally from the previous year: major increases to £3,340 (almost double) and then to £4,233, despite standing for Parliament in October 1959, did not occur until the following two years. These were mainly due to much-increased civil work, of which the preliminary paperwork formed a large part, replacing devilling, which ended almost completely by July 1957. A very useful additional source of income during this period was from licensing work under the Licensing Act 1911. There was usually opposition from the chapels and the temperance movement in North Wales to any application for a new licence to sell alcoholic liquor whether on or off the premises, and supermarkets had not yet entered the field on a significant scale. From a quite different standpoint, brewery companies everywhere were still very numerous and watched each other closely so that they were often ready to instruct counsel to oppose applications through the local licensed victuallers' associations on the ground of lack of demand.

Kerfoot-Roberts, who had a well-developed sense of humour and a distaste for teetotallers, introduced me to this field of activity early on by instructing me to apply for a licence for a new hotel in a residential area of Flint, knowing that this would stir up a hornets' nest. The chairman of the local magistrates' bench, Alderman H.R. Thomas, was a long-standing Liberal and friend of my father strongly opposed to any extension of drinking facilities. Kerfoot-Roberts' plan, therefore, was that I should make the application annually for a modest fee at the licensing sessions in February until the chairman had to retire from the bench on age grounds or miraculously had a change of heart. In the event we did have to continue applying until February 1960, by which time Thomas had retired; he had managed to carry the bench with him in refusing the licence throughout the intervening years.

By this time I was much better versed in the familiar licensing arguments and North Wales is dotted with licensed premises from the Lleyn Peninsula northwards over which I battled on one side or the other. Cheshire too was a good source of this litigation and there was always the possibility of an appeal to Quarter Sessions if one failed before the local justices. I was fortunate to be taken on by a successful Liverpool brewery called Bents, which had managed to evade takeover by a conglomerate, and I had several successful ventures on their behalf in expanding their territory.

The year 1957 was memorable also for a sybaritic summer holiday in the south of France, at Ramatuelle, where the actor Gérard Philipe is buried, just west of St Tropez, which was already booming but had not yet become the tourist honeypot of later days. The arrangements were rather complicated because Emlyn Hooson suggested that I should drive his car there in advance of him and his wife Shirley, who were to stay nearby at a hotel in Cavalaire-sur-Mer. My companion was Robin Day, to whom our destination had been recommended by a fellow newscaster, and we stayed at a pension on the beach called Chez Tony, composed of straw huts. We drove down in Emlyn's car via the route Napoleon without mishap, except for a brake failure in Grasse, which nearly ended our lives prematurely, and then swam and lazed on the beach for nearly a fortnight, drinking many bottles of the local Blanc de Blanc. We were joined latterly by my BBC producer, John Danvers, and emerged with satisfying tans, marred only in my case by a couple of medusa jellyfish scars that have faded slowly in the following 50 years!

The following year we were more adventurous because four of us, Robin, Emlyn and I plus Christopher Chataway, made off to the Club Méditerranée camp at Caprera off the coast of Sardinia for 18 days, travelling by train and stopping off at Rome en route. This is the island where Garibaldi spent his last days and his ashes were buried there. I remember that the sea was wonderfully unpolluted, a translucent blue green, in which my first attempts at snorkelling were especially rewarding. The food and wine were unpretentious but we enjoyed going native, using beads as currency, and Chris managed to deal quietly with the over-enthusiastic French youths who wanted to compete with him on our daily runs. Robin was so taken with the experience that he stayed later with his two sons at a different Club Méditerranée site.

On my return from Ramatuelle in 1957 a much more important event for me occurred because on 2 October I met my future wife, Sarah Ingram, at a party in Campden Street, W8, given by her friend from schooldays, Catherine Cave-Browne-Cave, whom I had met several times as a friend of Martin McCormack. Sarah was then 21 years old and had returned earlier that year from Tanganyika, as it was then known, where she had stayed for six months with her godmother, Lady (Luba) Fletcher, at Marangu on the slopes of Mount Kilimanjaro. Sarah's father, Captain Ernest (Inky) Ingram, was a popular breeder of racehorses from 1938 at Bletchley Park Stud, next door to the wartime intelligence centre, and with a well-known stallion, William of Valence, standing there; he had died on 22 November 1954, leaving his widow, Diana, to carry on the stud until it was overtaken by the development of Milton Keynes, whereupon she moved several miles north to Barracks Stud, Nash, just off the main road to Buckingham. Diana proved to be the most delightful mother-in-law imaginable and was a star in our family until her own untimely death at the age of 73 on 7 October 1984.

Sarah's family history was much more colourful than my own. Her father, born in 1892, was the son of a Coventry newspaper editor. He served as an officer in the West Yorkshire Regiment on the Western Front in the First World War and never returned to Coventry to live afterwards. Following periods in France and Italy, he moved to New York, where he married in the mid-1920s Dorothy Benjamin, the daughter of a US patent lawyer, Park Benjamin Jr, and young widow of Enrico Caruso, the world-famous tenor. A daughter, Jacqueline, who married a US naval officer (who became ultimately Admiral Porter), was born to them but the marriage was tempestuous, lasting only a year, and there was no contact between them afterwards.

Sarah was born on 9 July 1936, almost a year to the day after her parents had married. By this time Inky had established himself as a breeder of thoroughbreds, first at Ecchinswell near Newbury and then at Manton. Diana's maiden name was Leigh-Bennett and she was one of the four formidable daughters of Henry Woolley Leigh-Bennett of Donnington Grove in Berkshire and Thorpe Place in Surrey. All four sisters had been headgirl of Heathfield School (later called Heathfield St Mary) at Ascot and Sarah had reluctantly followed in their footsteps in that respect. Woolley's most relevant ancestor, Sir John Woolley, had been Latin secretary to Queen Elizabeth I and Chancellor of the Order of the Garter. Woolley himself had served in the Coldstream Guards during the First World War, after Winchester and New College, Oxford, and then qualified as a barrister at the Inner Temple. He had married in 1907 a naval officer's daughter, Elma Rose Price, of Trengwainton in Cornwall, and had acted for a time as land agent for Lord St Levan of St Michael's Mount, living at Devonport, where Diana was born on 15 February 1911.

The Price family is said to be descended from Cradoc Fraic Fras, a prince from between the Wye and the Severn, where Sarah and I now live, who was Knight of the Dolorous Tower and King Arthur's Round Table. What is more certain is that there were family roots in Breconshire and that Captain Francis Price, a Cromwellian soldier, arrived in Jamaica in 1655, aged 20, and settled there, acquiring a sugar plantation in St John's called Worthy Park in 1670. The plantation grew eventually from 840 to 12,000 acres and it remained in the family's hands until 1863. His grandson Charles (1708–72) inherited Rose Hall, Jamaica, through a Price aunt who married into the Rose family, and he became a man of great substance, a Jamaican baronet and Speaker of the House of Assembly for 18 years. The first English baronet was Sir Rose Price, of Trengwainton in the Cornish parish of Madron, who managed the Worthy Park plantation in his twenties but returned to Cornwall permanently in 1795; he was created a baronet by the Prince Regent (later King George IV) in 1815.

Elma was the daughter of George Edward Price, a grandson of the fifth baronet and MP for Devonport for 18 years after serving as a commander in the Royal Navy, and Gertrude Lawrence, the adopted daughter of another MP, Joseph Locke, and his wife Phoebe. To complete the picture, George Edward Price's mother was Emily Plunkett, daughter of the fourteenth Baron Dunsany. Of more contemporary interest, my mother-in-law's cousins included Lieutenant-Colonel Robert (Robin) Rose Price DSO, OBE, formerly of the Welsh Guards, and his brother the popular actor

Dennis Price. Robin's wife, Maureen, was a talented painter and the sister of His Honour Judge Lord Dunboyne.

The result of all this is that Sarah is much more cosmopolitan than I am. She has genuine Welsh blood as well as English and Irish whereas I am only Welsh by place of birth and association. She even has a Mackay in her Leigh-Bennett ancestry, and Gertrude Lawrence, the mother of Elma Price, is thought to have been French. Very little of this was known to me when Sarah and I met and she was late for the party because she had started work that day as an assistant to the editor of *Wheelers' Review*, Tony Wysard. Wheelers was a chain of about half a dozen excellent fish restaurants owned by Bernard Walsh, a long-standing and generous friend of Sarah's parents and whose father had owned oyster beds at Whitstable in Kent. The magazine was published from rooms above the still fashionable Ivy Restaurant in West Street and distributed free to Wheelers' customers, with whom it was popular because it covered general literary subjects and fashion as well as food and wine. Sarah remained with it for only a few months but it continued to be published, intermittently at least, until Bernard Walsh retired.

After the party we dined with others at El Sombrero in Kensington High Street and then went on alone to dance at the Royal Court Theatre Club, after which our relationship prospered. That autumn I was as busy as ever on circuit but I found time to pursue Sarah strenuously whenever I was in London and she soon met the rest of my family because she came to Sylvia's wedding to John Thompson on 12 December 1957 at Chelsea Old Church. He was sharing a flat then with Anthony Sampson, the *Observer* journalist and author of *The Anatomy of Britain*, in Sydney Street, Chelsea, where the reception was held.

A major complication in my life at this time was my adoption as the prospective Labour parliamentary candidate for the West Flintshire constituency. This was obviously only a trial run because the sitting member was Nigel Birch, then economic secretary to the Treasury and previously secretary of state for air, who had had a comfortable majority in the 1955 general election in a three-cornered fight. I was selected as candidate at a general management committee meeting held in Holywell on 2 November 1957, when only one other aspiring candidate was considered. Although the adverse majority to be bridged was over 8,000, the local party was full of optimism in the wake of the Suez catastrophe and I was expected to play a full part in nursing the constituency before the next general election, which was rightly assumed to be about two years away. An added point of interest, which did not strengthen my case against him, was that Nigel Birch resigned from the government with Peter Thorneycroft and Enoch Powell only two months after I became a candidate.

I enjoyed my time as a candidate despite all the pressures and I met a wide range of admirable people whom I would not otherwise have had the chance to know. The chairman of the constituency party was John Griffiths, the National Union of Mineworkers (NUM) delegate from Point of Ayr colliery, who was a sturdy leader with sound common sense, and the miners of this great colliery, stretching out under the estuary of the river Dee, provided the backbone of my support. There were stalwart helpers also in the vital centres of Rhyl and Prestatyn. I cannot pretend that my two years as candidate were out of the ordinary but there were highlights. I danced with Bessie Braddock, the Liverpool MP, at the Miners' Institute in Ffynnongroew and found that she was very light on her feet. Barbara Castle visited us during a tour of Wales and roused everyone with a fighting speech at Rhyl town hall. My most daunting task was to speak briefly on the same platform as Aneurin Bevan at Buckley in the neighbouring constituency of East Flintshire, where Eirene White was the sitting Labour member. She was always helpful and generous, speaking kindly of my brother Stuart, who had stood against her as a Liberal in 1950. The local newspapers drew attention to my father's likely embarrassment about my activities but he remained serene and did not disapprove of Hugh Gaitskell, who had succeeded Clement Attlee as leader of the Labour Party in 1955. My parents were also pleased to entertain overnight the ex-Liberal Dingle Foot QC when he came to speak for me.

Meanwhile, there were the demands of my practice to be met and 1958 proved to be a very busy year: solicitors did not seem to have been put off to any significant extent by my venture into politics and I began to nudge my way into South Wales, mainly with work in the County Court for the steelworkers' union. One northern case that caused me great distress was a charge of rape arising in Flintshire but tried at Chester Assizes in February 1958 before Mr Justice Salmon and a jury, in which I appeared for the prosecution. The complainant was a pretty bus conductress and the defendant, for whom Emlyn Hooson appeared, was a less than attractive Italian immigrant. There were difficulties about the prosecution case because the girl had left a dance with the defendant in his small car and the offence was alleged to have occurred in the car despite the limited space. The defence case was that sexual intercourse had taken place with the girl's consent and that it would not have been possible without her consent. She said in evidence that she had been a virgin until that evening and she seemed to me to be a very decent, conscientious girl. In my view, however, the excellent judge, who later became a Lord of Appeal, misjudged the case (unusually for him) and, in summing up the evidence to the jury, suggested that the girl might have agreed to sexual intercourse and then regretted profoundly losing her virginity. The jury acquitted the defendant and the tragic aftermath was that the girl jumped into the river Dee at Chester later that day and drowned. Those bare facts do not, of course, prove that a miscarriage of justice occurred but I certainly believe that the complainant felt that she had been wronged; the events do underline the unwisdom of judges making their own opinions too clear in jury trials of this kind if the evidence is adequate for a jury to consider. I know that the liberal and humane Mr Justice Salmon was deeply affected by what occurred.

A very different type of judge, Mr Justice Gorman, tried the most newsworthy case that I was involved in during this period at Chester Assizes in June 1958. This was an action by David Lloyd, the popular Welsh tenor, against the BBC following an accident that he had suffered on 4 June 1954 when preparing for a television programme called *Garrison Theatre* at the army camp at Kinmel, near Abergele. His case was that he tripped over a television cable on the floor of the stage when he arrived for a rehearsal and hit his head on falling, sustaining injuries that had disabled him from singing for a long period. The BBC was represented by a tenacious and able QC called John Thompson, who became a High Court judge in 1961 and who was known by the Bar as 'the wee scruple', leading another future High Court judge, Robert Gatehouse. Unhappily, the case for the BBC was that there had not been any cable to cause David Lloyd's fall and that he had simply collapsed, probably at the onset of an epileptic fit, attributable to excessive drinking over an extended period. The evidence of such excessive drinking by the plaintiff was very tenuous indeed but he did undergo an epileptiform attack very shortly after his fall. According to him, he had never suffered any similar attack previously; on 14 February 1954 he had suffered a minor head injury, requiring two stitches, when he had struck his head on a lamp-post whilst walking home at night in driving rain but he had not lost consciousness or suffered any other ill effects.

The background to the hearing was that Mars-Jones had advised Lloyd that he had little prospect of success on his own account of the accident because the presence of cables on the floor for an outside television broadcast could not be regarded as evidence of negligence on the part of the BBC. A second opinion had been sought from Gerald Gardiner QC, later Lord Chancellor, but (to our disappointment) he had addressed only the academic legal issues without appraising the factual circumstances realistically. The result was that legal aid had not been withdrawn and authority had been given for the case to proceed. The other misfortune was that the trial judge was an old fashioned northern Nonconformist who had been a Liberal MP for a short time in the 1920s and who was himself a teetotaller, as was leading counsel for the BBC. Alcohol-induced epilepsy was not a necessary part of the BBC's defence, in our view, and seemed to us to be a very speculative basis for it in the absence of compelling medical and other evidence. Moreover, it was highly damaging to David Lloyd's reputation but it was enthusiastically adopted by John Thompson and found a ready listener in Mr Justice Gorman. The unfortunate result was that Lloyd not only lost, as we had expected, but was stigmatised as an alcoholic, in effect, by the judge who accepted the BBC's case hook, line and sinker in a brief judgment after a hearing that lasted just over a week.

I am glad to say that David Lloyd was able eventually to resume his career and again attained immense popularity with audiences in Wales. He made his comeback at the Llangollen International Musical Eisteddfod in 1960 and toured the USA and Canada the following year, but died in March 1969 shortly before his fifty-seventh birthday. He would have achieved much wider success if the Second World War had not begun at the very moment when he was emerging on the operatic stage. Six years later, when he was demobilised from the Welsh Guards, he had missed a vital development period when he should have been learning operas and stagecraft. He was then 33 years old and it is not surprising, although regrettable, that he relegated himself to a less demanding concert career, unlike Sir Geraint Evans, who also sang with the Welsh Guards band but who was 10 years younger.

There was not much time in 1958 and 1959 for conventional social life and I am rather horrified now to see how much travelling I did in those years. I left 39 Roland Gardens on 1 November 1957 and moved to a small ground-floor flat at 31 Egerton Gardens, SW7, close to Holy Trinity, Brompton, for which the annual rent was £250. A great deal of my time was spent on the road and many weekends at my parents' home while I carried out constituency engagements. Sarah accompanied me to North Wales several times and I saw her almost daily in London when I was there but there was little time for anything else and I had to resign, to my great regret, from Denham golf club at the end of December 1957 after membership for only just over a year (and an undeserved handicap of 20) because of my other weekend commitments.

I stayed at Egerton Gardens for less than a year because I moved on 4 October 1958 to Flat 42, Vicarage Court, W8, just off Kensington Church Street, where Robin Day already had a flat and where Keith Kyle came to live on his return from Washington. It was a very comfortable and convenient flat and the rent was only £310 per annum. Robin moved soon afterwards to a new flat in Elm Park Gardens and I took over the responsibility for ensuring that the absent-minded Keith had at least one proper breakfast each week. My own move enabled Sarah to take over my flat at 31 Egerton Gardens and these were our last bachelor moves before we married 21 months later.

The dissolution of Parliament was announced from 10 Downing Street on 8 September 1959, the election day being fixed for 8 October. A major new factor in the campaign was to be the influence of television. This had been present via the BBC in 1955, after the great increase in television ownership associated with the coronation, but with commercial television in full swing in 1959 and effective provincial channels it was likely to have considerable impact. Members of the public were still accustomed, however, to attending public meetings and hearing the candidates in person so that full coverage of one's constituency had to be arranged, with at least two or three meetings nightly (but not on Sundays), except perhaps in borough constituencies. This required swift organisation at the outset in the face of competition from the other parties and made electioneering very exhausting after daily canvassing. It may be that political candidates of my generation spent rather too much time at public meetings but, for me, the experience was highly educational and enabled me to learn a great deal about parts of West Flintshire and its residents previously unfamiliar to me. It was exhilarating to be whisked from meeting to meeting and the enthusiasm of the loyal party workers was such that one became deluded into believing that even victory was a possibility.

In the end I came second in the four-cornered contest in West Flintshire and the result was very similar to that in the 1955 election, apart from the presence of a Plaid Cymru candidate for the first time, who gained only 4 per cent of the total vote. The full result was:

Nigel Birch (C)	20,446
Ronald Waterhouse (Lab)	12,925
Emyr Roberts (Lib)	4,319
Nefyl Williams (PC)	1,594

The national turnout was close to 80 per cent and the Conservatives and their associates received 49.4 per cent of the total votes cast (365 seats) against Labour's 43.8 per cent (258 seats) while the Liberal and Independent representation was unchanged at six and one seats, respectively. In Wales the swing to the Conservatives was only about half that in England but, rather surprisingly, Eirene White's majority in East Flintshire against a rather nondescript Conservative was reduced to 75.

It was at this general election that Robin Day made his only essay into national politics. Standing as the Liberal candidate in the Hereford constituency once represented by Frank Owen as a Liberal MP and much later by Paul Keetch, he fought a typically combative campaign against David (later Lord) Gibson-Watt, who had won a by-election there in 1956. Robin lost by almost exactly the same number of votes as I did, with the Labour candidate trailing in third place. His fellow newscaster Ludovic Kennedy also stood as a Liberal in Rochdale, failing by only 2,740 votes to defeat the sitting Labour member.

The 1950s ended with me back fully in harness at the Bar, involved in an increased amount of civil litigation, mainly in personal-injury cases with the inescapable paperwork to be done out of court hours. I see that November 1959 was a particularly good month because I notched up fees totalling over £750 and I was beginning to think that I might be able to afford to get married; but that big step deserves another chapter.

11

SETTLING DOWN

My urgent priority for the new decade was to get married, if Sarah would agree. Very fortunately for me, she did so early in 1960 but we thought that three months' engagement would be appropriate so we deferred the announcement until nearly the end of Lent on 12 April 1960. The Temple Church, right next to my chambers, was the obvious venue for our wedding and we fixed upon Saturday 16 July, a week after Sarah's twenty-fourth birthday, as the date. It was not a popular choice with racing friends because it coincided with the King George VI and Queen Elizabeth Stakes at Ascot (won that year by Aggressor) but there were only a few defaulters when the day arrived.

Our entry into the married state was miraculously free of difficulties because of the astounding generosity of Sarah's mother. Her home at Bletchley Park Stud was about to become merged in the new town of Milton Keynes, although the neighbouring listening post survived as a museum, and the stud was the subject of a compulsory purchase order. Diana insisted that Sarah should have half the proceeds on the questionable ground that Sarah's father would have wished this. The result was that, instead of having to search for a flat to rent, Sarah was able to buy from two Phillimores the 80 years' lease of a tall house at 3 Argyll Road, W8, off High Street, Kensington, one of five adjoining houses that had been reconverted to separate dwellings after wartime joint occupation. Even by the standards of 1960, the price was very reasonable and she was able to sell it with a capital gain of over 150 per cent 10 years later.

The weather was very fine on 16 July and we had close to 200 guests at the church and the reception afterwards at the Savoy Hotel. Many had travelled from North Wales and there was a good turnout from the circuit generally. I had become deputy circuit junior the year before and then junior (more or less equivalent to secretary) for 1960 and they clubbed together to give us a fine set of old silver cutlery. The legendary Temple organist, George Thalben-Ball, who had come to the Temple in 1919 as assistant to Sir Walford Davies before succeeding him in 1923, was unable to play for us because he had to attend a degree ceremony at Birmingham as university organist. However, this gave Sarah's school music teacher, the much-loved Charles Faulkner, the chance to fulfil a long-held ambition to play the Temple Church organ with the world-famous choir.

Ivan Yates made a very witty speech as best man without any of the usual embarrassments, and it was long remembered. Sarah's bridesmaid was Grania Bacon, the beautiful daughter of family friends; she herself subsequently married the diplomat Sir Alan Munro. My father survived the receiving line and the occasion generally very well at the age of 82 but he was to die within a year. This was long before the modern marathon wedding reception with dancing into the small hours. The wedding itself was at 2.30 p.m. and Sarah and I dined at the Connaught Hotel before catching a 9 p.m. flight to Paris, where we collapsed gratefully at a delightful hotel on the left bank, the Relais Bisson in the Quai des Grands Augustins.

We had decided to take an extended honeymoon in the long vacation, so this trip to Paris was a short one and I was to be back in court in London before Mr Justice Hilbery on 20 July. Fortunately, I was led by Malcolm Morris QC on this occasion for the defendants in a personal-injuries case against Murray Stuart-Smith so that preparation for the hearing was not allowed to mar our brief first honeymoon. In deference to Franz Lehar and the Merry Widow we dined at gay (in the old-fashioned sense) Maxim's with its three Michelin rosettes and then the next night at Laperouse, similarly praised, at 51 Quai des Grands Augustins for 75 new francs inclusive of service – equivalent to about £5.8s.6d. On our return to London Sarah joined me for a fortnight at Vicarage Court before we were able to move into 3 Argyll Road on 5 August. We were almost furnitureless, sitting on crates and boxes for a short time but our pride and joy, a Blüthner grand piano of 1898 vintage with aliquot scaling, which was Diana's present to us, arrived four days after we moved in and has remained with us, playing beautifully, to this day.

We had a special treat also on 7 August because Emlyn and Shirley Hooson took us to Glyndebourne for a performance of *La Cenerentola* with Juan Oncina, the Spanish tenor, as Don Ramiro and Ian Wallace and Hervey Alan. The latter was by this time Sarah's singing teacher because, after her stint at *Wheelers' Review*, she had enrolled in 1958 at the Guildhall

School of Music to train as a mezzo-soprano, receiving lessons from Esther Hulbert as well as Hervey Alan. She continued with this training for a couple of years until we became engaged; Hervey Alan suggested that, as a first step, she should apply to join the chorus at Glyndebourne but this was not an attractive prospect for a newly married woman.

Although Sarah had been to East Africa, she had not explored Europe before we married so we opted for an extended tour for our real honeymoon. In order to journey in proper style with my bride I acquired, as a very good bargain for £900, a 1949 Bentley convertible with a Park Ward body and electrically operated hood, which had been constructed for the Maharajah of Morvi and which had had only one subsequent owner. It was a splendid toy, greatly admired wherever we went in continental Europe, and never let us down. In the end I felt bound to sell it in 1966 because I was driving many miles on circuit, and it was bought by a Texan collector from Houston for £550, but I have never felt the same pride of ownership since. It was also a great pleasure to have it maintained by the gentlemanly Paddon Brothers in Cheval Place.

Thus equipped, we embarked on our ambitious trip via Dover and Boulogne on 23 August and restlessly travelled about 2,000 miles in the next three weeks, spending the first night at Le Grand Cerf in Evreux, the hotel where Harold Nicolson had retrieved the notes made by Mrs Simpson for her telephone conversation with King Edward VIII on leaving England in December 1936. Thence we sped westwards, interrupted only by a puncture in the vicinity of Chateaudun, and I remember with particular nostalgia staying and dining on the bank of the river Loire at Le Choiseul in Amboise, which is as welcoming as ever now, nearly 50 years later.

The 1960s were probably the busiest period of my life, so the timing of our marriage was not ideal but we were still able to enjoy ourselves to the full at 3 Argyll Road, where we stayed throughout the decade and where two of our three children first lived. It was a decade of great change for my family generally. My father died at 5 p.m. on 3 July 1961, when I was fortunate to be at Highfield with him. We held a private funeral for him at Tabernacle, the church he had attended all his life, and a thanksgiving service later the same day at Pendre Chapel in Holywell, to accommodate the very large number of friends and colleagues who wished to pay their respects. The service was conducted by Gwynn's father, the Reverend J. Ellis Williams, who was a long-standing friend. My father and my mother are both buried at Calcoed Chapel on Brynford mountain with my brother Tom, who died in 1923. An obituary of my father was published in *The Times* very promptly on 5 July 1961 and an account of his life by Gwynn

(Professor J. Gwynn Williams of Bangor) appears in *The Dictionary of Welsh Biography, 1941 to 1970.*

My father's brother, Uncle Horace, died on 22 April 1964, aged 80, after a life of continuous public service as a town councillor and secretary of the Tabernacle Church. His death brought to an end our direct family connection with Holywell. My mother had meanwhile moved to Helston in Cornwall to live with her brother Harold, whose wife May had died on 8 May 1962, my thirty-sixth birthday. Harold himself died on 15 February 1966, the day after my mother underwent a major surgical operation in London, and she then moved to live just off the Fulham Road at 24 Fernshaw Road, near my sister, who was established at 4 Edith Grove, SW10. My mother was to continue living there for nearly 24 years.

There were important changes in Sarah's family also during the 1960s. Her mother left Bletchley Park Stud in the summer of 1961, having bought Barracks Stud at Nash, with 97 acres, about five miles nearer to Buckingham, where she continued to breed racehorses until the summer of 1972, employing her long-serving groom, John Hutt, with his wife acting as cook when needed. An unexpected bonus from Diana Ingram's horse-breeding activities was that she leased a two-year-old filly to Sarah for the 1963 season. She was by Right Boy, a leading sprinter in 1958 and 1959, out of Diana's mare Turban, and Sarah cleverly chose for her the name Madame de Staël. Sarah took on her father's racing colours and Sir Gordon Richards agreed to train the filly. There was great excitement when she won the Ilsley Plate at Newbury first time out on 26 June with Scobie Breasley in the saddle. She gave Sarah a very rewarding season, winning again at Lingfield on 23 August, after finishing second at Brighton three weeks earlier; she earned her overall training fees in the four races in which she ran. The disappointment was that she did not fulfil her potential later as a broodmare.

By 1960 I was becoming a fairly senior junior barrister, with the large amounts of paperwork that inevitably accompany that status. Fortunately, the fax machine, email and the computer were unknown in chambers so that one could avoid the instant communication with solicitors that now occurs, except by telephone, and they were resigned to some delay by busy barristers in dealing with their work. Nevertheless, one's daily experience was to return to one's room in chambers filled with dozens of sets of papers awaiting attention, some of which had 'very urgent' markings.

This pattern of my life was fixed until I was granted silk at Easter 1969, after 16 years in full practice. In that period my earnings from the Bar rose from £4,363 in 1960 to £12,350 in 1967 and less in 1968 (£10,177) because I was off work almost completely for a month from mid-January

1968 undergoing an appendectomy followed by recuperation, with Sarah as my nurse, at Crans-sur-Sierre. I acquired also two part-time judicial appointments, as a deputy chairman of Cheshire Quarter Sessions in November 1964 and then the same office in Flintshire from June 1966. These provided a very agreeable introduction to judicial work in crime and a relief from daily advocacy. My only previous similar experience had been one brief stint as an assistant recorder at Birkenhead in November 1962 at the invitation of Mars-Jones, who was then the recorder. I was particularly lucky also to have friends of the calibre of Peter Thomas, Robin David, Philip Owen, David Pennant and Emlyn Hooson sitting as fellow deputy chairmen; the chairman of both county Quarter Sessions was Sir Francis Williams Bt, QC, who was, in effect, Chief Justice of Cheshire and most of North Wales for secondary crime for many years until the Crown Court took over in January 1972. The only blot on all of this was that I managed to put my right hand through a transom window at Mold after being sworn in there, imperilling the function of the hand, but I escaped with a night in Chester Royal Infirmary, where the severe laceration of my wrist was repaired, and a permanent scar.

The distribution of work on the Wales and Chester Circuit in the 1960s was quite different from that in the previous decade. The last of the four outstanding silks when I was called, Vincent Lloyd-Jones QC, became a judge in 1960 and we celebrated his appointment at a dinner on 1 October 1960 when Roderic Bowen QC, who succeeded him as leader of the circuit, made one of his wittiest speeches. In place of the original four silks, our main Queen's Counsel in the 1960s were Elwyn Jones, who became Attorney-General in 1964, Mars-Jones and Norman Richards with Emlyn Hooson, Alun Talfan Davies, Philip Wien, Philip Owen and then Tasker Watkins, Peter Thomas and Geoffrey Howe following on by the middle of the decade. Four of them were members of Parliament, as was the circuit leader, Roderic Bowen, until he became the national insurance commissioner for Wales in 1967, after nearly becoming Speaker of the House of Commons. There was still plenty of work for leading counsel: the legal aid authorities were not reluctant to provide for two counsel for a plaintiff or defendant in appropriate civil cases (or similarly in defended divorce proceedings) and all the silks I have referred to had successful practices, albeit of varying quality.

Inevitably, during the 1960s I was led by one of these QCs, most frequently by Mars-Jones, in the more interesting and substantial cases. My staple diet when appearing alone continued to be personal-injury cases, more often than not for steelworkers in South Wales and for miners in North Wales as well as members of the Transport and General Workers

Union. I had notably loyal solicitor clients in Ben Hooberman's Lawford and Co. in Gray's Inn and Russell Jones and Walker, who acted for the Police Federation as well as the steelworkers. On circuit I had a very wide spread of solicitor clients in Cheshire and North Wales, many of whom had transferred their former allegiance to Mars-Jones as a junior to me, and in Cardiff Leo Abse and Cohen became a very valuable source of work for me. There were also many criminal cases, and lucrative defended divorces were still quite prevalent for most of the decade until they became progressively obsolete following the enactment of the Divorce Reform Act 1967.

Although very frequent circuit journeys and the increasing pressure of paperwork were an ever-present strain, the contact with country clients and the camaraderie of the Bar were great compensations, and the general flavour of circuit practice remained unchanged until January 1972, when the Crown Court came into existence. I enjoyed particularly visits to Caernarvonshire and Anglesey, where litigation was always intense and one could normally expect a solicitor partner to be present to give one instructions. There were great rivalries between different firms in towns such as Porthmadog and Pwllheli, which added zest to trials, and the past always seemed to be just around the corner. In Wrexham the highly respected Cyril Jones continued to attend his office daily into his nineties and in Criccieth I breakfasted on one occasion, to my astonishment, with William George, the brother of David Lloyd George. William was born on 23 February 1865 and was very nearly 99 years old when I met him on 5 February 1964 while staying with his son to conduct a planning appeal (he lived on until January 1967). It was said that, a little earlier, the Assize judge at Caernarfon Assizes had made it clear that he intended to criticise some actions of William George junior (Wyl bach) in a civil case when the judge gave judgment. In order to deal with this threat William George senior was trundled into court the next day, where he sat glaring at the judge, who was so incredulous to see this living embodiment of history that his nerve failed him and the criticisms were left unspoken.

Some of my work in the 1960s as a junior was much more unusual. Perhaps the most surprising in this category was reading *Private Eye* fortnightly for libel, for which I received a fee of 10 guineas. The first issue of *Private Eye*, edited by Richard Ingrams, appeared in October 1961 and it survived, despite some hazardous moments, without any libel reader until 1966, when Lord Russell of Liverpool was awarded £5,000 damages for something said much earlier (in issue 13 in July 1962) in relation to his book *The Scourge of the Swastika*. *Private Eye*, by then solely owned by Peter Cook, launched a financial appeal to deal with the damages and costs and the question of a libel adviser was mooted at a dinner party at which my friend and neighbour Alistair Sampson suggested my name. The result was that I attended *Private Eye's* premises in Greek Street for the first time on 24 March 1966 and continued to do so every other Friday evening for the next three years, if I was available, until I took silk. Members of my chambers deputised for me when necessary and then took over from me in 1969.

It was great fun to meet Richard regularly with the luminaries who were the floating staff of his 'organ'. Outstanding, of course, was the brilliant journalist Paul Foot, son of Hugh and nephew of Michael, but there were other very memorable contributors such as Christopher Booker, John Morgan, Patrick Marnham (later Paris correspondent of the *Independent* and biographer of Jean Moulin and Georges Simenon), Richard West, the unique Willie Rushton and the very talented cartoonist Barry Fantoni. Our discussions were less about whether particular articles were defamatory (it was usually agreed quickly that they were) and more about the dubious admissibility of the evidence to support them and assessment of the risk of litigation. On the whole we had a charmed life in those three years, despite some uncomfortable threats of litigation and quite a few writs, even one from Lord Hailsham.

Our one significant failure was against two junior reporters of the *People* newspaper, who sued about a news story provided by Stuart Christie, the anarchist who had gone to Spain with the intention of throwing a bomb at General Franco. On his return to England after serving a sentence of imprisonment in Spain, he was captured by the *People* for his story and ended up in Edinburgh in the hands of the two reporters. He subsequently told *Private Eye*, without intending publication, that the reporters had taken him to a brothel, misinterpreting his needs after confinement in prison. We were mistakenly content to have the action tried by a judge alone (that is, without a jury, to which we were entitled if we wished). At the hearing, in order to explain how they had passed the time with Christie, the reporters said that they had taken him to a named restaurant and described their visit in circumstantial detail. Christie proved to be an excellent witness and, to our delight, we were able to call the manager of the restaurant to prove that it was closed that evening. Despite this remarkable 'own goal' by the reporters (to describe it too kindly), Mr Justice Brabin found in their favour and awarded them £500 damages each and costs. I was led very ably for *Private Eye* by Gwyn Morris QC against the redoubtable Sir Joseph Molony QC, so I was not a detached observer, but the only credible explanation of the judge's finding that I have heard is that he thought that it had been a dirty trick to publish the story that Christie had told them in confidence.

It was neither practicable nor wise for me to attend the famous *Private Eye* luncheons at the Coach and Horses except on isolated occasions but I did get to know the landlord, Norman Balon, whose gloomy outlook was notorious and who attended *Private Eye* cricket matches regularly. I was fortunate to be asked to turn out for them on several occasions and my junior clerk, George Hales, added considerably to their batting strength. There was an annual match against Richard's village team at Aldworth in Berkshire, at which Osbert Lancaster was always a spectator. Richard himself kept wicket; Paul Foot was an able all-rounder; Peter Jay (not yet our ambassador to the USA) was a formidable opening bowler; and Barry Fantoni was prepared to run anywhere, although he and Paul were soccer addicts. My own supreme moment came at another village, the name of which I cannot recall, where I opened the batting with Michael Parkinson and we put on a respectable number of runs. I missed greatly the opportunity to play regular village cricket but there was some compensation in turning out for the Bar team very occasionally (even for a Brussels weekend in 1971) and annually for Nigel Chamberlayne-Macdonald's home team at Cranbury Park, Winchester.

A quite different assignment, in which I was instructed by the Albany Trust via Lawford and Co., was to assist the Earl of Arran in presenting his private member's bill in the House of Lords in June 1965, which sought to legalise consensual homosexual acts by adults in private. The trust had been formed in 1958 and its secretary in 1965 was Anthony Gray. My most interesting role was to sit in the box on the floor of the House of Lords during the second reading debate and to advise Lord Arran as and when he required. The debate revealed a sharp division of opinion between many older peers such as Field Marshal Viscount Montgomery and Viscount Dilhorne, who were bitterly opposed to the bill, and the majority of younger peers such as the Marquess of Queensberry and the Marquess of Hertford, who were firmly in favour of it. Lord Queensberry was a particularly strong supporter, wishing to atone for the misdeeds of his kinsman, Lord Alfred Douglas in relation to Oscar Wilde. There was widespread support in the country for Lord Arran's bill but it failed to reach the Commons. However, after the 1966 general election Leo Abse obtained leave to introduce his own bill on similar lines and, having done so, was allowed time by the Labour government, with Roy Jenkins' blessing as home secretary, for the bill to pass through all its stages in both Houses on a free vote, emerging as the Sexual Offences Act 1967.

Very different drafting problems were presented by another Lawford and Co. client, the Electrical Trades Union (ETU). It was in 1961 that

John Byrne and Frank Chapple, represented by Gerald Gardiner QC and Jonathan Sofer instructed by Ben Hooberman, won their epic battle against Frank Foulkes and other officers of the ETU about election rigging. The particular election in dispute initially was that for the post of general secretary in 1959 but, when the hearing eventually began, the defendants did not seek to uphold that election: the issue left for trial was whether there had been a conspiracy between the union's officers to rig elections for a substantial period. Judgment in favour of the plaintiffs was given by Mr Justice Winn in a 40,000-word judgment only 12 days after the evidence and speeches had concluded. This inevitably caused a revolution within the union, to whom Lawford and Co. became solicitors, and I began to receive instructions to advise and to act in relation to a variety of union matters.

One of the recurring problems of trades unions in those days (and which may still persist) was that their main rules were dealt with at annual conferences, where issues of principle would be tackled but little thought might be given to detailed consequential amendments of the rules that might be necessary. Another problem was that, when a union executive had the power to make or change rules or by-laws, similar problems about consequential amendments would arise, particularly (it was said) if such matters were dealt with at an afternoon session after the executive members had refreshed themselves fully at lunchtime. It is not surprising, therefore, that internal union disputes about the interpretation of their rules were a fruitful source of litigation for the Bar. Rather oddly, the cases were assigned to the Chancery Division of the High Court and I was often led in them by my former Cambridge supervisor, Sydney Templeman QC, who took silk in 1964 and himself became a Chancery Division judge in 1972. Another doughty performer in this field was Peter Pain QC, a cousin of Tony Benn who became a Queen's Bench judge.

My involvement with the ETU led to many stimulating and rewarding encounters, notably with Frank (later Lord) Chapple himself and with Woodrow Wyatt, who had given strong support to the revolution in 1961 and who later became a neighbour of ours in Cavendish Avenue, NW8. I was even asked on one or two occasions to attend meetings of the ETU executive at their Kent headquarters to give them oral advice on specific problems. The only downside of all this was that I was asked as early as August 1962 to draft amended rules for the ETU, in anticipation of their annual conference, in order to enshrine the new democracy within the union and to minimise the possibility of future election rigging. It was a wearisome, but very important, vacation task and I have no very clear idea of how successful the amendments proved to be; but they did not give rise to much litigation, as far as I am aware, in the ensuing years and I comfort myself with that thought.

The more substantial cases in which I was led in the 1960s deserve a separate chapter but I must fill in some more domestic history here. Sarah and I were able to lead comparatively carefree lives at 3 Argyll Road for the first two years, but there was great joy when she gave birth to our son at 5.45 a.m. on Whit Sunday, 10 June 1962, in the Lindo Wing at St Mary's Hospital, Paddington. He was baptised with the names Thomas Hugh Ingram on 29 September at the Temple Church. We had a busy social life in London but, when we could, we set off for Barracks Stud, where Sarah's mother was always most welcoming and even willing to look after Thomas herself when we wanted to take a holiday elsewhere. We had become addicted to Italy by this time and we spent happy holidays there at the beginning of the 1960s. In 1961 we travelled in the Bentley via Evian and Locarno to Lake Garda, where we stayed at Gardone Rivera, and then on to Venice in late August and early September. On returning we managed to miss the car train from Lyons to Boulogne on 13 September but it was exciting to drive through the night via Paris, after a fortifying dinner at Mâcon, to Boulogne, where we were able to catch our booked ferry, enabling me to get to Pwllheli County Court the following day.

We returned in the Bentley to Italy in 1962, travelling by railway sleeper to Milan and then by road, via Florence and Siena, to Porto Santo Stefano. There we met up with our friend and neighbour Alistair Sampson and his Italian wife Marta, staying at the Albergo Filippo II on the shore. The port was still relatively unspoilt and the sea as enticing as ever. On the way home I was able to take Sarah to Rome for the first time and we spent five lovely warm September days and nights there; but a performance of *Rigoletto* was sadly below par.

These holidays provided a very necessary break from domestic routine for Sarah, not least because I was away on circuit for so many days during term time. These absences eventually reached a peak in 1966 when I was away for 145 nights in the calendar year (but the total was nearly as high,142, in 1969). My absences did give Sarah time to breathe, which was an advantage for her, but the demands of junior practice in one's thirties were certainly excessive for my own and immediately preceding generations.

Our domestic responsibilities were doubled in 1966 with the arrival of Sophia Alexandra (Sophie) at 4.10 p.m. on 13 July 1966 and it was a great delight to have a daughter to complement our son. At the vital moment I was appearing at Chester Assizes before Mr Justice Widgery for the defendants in a civil action but with the aid of my clerk I was able to catch the 5.30 p.m.

plane from Hawarden and to reach Sarah's bedside in the Lindo Wing by
8 p.m. The air service between London and Hawarden was of enormous
value to me in those years, allowing me extra time at home – as did the rail
sleeper service from Paddington – and I blessed it especially gratefully that
day. The courtroom in which I was appearing was that in which I had been
present only two months previously as junior counsel for the prosecution
in the case of Brady and Hindley ('the Moors murders') and the birth of a
daughter brought much-needed joy after the horrors of that trial.

Despite my legal and domestic preoccupations, my interest in politics
had not died completely. I see, rather to my surprise, that I took part in a
debate for Associated Television on 16 July 1961 in a series called *Forum*.
I had to propose the motion that 'The churches are playing no positive role
in modern life' against Norman St John-Stevas, with Julian Grenfell in the
chair. The series of 13 debates was organised by the barrister and MP Neville
Sandelson and the participants included Antony Howard, Geoffrey Howe,
Christopher Tugendhat, Brian Magee, Russell Johnston, Brian Walden,
Timothy Raison, Dick Taverne and Shirley Williams, to name but a few.

Hugh Gaitskell died on 18 January 1963, when only 56 years old,
to be succeeded as party leader by the very different Harold Wilson and
my enthusiasm for active involvement in politics began to diminish.
Nevertheless, the Campaign for Democratic Socialism (CDS) banner
was still being carried by men such as Roy Jenkins, Tony Crosland and
Bill Rodgers, with Denis Howell as a sort of chief of staff. The latter
had returned to the Commons in 1961 and both Bill Rodgers and Dick
Taverne had been successful in by-elections in 1962. They were interested
in getting sympathisers elected as Labour MPs, and Denis Howell, who
had great influence in the Midlands, arranged for me to be shortlisted for
the Wolverhampton North-East constituency, at the expense of Patricia
(later Baroness) Llewelyn-Davies, who had earlier fought Enoch Powell
unsuccessfully in the neighbouring Wolverhampton constituency.

The selection conference on 7 July 1963 was quite a terrifying occasion
for a rather naive stranger like me. It was held at a local elementary school
and the four shortlisted applicants waited in the headmaster's study before
being called to perform. The winner and obviously dominating character was
the flameheaded Renee Short, who regaled us with her recent adventures in
Moscow, and the others were Martin Ennals, brother of David and John,
and an AEU nominee whose name, regretfully, I do not recall. The audience
treated me quite kindly but I was obviously not the man for the job against
this opposition. I remember that, after it was over, I was taken by my friend
Robin Jenks and the highly amusing Douglas Graham, whose family still

own the *Express and Star* local newspaper chain, to the Oasis Club before catching a very early train to Chester the following morning.

Despite my reservations about Harold Wilson, I spoke on behalf of the Labour Party in both the 1964 election (in West Flintshire) and again in 1966 (in East Flintshire). Otherwise I attended, only occasionally when I could, meetings of the South Kensington local party. In 1969, however, the year when I took silk, vacancies were announced in two safe Labour constituencies in North Wales, where I had at least a chance of selection as the candidate. The first of these was Wrexham, where nominations closed on 15 March and the selection conference was held on 12 April, just over a week after my appointment as a QC had been announced. I spent several weekends in Wrexham, staying with my solicitor sponsor, Stanley Williams, and found unusually that I was attracting left-wing support against the NUM nominee, Tom Ellis, who was the manager of Bersham colliery. He was also, however, the chairman of the constituency party and, although I reached the final count on the day, he defeated me soundly by 42 votes to 26, much to Sarah's relief.

The next development was that Eirene White, who had been in the House of Commons for nearly 20 years, announced that she would not be standing again in East Flintshire. This was very much my home territory and Eirene urged me to have a go. I was very fortunate to have the support of the Transport and General Workers' Union via the highly respected Tom (not Jack) Jones, known affectionately as Tom Spain because of his brave membership of the International Brigade during the civil war, who had succeeded H.T. Edwards as regional secretary of the union. Under his guidance I did as much canvassing as I could that autumn but I had a strong opponent in Barry Jones, again the current chairman of the constituency party. In the event the outcome was the same as before at the selection conference on 6 December: I reached the last round but lost by 64 to 87 votes.

Looking back now it is clear to me that I had a very lucky escape. Indeed, a fortune teller who had accosted me earlier in a brasserie in Les Halles in Paris when I was lunching with Sarah had guessed correctly that I was a lawyer and told me that I would live to a great age but warned me to eschew politics. If I had been selected in 1969 in either constituency, I might have enjoyed the benefit of a safe seat for many years but I would have been subjected to the sterile Bennite heckling that characterised the 1970s and 1980s and would have had to decide whether to follow my CDS friends into the political wilderness, as Tom Ellis did. My feeling is that East Flintshire, on the other hand, was better served by Barry Jones, who remained in the party and is now a life peer, than it would have been by me. The result of my two failures was that I decided not to continue seeking a constituency: barristers were regarded, understandably, with suspicion by many Labour constituency parties and I did not relish yet another contest with a sitting constituency chairman.

The picture of my life outside court in the 1960s would not be complete without mention of the Garrick Club. Mr Justice Croom-Johnson had first suggested that I ought to become a member when I was marshalling for him in 1952. At that time I did not think that I could afford such a luxury. From 1958 onwards, however, I shared a room in chambers with Malcolm Morris QC and he began to urge me to join. Further impetus was given to the idea when Robin Day was elected in 1962; it was he who arranged that I should be proposed by Sir Geoffrey Cox, the distinguished editor of ITN, whom I had met on several occasions. Malcolm agreed to second me and I was lucky to be elected on 9 April 1964 before the waiting list for candidates lengthened enormously. Nearly 50 years on my wife and I remain devotees of the club and it has become a home from home for us since we gave up our last London residence in 2005.

Robin was an ebullient character to whom a minority reacted adversely but he was, in general, a very popular member of the Garrick, lunching there almost daily and serving as an elected member of its general committee. It was always a great joy to see him and he infused liveliness and banter into the company wherever he might be. After a succession of decorative girlfriends he married on 3 April 1965, in Perth, Australia, Katherine Ainslie, the clever daughter of a West Australian QC, and they held a great reception at the Garrick on 12 June on their return. Kathy had gained the top first-class honours degree in law at Perth University before coming to England. She taught for a time at Oxford University, where she had been introduced to Robin by Peter Carter, a leading law don. After her marriage she was called to the Bar and became a pupil of Brian (later Lord Justice) Neill before starting work as a parliamentary draftsman.

It was a great sadness when the Days parted eventually in 1983 but it is certain that they were under considerable strain from November 1978 onwards following a devastating accident at London Zoo when their elder son (my godson) Alexander, who was then just under five years old, fell about 20 feet from the Cotton Terraces and suffered severe head injuries. It is unnecessary to elaborate how this happened except to say that an au pair girl had taken Alexander and his brother Daniel to the zoo while Robin and Kathy attended the Blackstone lecture at Oxford at the invitation of Lord Devlin, who gave the lecture. Ultimately, the Zoological Society of London, which I was serving as a council member at the time, admitted liability and paid damages but Alexander has been left with severe permanent disabilities, of which the most alarming are recurrent attacks of grand mal epilepsy.

Our last family holiday abroad in the 1960s was in 1968 when we stayed with a friend of Bob and Mary Sloman's, Betty Franck, wife of a well-known *News Chronicle* writer, Stanley Baron, and mother-in-law of the actor Ian Richardson. She was then running a very efficient guest house at La Favière, immediately west of Le Lavandou, at which we stayed for three weeks. The company was highly entertaining because Clement Crisp, the ballet correspondent, was a fellow guest, and transient visitors included Trevor Nunn and Egon Ronay with his new wife. Clement Crisp was particularly kind to our children and we have been fans of his ever since. The only mishap during our visit occurred when I took Thomas and Sophie out in a pedalo with our large nanny, who could not swim. I found that I could not turn the pedalo back to shore because of the strength of the ebb tide and my passengers had to be rescued by beach guards who sped out to us. But there were other more enjoyable experiences, including a visit by Sarah's lifelong friend Catherine, who had introduced us, and her husband on their yacht, and lunch at a beach restaurant in the presence, to our astonishment, of Frank Sinatra, who dropped in from his yacht, accompanied discreetly by a posse of security men.

Thus the permissive decade sped towards its end, although I do not remember special permissiveness affecting us. Roy Jenkins was, in my view, a benign and enlightened home secretary in contrast to his more recent and inadequate Labour successors. After the theatrical excitements for me of the 1940s and 1950s, the 1960s was a rather tame decade. It began auspiciously, however, with my friend Bob Sloman's play, *The Tinker*, written with Laurence Dobie, having a successful run at the Comedy Theatre from December 1960, after a try-out at Bristol, and the two of them followed this up with *The Golden Rivet* at the Phoenix Theatre from June 1964, with Emlyn Williams' son Brook in a modest role. It was, of course, the decade of Joe Orton (*Loot* and *Entertaining Mr Sloane*), James Saunders (*Next Time I'll Sing to You*) and John Osborne (*Inadmissible Evidence*). The Establishment Club had its day and Joan Littlewood's Theatre Workshop produced *Oh What a Lovely War!* What surprises me most when looking back at theatre programmes is that Sarah and I managed to see a series of excellent productions at the National Theatre and at the Royal Opera House, Covent Garden, despite other distractions; we have never been able to attend either on the same scale since.

12

SOME NOTABLE TRIALS IN THE 1960s

The more important cases in which I was involved in the 1960s deserve a separate chapter because they were all of special interest and cannot be dealt with very briefly. These cases seemed to occur more or less annually but they did not generally last as long as so many contemporary cases. No doubt life has become more complex because of modern technology and wider sophistication, including the excessive use of emails, but I cannot see any excuse for the amount of paper that is now introduced into almost every form of litigation. It began with the use of the simple photocopier but has accelerated out of control with the result that judges at all levels and juries are burdened with large files of documents, most of which are not referred to in any detail; this happens even in interlocutory hearings, in which short procedural points have to be decided.

An early unusual case was a public inquiry conducted by Lord Cameron of the Scottish High Court bench with three assessors, which was held in London over the course of eight weeks in April and May 1963. The inquiry, ordered by the Minister of Labour, was into a complaint made a year earlier by the National Union of Bank Employees (NUBE) to the International Labour Organisation (ILO) to the effect that the British government was failing to ensure that various provisions of an ILO convention about the right to organise and to bargain collectively were applied by the District, Martins, National Provincial and Yorkshire banks. I was instructed by Lawford and Co. as junior counsel for NUBE with Elwyn Jones QC as my leader; the legal representation generally was remarkable because, of the total of 15 barristers who appeared for the interested parties, two had been or became law officers and seven became High Court judges, two of whom advanced to the Court of Appeal and another to the presidency of the Family Division.

The outcome of this major forensic battle became known six months later when Lord Cameron's report was presented to Parliament. He considered that the specific allegations of breaches of article 2 of the ILO convention had not been proved. However, the president of NUBE had said that the purpose of the complaint was to achieve recognition by the banks and to secure national negotiating and conciliation machinery with exclusive staff representation reserved for NUBE. Lord Cameron was critical of both these objectives, linking them to the background of prolonged hostility between the union and the staff associations, but he went on to encourage a reappraisal of relations between the banks and NUBE in the light of his factual findings, and he suggested a route by which the four banks might agree to accept oral representations from NUBE, paving the way to a form of recognition. Thus, NUBE undoubtedly lost the battle, but it is arguable that it won the war because recognition did follow quite quickly and industrial relations within the banks improved considerably in the ensuing years.

An unusual result of my appearance in this case with Elwyn was his suggestion that I should stand in for him in May 1963 at a trial in Lisbon, which he had been asked to attend as an observer on behalf of the Council for Freedom in Portugal and her Colonies. This was the trial of a young communist student, José Bernardino, and I flew to Lisbon on my thirty-seventh birthday, rather rashly taking Sarah with me. In the event it was a distressing venture and gave us vivid direct evidence of the Salazar regime at work. We attended the trial for two days in the company of a liberal-minded Portuguese lawyer but our guide, who was closely related to the governor of Goa at that time, was soon warned to leave the capital because he was likely to be arrested by one of the seven police forces then in operation. We ourselves were followed wherever we went and, on the second day, witnessed a brutal assault upon Bernardino in the dock by about a dozen security guards, who had been sitting in the public seats nearby. The ostensible reason for this assault was that Bernardino was ignoring the judges' direction that he should not seek to mitigate his actions.

The weekend then intervened towards the end of the trial and I decided that I was not prepared to expose Sarah to further risk and unpleasantness so we flew home, pausing in Paris for 24 hours to recover our composure and sense of well-being. When we returned I held a press conference, which did not attract much attention, and presented a report to the council on whose behalf I had attended the trial. I received an interesting letter subsequently from Peter Benenson, the much-admired founder of Amnesty International, in which he said that a plausible explanation of the vicious physical attack on Bernardino was that it was planned in advance to deter foreign observers from attending similar trials in future because they might provoke a repetition of such brutality.

The next year, 1964, produced two cases of general interest and the facts of the first were surprising even in the world of crime. The defendants at Chester Assizes before Mr Justice Nield and a jury were the actor and producer Norman Williams and his 72-year-old father, who had been secretary of the John Summers Building Society, associated with the steelworks. The essence of the prosecution case was that the father was responsible for a shortfall of over £60,000 in the society's funds and that over £25,000 had found its way to his son or to his son's creditors. In short, it was said that the father had become very proud of his son's career and had taken on the role of a theatrical 'angel' without funds of his own, using money deposited by clients of the building society. The father pleaded guilty to eight specific charges but both defendants pleaded not guilty to a joint charge of conspiracy.

Norman Williams was a good-looking man in his mid-forties when he was tried; he was married to a very attractive actress, who stood by him throughout. He had acted in many successful films and plays earlier, after discharge from the army in 1941 on medical grounds. He had then become a film producer from about 1953 onwards, producing, for example, an Errol Flynn series and a White Hunter series, joining Sidney Box in 1958 before forming a film distribution company in 1961. His evidence was that he had received from his father overall only £2,040 for his personal use and a total of £11,400 for various plays and films without ever realising that the source of the money was the building society; and he was appalled when he learnt later how little his father was paid as the secretary.

Despite the complexity of the evidence the prosecution had to produce to prove its case, the trial lasted only seven days because of the efficiency of both Mr Justice Nield and the prosecution, in the hands of Phillip (later Mr Justice) Wien QC and Robin David. Both defendants were found guilty: the father was sentenced to three years' imprisonment and his son to half that term. Norman Williams had, of course, many contacts in the theatrical and film world who were very concerned about him and they were keen that there should be appeals against these convictions. Eventually Lord Gardiner QC, who was soon to become Lord Chancellor, agreed to take on this forlorn task and Mars-Jones stepped aside. The appeals were heard expeditiously by a court presided over by the Lord Chief Justice, Lord

Parker, and inevitably failed despite Lord Gardiner's eloquence. To our surprise, however, Lord Parker invited an appeal against sentence by the father in view of his age and state of health and his concurrent sentences were reduced very mercifully to 18 months. The two defendants then served their sentences at Ford open prison, near Arundel, from which the father emerged in much better health. Norman Williams was one of those rare clients who wrote to me from prison to thank Mars-Jones and myself for our efforts on his behalf. His letter contained some interesting and amusing comments on the course of the trial and the appeal.

Later that year, I had my first close experience of libel litigation, although the action was settled early in the trial. The plaintiff was Brian Glanville, the novelist and football correspondent, then only 33 years old and at an early stage of his career. He had published in 1958 a novel called *The Bankrupts*, depicting the life and difficulties of the daughter of rich Jewish parents in north-west London and describing local society there as unpleasantly selfish and materialist. Then in 1962 he published another novel, *Diamond*, about the interplay of characters in a Jewish family seen, as in *The Bankrupts*, through characters in the book. This later book was reviewed in April 1962 in a recorded BBC programme called *The World of Books* by the well-known actor David Kossoff, who was highly critical of it because of the picture that Glanville gave of the Jewish community when he himself was a member of that community. Glanville thereupon sued both the BBC and Kossoff personally for libel and I was instructed to appear for both defendants, led by an eminent specialist in defamation cases, Peter (later Mr Justice) Bristow QC.

I must confess that, as a brash young barrister inexperienced in the field, I thought that we had a good chance of defending the action successfully on the ground that what Kossoff had said amounted to 'fair comment' in the special legal sense and he himself held that view strongly. However, the case for the plaintiff was opened to the jury before Mr Justice Hinchcliffe by David Hirst, my Cambridge contemporary, in his typically pugnacious style. He was careful to point out that Glanville's complaint was not about Kossoff's comments on the book, whether or not the jury agreed with them, but about the alleged attack on Glanville's motivation. Hirst suggested that, in effect, Kossoff had alleged that Glanville had offered an anti-Semitic handbook in order to make money and was, amongst other things, a coward, and that Kossoff had taken advantage of his position as a reviewer to publish an injurious and false attack on Glanville.

This was indeed powerful stuff and a good example of David Hirst's strength as an advocate. He went on to call Glanville, who proved to be a good witness who did not weaken significantly under cross-examination. My leader took the view, therefore, that the defendants would be wise to settle the claim, and he was probably right, because we were able to do so for what was a modest amount even as long ago as 1964. For me, the experience was very valuable as an introduction to a form of litigation that was to become important to me when I took silk.

Negotiating a settlement is one of the less comfortable tasks that a barrister has to perform frequently. In my time there was no formal training in the art, and the process was repugnant to many barristers. On my circuit the barrister who probably enjoyed it most was Sir Alun Talfan Davies QC, who relished the market place and was an early barrister entrepreneur when business activity by the Bar was still rather frowned upon. I never regarded myself as a sophisticated negotiator but I did respect the wise views of Phillip Wien QC, who led me frequently, particularly on behalf of steelworkers in personal-injuries cases. He was clear that one should make a definite discount for the hazards of litigation when considering an offer, even when one had a strong plaintiff's case, in order to avoid the torment of ultimate possible failure if the offer was rejected.

The next two years in court were dominated for me by two very notorious cases, the Moors murders and the Aberfan inquiry, in both of which Sir Elwyn Jones QC led as Attorney-General with a Wales and Chester Circuit silk as second leader. In *The Queen v. Brady and Hindley* the circuit silk was Mars-Jones and I was the junior counsel for the prosecution at the trial. I was not permitted to appear in the committal proceedings at Hyde Magistrates' Court because I was already a deputy chairman of Cheshire Quarter Sessions and Monro Davies, my Farrar's Building colleague, appeared in place of me. I was fully involved from then on, however, in the preparations for trial and visited the moors with police officers on 22 March 1966.

The trial took place at Chester Assizes before Mr Justice (Fenton) Atkinson and a jury from 19 April to 6 May. The facts of the case were so horrific that it attracted worldwide attention, and press facilities at Chester Castle had to be specially created to cater for the throng of journalists; the courtroom itself looked like a fortress because of the need to protect the defendants. The trial brought to the court several well-known authors, such as Emlyn Williams, Pamela Hansford Johnson, Mary Hayley Bell (the wife of the actor John Mills) and Gerald Sparrow, all of whom wrote books about it. My firmest recollections of it now are of the immaculate and expeditious way in which Mr Justice Atkinson tried the case and the nightmare of listening to the recording made by the defendants of a young girl's protests and screams shortly before she was killed.

Elwyn Jones himself conducted the prosecution throughout and I was greatly impressed by his application to the case: he was tireless each evening in preparing for the next day, discussing every possible eventuality in consultation until a late hour. It was the first case in which more than one murder was tried at the same time; we had won the argument about this before the judge and it established an important precedent for later cases, beginning with the 'black panther' case, which Mars-Jones himself tried when he became a High Court judge.

Ian Brady was 27 years old at the time of the trial and had been employed as a stock clerk from 1959. He had convictions for dishonesty and had undergone Borstal training but he had no history of violence. Myra Hindley was four years younger and had become infatuated with Brady when she joined, as a shorthand typist in 1961, the firm by which he was employed. Brady could not or would not drive so that she became his chauffeur and abandoned her Roman Catholic faith. Both were charged with the murders of three children, John Kilbride, Leslie Ann Downey and Edward Evans, but there was an alternative charge against Hindley in respect of Kilbride of being an accessory after the fact. They were both convicted of the murders of Downey and Evans; on the Kilbride charge, Brady was found guilty of murder but Hindley was convicted of the lesser offence.

I will not rehearse again the appalling story of the defendants' sadistic cruelty to their victims. That story has been brilliantly told by Emlyn Williams in *Beyond Belief*, which took him a year to write and which is dedicated to the two leading Cheshire detectives in the case. There are, however, some special points that stick in my mind. One is a mental picture of Detective Superintendent Talbot following up a telephone call to Hyde police station from Hindley's brother-in-law, borrowing a white coat from a bread roundsman early in the morning to approach and enter the house where Edward Evans had been butchered the previous night and where his body lay in a back bedroom. Other recollections are of the trial itself, particularly of Hindley's cold, blue unblinking eyes (Gerald Sparrow described her face as a death mask) and the absence of any apparent remorse on the part of either defendant.

Brady admitted from the outset, as he was bound to do, that he had killed Evans, because he had been almost caught in the act, but he tried to implicate Hindley's brother-in-law, Smith, who gave evidence for the prosecution, and Brady sought also to exonerate Hindley. She, on the other hand, made no incriminating remarks to the police and stonewalled similarly when she gave evidence, although she did admit cruelty in relation to the recording that they made of Downey. Hindley alone appealed against the convictions and, in the end, only one ground of appeal was pursued, namely, that the trial judge should have ordered that she should be tried separately from Brady because a large body of evidence was allegedly admissible against him but not against her. The Court of Appeal Criminal Division, made up on this occasion of the Lord Chief Justice, Lord Parker, with Lord Justice Winn and Mr Justice Widgery, had no hesitation in dismissing this tenuous argument.

One of my duties as junior counsel for the prosecution was to read the correspondence between the defendants in prison in the hope that there might be clues to the whereabouts of other missing children whose disappearance was thought to be linked to the defendants. Unhappily, the letters were much too guarded to give that kind of help, but I was dumbfounded by the intellectual pretensions of the pair and I remember that Hindley's solicitor had seen fit to give her a copy of Wordsworth's poems as a Christmas present.

Part of the background to the case was Brady's interest in the activities and writings of the Marquis de Sade and his apparent admiration for the views of Adolf Hitler, including his anti-Semitism, which seemed to be shared by Hindley. It was bizarre, therefore, that she was defended by a distinguished Jewish Queen's Counsel, Godfrey Heilpern, the leader of the Northern Circuit. We were all deeply shocked during the trial when Heilpern's own sister-in-law was murdered while travelling on the upper deck of a Manchester bus.

Gerald Sparrow called his book about the trial *Satan's Children*, and I would not criticise that description of the defendants. In the last paragraph of his account of the trial he said:

> I travelled back to London with a friend who had covered the trial as a journalist. We compared notes and both of us felt that for 14 days we had been in the presence of overwhelming blind evil.

This trial took place just before the birth of our daughter Sophie in July 1966. Scarcely had we started to breathe again after this excitement when the disastrous mudslide at Aberfan occurred on Friday 21 October, and was to require most of my attention for the next six months. At about 9.15 a.m. on that day many thousands of tons of colliery rubbish swept with a horrific roar down Merthyr mountain, submerging two occupied farm cottages, engulfing Pantglas junior school and 18 houses below and damaging another school and other properties in the village. As a result, 116 children and 28 adults lost their lives and 29 other children and six adults were injured. That colliery rubbish came from a tip – referred to as No 7 at the inquiry – which had been established from April 1958 to receive waste from the nearby Merthyr Vale colliery. Heavily saturated material in the tip had become liquefied: the lower parts of the tip had changed to a heavy liquid carrying upper parts of the tip with it so that it plunged rapidly down the mountainside over a railway embankment and a disused canal into the village.

The colliery had been established in 1875, when two shafts had been sunk, and its last owners before nationalisation had been Powell Duffryn Limited. Tipping waste on the mountain had been going on for 50 years. Various estimates were put forward of the amount of waste deposited in tip No 7 up to October 1966: they were in the range of 300,000 to 400,000 cubic yards or about 500,000 to 700,000 tons by weight. Fatally, the tip had been extended over the years to cover a spring draining the Brithdir sandstone of the mountain. A major incident had occurred in November 1963 when a flow of wet material from the base of the tip's toe had resulted in the collapse of overlying material, and frequent minor subsidences had followed. Then, heavy rainfall on 18 and 19 October 1966 caused subsidences of as much as 20 feet of material on 21 October, culminating in complete failure of the tip, the lower part of which had become saturated by the increased yield of the spring.

The ensuing chaos and the massive, but largely fruitless, rescue operations compelled world attention and the secretary of state for Wales, Cledwyn Hughes, responded very quickly within five days by establishing, with the authority of both Houses of Parliament, a tribunal of inquiry into the causes and circumstances of the disaster. Lord Justice Edmund-Davies, who had just been elevated to the Court of Appeal and who had been brought up at nearby Mountain Ash, agreed to preside over this tribunal, and the two other members were a leading consulting engineer and the recently retired clerk of Monmouthshire County Council. As is the usual practice, the Attorney-General appointed, with the approval of the chairman, counsel for the tribunal to assist it by presenting the evidence and making submissions on the facts. In this case, because of the gravity of the matter, Sir Elwyn Jones decided to act as leading counsel for the tribunal by making the lengthy opening statement, and three counsel were nominated to appear under him, namely, Tasker Watkins VC, who had taken silk the previous year, with Breuan Rees and myself as junior counsel. As I said earlier, Breuan, who practised from chambers in Swansea, was arguably the ablest junior on the circuit in my time. Very sadly, however, he had a fatal heart irregularity and died on a Yugoslav beach on 23 August 1967, within four months of the conclusion of the tribunal's hearings.

Sir Elwyn opened the proceedings at Merthyr Tydfil with his statement on 29 and 30 November 1966, which was in itself a considerable feat because a mass of evidence had had to be obtained by the Treasury solicitor's staff beforehand. In the end, statements were taken from 250 persons, of whom 136 were called to give oral evidence, and the hearings occupied 76 days until the end of April 1967. We sat at Merthyr Tydfil initially for the convenience of local residents who were to give evidence but after Christmas the hearings were at the Cardiff College of Food Technology (as it was then known) in Colchester Avenue, which proved to be a very convenient base.

The puzzling mistake made by the National Coal Board was to refuse at the outset, and for a substantial period after that, to admit liability for the disaster, despite the forceful advice that they should do so given by their own counsel, Phillip Wien QC, leading Norman (later Judge) Francis and John (later Lord Justice) Roch, a formidable and very balanced team. A degree of responsibility for this error, which lengthened the inquiry and added to the heat of exchanges, must lie with the chairman of the board, Lord Robens, who was fully in touch with the proceedings and who gave evidence to the inquiry. In all, eight parties, other than the tribunal itself, were represented at the hearing by 16 counsel, 12 of whom ultimately became full-time judges. All of them were able advocates, and a prominent role was played by Desmond Ackner QC, later a Lord of Appeal, who assuaged the anger and sadness of Aberfan parents and residents by his strong presentation of the case against the board and some of its senior officials.

It was inevitable that the National Coal Board would be held to blame because the evidence indicated that the tip had been established in an extremely unsafe place, riddled with springs and watercourses, that there had been earlier slides and other warning signs at No 7 tip and other comparable tips, from which no appropriate lessons had been learnt, and that there was no established system of inspection directed at the stability of the tip. In the tribunal's report, which was presented to Parliament very expeditiously on 19 July 1967, blame was attributed also, with some regret, to a number of Coal Board officials with varying expertise, from the unit mechanical engineer upwards, but the men actually working on the tip were acquitted of blame in the absence of any adequate instruction or training. With greater hesitation the tribunal acquitted Merthyr Borough Council officials: they had been concerned from 1957 onwards about the extent of the tipping area and had later secured a promise that the tipping of 'tailings' (a particular cause of instability) would be stopped but had accepted assurances from high-ranking Coal Board officials that nothing was wrong with the stability of tip No 7.

My recollections of the inquiry are now very diffuse but I have a vivid memory of visiting Aberfan and the tip with Tasker Watkins on Sunday 6 November before starting a disputed public footpath case for the British Railways Board the following day at Carmarthenshire Quarter Sessions. Tasker climbed the slurry like a stag while I laboured behind him; the general scene of desolation was almost indescribable. The atmosphere of the hearings at Merthyr Tydfil before Christmas was highly emotional and intense and the grief of so many residents was greatly affecting. Later, as the inquisition into fault proceeded at Cardiff, there was great concern on behalf of the many decent but potentially blameworthy officials who had had some responsibility for the tip from time to time. Nevertheless, the atmosphere was to some extent lighter, as it has to be if one is to retain one's balance; and we found some light relief in the terrier-like pursuit of Merthyr Tydfil officials and some other witnesses by the local government member of the tribunal, who was not at all disposed to succumb to the blandishments and broad generalisations of Alun Talfan Davies QC, then recorder of the borough, who represented the council and its officials at the inquiry. We thought that the ultimate acquittal of the council owed much to the fair-mindedness and balance of the tribunal chairman.

Tasker Watkins yet again rose to the occasion, cross-examining virtually every witness on behalf of the tribunal and shouldering his very heavy burden, including making final submissions on the evidence, without visible strain. Although he had only a year's experience as a QC, he demonstrated all the qualities of a commanding leader, and the tribunal placed great reliance upon his judgement. Breuan Rees and I, on the other hand, had much more discreet roles, which were interchangeable; usually one of us would be with Tasker in the inquiry room while the other would be backstage working ahead with the evidence to come or drafting submissions. None of us, however, was required or expected to assist the tribunal in drafting its report and, needless to say, Lord Justice Edmund-Davies played the dominant role in this.

One of the features of tribunals of inquiry of this kind under the Tribunals of Inquiry Act 1921 was that everyone closely involved was supplied with a full transcript of the proceedings provided by a team of shorthand writers sitting in turn for short periods and then retiring to transcribe that part of the hearing. I have always found this to be a rather mixed blessing: the transcripts are usually of very good quality but time can be wasted reading them and sometimes counsel are invited to propose corrections, which quite often prove to be face-saving for counsel rather than strictly necessary. I was very impressed, however, with the discipline and vigour of Desmond Ackner, whose practice was to take the previous day's transcript to his hotel room early each evening and to dictate from it into a tape recorder the passages (with page references) that he intended to rely upon later, particularly in his final speech. The record was then typed up by his chambers staff in London and returned to him so that he had before him in convenient accessible form all the material that he needed without having to trawl again through the long transcripts.

No succeeding cases were likely to match those in 1966/67, but there was a great deal of interesting work to keep me busy in the two years after the Aberfan inquiry ended, apart from an interruption lasting about a month in January and February 1968 when I succumbed to appendicitis while being led in a Customs and Excise case by Malcolm Morris QC against Treasury counsel, then Nigel Bridge (later Lord Bridge of Harwich). I was operated upon immediately by Sir Ralph Marnham, the Serjeant Surgeon to the Queen, and brother of Harold Marnham QC, at University College Hospital. Fortunately, there were no serious complications and I see from my diary that I applied for silk while in hospital. One was allowed to stay in hospital much longer in those days and I was not discharged until 10 days after the operation. A week later I flew with Sarah, who was permitted a foreign travel allowance to act as my nurse, to Geneva and thence by train to Crans-sur-Sierre, east of Montreux, where we spent a most enjoyable and relaxing week and saw the Russian film version of *War and Peace*.

I was crestfallen not to be appointed a Queen's Counsel at Easter 1968 but I had no substantial ground for complaint and, in the end, I think that my appointment the following year was better timed. The two barristers from the Wales and Chester Circuit who were successful in their applications in 1968 were Raymond Phillips MC and Robin David, both of whom had prior claims to mine. Raymond was 10 years older than I was and had been junior counsel to the Inland Revenue for 10 years, while Robin was four years older than me and also senior in call to the Bar. Raymond became a High Court judge in 1971 and Robin was undoubtedly offered appointment as such by Elwyn Jones when he was Lord Chancellor but was unable to accept at any relevant time because he had to care for his wife, as I have mentioned earlier. Instead, Robin became the first full-time chairman of Cheshire Quarter Sessions and then for many years from 1972 the highly respected senior Circuit judge in Cheshire and a deputy lieutenant for the county.

My failed application meant that I was faced with another year's grind at paperwork, but there were important compensations. One of these was to be briefed by the Treasury solicitor as junior to Sir Joseph Molony QC, the long-time Attorney-General to the Duchy of Cornwall, and the leader of the Western Circuit, who was a son of a former Lord Chief Justice of Ireland. It may be that he was not made a High Court judge here because it was doubted whether he had the necessary judicial temperament but he was certainly a brilliant man and I found him to be charming and generous in all his dealings with me. Our joint task for the Ministry of Transport was to put forward the case for a new motorway, the M53, at a public inquiry. This motorway was to run for 10.5 miles through the Wirral peninsula to the Mersey tunnels and there were some 42 organisations and individuals who appeared at the inquiry with objections to the scheme or details of it. Apart from Cheshire County Council and Bebington Corporation, the objectors included Viscount Leverhulme (HM Lord Lieutenant) and the neighbouring Leverhulme estates, comprising over 5,000 acres, represented by Andrew Rankin QC; Roger Lancelyn Green, the well-known author, represented by Michael (later Mr Justice) Morland; and a Sangster, son of Vernons Pools, who had an interest in a farm that would be affected by the motorway, and who was represented by David (later Mr Justice) McNeill QC.

It was a tribute to Sir Joseph's skill that the public inquiry at Birkenhead, which began on 15 May 1968, was over by 31 May, despite the number of objectors and witnesses that had to be heard. I doubt whether similar speed would be achieved now, even though the technical equipment available has been transformed in the intervening years. Another firm recollection is how undemanding Sir Joseph was as a leader. I had become used to considerable demands for preparatory work as a junior, particularly from Mars-Jones, but Molony's style was very different: he was certainly master of his brief but he did not make voluminous notes and his ability to cross-examine expert witnesses, apparently extemporarily, was very impressive, although I did not aspire to imitate it. I remember that he dealt particularly trenchantly with one or two of Lord Leverhulme's experts who were concerned that a specially planted avenue of trees would be severely affected and who argued strongly in favour of one of three alternative routes for the motorway.

Professionally, the most important events for me in 1969 were the appointment of Mars-Jones as a judge of the Queen's Bench Division from St David's Day, 1 March, and my own appointment as a QC a month later at Easter. On this occasion my application had been supported by Lords Justices Widgery and Edmund-Davies and I could not have wished for more authoritative backing. Despite this important advancement, however, my own professional preoccupation for the first six months of the year was work in which I was briefed as a junior to Tasker Watkins QC. That work was the prosecution of the leaders of a curious rebel organisation calling itself the Free Wales Army, which took place as preparations proceeded for the investiture by HM the Queen of Prince Charles as the Prince of Wales at Caernarfon Castle on 1 July.

An important concern for me at that time, apart from my political forays in Wrexham and East Flintshire, was the future of Thomas' education. Sarah and I had made the usual attempts to provide for this by putting his name down for various preparatory schools but we were very reluctant to send him away to school at the age of eight. He had started off at a dame school, but we had enrolled him in the autumn of 1967 at the Fox Primary School in Kensington Place to see how he would fare in the state system. He did not settle down well and so we decided that a London preparatory school would provide the best solution. Our choice fell upon the Hall School, partly because its headmaster, Raymond Cooper, with a Military Cross won in the Burmese jungle, looked very like Trevor Howard, but mainly because of his and its excellent reputation.

To our great relief, Thomas was accepted just before Christmas 1969 for admission to the junior school the following term, which was two terms earlier than had been promised. In the meantime we had already been making preparations to move from Kensington to St John's Wood in order to be nearer Thomas' school. We sold 3 Argyll Road eventually in April 1970, but we had already lighted upon 12 Cavendish Avenue, NW8, in June 1969 as our next home and we completed the purchase of that house in September 1969. We needed to carry out some work on it, including the installation of central heating, and it was convenient to stay at 3 Argyll Road until a purchaser had been found, so we did not actually move house until 6 March 1970.

The nomination of counsel for the prosecution in all the more important cases, which were in the hands of the Director of Public Prosecutions (DPP), was always made by the Attorney-General from a list of counsel on the relevant circuit, who were graded on the basis of their ability and experience. I counted myself very lucky, therefore, to be nominated as junior to Tasker in the Free Wales Army (FWA) case. The nature of the case was rather odd, not only because of its basic facts, but also because of the type of evidence that we had to rely upon to establish those facts. The Free Wales Army had been formed in or about 1963 and was first seen exercising in October that year at Trywerin in Merionethshire, where the controversial dam that drowned the village of Capel Celyn had been constructed in the 1950s to supply water to Liverpool. The army's subsequent activities were chronicled mainly in newspaper colour supplements and magazines when it carried out training exercises and manoeuvres in front of any journalists who could be persuaded to follow it for weekends in the Welsh mountains.

The more serious charges laid against the main defendants, Cayo Evans and Dennis Coslett, were of taking part in the control or management of a quasi-military organisation and of organising and training that organisation, all of which were offences specified in the Public Order Act 1936. Five other defendants were charged with either one or two of these offences but only one of these others was convicted of an offence under the Act of 1936. There were also 12 other charges against Evans and Coslett and seven of the other defendants of possessing explosives, in the case of Coslett, and firearms in respect of the others.

It will be apparent from what I have already said that to prove these charges the prosecution had to rely upon the reluctant evidence of journalists who had written highly coloured accounts of the FWA exercises while enjoying themselves in the hills. There was, however, a serious background to the case because there had been an increasing number of violent incidents in Wales following explosions at the Clywedog dam in March 1966. These had been followed by three explosions in 1967 and seven incidents involving explosives in 1968 as well as a smoke bomb incident. It was not the prosecution case that any of the defendants had been involved in these offences but it was a matter of grave public concern that their illegal FWA activities were being given wide publicity as the investiture of the Prince of Wales approached; the nine defendants were chosen on the basis that they were alleged to be the leading figures in that organisation.

Cayo Evans was a 31-year-old farmer and horse breeder from Lampeter and the head of the army, while Coslett was an unemployed fantasist, aged 29, from Llangadog, who regarded himself as a commandant under Cayo. The others were a very mixed bag of Welsh extremists, including another Lampeter farmer, a plumber known as 'Dai Bomber', two men from the Corris area of Merionethshire and three others from Swansea, Bridgend and Cwmbran, one of whom had experience in the Territorial Army. The committal proceedings in Cardiff in March 1969 took only a week but the trial at Swansea Assizes before Mr Justice Thompson and a jury lasted 52 days from 16 April until 1 July, the day of the investiture.

The trial began the day after I had been sworn in as a Queen's Counsel by the Lord Chancellor, Lord Gardiner: a hectic day on which I travelled to Cardiff after a celebratory lunch party, by the 8 p.m. train, to stay overnight with Tasker and work until 1 a.m. In view of my change of status a replacement junior for the prosecution had been nominated: Michael Gibbon, an old friend and a prominent barrister, who later became the first full-time Recorder of Cardiff and a senior Circuit judge. We were, therefore, a very contented team under Tasker's calm and good-humoured leadership, arrayed against a galaxy of leading counsel representing the defendants other than Cayo Evans, who was well defended by a junior barrister, James Mulcahy.

Most prominent of the defending leaders was John Mortimer, already famous as a playwright, before Rumpole and the novels, who refreshed himself with a swim most mornings in court time and who departed for the south of France during the Whitsun break to stay on Sam Goldwyn's yacht in order to refashion someone else's screenplay. He represented Coslett, and a rather bizarre incident occurred during his witty final speech to the jury: he tried to laugh the case out of court by mocking his client's activities, not realising how affronted Coslett would be. At the luncheon adjournment Coslett asked to see Mortimer with a view to changing his plea to guilty rather than endure further witticisms at his expense and was only dissuaded from doing so with difficulty.

The other leading counsel, John Davies, John Gower, Aubrey Myerson, Philip Owen and Andrew Rankin, were all notable in their respective fields and the last named had an additional skill because he was a reliable racing tipster whose daily advice greatly benefited a number of police officers attending the court. The curtain raiser to each day's hearing was a chorus of complaints by the defendants through counsel about their conditions in Swansea prison; John Davies' client, Dai Bomber, was particularly obsessive about the lack of toilet accessories available to him because he took great pride in his personal appearance and hygiene.

It was by no means easy to extract any precise evidence from the journalists, whose sympathies and indeed affections appeared to lie with the defendants rather than the prosecution: the process was like drawing a difficult tooth. I remember particularly being hectored rudely by a woman journalist whom I was trying to examine-in-chief, with the result that the trial judge intervened with the question, 'May he continue, Miss Howard?' to the great amusement of the jury and everyone else. In the end, however, the photographic evidence largely proved itself and most of the defendants were convicted by the jury, after it had retired for just over four hours, of at least one charge. Evans and Coslett were both convicted of the Public Order Act charges as well as firearms offences (and, in Coslett's case, two explosives offences), for which they were sentenced to 15 months' imprisonment. Another defendant, from Corris, who was only 22 years old but who had claimed to be director-general of the FWA, received nine months' imprisonment for organising it, and three others were given various short suspended prison sentences while the other three were acquitted.

In the event I believe that honour was satisfied and no more was heard of the Free Wales Army. Evans and Coslett died in March 1995 and May 2004 respectively and they would no doubt have been proud if they had known that their deaths would be marked by obituaries in national newspapers. The investiture of the Prince of Wales proceeded safely as a result of the vigilance of the police, but about five bombs were planted in relevant places, apparently by members of a parallel militant organisation. One that exploded killed the two persons who planted it. For me, the end of the trial meant that I was free to embark properly on my new career as one of Her Majesty's counsel.

13

IN THE FRONT ROW

Many judges say that the most rewarding period, in a non-mercenary sense, of their professional career was in practice as a Queen's Counsel; I do not dissent from that. Certainly, the years between 1969 and 1984, that is, to the end of my tour of duty as a presiding judge and roughly coincident with the period when we lived at 12 Cavendish Avenue, were the most fulfilling for me.

My first appearance as leading counsel was in May 1969, when I was given two days' leave from the Free Wales Army case to defend a lorry driver charged with causing death by dangerous driving before Mr Justice Brabin at Chester Assizes. Fortunately, my absence from Swansea proved to be worthwhile because the driver was acquitted. But my first leading case of substance followed a week after the FWA trial, this time at Caernarfon Assizes, in the shadow of the castle, before Mr Justice Lawton. The seven charges against my client were the very grave ones in rural eyes of sheep stealing and there were seven alternative charges of receiving stolen sheep.

This was the most interesting agricultural case in which I was ever involved and it required the trial judge and counsel to become familiar with a host of earmarks, identified by descriptions in Welsh, denoting the ownership of the sheep. The defendant, whose day job was as a waterworks attendant, was a hill farmer in Snowdonia with grazing rights on the mountain above his farm, Mynydd Du, in front of Carnedd Dafydd above Lake Ogwen, and the case against him was that he had persistently changed the earmarks of his neighbours' sheep so that they looked as if they belonged to him.

Counsel for the prosecution were my friends Peter Thomas QC, who was to become the secretary of state for Wales on the return of the

Heath government in June the following year, and Bertrand Richards. Both had local roots, having been brought up in Denbighshire, and they enjoyed particularly, as did the judge, the accounts of sheep shearing on the mountains and the major events of each year given by the patrol shepherd. Altogether, the trial lasted an eventful 11 days and the evidence against the defendant was too compelling for me to gainsay: the jury returned verdicts of guilty on five counts of theft after retiring for four hours and the defendant was sentenced appropriately to three years' imprisonment. I use the word 'eventful' because in the course of the trial Armstrong became the first man to land on the moon and we bought 12 Cavendish Avenue after a failed auction. I managed also, rather surprisingly, to play cricket against Anglesey solicitors at Chester and for another team at Mill Hill at weekends just before and during the trial.

Sarah and I decided that we should opt for a bucket and spade holiday in 1969, so we took Thomas and Sophie to the Belgrave Hotel on the front at Tenby for a fortnight. The weather was patchy but there were some fine days so that we were able to spend quite a lot of time on the excellent beaches. I did not know then that I would have to defend the borough council nearly four years later about the state of the diving board that it provided on Goscar rock on the beach in North Bay. We did most of the appropriate things: visiting Caldy Island, St David's Cathedral, Dylan Thomas' Boat House at Laugharne and Pembroke Castle; and, despite the caravanners, Tenby was not too uncomfortably crowded.

Any anxiety that I may have had about not being fully occupied in term time had disappeared before the opening of the new legal year on 1 October 1969. This was because I had taken on the first of a number of governmental tasks that came my way as a silk. It came at the suggestion of an able Board of Trade lawyer, John Trapnell, and it proved to be by far the most arduous. My official designation was as an inspector to carry out, with an accountant inspector, an investigation under section 165(b) of the Companies Act 1948 into five building and development companies. My fellow inspector was J.C. Steare CA, a partner in a firm practising at Ralli House in St Paul's Churchyard. We were appointed initially on 2 July 1969 to investigate two building companies, Dwell Construction Limited and Yorks and Lancs Construction Co. Limited, within a group of companies controlled by Gerald Israel Ronson, an uncle of the better-known Gerald Ronson of Heron International, who was not involved in any way with the companies whose activities we had to investigate. The appointment of inspectors was not unusual and the best-known investigation up to that time had been that of the Pergamon Press and Robert Maxwell by Owen Stable QC and a senior accountant, on which they reported in 1970 in highly critical terms that have been fully and further justified by later events.

In our case there had been mounting criticism of the conduct of the building companies in the development of residential building sites in the south of England and Yorkshire, some of the criticism coming from purchasers and from building societies. In consequence, the companies were removed from the National Housebuilders Register in June 1969. There were also very numerous complaints from sub-contractors, reported in newspapers and to MPs, that the companies were unjustifiably refusing to pay them. A joint meeting of creditors had been convened in Coventry on 31 May 1969 and petitions were presented in July 1969, leading to winding-up orders in respect of both companies on 6 October 1969. At creditors' meetings on 18 November 1969 approximately 170 claims totalling £80,000 against Dwell Construction were disclosed and 160 claims totalling about £100,000 against the other company.

The major difficulty about our investigation was that almost all of these claims were disputed by the two building companies in whole or in part so that we were faced with the prospect of adjudicating on a host of potential civil actions. Moreover, the only known assets of the building companies were possible claims against the development companies within the same group for which the building work had been carried out. It followed that our investigation had to extend to the two development companies mainly involved; this was arranged early on in July 1969, and then in September 1972 yet another company outside the group was added. In the end we had to investigate the affairs of 17 companies and we commented in our report that our inquiry had been painfully and embarrassingly prolonged because of the complexity and disorder of the companies' affairs. It is not surprising that our report extended to 640 pages with 83 appendices covering another 1,013 pages and that we were not able to present it until 1 July 1975, six years after our initial appointment.

Our conclusions about the matters were set out in chapter 27 of our report. In our view the evidence that we had gathered justified to a very substantial extent the complaints made by sub-contractors and house purchasers. We did not accept that the building developments had been conceived initially in fraud but we were highly critical of the conduct and management of the companies under investigation, for which Gerald Ronson and his son Howard bore the overall responsibility. We were particularly critical of the conduct of the two building companies and concluded that their failure was directly attributable to gross mismanagement by the two Ronsons.

My own misgivings about this company investigation procedure were and remain many and various. A basic objection to it is that conclusions about alleged misconduct are expected, however guardedly they may be expressed, so that the investigation has the attributes of a trial by Inquisition without many of the safeguards to which a defendant in a criminal trial is entitled. Secondly, the investigation is very frequently highly complex because of the nature of the complaints that have been made, and so it is prolonged. The result is that by the time the inspectors' report has been received it is too late to mount an effective and fair investigation by the police and prosecution of the case to trial, even if there is strong evidence of criminality (by saying this, I am not imputing it to the Ronsons). Thirdly, the inspectors have neither the powers nor the resources of the police in carrying out an investigation, so delays and some procedural errors are very difficult to avoid. Fourthly, the demands made upon the time of professional men who have their own practices to pursue (and, in the case of accountants, their duties also towards their partners) are such that it is very difficult to ensure that investigations are completed in the shortest practicable time.

Some of these problems are being met by new provisions of the Companies Acts 1985 to 2006. In particular, an investigation can now be halted to enable the police to investigate the case promptly. It may be too that departmental inspectors are more frequently used now: it seems that 24 non-departmental inspectors were appointed between 1985 and 1993 but there was then a gap of six years before the next such appointment in January 2000. It is likely, however, that many of the procedural difficulties and shortcomings remain.

My most noteworthy leading brief in 1969 was for a police superintendent named Thomas Rimmer, who was the defendant in a civil action for malicious prosecution brought by a probationary constable, Michael David Conway, who had been prosecuted for the theft of a torch at a police station. He had been tried at Chester City Quarter Sessions in April 1965, just before the end of his probationary period, when the jury had stopped the case, with the result that he had been acquitted without having to present any evidence. Nevertheless, he had been told by the assistant chief constable that he was 'out of the force': he had been offered the option of resigning but, on refusing to do so, had been discharged by the chief constable.

Robin David QC had been briefed for Rimmer originally but, by the autumn of 1969, he had become a full-time judge and I was asked to take over as leading counsel. The case was already famous within the legal profession because it had been to the House of Lords in May 1968 on a question of law about the range of compulsory disclosure of documents in a civil action. The Home Office had claimed crown privilege in respect of four reports made about the plaintiff during his period of probation and a report made by the defendant to the chief constable about the case against the plaintiff in relation to the torch, which was to be submitted to the Director of Public Prosecutions. This claim was based on the assertion that there was at least a possibility that it would be prejudicial to the public interest for an order to be made requiring confidential documents of this kind to be disclosed. The arguments in the House of Lords were complex and the report of the case at (1968) AC 610 occupies 86 pages of that year's volume. But their Lordships decided in the plaintiff's favour, having ruled that they were entitled to look at the documents in the balancing process of deciding for or against disclosure.

In the end the case came on for trial before Mr Justice Cumming-Bruce and a jury at Chester in December 1969. I knew that the defendant was quite unpopular as a senior police officer and was disliked by a number of my colleagues, and I was apprehensive that, if he gave evidence, he might well give an unfavourable impression to the jury, who were likely anyway to be sympathetic with the acquitted constable. It was important, therefore, that I should try to demonstrate that there was no evidence that the defendant had acted 'without reasonable and probable cause' or with 'malice' in the legal sense in going ahead with the prosecution, about which the DPP had been consulted. Very fortunately, the judge (with some courage) accepted my submission to this effect at the conclusion of the plaintiff's case and so we won without having to call Rimmer to give evidence.

Thus, the decade ended for me on a winning note and we were able to enjoy a family Christmas with my mother-in-law at Nash with the news that Thomas had been accepted for entry to the Hall School the following month. My gross earnings for the calendar year were higher than ever before at £15,584 but, in achieving this, I had had to spend 142 nights on circuit. That pattern was to continue through the next decade but my professional travels from 1972 onwards were to extend as far as Singapore.

The main domestic event of the new year for my family was our move on 6 March 1970 to 12 Cavendish Avenue, which was to provide a very happy home for us for the next 15 years. Sarah and I had been struck by its cheerful atmosphere when we first saw it and its broad layout was appealing after living in a narrow five-storey house. The vendor was a French widow who had used the drawing room as a commercial picture gallery, and she behaved rather like a concierge on leaving by taking even the electric light bulbs with her, but this did not darken our spirits.

Cavendish Avenue runs from the St John and St Elizabeth Hospital to the nursery end of Lord's cricket ground in St John's Wood; it now has the two parts of the Wellington Hospital close to either end. We were roughly in the middle of this avenue on the Wellington Road or poorer side. It was a very convenient location and the only disadvantage was the considerable building development taking place along the western side of Wellington Road; but we were lucky to have a freehold and the development eventually provided a welcome shield from traffic noise.

There was also the attraction of varied and quite exotic neighbours. Directly opposite us was David Astor, the editor of the *Observer*, and next to him was John Platt-Mills, a former New Zealand Rhodes scholar at Oxford who became a QC and the left-wing Labour MP for Finsbury until he was expelled from the Labour Party at the time of the Nenni telegram. Another Labour MP neighbour was Leo Abse, whose Cardiff firm of solicitors was already an excellent client of mine. Soon these neighbours were joined by Paul and Linda McCartney and, after the departure of the Platt-Mills family, by Mark and Arabella Lennox-Boyd. Mark was already known to me as a young barrister and was to become a Conservative MP and parliamentary private secretary to Prime Minister Thatcher. We were rather apprehensive about the McCartneys' fan followers but they were surprisingly well-behaved (many of them Japanese) and the Abbey Road Studios nearby, but far enough away from us, were a convenient Beatles counter-attraction.

Oddly, on the very day that we moved in, I found myself holding a press conference in relation to another ad hoc government appointment. The previous day I had attended upon Cledwyn Hughes, then Minister of Agriculture, Fisheries and Food, when he had invited me to preside over an inter-departmental committee of inquiry on rabies. The committee was inter-departmental because it extended to Scotland and the secretary of state for Scotland, William Ross, shared in the appointment.

The background to this inquiry was that rabies had been diagnosed in two imported dogs, in October 1969 and February 1970, after they had left quarantine kennels. In the first case a collie had arrived from India and died of rabies in quarantine kennels three months later (it had been involved in a fight with a stray dog in India one month before importation); then six months later another imported dog died of rabies 10 days after its release from the same kennels, having killed a cat near Camberley. A third dog in those kennels showed signs of rabies the following month, which was later confirmed, and the dog was destroyed at the owner's request. The other case outside quarantine occurred at Newmarket. The bitch had been released on the last day of November 1969, without showing any symptoms but had died of dumb rabies three months later.

The membership of the committee was particularly interesting and two of them became my friends for many years. The first of these was Sir Solly (later Lord) Zuckerman OM, KCB, FRS, the chief scientific adviser to the government, a man for whom the descriptions 'charismatic' and 'polymath' might have been invented. He had come to the UK from South Africa at the age of 22 and it is impossible to summarise his immense achievements after that. When I first knew him he had three bases: the first was at the Cabinet Office, whence he exerted international influence for the good in matters such as the nuclear arms race; the second was at the Zoological Society of London, of which he was the secretary for many years and then its president, and which owes him an enormous debt for its survival; and thirdly, at the University of East Anglia, where he was described as professsor at large, having earlier been professsor of anatomy at Birmingham University for 25 years. Solly gave me great help and support on the committee and then showed overwhelming kindness to me, drawing me on to the council of London Zoo, which remained a great interest for the next 20 years. His wife, Lady Joan, a granddaughter of the great Rufus Isaacs, was herself a talented artist and she too showed great kindness to Sarah and me, acting as a splendid hostess for Solly on many notable occasions.

The other friend was Dr Gordon Smith, then director of the Microbiological Research Establishment at Porton Down but soon to become dean of the London School of Tropical Medicine and Hygiene for nearly two decades. He was always a most entertaining companion and wore his great academic distinction lightly. But to disregard other members of the committee would be a grave injustice. They were most agreeable and made my task very much easier than I had expected it to be; they included very able men such as Professor William Jarrett FRS of Glasgow University, Professor Andrew Semple of Liverpool University and Captain Sir Thomas Barlow Bt, DSC, a grandson of Sir Charles Darwin.

We needed to be agreeable company because we travelled quite widely together. Rabies in the fox population had spread quite rapidly after the Second World War from eastern Europe into Germany, Switzerland and France and was moving towards the English Channel; it had also moved north from Germany into Denmark. Thus, it was necessary for us to visit major affected countries to discuss methods of control, and we visited in turn Paris, Lyon, Amsterdam, Copenhagen and Tübingen University, near Stuttgart, as well as the World Health Organisation in Geneva.

In Paris, Solly stayed with our ambassador, Sir Christopher Soames, while the rest of the committee were very well boarded in the Prince de Galles Hotel, next door to the George Cinq. Sir Christopher was kind enough to invite me for a drink with him at the embassy. He was very much at work, in his shirt-sleeves and braces, and I was amused that his main concern was to try to avoid quarantine for two particularly handsome Labradors given to him by his friend the Baron de Rothschild. Unfortunately, I could not help him despite my sympathy for his objective. Our visit to France was memorable also for the sumptuous dinner to which we were entertained by the Institut Mérieux at the restaurant of Paul Bocuse (still meriting three Michelin stars now) at Collonges-au-Mont-d'Or on the banks of the river Saône, near Lyon.

Altogether we held 35 full committee meetings, mainly at our head-quarters in Russell Square House in London, and we presented two reports, an interim report on 21 July 1970 and our final report on 10 May 1971. It was therefore rather a hectic time for me, in view of the other matters on my plate, and, as Solly Zuckerman had predicted, I had to take full responsibility for the drafting of the reports, despite our secretary's valiant preliminary work. In that process I was greatly impressed by Solly's own drafting expertise: his clarity of mind was such that he could transform inept sentences with the minimum transposition of phrases and alteration of words.

The result of our deliberations was that we recommended the retention of compulsory quarantine for six months for imported animals susceptible to rabies with very few exceptions. We were against extending the period, even though the incubation period was known to exceed six months on occasions, because of the increased temptation there would be for owners to attempt to evade the requirement and the increased risk of failure of detection. Encouraged particularly by our Kennel Club member, we also recommended considerable defined improvements in the hygiene requirements of quarantine kennels. This was, of course, long before the adoption of the microchip as a means of identifying animals and at a time when some radical improvements in vaccination were still at an experimental stage. In fact, the Rabies (Importation of Dogs, Cats and other Mammals) Order 1974, which followed our recommendations, remains in force over 30 years later with the requirement of six months' quarantine on arrival in Great Britain. The order has, however, been amended and it is now possible to avoid the quarantine requirement in specified circumstances under the pet travel scheme.

The relaxation for vaccinated dogs, cats and ferrets was introduced for some European countries at the end of February 2000 after a long campaign led by Lady Fretwell, with which I sympathised. It has since been extended to other countries, including Canada and the USA, with the result that our daughter Sophie was able to import her dog and cat, both born in Rhodes, from California to the UK in 2006 without either of them undergoing detention in quarantine. The importance of all this is that animals at large in the UK, other than humans, have remained rabies free since 1922, except for those that led to the appointment of our committee; and in all the cases in which humans have been diagnosed as suffering from rabies it is clear that the disease was contracted abroad.

By the time that we presented our final report I had been in practice as leading counsel for two years and my clerk had had to show great ingenuity in arranging my timetable. Juggling two government inquiries and sittings at two county Quarter Sessions with my 'proper' work as a barrister was no mean feat, not least because many of my court appearances continued to be on the Wales and Chester Circuit and elsewhere in the country at Assizes. More remarkably, in addition to the usual run of personal-injury and criminal cases, I became involved for the Board of Trade in a 10-day prosecution at Mold in April and May 1970 for fraudulent trading, a 32-day libel action in London in November 1970 and a nuclear power station public inquiry lasting 20 days, again at Mold, in March and April 1971. To my surprise, I was drawn also into the specialist field of libel quite early in silk and this led to half a dozen cases, all of which attracted public attention for a variety of reasons and most of which had rather odd features. For these reasons I will deal with them in the next chapter and here I will mention only the public inquiry.

The proposals by the Central Electricity Generating Board (CEGB) in 1971 for a nuclear power station at Connah's Quay, broadly on the site of an existing coal-fired power station, brought into question major developments on the Welsh side of the Dee estuary and necessitated appraisal of the likely long-term future of a wide area of North Wales. The intention of the CEGB was to provide a base-load power station generating 2,500 MW, which would take five years to build once the preliminary statutory procedures, including the public inquiry, were completed. The main building would be 800 feet long and 200 feet high and there would be eight cooling towers, each 375 feet high and 300 feet in diameter. Furthermore, the application was made on the footing that electricity demand had doubled every 10 years since 1920 so that an additional 20,000 MW would be needed in the period 1976–80, of which 15 per cent should be in the relevant Manchester grid control area; it was said that by that time all power stations would be nuclear or oil-fired.

The CEGB's application was presented by Charles Sparrow QC and Michael Fitzgerald at a public inquiry in Mold Civic Centre before the deputy chief inspector of the Department of Trade and Industry and a senior planning inspector. It was opposed by all the major local authorities, led by Cheshire County Council, for whom David Widdicombe QC and Charles Fay appeared, and Flintshire County Council, for whom I led Eifion Roberts, later a QC himself and the senior Circuit judge for North Wales. A major factor in the opposition, apart from the obvious visual impact of the development over a large area, was its likely adverse effect on the more general development of Deeside and the estuary of the river itself. The inspectors had to hear evidence, therefore, about wide-ranging proposals for the area, and it is particularly interesting now, nearly 40 years later, to read again what was envisaged then.

One of the central planks of the opposition was that a new crossing of the river Dee was required to relieve the traffic flow from Cheshire and Merseyside and that this would have the effect of opening up Deeside to further intensive development. The site of the crossing had not been decided but it was likely to be from Burton to Flint or from Gayton to Greenfield. There had been two important studies, in 1967 and 1970, respectively, of the future needs of Deeside and it was expected that the population would rise to 250,000 by the end of the century, with the increase almost wholly in East Flintshire. It was also suggested that a single new town, based on Flint, might emerge with a total population of up to 280,000.

The objectors argued that these long-term plans would be drastically compromised if the erection of the nuclear power station were to be approved, because of the population safety limits that were regarded as acceptable in the vicinity of such a power station. These would reduce the physical capacity for population growth in East Flintshire from 212,000 to 130,000 and would require the urban complex to be divided into two, destroying planning flexibility.

The hearing was probably the most instructive for me of all those in which I was involved at the Bar, and Charles Sparrow was a sprightly opponent with whom one was able to quarrel daily without any lasting ill feeling so that I enjoyed my overall role in what I regarded as a good cause. It was not until 15 months later that the decision to reject the application became known. It was particularly important that the CEGB's fall-back suggestion, of postponement of a decision until the proposals for a new Dee crossing had been finalised, was also rejected.

In the end the coal-fired power station was demolished in the early 1990s and replaced, at a cost of £580 million, by a gas-fired power station, which opened in March 1996. This 1,420 MW station runs on natural gas from Liverpool Bay via an 18-mile pipeline from the Point of Ayr refinery. There is a similar 498 MW power station, the Deeside power station, one mile to the east on the north bank of the river, on land previously forming part of Hawarden Bridge steelworks. This power station cost £200 million and opened in November 1994. The second river crossing is provided by Flintshire Bridge, built between 1994 and 1997 at a cost of £55 million, which runs between the two power stations and is described as visually stunning. North Wales has become very readily accessible from north-west England as a result of this last development and the transformation of the A55 road into a dual carriageway from Chester to Holyhead. Commuting from Liverpool and Manchester is now commonplace but I do not have up-to-date information about the increase in population on Deeside and a large-scale new town has not yet emerged. A recent demographic study indicates that the major population flow in the sub-region is into Flintshire, with a secondary flow from Flintshire into Denbighshire.

All this professional activity did not leave much time for normal domestic life, although we tried to make the most of our weekends now that I was free of most paperwork; Hampstead Heath and Regent's Park were conveniently near for us. For our summer holiday in 1970 we returned for 10 days to the Belgrave Hotel at Tenby, but the weather was disappointing. We were more adventurous the following summer, when we rented a villa at Benodet in Brittany and spent a little extra time touring. The famous Pont de Cornoueille across the river Odet was then under construction and the two wings of it had not yet met in the middle. Benodet has one of the best beaches in Brittany and is a good centre for exploring Finistère. A high point of the holiday was a visit from Dick and Janice Taverne, who called on us in their elegant yacht and took us for a trip. Earlier in the year, Sarah and I had managed to take a much-needed week's break at the beginning of June by revisiting a favourite hotel, the Sirenuse at Positano, which did much to enliven me before a major libel action later that month.

1 Portrait of Sir Ronald Waterhouse in evening dress, wearing the insignia of the honour of Knight Grand Cross of the British Empire (GBE), given to him in the 2002 New Year's honours list.

2 The author in the garden of the Middle Temple in the year that he was Treasurer, 1995.

3 The author in his robe as GBE at the service of dedication to the Order, held at St Paul's Cathedral every four years. The photograph was taken by Peter Holland, who covers many of the royal occasions.

4 Cambridge Union Society, Michaelmas term, 1950, when the author (*seated, centre*) was president. The president of the Oxford Union, Godfrey Smith (*seated, second from left*), became a well-known author and journalist and a lifelong friend of Ronald Waterhouse. Also present are: Percy Cradock (*seated, second from right*), who later had a distinguished career at the Foreign Office and was chief adviser to Margaret Thatcher; Jack Ashley (*seated, left*), later MP and peer; and Greville Janner (*standing, left*), later Lord Janner.

5 Robin Day and Norman St John Stevas at the Oxford and Cambridge Union Boat Race.

6 The author on his graduation day, 1951.

7 Portrait of Sir William Mars-Jones wearing the clothes of a Queen's Counsel. He took silk in 1957 at the age of 41 and became a High Court judge in 1969. He was pupil master to the author when he started at the Bar in 1952.

8 Sarah Ingram, engagement picture, 1960.

9 Wedding of the author and Sarah Ingram at the Temple Church, London, on 16 July 1960. *From left to right*: Thomas Waterhouse (author's father), Grania Bacon (bridesmaid, now Lady Monro), Doris Waterhouse (author's mother), the bridegroom and bride, Diana Ingram (bride's mother), Ivan Yates (best man) and Edward Bacon (cousin by marriage to the bride), who gave her away as her father had died in 1954.

10 The author dressed as a Queen's Counsel on the day he took silk, 1969, with Sarah on the steps of their home in Cavendish Avenue, London.

11 At the baptism of Alexander Day, June 1974 – the author was Alexander's godfather. *From left to right:* the author, Robin Day, Mrs Ainslie (grandmother to Alexander), Katherine Day, Lord Blaker and Sara Ricketts (godparents).

12 The author as QC leading Leon Brittan in a libel case at Sheffield, 1976. Arthur Scargill had sued the *Sheffield Star* for libel, and the author appeared for the newspaper company. Leon Brittan became QC, MP, vice-president of the European Union and later Lord Brittan of Spennithorne.

13 The author at the House of Lords on the day he was sworn in as a High Court judge by the Lord Chancellor, 9 January 1978. *From left to right*: Thomas Waterhouse (son), Doris Waterhouse (author's mother), Laura Waterhouse (daughter), Sarah (wife), Sophie Waterhouse (daughter) and Arthur Hathaway (head clerk to the author's chambers at Farrar's Building, Temple).

14 The author with daughter Laura and Orlando in Regent's Park, early 1980s.

15 The author was president of the Llangollen International Eisteddfod, to which Pavarotti and his father came in July 1995. Pavarotti sang on two nights of the festival. He had been there previously at the age of 16 with a choir from his hometown, led by his father. *From left to right*: the author, Pavarotti senior, Luciano Pavarotti, Harvey Goldsmith the impresario and H. Gethin Davies (chairman of the eisteddfod). Pavarotti was still in good voice and full of warmth and charm.

16 The author at a holiday house in L'Isle-sur-la-Sorgue, Provence, relaxing after a very busy summer, 1995.

17 The author with his wife Sarah at Buckingham Palace to receive his GBE from the Prince of Wales, 17 April 2002.

18 The author with Sarah at the Middle Temple Hall for a dinner in honour of Gavin Arthur, a member of the Middle Temple who had become Lord Mayor of London, November 2002.

19 Laura Waterhouse's wedding in May 2003. She married Andrew Shakeshaft in Lincolnshire. The author and Laura had arrived in the horse-drawn carriage for the ceremony. The horse had been rather frisky on the way there, but this fact is not mentioned by the author in the text!

20 The countryside near the author's home in Herefordshire, looking towards the Black Mountains in Wales and the twelfth-century Goodrich Castle. The river Wye is at the bottom of the hill.

21 The author in his garden in Herefordshire with daughter Sophie and their beloved Labrador, Benjy, who died in 2007.

22 Thomas Waterhouse in New York in the 1980s.

23 The author's grandsons: David, James and Mark.

24 Sophie Waterhouse in an olive grove in Rhodes, 1993

25 Sophie in Lindos, 1993.

26 The author and Sarah in Herefordshire, early 2000s.

27 Breakfast in Herefordshire in 2009 with the author, Laura and Andrew Shakeshaft.

28 The author at one of his favourite restaurants in Venasque, in Provence. The photograph was taken by Sarah on their last visit to the area in October 2007.

14

THE PERILS OF
LIBEL LITIGATION

If one's practice as a junior barrister lies in a specialist field of the law, it is unlikely that there will be much change in that when one takes silk but there is a much greater unpredictability about what will happen at that stage if one's practice is more general. The element of chance is much bigger and it was chance that led me into the field of libel early in my career as a QC.

As a junior, my experience of libel had been limited to my work for *Private Eye*, including the Farmer and Cassidy action against it, the Brian Glanville case against the BBC and one or two settled cases for Robin Day, who was quite quick to sue any newspaper that overstepped the mark. However, in November 1968 I received instructions to draft the defence in an important libel action that did not come to trial until after I had been granted silk. The plaintiff was the formidable and litigious Church of Scientology, which was pursuing a campaign for recognition as a church and hence registration as a charity. The defendant was Geoffrey Johnson Smith, a friend of Robin Day who had partnered him on an Oxford Union debating tour of United States universities and colleges in 1949. By 1968 he was the Conservative MP for East Grinstead and a vice-chairman of the party. He had earlier worked for BBC television as an interviewer and reporter and was known to me socially through Robin.

It was Johnson Smith's misfortune that the UK headquarters of the scientologists were, and still are, at St Hill Manor in East Grinstead. They had also sued on a separate occasion Peter Hordern, who was the MP for the neighbouring constituency of Horsham. The case against Johnson Smith related to an interview that he had given in the BBC television programme

Twenty-Four Hours, which was similar to the contemporary *Newsnight*. He had put a question in the House of Commons to the Labour Minister of Health, Kenneth Robinson, asking him what action he proposed to take in regard to the scientologists. In a written answer on 25 July 1968 the minister had made a statement of government policy banning all immigration by scientology students; he had cited an Australian inquiry report that had found, rightly or wrongly, that scientologists 'direct themselves deliberately towards the weak, the unbalanced, the immature, the rootless and mentally or emotionally unstable'. The Minister's answer was widely reported by the media and the BBC invited Johnson Smith to appear that evening on their leading news programme because he was the local MP.

In that interview Johnson Smith was asked what the minister could do (he had talked about clamping down) and Johnson Smith merely repeated what the minister had said he would do. Then Johnson Smith was asked whether that was going to be enough and 'Could you put it into some sort of order?' in response to which he explained what matters of concern there were to the minister and other responsible persons, quoting the Australian finding. The interviewer asked also whether he had come across any alienation within family and he replied that it had been the disturbing trend of correspondence that he had received, stretching back almost three years, mentioning also that Peter Hordern had detected the same theme. But he favoured an inquiry rather than a bar, and an inquiry by Sir John Foster QC, MP announced early in 1969 resulted in a report that was quite favourable to the scientologists.

Little did the defendant realise in July 1968 that his careful words in answer to the questions put to him would provoke a libel action, the trial of which eventually took 32 days (and one in which the BBC was not joined as a defendant, even though it had broadcast the words complained about). One of the issues that arose was the question of parliamentary privilege and Sir Peter Rawlinson QC, the Attorney-General, had to intervene at an early stage to assert successfully that words said in Parliament could not be used as a link to other words in order to establish malice against an MP. Nevertheless, the evidence called was extremely wide ranging and the preparation for the case was probably more elaborate than for any other in which I appeared at the bar.

In view of the fact that I had become a QC early in the preliminary proceedings, Bernard Braithwaite of my chambers, who became a County Court judge very soon after the trial, was taken in as junior counsel and our most irksome task was to read a dozen or so of L. Ron Hubbard's indigestible books in which he expounded his theories, in order to prepare for cross-examination. Geoffrey Johnson Smith was very courteously willing for me to lead his defence but I recommended very strongly that Sir Elwyn Jones, who had been Attorney-General until June 1970, should do so, and he performed with great charm, skill and judgement at the trial, which began before Mr Justice Browne and a jury on Guy Fawkes' Day 1970 and ended, with victory for the defendant, thankfully, only four days before Christmas.

A rather bizarre feature of the case was that the scientologists were represented by a comparatively junior barrister called Ronald Shulman, who disappeared later in mysterious circumstances unconnected with our case. He was thought to have behaved oddly, to use a neutral word, in relation to the will of a man who died in a private plane crash when en route to France. Shulman was last seen, to my knowledge, by a barrister friend of mine, James Crespi, breakfasting at the Great Eastern Hotel: it was speculated that he ended up in Brazil and I have not heard of him now for over 35 years. He opened the case against Johnson Smith high, as you would expect, declaring that it was the freedom trial of the century, but Elwyn was very ready to deal with that sort of assertion and reminded the jury of L. Ron Hubbard's advice in the event of any inquiry into his organisation: 'Refuse to describe it or to discuss scientology'.

An early consequence of this victory was that I was drawn into another complex libel action. This was an action by a limited company and eight of its directors against Associated Newspapers Limited, the owner and publisher of the *Daily Mail* newspaper. The plaintiff company was originally called the Phonographic Equipment Company Limited but changed its name to Associated Leisure Limited on 2 December 1969; three of its main directors were Cyril Shack, Gordon Marks and Max Fine, the first and last of these being brothers. The plaintiffs' ground of complaint was that the company had been described in an article in the *Daily Mail* on 5 December 1968 in effect as 'a Mafia company'. Initially the defendant did not seek to assert that this description was true and merely put in issue formally such matters as identification, meaning and damages. However, many months after this written defence had been served on the plaintiffs, the defendant came into possession of evidence that it thought would establish that the words used in the newspaper article were true; and leave was obtained in May 1970 from a strong Court of Appeal headed by the Master of the Rolls, Lord Denning, to amend the defence to plead 'justification', that is, that the words complained of were true in substance and in fact, with the alternative rather technical defence of 'fair comment' as a precaution (see (1970) 2 QB 450).

At that point the defendant was represented by Peter Rawlinson QC and a very able junior, Bryan Anns, who sadly later drowned in the swimming pool of a Singapore hotel when out there for a preliminary hearing in a case in which I was leading him. As the Associated Leisure case approached trial, Rawlinson became Attorney-General and he recommended that Sir Elwyn should replace him as leader for Associated Newspapers. Sir Elwyn then asked that I should be briefed as second leader in view of the fact that we had worked together successfully in the scientology case.

The background to the case was that Shack and Marks had started a hire purchase business to finance the purchase of refrigerators in 1952 and had expanded into jukeboxes two years later. In 1960 they had started diversifying into various types of gambling machine. At first, their purchases of these machines were mainly from Germany but in 1962 the company started doing business with Bally Manufacturing Corporation based in Chicago, initially buying fruit machines and then, from 1964 onwards, mainly machines providing amusements with prizes. The other relevant business in which the plaintiffs became involved was that of the Colony Club in Berkeley Square, London W1, the premises of which were owned by the Tolaini brothers, both of whom were British citizens. Cyril Shack was approached by an American called Dino Cellini, who was an expert in running gaming establishments, with the suggestion that he should become a shareholder in the Colony Sporting Club, already registered in February 1966, which was to run a gaming club at the Berkeley Square premises.

The upshot was that Shack and Marks put up some of the money required (with other English shareholders) and the Colony Club opened with Alfred Salkin, who had been with Crockfords, as managing director; the film star George Raft, who received a Home Office residence permit for the purpose, became the host. Then, in 1967, the Home Office withdrew its permits for both Raft and Cellini, and in the same year Cyril Shack asked Salkin to look for a buyer for the financial interests of those of the plaintiffs who were involved. It was not until the following year, however, that a buyer was found with the help of Maxwell Joseph: there was a members' voluntary liquidation of the Colony Club company and it passed into the control of Curzon House, another well-known casino nearby in Park Lane.

The *Daily Mail* article in December 1968 was not provoked by any of the events in 1967 but by the widely publicised news in the late autumn of 1968 that the plaintiff company was planning a takeover bid for Butlins Limited, and the actual offer, in a formal document, was sent out by the plaintiff company to Butlins' shareholders a week before the *Daily Mail* article appeared. The general tenor of that article was that the Mafia and American gangsters were acquiring interests in gambling in London. The article was headed 'West End Mafia Faces an Attack by Sir Rasher', a reference to Sir

Ranulph Bacon, who was a member of the Gaming Board, after serving as deputy commissioner of the Metropolitan Police. The article went on to allege that American gangsters could wind up owning London, adding, 'Already it is thought that the Mafia has quietly acquired interests in several London casinos.' Later, the article went on to state: 'It's only a few weeks ago that a Mafia takeover bid to get hold of one of our big entertainments companies made the front-page headlines. Except that only a few people knew about the Mafia part of it.'

The defendant's case as pleaded in the amended defence ran to many paragraphs of particulars; Mr Justice Lawton described it in his summing up to the jury as being divided into four acts, which were:

(i)   trading with the Mafia, referring to an incident involving the Las Vegas Coin Company;
(ii) involvement with the Mafia in gambling, which referred to evidence about the Colony Club;
(iii) partnership with the Mafia in dealing with Bally Manufacturing Corporation;
(iv) joining with the Mafia to get hold of Butlins.

As Lord Denning summarised in his judgment on the application to amend the defence, the allegation was that 'the attempted takeover was for the purpose of gaining for the Mafia a substantial interest in the gaming and leisure industry of the United Kingdom.'

The trial before Mr Justice Lawton in the famous Queen's Bench Court 14 of the Royal Courts of Justice began on 21 June 1971 and lasted nearly a month to 19 July. The plaintiffs were represented by the highly experienced David Hirst QC and Tony Hoolahan, both well-known specialists in the field of libel. By then several favourable developments from the plaintiffs' point of view had taken place. One was that Bally Manufacturing Corporation had become a public company in the USA after an investigation by the Securities and Exchange Commission of its alleged Mafia connection. Another was that the plaintiff company had been granted a licence by the British Gaming Board in connection with its machine-vending business, the board having been supplied by the plaintiffs with a copy of the allegations made against them in the libel action. As for the individual plaintiffs, only Cyril Shack remained involved with the plaintiff company as its managing director, and Lord Jessel had become its chairman.

Before the trial began I had an unusual task because the defendant wished to be able to call George Raft to give evidence, if necessary, but he was still a prohibited immigrant in relation to the United Kingdom. We were informed, therefore, that Sir Elwyn and I would have to provide a joint opinion for submission to the Cabinet confirming the need for Raft's attendance. In the event, permission for this limited purpose was granted and he was flown from California to New York to await his possible call to London but we were able eventually to dispense with his evidence because of the testimony given by another American, Herbert Itkin. I should add, however, that calling him would have been a rather desperate last resort because it is very unlikely that he would have wished to assist the defendant.

In opening the case, David Hirst gave a masterly account of the plaintiffs' history and the issues raised by the pleadings and Cyril Shack gave the main confirmatory evidence on behalf of the plaintiffs. It was soon apparent that act (i), the company's dealings with the Las Vegas Coin Company, was of very minor relevance and that any justification for the allegation of Mafia involvement in the Butlins bid depended almost wholly upon acts (ii) and (iii) as they were later defined by the trial judge. From my point of view, the trial proceeded conventionally for the first week, which was occupied mainly with the evidence of Shack. He was followed by his brother, Max Fine, and much of my weekend was spent with Elwyn Jones and Bryan Anns preparing for the cross-examination of Fine. However, when I returned home late on Sunday evening I was thunderstruck to be told that Dennis Walsh, the senior partner of our instructing solicitors, had telephoned my wife to inform her that it was his wish that Elwyn should withdraw from the case, leaving me to lead for the defendant.

There is no doubt that, at that point, Mr Walsh was overwrought: he thought that the case for the defendant was going badly and he was more than usually involved emotionally because (I believe unknown to me at that time) he had been the co-respondent when Lord Jessel divorced his wife. A particular cause of his agitation was that I had been prompting Elwyn frequently as he cross-examined Cyril Shack. This was not due to any lack of preparation by Elwyn, who had worked full out both before and throughout the hearing, but because he had made only rare appearances in court during his long period as Attorney-General and was, therefore, rusty in the practice of cross-examination. We had worked together similarly in the scientology case and Elwyn regarded the prompting as helpful.

This was certainly my most embarrassing moment at the Bar and particularly distressing because of my affection and regard for Elwyn, who had brought me into the case and was always a most effective jury advocate. My own wish was to withdraw from the case, if the request to Elwyn was pursued, but we went to see Lord Justice Edmund-Davies, the former head of Elwyn's chambers, and he told me very firmly that I could not withdraw without committing a grave breach of the Bar's rules of conduct. The result was that we informed Mr Justice Lawton in private of the position and a bland formula was agreed by counsel on both sides to explain Elwyn's departure to the jury. Recollection of these events still saddens me and I felt ever afterwards that it clouded an important friendship in my life although Elwyn always behaved most generously to me and never gave any hint of antagonism because of it. The one good outcome was that he was immediately instructed to appear in the important Vehicle and General Insurance Company public inquiry and no criticism of his performance in the libel action emerged publicly.

Altogether 22 witnesses were called for the plaintiffs, including the eight individual plaintiffs and three of their wives and the president (chief executive) of Bally Manufacturing Corporation. In response, seven witnesses were called for the defendant but only one of them, Herbert Itkin, was crucial and it is fair to say that the whole of the defendant's case rested upon his evidence.

By any standards Itkin was an extraordinary man. He was born in Long Island in 1926 and raised in Brooklyn. He then worked as an office boy in a law firm, working his way through college and graduating from Brooklyn Law School in 1953. For the next 10 years he practised mainly in the personal-injury field, starting up his own firm in 1957 in rather dubious circumstances; from 1963 onwards his activities became much more exotic, wherever the truth may lie. In trying to give a brief account of him now, it is really impossible for me to separate fact from fiction and it is safer merely to explain how he presented himself to the defendant's solicitors and to the jury when he gave evidence in the libel action.

In brief, Itkin said that he was a New York lawyer who had become an agent for the American CIA and the FBI. He undertook various projects for the CIA from 1963 onwards but, more relevantly, the FBI wanted him to infiltrate gambling activities in England and to report regularly what he found out about American criminal, particularly Mafia, involvement. This FBI project was on hold because of his other concerns until March 1965, when he began to try to get involved in gambling and he alleged that he met Shack and others on several occasions in Miami and London. Matters proceeded more urgently from May 1966 when he met a prominent member of the Mafia called Antonio Dux Corrallo, and Itkin went on to refer to numerous visits that he said that he had made to England between October 1966 and January 1967 after Corrallo had agreed to get involved in the gambling project on certain specific terms.

Itkin spoke of many meetings in this period in London and elsewhere at which Shack, Fine or Marks had been present with named members of the Mafia, including Angelo Bruno, head of a Mafia family in Philadelphia, and other criminals, among whom a man called Albert Dymes or Dimeo was prominent. Eventually, Corrallo had flown with Itkin and a bodyguard to the UK on 18 January 1967 but had not been permitted to enter. Instead, another Mafia man, Dick Duke, had flown to London and had met Fine and Dymes with Itkin at the Tavistock Hotel to discuss a Spanish casino project that had been talked about from the previous November. Fine reported that no more money was forthcoming from his contacts and Duke walked out. None of the plaintiffs was present at a later meeting in Dominica but he did see Marks in the company of Angelo Bruno in a New York hotel on a day between 27 May and 2 June 1967.

There can be no doubt that the members of the jury were highly intrigued by these apparent revelations of underworld life. Itkin was a very professional witness, having given evidence in several important trials in the USA, and he appeared to be ready to admit shortcomings in his own conduct when cross-examined about them. There was also the point that he was still at that time a member of the New York Bar, despite the fact that he had been under investigation by the Bar authorities. Mr Justice Lawton summed up the case to the jury very fairly, rightly emphasising the central issue as the credibility of Itkin. The jury retired at 2:55 p.m. on 19 July and returned with their verdicts three hours later: they found that the words complained of had referred only to the plaintiff company and Shack, Fine and Marks (that is, not to the other plaintiffs) and that the defendant had proved that the words were true. The judge therefore entered judgment for the defendant with costs.

The result was an enormous relief to the defendant because the damages would have been very substantial indeed if the defence had failed. It was a special relief to me also because of the circumstances in which I had taken over a leading role. The defendant's chairman, Viscount Rothermere, showed his appreciation by entertaining Bryan Anns, Dennis Walsh, the latter's legal executive Tubby Brotherton and me to dinner at his Eaton Square flat two months later.

The impact of the jury's verdicts on Shack, Fine and Marks was, of course, devastating. They had denied in their evidence all of Itkin's assertions about the meetings and discussions at which he said that they had been present, and David Hirst had been able to demonstrate that a number of Itkin's alleged identifications were plainly incorrect. But Itkin had been quite agile in explaining away these 'errors' and had not brought any documents such as notes, diaries or even his old passport to confirm his evidence.

The plaintiffs duly appealed and the appeal was heard over a period of 18 days in January and February 1972. Perhaps the strongest point made by David Hirst on the plaintiffs' behalf was that, before the jury trial, they had been misled by the particulars of the defence of justification supplied by the defendant into thinking that Itkin, of whose existence they were aware, could not be called to give evidence so that they had not made the exhaustive inquiries necessary in order to cross-examine him effectively. It was said that the plaintiffs had secured much adverse information about him after the trial and that there ought to be a fresh hearing to enable this evidence to be put before a new jury. This and the other very full submissions for the plaintiffs were rejected, however, and the appeal was dismissed in a unanimous judgment delivered on 23 March 1972, the day when Sophie, aged five years eight months, passed her test for admission to Francis Holland School, Regent's Park.

An unexpected offshoot of this libel action was that I was asked a year later to help the United States government in the prosecution of the notorious Mafia leader, Meyer Lansky, who had been deported back to the USA by Israel, and Dino Cellini, who had been involved in the opening of the Colony Club until he had been required to leave the UK in 1967. The case against these men was for tax evasion and the United States government wished to have evidence taken by a commissioner in London from Alfred Salkin, who had been managing director of the club. For this purpose I was sworn in as a temporary district attorney and a hearing was held in my chambers on 6 March 1973 with an American lawyer representing Lansky and Cellini. The hope of the prosecution was that Salkin would disclose that there had been a 'skim' or secret rake-off of part of the casino's takings that was not disclosed to the Revenue but was taken by those who were 'party to the action'. However, Salkin unsurprisingly denied that there had been any such arrangement and the evidential exercise was fruitless from the prosecution point of view. The prosecution went ahead on other evidence, particularly that of a quite senior member of the Mafia called Vincent Teresa, but a jury acquitted Lansky in July 1973 (Cellini remained in Europe and was never tried). A further unexpected development for me was that I received from Vincent Teresa a copy of his book, *My Life in the Mafia*, published in 1973. He had inscribed it, rather embarrassingly, 'RG Waterhouse. To our London Counsel, I hope you enjoy this Book, Good Luck and Thank you. Vinnie'!

I would have left my account of this libel action there but for the admirable persistence of Cyril Shack, who has never ceased to assert that a grave miscarriage of justice occurred. He has sought out every detail available to him of Herbert Itkin's chequered history and enlisted on the way the interest and sympathy of Sir John Foster QC and Lord Justice Lawton (as he soon became). More recently, on seeing that I had attended the thanksgiving service for the latter's life, he sent to me the more important material that he had gathered. Much of it is very detailed because Itkin was involved in proceedings in France and Australia as well as several trials in the USA and at least one other court hearing in this country, so it would be inappropriate to try to recapitulate it here. It is necessary for me to say, however, that although the defendant in the libel action and its lawyers acted in good faith throughout the trial and the appeal, I am convinced now that Itkin was an accomplished liar and that, if this could have been demonstrated to the jury at the trial, they could not have found in the defendant's favour.

I am very conscious that this is an unusual statement for an advocate to make about one of his former cases because it is not his business to adjudicate upon the veracity of witnesses called in support of his client. The issue has, however, been forced upon me, so to speak, by the endeavours of Mr Shack and it would be churlish of me to avoid it. Most importantly, it does not involve any breach of confidence on my part and is based on information that is now within the public domain. I am fortified in my conclusions also because it accords with the opinion of Lord Justice Lawton, one of the most experienced jury trial lawyers of his generation, who heard all the evidence presented in the case.

Lord Justice Lawton had undoubtedly been uneasy about the credibility of Itkin during the trial itself, despite Itkin's continuing status as a barrister, and he cited the Associated Leisure case soon afterwards, when giving evidence to the Faulks Committee on the law of defamation, in support of his opinion that defamation actions should be tried by a judge alone without a jury, save in specified circumstances that are not relevant to the point that I am making (see the report of the committee, 1975 Cmnd. 5909, at paragraph 464). He said, *inter alia*, 'To say, as it has been said – and of me in particular – by one well known journalist that it is presumptuous of judges to think that they can decide complicated issues of fact better than jurors is, in my opinion, romantic twaddle.'

At some stage Cyril Shack wrote to the judge drawing his attention to much of the material about Itkin that he later sent to me. It is clear from copies of the correspondence between them that I have seen that Lord Justice Lawton was fully persuaded that a miscarriage of justice had occurred and it is intriguing that a warm friendship developed between them, embracing also Cyril's son, Jonathan. I have also seen a photocopy of a letter written by the Lord Justice to Lionel Swift QC as recently as March 1997, after considering the latter's 21-page written opinion in the matter, in which he expressed his agreement with Swift's conclusions.

Swift's opinion was that no jury could or would have placed any reliance on Itkin's evidence if they had been informed of the material about him to which I have referred and which Swift had considered in detail. He summarised his consideration of Itkin's evidence in seven highly critical paragraphs. He referred also to the fact that Itkin was not a practising member of the Bar at the time of the trial because there were proceedings against him that had been suspended temporarily, and he was disbarred in 1974 with his consent. Moreover, Itkin was never an FBI or CIA agent: he was merely a voluntary informant and his evidence about reporting matters to the FBI in London was expressly refuted by the FBI representative, as was another part of his evidence by a Metropolitan Police commander. These references are sufficient for my purpose and it is of interest that Itkin's evidence in a United States prosecution for perjury very shortly after the Associated Leisure case was disbelieved by the jury because the defending counsel had extensive material on which to cross-examine him and was able to demonstrate that he was a liar, with the result that he was not used as a prosecution witness subsequently.

My other experience of libel actions at that time was rather different because I appeared against litigants in person, which is always a difficult exercise and particularly so in a technical sphere such as defamation. The first of these to come to trial was an unusual action by a claims assessor (a category of occupation rudely called 'ambulance chaser' by some lawyers) against Leo Abse, the well-known Labour MP and my neighbour in Cavendish Avenue. The action was for damages for slander in the way of the plaintiff's business on the basis of statements alleged to have been made by the defendant to two journalists on 25 June 1964 about the plaintiff's advice to a man called Mifflin in respect of his claim for personal injuries. Special features of the case were that, first, there was no claim in respect of republication by the journalists of the defendant's words in their respective newspapers, the *Western Mail* and the *News of the World*, because the plaintiff, Gerald Wheeler, had failed in separate libel actions against both and had not issued a writ against Abse until an attempt to appeal to the House of Lords in the second action had failed. Second, in his Statement of Claim the plaintiff sought to rely, in proof of an alleged extended meaning of the alleged defamatory words, upon other words spoken by the defendant two days earlier in the House of Commons; and this raised potentially the question of parliamentary privilege, which had been in issue also in the scientologists' case.

The defendant's written defence was drafted by Leon Brittan, then an eminent junior in defamation but not yet a Conservative MP. The main defence was that any words actually spoken by the defendant to the journalists were true in substance and in fact. I cannot now recollect whether we took the point about privilege but, in the event, it became unnecessary for the defendant to pursue the matter.

The trial took place before Mr Justice Browne, sitting without a jury, in October 1971, and the plaintiff's case collapsed towards the end so that it was unnecessary for the defendant to give or call any evidence. Two journalists gave evidence of what the defendant had said to them and it emerged that he had met both of them in the lobby of the House of Commons after they had telephoned him separately, but they did not prove that he had spoken the words complained of by the plaintiff, and the judge refused his application to amend his Statement of Claim, commenting that it was seven and a half years since the conversation had taken place. Another development was that the plaintiff belatedly accepted that he had advised Mifflin to accept £10 in settlement of his claim whereas a solicitor obtained £75 for him, as alleged in the defence. The plaintiff was thus left without any effective case and the trial judge ruled that the words spoken by the defendant as proved were not capable of being defamatory. He entered judgment for the defendant and the plaintiff's appeal, heard in May 1972, was inevitably dismissed.

I will mention only two other libel actions in which I was involved as a silk, the first because of the notoriety of the plaintiff and the second because it posed a very difficult question of professional etiquette for my junior and me. In the first case my client was Sheffield Newspapers Limited and my junior was again Leon Brittan, by this time a rising Conservative MP and opposition spokesman; our opponents were Michael Kempster QC and Peter Bowsher, both libel specialists who later became judges in different spheres. The trial, which lasted 12 days in March 1976, took place in Sheffield Crown Court before Mr Justice Waller (senior) and a jury. The plaintiff on this occasion was Arthur Scargill, then president of the National Union of Mineworkers, and his complaint was about an article that had appeared in the *Sheffield Star* on 27 February 1974, the eve of a general election, in the course of the miners' strike and quite shortly after his election in 1973 as president.

The article was headed 'Scargill Must Quit Demand Miners' and it contained the following passage:

A branch spokesman referring to Glasshoughton Colliery told *The Star* today: 'There is a lot of ill feeling about the way picketing is being run, not only at our own pit, but at many others as well.' One thing that has angered many branches is the claim that 'plum' picketing jobs in East Anglia and other parts of the country have not been distributed fairly. 'It seems that jobs like these have been given to a small clique and this has really upset some of the men.'

An interesting background feature of the case was that the executive of the Yorkshire area of the NUM had agreed to underwrite the plaintiff's liability for costs in the libel action, even though it was his personal action for damages, and the union's risk in respect of the costs was very substantial.

My most onerous task was to cross-examine Scargill for two full days in support of the newspaper's defences of justification and fair comment. It was a tedious process and Scargill presented himself somewhat unattractively as a union bureaucrat who had merely followed decisions made by the appropriate bodies of the union democratically in accordance with the rules. It was not disputed that there had been an angry meeting of the Glasshoughton colliery branch at which dissatisfaction with the plaintiff had been expressed. The main factual issues in the case were as to:

(a) the circumstances in which and by whom it had been decided that picketing in East Anglia was to be carried out by members from the Barnsley area, in which the plaintiff had been employed for many years at Woolley colliery and

(b) his role and that of the NUM in deciding that, in general, pickets would not be paid except, relevantly in this case, limited sums for picketing in non-mining areas such as East Anglia.

Altogether 13 additional witnesses were called on behalf of the plaintiff, including a left-wing Sheffield MP, Martin Flannery, and eight witnesses gave evidence for the defendant, including the branch delegate of Glasshoughton colliery and other NUM members, mainly from North Yorkshire branches. At the end of it all we thought that we had presented a strong case as the result of the miners' courageous willingness to speak out against Scargill. To our dismay, however, Mr Justice Waller, who was widely experienced in the general common law but had little, if any, familiarity with libel, failed to give the appropriate direction to the jury about the very wide meaning to be given to 'fair comment' as a legal defence, although his summing-up was otherwise unfavourable to the defendant. Whether or not this omission did affect the verdict of the Sheffield jury I know not, but they found in the plaintiff's favour and awarded him £3,000 damages. Although the defendant could have appealed successfully because of the judge's omission, it would have only been able to obtain an order for a retrial with all the attendant risk and expense so it was decided very sensibly to let the matter rest there.

The other libel action that I want to mention had the flavour of a law examination question on its basic facts. My client, the defendant, was a bookmaker with the unusual name of Joseph (widely known as Chummy) Gaventa; two other defendants were his company and an employee who were also represented by me but need not be mentioned again. The brief had been passed to me by the clerk to Robert Alexander QC (later Lord Alexander of Weedon) and my opponent was Leon Brittan, representing the plaintiff, Milton Shulman, the well-known writer and theatre critic.

One of the plaintiff's forms of relaxation was to watch horse racing on television and to place bets by telephone as the afternoon went by, but he was dilatory in paying up and, according to his own evidence, often gave a series of post-dated cheques to major bookmakers and the Tote. The defendant, however, tired of this practice and may himself have been feeling the pinch late in 1971 and early in 1972. Whatever the reason, he threatened to report the plaintiff to Tattersalls if he did not settle his debts to the defendant in full and eventually did report him. This letter was the main foundation of the plaintiff's action for libel in which he asserted that, by sending it, the defendant was, in effect, alleging that the plaintiff had refused to pay or had shown a fixed and permanent intention not to pay.

The defendant's case was that he had taken the only course open to him in seeking to recover the money owed to him. Gambling debts were not actionable in the courts because gambling was then unlawful in English law and reporting to Tattersalls was the accepted procedure for dealing with defaulters: in reporting the plaintiff he had acted without any malice towards him.

The action was heard by Mr Justice (later Lord) Griffiths and a jury over the course of four days in February 1975 and my dilemma arose as Leon Brittan was cross-examining the defendant specifically on the issue of malice. Leon asked the defendant whether he himself had ever been reported to Tattersalls and the defendant denied it. That afternoon we had in court the secretary of Tattersalls because we intended to call him as a formal witness to prove the procedure and the jurisdiction of his committee and, to my surprise, a note from him was handed to me via my solicitors and my junior posing the question 'What is my duty when I go into the witness box if I know that a witness I have heard has lied?' Either in the note or on further inquiry it was made clear to me that the defendant had been reported to Tattersalls previously.

I had never been placed in this or any similar position and I was greatly troubled about the proper action to take. After consultation with my junior, John Phillips, who later died when still very young, and my instructing solicitors, I decided to ask Leon Brittan and the trial judge for permission to speak to the defendant on the assurance that it would not be detrimental to the plaintiff. Permission was forthcoming and, at the adjournment of the court, the defendant admitted that the secretary of Tattersalls was correct. Rightly or wrongly, I then warned the defendant that my junior and I could not continue to represent him unless he corrected his evidence. He agreed to do so and we continued to appear for him but it was inevitable that the jury would find against him and award damages to the plaintiff, which they did in the modest sum of £1,200.

I believe that I discussed my problem with the head of my chambers, Malcolm Morris QC, early that evening and that he approved what I had said to the defendant but I have had doubts about the correctness of my action ever since. It is certainly arguable that I had no right to threaten to withdraw from the case and, when I consider what would be the parallel duty of defending counsel in a criminal case, I find it difficult to justify my action. It may be that the same result would have occurred if the secretary of Tattersalls had been called to give evidence despite his disclosure but that is not an answer to the point.

Sir Robert Megarry, the vice-chancellor of the Chancery Division, used to entertain students and members of the Bar in very stimulating after-dinner talks in the Inns of Court, in the course of which he would pose practical problems of the kind that confronted me and invite members of the audience to respond. My recollection is that on one occasion in the Middle Temple he posed the very same problem that I had faced and that he acquiesced in the type of action that I had taken, although I did not have the courage to intervene in the discussion myself. However, my recollection of this may be incorrect and it would be unfair to the former vice-chancellor to cite him in my defence.

Altogether, my experience of defamation actions as an advocate brought home to me the unpredictability of the results both on liability and the quantum of damages. Such speculative litigation should only be embarked upon by persons with either a cast-iron case that must succeed or very substantial financial resources. Otherwise, they should be content, for their own peace of mind, with any apology that they may be able to secure or, failing an apology, any rebuttal that they can get published.

15

FORAYS TO SINGAPORE

One of the great spurs at the Bar, particularly as a silk, was the possibility of unexpected assignments, and the most exciting for me came early in March 1972. My star must have been in a particularly favourable position at that time because I had just won the appeal in the Associated Leisure libel case and had followed it with a delightful stolen holiday with Sarah in Megève because another appeal, in which I had inherited the respondent plaintiff's brief from Tasker Watkins on his appointment as a judge, had come to an abrupt end on the intervention of the court to prevent unnecessary costs being incurred. The unexpected new assignment for me was to lead the Singapore Solicitor-General, Wahab Ghows, in the prosecution of a British stockbroking firm and one of its directors.

The firm of stockbrokers was Fraser and Company, incorporated in Singapore in 1955 but established long before that in 1873, and the director was Tony Measor, who had emigrated to Singapore in 1955, immediately after qualifying as an accountant. He had joined Fraser and Company as an assistant in 1960, becoming a director in 1962. The case against both the firm and Measor was based on alleged breaches late in 1971 of the provisions of section 366 of the Singapore Companies Act 1967, which was in the same terms as section 13 of the British Prevention of Fraud (Investments) Act 1958 and its 1939 predecessor. In short, the charges were of recklessly making statements or forecasts that were misleading and thus inducing or attempting to induce a person to buy company shares. In this case the shares were in a company called the Singapore Traction Company (1964) Limited, incorporated in Singapore and with a quotation on the stock exchange; the person whose share dealings on Measor's initiative formed a central plank of the prosecution case was Shen Yuen Pai, a wealthy Brunei civil engineer with a Shanghai University degree, who had built up a very successful construction business from 1958 onwards and was a well-established client of Fraser and Company from 1966.

STC (as I will call it) had succeeded an earlier company of the same name and its main activity was in operating bus services: it had a franchise covering many roads in the central part of Singapore (37 bus services) but this franchise was brought to an end by legislation early in 1971 and, to make matters worse, a new fare structure severely affected the company's revenue. The result was that it began to add heavily to already substantial accumulated losses and, under government direction, the company started to negotiate with other bus companies for the sale of most of its buses. This in turn led to feverish speculation about the future of STC, triggered by an article in a Singapore newspaper and evidenced by very high daily turnovers in its shares from 16 November to early December 1971, at which point dealings in the shares were suspended at the request of the Monetary Authority.

The misinformation about STC's net asset value conveyed by Fraser and Company and Measor to the firm's clients related mainly to the value of its two pieces of land in Singapore. Although the directors of STC vigorously denied that any sale of the company was contemplated, it was almost inevitable that outsiders would make attempts to value the company once its buses had been sold and Measor, on behalf of his firm, tried to do so but made substantial errors in relation to the size of both pieces of land. He applied also an excessive multiplier of four or five to what he wrongly thought was the latest previous valuation in 1964, arriving by these means at S$1.10 per share 'on a conservative property valuation'.

This erroneous assessment was set out by Measor in a weekly circular distributed by Fraser and Company to about 3,000 clients and institutions on or about 20 November 1971. Moreover, it was a basis, at least in part, of discussions between Measor and Shen from 24 November during a period of just over a week in which Measor increased Shen's holding of STC shares from 80,000 to a total of 2.5 million by 3 December, representing 17.5 per cent of the company's issued capital. Then, on 15 December a receiver was appointed by Chung Khian Bank to secure the company's overdraft and it was still in the hands of the receiver at the time of the trial.

That is a sufficient summary of the basic facts to give the general flavour of the case in which I was instructed for the prosecution and for which I flew out to Singapore on 30 March 1972. Two of the many advantages of appearing for the government of Singapore were that it had substantial interests in both Singapore Airlines and the Shangri-La Hotel, so I was very comfortably transported and housed. It was my first experience of the barrister's 'taximeter' ticking over daily, including weekends, from the moment I stepped onto the aeroplane at Heathrow. Another pleasant aspect of the case was that both defendants were represented by Owen Stable QC, the brother of my old friend Philip Owen QC, who did so skilfully and tenaciously. He was already a bencher of my Inn, the Middle Temple, of which Singapore's Prime Minister, Lee Kuan Yew, had been elected an honorary bencher; the unexpected result was that Owen and I were invited to dine on 19 April with Lee and his wife, both of whom were contemporary law students of mine at Cambridge, at the prime minister's official residence, Sri Temaset, in the grounds of the Istana.

The trial began on 3 April in District Court No 1 before Judge T.S. (Sam) Sinnathuray, who became a judge of the Supreme Court in 1978, and it lasted until 10 May, including Saturday morning sittings. The long absence from home was considerably mitigated by Sarah's arrival on 8 April for just over a week, and throughout my visit I was entertained very generously by a host of new friends in the legal fraternity. Highlights included two visits to race meetings at the Singapore Turf Club, dinner with Owen Stable at Raffles Hotel and innumerable other excellent dinner parties, a cruise around the harbour and a visit to a rubber plantation over the Causeway. I spent as much time as I could in the Shangri-La's swimming pool but there was a great deal of work to do in between.

The trial itself was of absorbing interest because of the clash between Measor and Shen. There was a considerable amount of money at stake ultimately because the market price of STC shares had been at a peak, albeit briefly, of 87 cents per share on 19 November 1971, whereas the valuation of each share late in March 1972 was said to be just under 20 cents. The defendants' case was that Measor's assessments had been made conscientiously on the basis of the information available to him at the time and that the errors about the size of the STC sites had been corrected when they became aware of them. There were, however, very many issues of fact between Shen and Measor about what had been said in their discussions.

Judge Sinnathuray delivered his 127-page judgment on 16 June 1972 and predictably found for the prosecution on all six charges. Although Measor had appeared to be quite a decent, amiable young man when giving his evidence, he was faced with a very shrewd, not to say wily, client in Shen, whose successful career demonstrated his considerable ability, and it is not surprising that the latter's evidence was preferred. The prosecution did not allege dishonesty on the part of Measor or his firm and honour was satisfied by the imposition of fines totalling S$37,000. The Singapore government was anxious to establish the stability of the local stock exchange as a major international institution and the prosecution played some part in discouraging the tendency of some investors there to indulge in feverish speculation.

My first case in Singapore led to other work there and in London over the next five and a half years until I was appointed to the High Court bench, and my major regret on taking that appointment was that it brought to an end the possibility of further professional visits there. My good friend Tan Boon Teik, the Attorney-General, who became chairman of Singapore's International Court of Arbitration, did arrange for me to be included in their list of arbitrators but, as I have lacked sponsoring litigants, my services have not been called upon.

My next visit occurred a year later when I appeared for the defendants in a civil action brought by a Slater Walker company, Motor and General Underwriters Investment Holdings Limited (M&G), about the purchase of shares in a new multi-storey building in Clemenceau Avenue, known as the Glass Tower. M&G was represented by a Chancery silk, John Balcombe, who became a fellow judge with me in the Family Division and then a Lord Justice of Appeal; the company's managing director was a young man called Ian Tamblyn, who became a proposed defendant in the extradition proceedings to which I refer later in this chapter but who was then absent from the UK.

The four shareholder defendants that I represented were companies that had invested in Fort Development Limited, the developer of the Glass Tower. M&G claimed to have bought all the shares in that company in November 1972. The moving spirit behind the development, however, was Lim Cher Kheng, the managing director of the developer company, who had been a member of the legislative assembly prior to 1959 and quite a prominent politician. The seven-storey building with a basement and two penthouses should have been completed by 14 August 1972 but financial problems arose and on 22 November of that year M&G agreed with the four defendants to buy the developer company. The case for M&G was that the completion date for this agreement was put back, for the defendants' convenience because of various difficulties they were experiencing, until 31 January 1973; but the defendants tried to change certain clauses in the agreement and then, in breach of it, gave notice on 1 February that they did not intend to proceed with the sale of the shares. M&G therefore claimed specific performance of the agreement while the defendants put forward a rather tenuous defence on the footing that 'time was of the essence of the contract' and that M&G had broken the agreement by failing to complete the purchase on the date originally agreed. The defendants therefore counter-claimed damages for alleged loss that they had suffered in consequence.

The hearing of this action in the Singapore High Court before Mr Justice Tan Ah Tah began on 9 May 1973, the day after my forty-seventh birthday, so that my actual birthday was spent in consultations with my clients, but Sarah had followed me out the previous weekend and we were able to celebrate it together. It soon became apparent that more than the allotted time was needed to complete the case and Sarah and I flew back to London on 15 May, after which it was arranged that the hearing would resume on 23 July. During our May visit we stayed in a ground-floor room at the Goodwood Park Hotel, much favoured by English visitors, and enjoyed dining romantically by one of the hotel's swimming pools. It was a great pleasure also to renew friendships begun a year earlier with Tan Boon Teik and his wife Sookyee, Alan Daniel, the government's British legal adviser, the Karthigesus and many others prominent in Singapore's legal life.

I returned to Singapore alone on 20 July for the resumed hearing, staying this time at the Shangri-La Hotel. Singapore was as delightful as ever but I found the litigation oppressive. For me, it was late in the legal year and I was anxious to join Sarah and the children for the long vacation in Italy. The case for my clients was manifestly weak, bearing in mind the developer's financial difficulties and the suspected wish of Lim Cher Kheng to arrange for M&G to be 'gazumped' at the time when he refused to allow M&G to complete the purchase. Another anxiety was that Lim seemed to spend most nights playing mah-jong and drinking brandy, testing his mental stamina to the utmost limits. However, my junior, Ramanujan, was a particularly witty and relaxed companion who did not allow me to become distraught. It was a great sadness when he died in April 1979, at the age of only 49, on a trades union mission to Manila.

To my relief, after a 15-day hearing, we were able to negotiate a settle-ment of the case while Lim was giving his evidence. The defendants accepted the substance of M&G's claim for specific performance of the agreement at the agreed price of S$4 million, subject to the deletion of some clauses in it, and agreed to pay S$20,000 damages. This was announced in court on 8 August and that evening I flew to Pisa via Rome to join my family at Nugola Vecchia in Tuscany, where we had rented a house for the month.

That proved to be the most social of all our family holidays. We had been persuaded to rent a small house there by Leo and Marjorie Abse, who had a house in the same village, and other neighbours were Woodrow and Verushka Wyatt, who had Elizabeth Jane Howard, the novelist and then wife of Kingsley Amis, staying with them. To cap all this, Bill and Silvia

Rodgers were installed with their daughters in another house nearby and Roy Jenkins arrived to stay with them for a couple of days, with the result that we played cricket (Sarah caught him out, literally!) and dined with him. The weather was particularly hot and we spent most days on the beach at Tirrenia with Thomas and Sophie, aged 11 and 7, and our respective mothers, who visited us in turn. Towards the end we were joined in swimming by Robin and Kathy Day, who stayed with the Abses and then with Sarah's Heathfield contemporary, Edwina Sandys, in a delightful house above Lucca. We all enjoyed a spectacular party that Edwina gave when Perry Worsthorne and his wife were also staying with her. Altogether, it was a very memorable holiday but I vowed not to return to Tuscany in the heat of August and our subsequent visits have been in the gentler month of May.

My later visits to Singapore were all in relation to criminal cases involving company law and, in all but one of them, I acted for the Singapore government. During this period, when Singapore's reputation as a sound financial centre was being established, Alan Daniel was very active as an adviser to the Attorney-General and the government as a whole, and Singapore looked to Australia as well as the United Kingdom for legislative models in company law. A particular concern was to outlaw and punish 'insider trading', which was thought to be rife, and in pursuing this aim actively Singapore was significantly ahead of us at the time.

An early example of this involved the Sime Darby Group and its chairman and managing director, Dennis Pinder, about whom I was asked to advise the Attorney-General in June 1974. Attention had been focused on the financial affairs of the group in September 1973 when the senior partner of a highly respected Singapore firm of accountants, who were the auditors of Sime Darby Holdings Limited, committed suicide and left two letters alleging that he had been duped and deceived by Pinder in relation to the audit of the Sime Darby Group. An investigation by the commercial crime division of the CID followed and eventually, having considered reports by a senior police officer (who later became a barrister of the Middle Temple) and the Assistant Registrar of Companies as well as the auditors' report, I approved charges of criminal breach of trust by Pinder involving over S$3 million and five charges under the Companies Act of making false statements to the auditors.

The nub of the prosecution case was that Pinder had played the leading role, with another director no longer in Singapore, in setting up the Simit Welfare Fund in the Bahamas for the benefit of Sime Darby's expatriate staff and had insisted upon the utmost secrecy about the nature and source of this fund. Remittances via Chartered Bank from the group to the fund were camouflaged, using an account in London: they were shown in Sime Darby ledgers as payments to a London commission suspense account and fictitious debit notes were issued to back them up. Moreover, many of these payments did not end up in the Simit Welfare Fund but were diverted to accounts in the name of Pinder or the joint names of Pinder and one of two other directors. When the investigation was pursued by the auditors Pinder told a number of lies, which were the basis of the Companies Act charges. He was dismissed from his offices with the group at the end of October 1973.

It had been the intention of the Attorney-General that I should lead for the prosecution at Pinder's trial, Owen Stable having again been retained to lead for the defendant. To my disappointment, however, the Finance Ministry refused to sanction the expense of instructing me, on the ground that a recession was looming. The prosecution was undertaken instead by an able member of the Attorney-General's chambers, S. Rajendran, later a Supreme Court judge. The judge was again the senior District judge, T.S. Sinnathuray, and the hearing began at the end of March 1975 but it was adjourned early on to enable discussions to take place. These resulted in changes of plea by Pinder: he agreed to plead guilty to three amended charges and the prosecution dropped the others, taking into account Pinder's alleged deteriorating health. He agreed also to transfer certain property to the Sime Darby Group and it was said that the amount recovered by the group from him and the other former director totalled S$2.8 million. In the light of these developments Pinder was sentenced on 20 October 1975 to 18 months' imprisonment; I believe that he claimed that his health had improved significantly when he emerged from prison after his enforced rest.

A financial scandal in Singapore with wider overseas aftershocks was already beginning to erupt by the time that Pinder was sentenced. The company involved was Haw Par Brothers International Limited (HPBIL), which was controlled at the relevant times by Slater Walker personnel, although the shareholding of Slater Walker Securities Limited was only in the range of about 19 to 30 per cent from time to time. I was asked to advise the Attorney-General in the matter as early as September 1975 because inspectors appointed to investigate HPBIL were refusing to disclose incriminating evidence that had come to light in the course of their investigation until they presented their report. In the event, the affairs of Slater Walker and HPBIL were to preoccupy me from then on until I became a judge in January 1978.

The investigation under the Companies Act was begun by two inspectors, a leading Singapore lawyer and a partner in Price Waterhouse and

Company, appointed by the finance minister. The lawyer had to withdraw in the course of the investigation because of a possible conflict of interest and it was concluded by the accountant, P.G. Grundy, in or about March 1976. I had by then given three further written opinions on various aspects of the matter and on 28 March, immediately after the Scargill libel trial, I travelled out to Singapore to discuss and draft charges to be preferred against five Slater Walker personnel, namely, James Slater himself, Richard Tarling, Donald Ogilvy Watson, Ian Tamblyn and Patrick Goodbody. My visit lasted four days, at the Shangri-La Hotel as usual, but there was little time for leisure activities. Our discussions resulted in the formulation of a wide range of charges, eventually 68 in all, against the intended defendants. Some amendments were made in the following month but they were finalised by June 1976, at which point warrants for the arrest of the persons charged were issued in Singapore.

The home secretary granted authority to proceed on 6 October 1976 and by that time only Slater and Tarling were accessible in the United Kingdom, and so only they could be served with the charges. Slater had to face possible extradition on six charges and Tarling on a total of 17, six of which were in similar terms to the Slater charges. The applications by the Singapore government for extradition were heard, as was customary, by the chief metropolitan magistrate, K.J.P. Barraclough, at Horseferry Road Magistrates' Court in January 1977.

There were two distinct parts to the government of Singapore's case. The first related to the creation of a secret fund for the benefit of the five intended defendants and a small number of other Slater Walker personnel in a company called Spydar Securities Limited. The second was concerned with alleged manipulation of the accounts of various companies and Melbourne Unit Trust to present a distorted picture of increasing annual profits being made by HPBIL.

The six charges against Slater and the first six against Tarling all related to the secret Spydar fund, as did four additional charges against Tarling alone. Slater was executive chairman of the Slater Walker Group and of Slater Walker Securities Limited (SWS) at all relevant times, while Tarling was a director of SWS and chairman of HPBIL, in which the Slater Walker Group had acquired a substantial shareholding in 1971. Then, in February 1972 HPBIL acquired seven million shares in Kwan Loong and Company (Hong Kong) Limited and, shortly afterwards, an HPBIL subsidiary in Hong Kong, Haw Par Brothers (Hong Kong) Limited, purchased 6,663,000 shares in King Fung Development Limited. However, on 15 or 16 March 1972 Slater, Tarling and Ogilvy Watson met with another Slater Walker man, Johnson-Hill, and agreed to obtain an existing company into which 10 per cent of the Kwan Loong and King Fung shares would be transferred at cost price for the benefit of named Slater Walker personnel, including Slater and Tarling. The agreement was modified about a week later in Australia, reducing the proposed capital of the new company slightly, but the basic scheme remained the same and 725,000 Kwan Loong shares and 612,631 King Fung shares were subsequently transferred to Spydar Securities Limited, a Hong Kong company which had been obtained, with a change of name, for the purpose. Declarations of trust were made later in respect of the share capital of Spydar in favour of the Slater Walker parties to the agreement.

As a result of these manoeuvres, very substantial distributions were made between January and December 1973 to the five intended defendants and Johnson-Hill, and some payments to other Slater Walker executives. Slater or a company of his received over HK$2.25 million, as did Tarling; the total profit made by Spydar from the shares amounted to over HK$11 million. These transactions were kept secret from the board of HPBIL, other than the beneficiaries, and from its shareholders; false documents were created to assist the concealment. It is noteworthy also that the declarations of trust in favour of the Spydar beneficiaries were not made until 30 September 1972, after all the King Fung shares (sold on 26 May) and a substantial proportion of the Kwan Lung shares had been sold at a considerable profit. Spydar Securities Limited went into voluntary liquidation in July 1973.

The charges against Slater and Tarling alleged conspiracy to steal the Kwan Lung shares and the proceeds of sale of the King Fung shares allocated to Spydar (charges 1 and 2) and conspiracy to cheat and defraud HPBIL by dishonestly concealing the existence of the relevant agreements (charges 3 and 4). They were also accused in charges 5 and 6 of furnishing false and/or misleading statements to the shareholders in a circular dated 24 March 1972. Tarling faced four additional charges of wilful non-disclosure as a director of HPBIL of the benefits that he received in 1972 and 1973 from Spydar.

The second part of the Singapore government's case was based on manoeuvres by Tarling and some of his fellow directors to deal with the very large profit made on the sale of the other 90 per cent of Kwan Loong and King Fung shares. By June 1972, as I have said, all of the King Fung shares and a large proportion of the Kwan Loong shares had been sold, and Tarling and the other directors did not wish to show this profit in the accounts of HPBIL for 1972. They took elaborate steps via a number of companies and the creation on 28 June 1972 of Melbourne Unit Trust (MUT) to conceal the profit; they then used MUT to pump back the profit into HPBIL in the following two years to give a false picture of satisfactory profitability by HPBIL. The true picture in the years 1972 to 1974 would have been of rapidly decreasing profits after a peak in 1972 of S$41,775,000.

Tarling faced seven charges on this part of the case. One was a general charge of conspiracy to induce investment in HPBIL by misleading statements about its current profits and dishonest concealment of material facts. There were also five alleged breaches of section 169(6) of the Companies Act by wilful failures to disclose in the 1972 and 1973 accounts of HPBIL. Finally, there was a further allegation of conspiracy to induce investment by dishonest concealment of material facts because in January 1970 HPBIL reported in an offer document the false statements about its profits that had appeared in its annual accounts. This was an offer document sent to the remaining shareholders of another Slater Walker company, M&G, the owner of the Glass Tower development to which I have referred earlier in this chapter.

The Attorney-General of Singapore appointed his usual London agents, Charles Russell and Company, and they in turn instructed a junior barrister to appear with me but he disagreed about the strength of the case against Slater and withdrew. On my recommendation, therefore, Alexander (Derry) Irvine, then a very successful junior, was instructed in his place and we had to assist us a second junior, David (now Mr Justice) Lloyd Jones, who was still then an active fellow of Downing College, Cambridge, as well as a practising barrister. The stage was thus set for the extradition proceedings, which occupied almost the whole of January 1977, consequentially my most profitable month at the Bar. A very surprising aspect of the hearing was that Derry had two pupils attending court with him daily: they were Tony Blair and Cherie Booth, who were soon walking hand in hand, and I came to know them quite well at lunch and tea in the course of the proceedings. It is sad that Cherie should now write so unkindly and unfairly in her autobiography about Derry, who was entrusted by her husband with the office of Lord Chancellor for over six years and who has not, as far as I am aware, voiced any public criticism of either of them.

The proceedings attracted very wide public attention and it was generally recognised that the government here and the Bank of England viewed them with considerable concern because of the extent of the involvement of the City in the affairs of the Slater Walker Bank, which was thought to be near collapse. The Bank of England's view was that such a collapse would have widespread damaging effects in other financial sectors: James Goldsmith had been active from the autumn of 1975 on behalf of his friend Slater and it became known later that the Bank of England provided a substantial lifeline to SWS to keep it afloat.

As one would expect, there was strong representation for the defendants. Slater's leading counsel was John Matthew, the First Senior Prosecuting Counsel to the Crown and the son of a former Director of Public Prosecutions, and his junior was another Treasury counsel, David Tudor Price. Tarling was represented by my fellow Middle Temple bencher, Andrew Bateson QC, a former counsel to the Board of Trade, and Michael Burton (both he and Tudor Price became High Court judges). As was usual in extradition proceedings, the governor of Brixton prison was also represented, this time by Kenneth Richardson and Clive Nicholls, both Treasury counsel at the Old Bailey.

Slater's defence essentially was that, whilst he had taken part in the initial agreement to set up Spydar, he had left the subsequent implementation to the Slater Walker executives in Hong Kong and Singapore and assumed that they would ensure that local legal requirements were complied with. In particular, he asserted that he was not a party to the concealment of Spydar from shareholders or the creation of any false documents. Many detailed submissions were also made on his behalf on the nature of the transactions, the issue of dishonesty generally and the complex jurisdictional issues in respect of Slater, who had visited Singapore and Hong Kong in March 1972 only. Overall, it was said, the Spydar arrangement was a legitimate and proper way of compensating the relevant Slater Walker executives for entering into covenants restricting their right to trade in shares for their own benefit and providing an incentive scheme. Slater himself joined in at the invitation of the others to give the scheme his clear blessing.

Tarling's case in relation to the Spydar scheme was that he was a willing participant but was unaware that it had to be disclosed to shareholders or to non-European members of the board of directors who were not participants. He and his colleagues relied heavily on the advice of local accountants and lawyers in Hong Kong and Singapore as to local law and understood that disclosure had not been required in respect of a similar scheme in the UK, referred to as the 'Tokengate concept', although disclosure requirements were generally far more onerous in the UK. The direction of HPBIL had been delegated by its board to an executive committee so that information about particular transactions was usually confined to members of that committee.

On the alleged falsification of HPBIL's profit record, it was argued that no responsible director would have incorporated the profit in the Kwan Loong and King Fung shares in HPBIL's accounts for 1972. The money did not belong to HPBIL until it was transferred by MUT to HPBIL as a dividend. Moreover, MUT was vetted by accountants and auditors before it was established and Tarling himself was not involved in the details during the mere 18 days that he spent in the Far East in the course of 1972 and 1973.

At the end of a very detailed examination of this complicated history, the chief metropolitan magistrate reserved his decision for four days and then announced it in a brief judgment on 26 January. The magistrate's decision was that Slater had no case to answer on the six charges against him on the grounds that he was never a director of HPBIL and that he was not charged as an aider and abettor. It was the magistrate's view also that the evidence did not establish a *prima facie* case of conspiracy by him to steal and cheat in relation to the Spydar scheme. Tarling, however, was found to have a *prima facie* case against him on 15 of the 17 charges laid against him. The two exceptions were charges 5 and 6 alleging the furnishing of false and misleading statements to shareholders about the acquisition of Kwan Loong and King Fung shares. He was ordered to be detained in custody with a view to his extradition to Singapore for trial, the final decision resting (as always in these cases) with the home secretary.

Tarling indicated immediately that he intended to apply to the Queen's Bench Divisional Court for a writ of *habeas corpus ad subjiciendum* in order to have the magistrate's decision quashed, and he was admitted to bail by that court the same afternoon pending the hearing of his application. It was obvious that it would be opposed by the Singapore government but we were in a dilemma about the position of Slater because we were mystified by the magistrate's stated reasons for distinguishing between him and Tarling on the charges common to both of them. I am glad to say that all five of the Law Lords who later heard the case found it difficult or impossible to understand how the chief magistrate could have come to different decisions in respect of Slater and Tarling on the first four charges, a view apparently shared by Professsor J.C. Smith, as he then was, the leading academic criminal lawyer.

Our problem was that there was no reported English case in which the divisional court had reversed an acquittal by an examining magistrate in an extradition case. It was reasonably clear that the appropriate application would be for a writ of *certiorari* to quash the decision (now it would be for judicial review) but it had been expressly held in two Irish cases that it could not be used to reverse the decision of magistrates not to commit for trial. When we were asked to advise whether an attempt should be made in the divisional court to reinstate the case against Slater, Derry Irvine drafted a very learned joint opinion, which we both signed, putting the prospect of success no higher than 25 per cent in view of the hurdles to be overcome (including the British distaste then for double jeopardy).

Before this opinion was signed on, however, I had received an early morning telephone call at home urging an appeal in Slater's case. Tan Boon Teik was on friendly terms with Lord Shawcross, who was then chairman of the Panel on Takeovers and Mergers here, and I learnt that he had expressed the view to Boon Teik that we should appeal. It is not surprising therefore that our instructions to proceed against Slater were confirmed late in March.

Our applications for *certiorari* and *mandamus* in respect of the Slater decision and Tarling's for *habeas corpus* came before a divisional court presided over by Lord Justice (Sebag) Shaw, with Mr Justice Nield and Mr Justice Stocker as his fellow judges, on 25 April 1977. We had informed Slater's counsel of our applications and he was permitted to intervene with the same representation, except that John Mathew had taken silk in the interim. The applications against Slater were taken first and refused the following day on the ground that there was no basis for granting a writ of *certiorari*. The Tarling application lasted until 17 May, however, during which time I addressed the court for about six days.

The judgment of the court was delivered by Lord Justice Shaw two and a half months later, on 29 July, when Tarling was discharged from custody in respect of the eight Spydar charges that had remained against him but the court dismissed his application for release in respect of six of the seven MUT charges. Applications for leave to appeal by both sides were refused and Tarling was released on bail pending renewed applications to the House of Lords for leave to appeal. There was no attempt to appeal further against the acquittal of Slater.

The basis for acquitting Tarling on the Spydar charges was partly, in the court's view, the absence of 'appropriation' necessary to constitute stealing and partly insufficient evidence of dishonesty to justify conviction. There was also an absence of relevant acts in Singapore to found jurisdiction to try the alleged crimes there. Finally, on charge 11, which alleged a fraudulent intention, the divisional court made a finding of fact that was surely not open to it on the issues before it, in the following terms:

> Mr Tarling's complicity appears to us to derive from errors of judgment and the exercise of too intermittent and remote control rather than from any dishonest intention.

However, the divisional court did reject the allegation made by Tarling quite unjustifiably that the applications by Singapore against him were politically motivated and made in bad faith.

Leave to appeal was granted by the House of Lords to both the Singapore government and Tarling in October and I spent many hours during my last three months at the Bar considering the necessary documentation and the printed statement for the appeal. On 1 December, however, I was asked to see the Lord Chancellor, Lord Elwyn Jones. Fortunately, my case at Cardiff settled early the next day and I was able to see the Lord Chancellor at 4.30 p.m., when I accepted appointment as a judge of the Family Division of the High Court. By then the appeals in the HPBIL case were due to be heard in January 1978 and I did ask whether my appointment could be postponed for a short period to enable me to complete my role in them but I was told that this would not be possible. This meant that I had to inform Derry later, on the eve of the announcement, that I would not be available to lead him. He has never quite forgiven me for this but I would say in my defence that in the event he was able to strengthen his already formidable case for the grant of silk at Easter 1978, which duly occurred.

To complete the story, Tarling quarrelled with his leading counsel and was represented by his junior, Michael Burton, leading Michael (now Mr Justice) Supperstone, in the House of Lords, while the government of Singapore was represented by Derry leading David Lloyd Jones and Richard (now Mr Justice) Field. The upshot was that Tarling succeeded in getting rid of charge 17, relating to negotiations about HPBIL shares with M&G shareholders, and Singapore failed to obtain reinstatement of any of the charges dismissed by the divisional court (mainly the Spydar charges); but Tarling still had to face the five surviving MUT charges and was eventually extradited to Singapore in March 1979. He was sentenced to six months' imprisonment on 20 November that year, after a 59-day trial.

I have probably taken up too much space in giving my account of the Slater Walker affair but it was the major preoccupation of my last 18 months at the Bar and is of general interest because of an extraordinary conflict of opinion between the Law Lords on the meaning of the word 'dishonesty'. Up to that time the Court of Appeal, criminal division, had repeatedly told trial judges of all kinds not to attempt to explain to juries the meaning of this perfectly familiar English word: it was to be interpreted by the good sense of the jury applied to the facts of the particular case before them. Yet, in the Tarling case the underlying facts were not unduly complicated but the Law Lords divided 3:2 in deciding whether there was a *prima facie* case that the Spydar scheme and the MUT scheme were, or (more strictly) could properly be regarded as, dishonest.

In short, the conclusion of Lords Wilberforce, Salmon and Keith of Kinkel was that Tarling should not be required to stand trial on any of the Spydar charges and one of the six surviving MUT charges. All of these involved allegations of dishonesty on the part of Tarling. However, Viscount Dilhorne, who gave a full review of the relevant evidence, and Lord Edmund-Davies took the opposite view on all those charges and were in favour of upholding Singapore's application for extradition in respect of them as well as the five charges that survived Tarling's appeal.

Lord Edmund-Davies said at the outset of his speech:

> A majority of your Lordships have concluded that Mr Tarling should not be called upon to answer any of these [six] charges. In these circumstances, I would not comment on them if I could properly avoid doing so. But I find that course impossible, so strong are the misgivings created in my mind by the deplorable conduct of the appellant and others which led to the preferring of these six charges, and my dismay that such conduct should be regarded as stopping short even of the appearance of dishonesty.

It would be inappropriate for me to comment further on the outcome. There followed some delay before the home secretary, Merlyn Rees, made the decision that the extradition should proceed; it was prefaced by fairly extensive adverse newspaper comment about Tarling's prospect of a fair trial in Singapore. In the end, however, he chose to accept his modest prison sentence rather than to have to remain in Singapore for a further period pending an appeal.

It is difficult now, 30 years after the event, to convey the atmosphere of tension in City circles that the prosecution generated. Two recent articles by 'City Slicker' in *Private Eye* have nevertheless drawn attention to some surprising facts about the Slater Walker crisis now disclosed under the '30 year rule' and the Freedom of Information Act. They show how James Goldsmith, Slater's friend, was accepted as negotiator on his behalf and was granted access on the subject to UK government ministers, even including the prime minister, Harold Wilson.

Although the Slater and Tarling case was my main preoccupation in 1977, I was able to pay a last professional visit to Singapore for a fortnight in June of that year when I appeared in committal proceedings for the defence of a rather extraordinary Malay entrepreneur who was later sentenced to seven years' imprisonment. It will have been seen therefore that I had very mixed fortunes in my Singapore cases but I have remained very grateful for having been given the chance to practise there intermittently in the 1970s. No doubt the influence of Lee Kuan Yew on the administration of justice was thought to be oppressive but the framework of an excellent court system has been established and one can hope that it will eventually become fully free from political pressure, as it now is in a substantial part of its work.

Lee is, of course, notoriously authoritarian but it was his difficult mission from the early days of the republic to ensure that Chinese communism did not take over in Singapore, as it might well have done. The remarkable growth of Singapore as a financial centre under Lee may enable his political successors to adopt a more liberal outlook and, particularly, to recognise the value and importance of the separation of constitutional powers.

16

SOME PUBLIC DIVERSIONS

My main public work in the early 1970s, apart from the rabies committee, was the inquiry into the Ronson companies, which was increasingly demanding for me throughout 1973 and 1974 because of the length of the report. On circuit the new procedural arrangements recommended by the Beeching Commission came into force on 1 January 1972. The Assize system that had prevailed since the reign of King Henry II came to an end and Quarter Sessions also ceased to exist so that I no longer sat as a deputy chairman in Cheshire and Flintshire for up to 40 days a year. However, I was appointed more or less automatically, as a recorder of the new Crown Court from 1 January 1972. This involved a slightly reduced commitment to sit not less than 30 days annually and I was able to vary the places at which I sat. I was attached to the Wales and Chester Circuit as a part-time judge but I was permitted, for example, to sit for the week of the general election in February 1974 as far away as Ipswich, where my old circuit friend Judge Bertrand Richards reigned as the senior Circuit judge and with whom Peter Thomas also came to stay on relinquishing office as secretary of state for Wales.

I was hesitant about taking on any other public work until the Ronson investigation was completed but an invitation from Solly Zuckerman, my colleague on the rabies committee, could not be refused. This was to join the council of the Zoological Society of London, of which I had become an ordinary fellow (member) at his urging in November 1970. In the end I served on the council from 1972 to 1993, for periods of three or four years with compulsory gaps in between and two periods as a vice-president. It was a considerable honour to serve then with HRH Prince Philip as president and Solly as secretary until he succeeded Prince Philip as president. The

18-member council itself was an august body with members ranging from the Duke of Northumberland to Woodrow Wyatt; I am amused to see that in 1970/71 it embraced virtually every rank that Debrett and Burke would recognise, from royal prince to officer of the Order of the British Empire.

The duties of an ordinary council member were not then very arduous, with about 10 meetings to attend each year, but I was particularly grateful to Peter Scott, the artist and conservationist, for his kindness to me as an ignorant newcomer. His sketching of birds was compulsive and he would carry on doing so next to me whilst listening attentively to the business in hand. Later on, after I had become a judge, I became more closely involved in the affairs of the society and its financial problems began to loom large. Meanwhile, in the 1970s the zoo, properly described as 'the learned society', was a happy ship. Solly, ennobled in 1971 and a member of the Order of Merit from 1968, had a genius for persuading rich benefactors to make large donations and there were excellent dinners from time to time to thank them for doing so, fully justifying the expenditure. There was also a grand occasion on 3 June 1976 when HM the Queen and Prince Philip attended a reception and dinner to mark the hundred and fiftieth anniversary of the founding of the society.

Soon after the 1974 election my public commitments began to multiply, undoubtedly because I was a known Labour supporter. The first development was that the newly appointed secretary of state for Wales, John Morris, who had been a pupil in my chambers, asked me to take on the chairmanship of the Local Government Boundary Commission for Wales, established under the Local Government Act 1972. His predecessor, Peter Thomas, had already appointed the members of the commission provisionally during the run-up to the election but it was for John Morris to confirm or reject his nominees. In the event all except the proposed chairman were confirmed and I agreed rather hesitantly to replace him, encouraged by the fact that Michael Gibbon, who had just taken silk and was about to become a godfather to our newly born daughter Laura, was to be the deputy chairman. He succeeded me as chairman in 1978 and later became a senior Circuit judge and the Recorder of Cardiff.

The first task of the new commission was to conduct a review of the boundaries of all the local government parishes (renamed 'communities' in Wales), and I was expected to devote a day per week on average to the work. Needless to say, that was an under-estimate but I never regretted my decision to accept because the work was interesting, involving visits all over Wales to launch the review of community boundaries within each district, and my fellow members proved to be very congenial. The most influential undoubtedly was Dr Elwyn Davies of Tenby, a distinguished geographer, who had been secretary of the Council of the University of Wales for many years before becoming Welsh secretary of education. He had retired from the latter office in 1969 but was still a leading figure and became president of the National Library of Wales in 1977. The other two members were in a sense political nominees: Winifred Matthias was a former Conservative Lord Mayor of Cardiff and Bill Coleman was a prominent Labour councillor from Gelligaer, but neither demonstrated any political bias in our discussions and they were always very helpful in formulating our unanimous recommendations.

Headquarters were established for us close to the new Queen Street pedestrianised area of Cardiff, and we were provided with efficient senior staff led by D.T.M. Davies. Our normal practice was to meet in Cardiff on Fridays and I made a day trip from London by train for this purpose, lunching whenever possible at the very agreeable Cardiff and County Club, of which I had become a member in March 1972. Beginning with John Morris' own constituency in the district of Afan (Aberavon/Port Talbot) and Anglesey, we reviewed the community boundaries within most of the Welsh districts during the four years of my chairmanship. In a sense we were formulating a Domesday Book for Wales, as Charles Quant noted in the *Liverpool Daily Post*, and we had to deal with a wide variety of communities, many of which had no council and relied simply on occasional community meetings for their governance. Moreover, the boundaries were often based on natural features such as rivers and ignored the development, for example, of settlements on both sides of a river at a bridgehead, forming a single town.

In my period as chairman we also conducted reviews of parts of the boundaries of five of the districts, so we carried out most of the initial work expected of us, but there was still a great deal of tidying up to be done when I handed over to Michael Gibbon before the next phase of the commission's work could be embarked upon. The disappointing aspect of our work was the negative and conservative response of the local representatives of all the main political parties. I say disappointing because I do not believe that most local issues ought to be decided on party political lines and there is much greater scope for a pragmatic approach than there is on many national issues. Boundary changes, however, were likely in many cases to affect electoral results in varying degrees and many of the defensive responses that we received were predictable.

Another public work commitment that I was asked to take on towards the end of 1974 was less demanding but highly sensitive and worrying. The home secretary, Roy Jenkins, asked me to be one of his two advisers under the Prevention of Terrorism (Temporary Provisions) Act 1974, the other being Lord Alport, a former British High Commissioner for Rhodesia and Conservative minister. The arrangement was made on 6 December in the wake of the Guildford and Birmingham public house bombings and at a time when about 60 people were either in custody or helping police with their inquiries in relation to these events. I did wonder whether the appointment would have any security implications for me personally but, ironically, it was Sarah who came nearer to danger than I because she was in Harrods completing her Christmas shopping on 21 December 1974 when a bomb went off in the store. I myself did not need, and was not given, any special protection but I was told to take certain routine precautions in respect of my car and so on.

Each adviser was required to act independently of the other in advising about the case of any detainee upon whom an exclusion order under the Act had been served. One of the two advisers was assigned to each detainee who chose to appeal against the order and it was then the duty of that adviser to investigate the detainee's grounds of objection and to advise the home secretary whether or not the order should be revoked. This brief description of the adviser's task is sufficient to underline the difficulty of his role and predictably the Law Society's *Guardian Gazette* attacked the legislation as an unfair encroachment on liberty. My own procedure was to attend at the Home Office to read the relevant file of information on which the exclusion order had been based in order to know as precisely as possible the grounds for it. I would then see the detainee in prison by appointment, usually alone but in the presence of a solicitor if that was what he required. The detainee's obvious difficulty was that he had not been served with a statement of the alleged facts on which his exclusion order was based because such a statement might well have alerted him to the likely source of the information. I was similarly constrained in what I could say to him but needed to get him to talk about relevant events in which he had been involved in order to understand whether he could realistically challenge what had been said against him.

I cannot pretend that this was a satisfactory procedure or that I had any special skill in carrying it out but I did not see how it could be improved without breaching security and so I just did my best to try to achieve fairness. In fact, the very first case assigned to me illustrates the many problems that stem from anti-terrorist legislation. The case was very directly linked, allegedly, to the Guildford bombings and heavy reliance was placed by the police on the confession statements said to have been made by 'the Guildford four', copies of which I read. Not surprisingly, although the detainee was a London resident, I felt compelled to advise that the exclusion order should be upheld. In saying this, I am not myself disclosing any secret because the case itself was the subject of newspaper comment then and has been again since the successful attack on the confessions and the quashing of the convictions of the Guildford four. Indeed, the whole police investigation was the subject of a public inquiry later under Lord Justice (John) May.

I have no wish now to get involved in political arguments about appropriate responses to threats of terrorism from whatever source. I must say, however, that I found Roy Jenkins to be both conscientious and fair minded in responding to the advice that I gave to him. He accepted my opinion that one particular exclusion order should be revoked – in difficult circumstances in which another politician could well have declined to do so on arguable grounds.

My work as an adviser continued until I became a judge in January 1978 and shortly after that Lord Shackleton was asked to prepare a report on the working of the Act of 1974, which provides helpful information on the detentions and exclusions that had occurred up to that time. The Act came into force on 29 November 1974 after 110 bombing and shooting incidents that year in Great Britain, resulting in 23 deaths and injuries to 180 persons (the Birmingham bombing took place on 21 November). Subsequently, up to the date of the Shackleton Report, 3,259 persons were detained but only 111 exclusion orders were made during the period when I was an adviser (most removals were to Northern Ireland but about one-fifth were to Eire). A small number were not served and 19 applications for orders were refused.

What is surprising is that representations against the orders were made in only 22 cases, and seven of the orders were revoked after representations had been made, so only 15 of those appealed against were enforced. It seems that I advised in 10 of the cases and recommended revocation in two of them. Thus, although the remedy of exclusion could be regarded as draconian, it was implemented as sensitively as possible on the available evidence under the Jenkins regime.

Roy Jenkins telephoned to ask me to undertake one other difficult role during this period, namely, to conduct the public inquiry into the conviction of James Hanratty for the A6 double murder in August 1961 but I was compelled to refuse because my friend Paul Foot, whom I had met often when reading for *Private Eye* and with whom I had played cricket, was one of the main challengers of Hanratty's conviction and had written a book on the subject. There was also the embarrassment that Ludovic Kennedy, another critic of the conviction, was known to me as a close friend of Robin Day. Roy Jenkins could be very persuasive but I am sure that I was right to refuse. The chalice was handed instead to Judge Lewis Hawser QC, who reported that the conviction appeared to be sound, and it has survived further scrutiny by the Court of Appeal Criminal Division, in the light of some family DNA evidence, as recently as May 2002.

Fortunately, my public commitments in the 1970s did not involve many consecutive nights away from home because it was a most important decade from our children's point of view and 12 Cavendish Avenue was the favourite home of all of us. Thomas continued at the Hall School until July 1974 and played for the first XI at cricket, batting on occasions with J.D. Carr, the son of D.B. Carr and later a Middlesex player himself. Thomas then went, in September 1974, to an excellent crammer run by Hugh Glazebrook and known as Millbrook House School at Milton, near Abingdon, where he shared a small dormitory of four with Viscount Linley, amongst whose regular visitors was the Queen Mother. When Thomas passed the Common Entrance Examination in November 1975 we opted for Uppingham, with its excellent playing fields, as the most suitable school for him, and he began there in Fircroft House in January 1976. We were very pleased with Millbrook House, which gave Thomas a gentle introduction to boarding at the age of 12, and it is sad that the next generation of Glazebrooks had to close the school because of declining numbers in the summer of 2003.

Sophie started at Francis Holland School, Regent's Park – where the glamorous Heather Brigstocke reigned as headmistress – in September 1972 at the age of six and astonishingly remained there for the following 12 years. She had previously been, from September 1970, at a pre-prep school in Langford Place, St John's Wood, run by an efficient (and amusing) Irish lady called Mrs McCaffrey. She believed in education on traditional lines and both our daughters received excellent grounding in her establishment.

September 1972 was notable also because it was the month in which my mother-in-law Diana left Barracks Stud at Nash. This ended the Ingrams' major activity as breeders of racehorses for the flat but Diana did retain a couple of mares for a short further period and sent them to Eire. For us, the sale of Nash meant the loss of our much-loved and accessible weekend retreat. However, by Easter 1973 Diana had rented a bungalow called Downside in the training stables of Frank Cundell at Compton in Oxfordshire, not far from Thomas' crammer and next to Richard Ingram's village of Aldworth. This remained her country home for the next five years until the Cundells took over Downside themselves. It was, of course, a great benefit for us, with the use of the Cundells' swimming pool and excellent walks nearby on the Ridgeway, much appreciated by our golden cocker spaniel Orlando, which we acquired at Tintern in the Wye valley at Christmas 1973.

Our family was completed by the arrival of Laura on 3 May 1974, when I am glad to say that I was nearby at home and able to rush to St Mary's Hospital, Paddington. It had not become fashionable then for a father to be present at the birth. Orlando did not react to her arrival in a hostile manner, although he did bite each of us in turn eventually in moments of hysteria that he regretted immediately afterwards (and none of us was significantly injured). In the new fashion Laura started attending a nursery school in Grove End Gardens when she was only two years and eight months old and went on to McCaffrey's a year later, on 11 January 1978, the day after I was sworn in as a judge. She stayed there three years before following a different route from Sophie to Francis Holland School. That was via St Mary's Convent (now school) in Fitzjohn's Avenue, established in 1926 by the Institute of the Blessed Virgin Mary, where she stayed until the end of the summer term 1985. It was an excellent school, patronised by an interesting range of parents, including Judi Dench, Edward Fox and Jeremy Irons; and thus well prepared she went on to Francis Holland School at the age of 11 years in September 1985, by which time Ann Holt had succeeded Heather Brigstocke as headteacher.

Holidays with our growing children were, of course, very important for us in the 1970s and were over all too soon. I have written earlier of our visits to Tenby in 1969 and 1970 and then to Benodet in 1971. In 1972 we rented a floor of a chateau near Moulins, owned by the Baron de Segonzac, with our Foreign Office friends, Kenneth and Teresa James, for three weeks from mid-August. In later years we spent three fine summer holidays at the Gidleigh Park Hotel on the edge of Dartmoor at modest expense, although it is now well beyond our means (£480 daily upwards for double occupancy demi-pension); and in 1974 we enjoyed stays at Eglwysfach and Portmeirion.

By the time that I entered my fifties in the second half of the 1970s extra-mural duties seemed to descend on me continuously. I had become head of my chambers in October 1975 on the elevation of Kenneth Jupp QC to the High Court bench. I had also become treasurer of my circuit in 1973 and this involved quite considerable repetitive work in recording (and chasing, some of the time) circuit subscriptions and the special fees that had to be paid by non-members who appeared in court on circuit. There were also other duties because I had joined the management committee of the Greater London Citizens' Advice Bureau in March 1976 and remained on it until I became a judge. To cap all this, I had been put on the executive committee of the Zoological Society of London in June 1976. Altogether, therefore, I was beginning to feel oppressed by my work load and, like many other 50 year olds, began to worry about where it was going to lead.

It was at this point, that is, early in 1977, that I was approached by the Attorney-General, Sam Silkin QC, about the succession to the retiring Director of Public Prosecutions, Sir Norman Skelhorn KBE, QC. The Attorney-General explained to me that he planned to establish a national prosecution service which would be led by the director and asked whether I would agree to be one of the possible candidates for the appointment. I was, of course, flattered to be asked but it was a difficult decision to make because I would be subject to the normal retirement age for a civil servant (60), unless I was given exceptional permission to carry on. Moreover, the pension earned in nine years or so would be very small in comparison with a judicial pension; and with income tax at 83 per cent and the investment surcharge at 15 per cent I had not been able to establish any substantial private pension entitlement. Nevertheless, after a weekend's reflection I wrote to say that I would like to be considered and there followed a meeting with the Attorney-General in great secrecy in his room at the House of Commons on 21 February 1977. In the end I was saved from making a great mistake because I was not chosen. Sam Silkin wrote a charming letter to me at the end of March, explaining that he had chosen Tony Hetherington (whom I had come to know as the very able legal secretary in the Law Officers' department before he became deputy Treasury solicitor) because of his familiarity with the 'corridors of power', which would be particularly helpful in piloting the changes that Sam had in mind.

As a matter of history, Sam Silkin was not able to establish the Crown Prosecution Service during his period as Attorney-General and it was not created until the Prosecution of Offences Act 1985 was implemented in 1986 under a Conservative government, but I had no reason to quarrel with his decision. Tony Hetherington proved to be a successful DPP and Sam was kind enough to say in his letter to me that I would have been 'the choice' if it had been a practising barrister.

From late 1974 until the end of the decade, weekends were focused on the children, particularly Thomas. It was not much fun for him to linger about hotels and cinemas when we visited him at school. Instead, I eventually adopted the practice of driving to Uppingham on Saturday mornings, watching him play games in the afternoon and dining with him before staying overnight but then driving him home for the day after school chapel on Sunday and making the double journey to take him back in the evening. It was a strenuous routine but the benefit for Thomas of a few hours at home was worth the effort.

Amongst the liveliest social events for Sarah and me were dinners as guests of Woodrow and Verushka Wyatt, who were neighbours and generous hosts at 19 Cavendish Avenue, fortunately before Woodrow began recording his daily thoughts in journals that started in October 1985. Our own dinner parties were on a much more modest scale but we did have a large gathering in February 1973 of contemporaries to celebrate the twenty-first anniversary of our call to the Bar, and the guests included Geoffrey Howe, Robin Day, Peter Blaker and Poppy Jolowicz, formerly Stanley. That was excelled only by a party that we gave earlier, in July 1971, for Kenneth and Teresa James three days after their return from Saigon, when Kenneth became head of the Western European department of the Foreign Office. Amongst the diplomatic luminaries that attended were Julian and Margaret Bullard, Crispin and Chloe Tickell and Dick Stratton, as well as other friends of Kenneth and Teresa such as Leo de Rothschild and Alistair Horne. We dined in the garden and danced to the music of the Alan Clare trio late into the night, even though I was presenting the defendant's case in the Associated Leisure libel action at the time.

Thus passed one of the most important decades of Sarah's and my lives but, before I move on, I must give some account of the more conventional part of my professional life in the 1970s.

17

FAREWELL TO THE BAR

I continued to appear in many typical common law cases during my nine years in silk. Most of these were heard at first instance at Cardiff, Newport, Swansea or Chester but there were quite frequent visits to other Crown Courts in Wales and elsewhere. The longer cases were fairly evenly balanced between civil actions and criminal trials and they led to quite regular appearances in both divisions of the Court of Appeal. In my first full year in silk I earned £16,865 gross and this more than doubled (£37,267) by 1972. My earnings remained at about that level in the following years, apart from a less successful year in 1974, when I had to spend a great deal of time completing the report on the Ronsons for the Department of Trade and Industry, and they rose to a peak of £56,701 gross in 1977, when the salary of a High Court judge was £18,000.

The case in which I appeared during this period that attracted most newspaper attention, apart from the extradition proceedings against Slater and Tarling, was a motion in the Queen's Bench Divisional Court to commit Paul Foot and the publisher of the *Socialist Worker* newspaper for contempt of court. This motion was brought by the recently appointed Attorney-General, Sam Silkin QC, in October 1974, leading Treasury counsel, Gordon Slynn. The background was that Paul Foot had named in an article in the newspaper two prosecution witnesses, one of whom was a hereditary peer, who had given evidence in April 1974 in the trial of Janie Jones for blackmail before Judge King-Hamilton QC and a jury at the Central Criminal Court. The prosecution case there was that Jones ran a brothel in Kensington that pandered to various sexual fantasies of customers, including the wearing of gymslips by prostitutes, and that Jones had subsequently demanded money from the two relevant witnesses, threatening to publicise what had occurred. There were five charges against her of blackmail but she was acquitted by the jury of those alleged offences. A complication in the case was that she had been tried earlier by the same judge on charges that she had exercised control over the movements of prostitutes and had attempted to pervert the course of justice, which the judge had ordered to be tried separately from the blackmail charges.

In this earlier trial, in response to an application by counsel to the contrary, Judge King-Hamilton had directed that the witnesses should be referred to in evidence by the letters Y and Z and not named. It was accepted, however, that he had not given any direction to the press about the matter. What he had said was 'May I say, before the jury comes in, that if by accident any counsel happens to mention the name of a witness other than by letter I hope – I have no juridiction over the press – but I hope that they will not mention the name if it slips out accidentally as sometimes happens.' In the second trial, before a different jury, no further mention was made of the matter but the two witnesses were again referred to as Y and Z.

Paul Foot did not attend either trial, except on one occasion after his article had appeared, but he took the trouble to find out what the judge had said about naming the witnesses. He knew who both the 'anonymous' witnesses were and that the judge had not given any direction to the press in either the first or the second trial about the disclosure of their names. It was his view also, as the judge himself had said, that the judge had no power to make an order binding on the press to prevent such disclosure.

At the contempt hearing, before Lord Widgery, the Lord Chief Justice, Mr Justice Milmo and Mr Justice Ackner, Stephen (now Lord Justice) Sedley appeared for the newspaper publisher and I appeared for Paul Foot with Michael Lewis, the brother of Esyr, as my junior. I was fortunate to go first in answer to the Attorney-General and I had the luxury of echoing Paul Foot's view of the case, having spent several days researching the matter. As the Attorney-General conceded, the case was unusual and was not covered by any binding legal authority, but it seemed to me clear that the trial judge had not had any power to make an order preventing the press from publishing the names of witnesses who gave evidence at a hearing in public: the only way for the court to ensure non-disclosure was for it to sit 'in camera', which would, of course, have been highly objectionable on many grounds. In this particular case there were additional strong arguments based on the absence of even a purported direction to the press in either trial: there had merely been an expression of hope in the first, quite separate trial.

The Divisional Court, however, was determined not to allow Paul Foot to get away with it and he and the publisher were both found guilty of contempt and fined £250. Giving the reserved judgment of the court, Lord Widgery said that they were not giving credence to the idea that blackmail charges should be heard 'in camera', which would be disastrous, nor were they ruling on the basis that the trial judge had made an order that had been disobeyed. Accepting that the case had 'ventilated a somewhat dark corner of the law of contempt', Lord Widgery said that Paul Foot had acted recklessly and the Divisional Court was satisfied that naming the two witnesses was an affront to the authority of the court and calculated to interfere with the course of justice because it would destroy the confidence of witnesses in future blackmail cases.

This is not a decision likely to be regarded as a binding or persuasive authority in any future case and it is significant that anonymity for rape victims in criminal trials was only achieved subsequently by legislation: there was no rule enabling anonymity to be conferred by a judge at the time of the Foot case. There were many critics of the Divisional Court's reasoning, notably Lord Edmund-Davies five years later in his speech in the House of Lords in *Attorney-General v. Leveller Magazine* (the Oz case). It was criticised severely also by Bernard Levin, no friend of Paul Foot, in an article in *The Times* headed 'The Day the Judges Took an Extra Helping of Power', even though he regarded the naming of the witnesses as 'deplorable and indefensible'.

Personal-injuries litigation was rarely glamorous but it was frequently of overwhelming importance to the claimants, providing the only possible mitigation of the effects of their injuries, and representing them was highly responsible and taxing work. Although barristers appearing in these cases learnt a great deal about working practices, in such industries as coalmining and steelmaking in my case, the facts of individual cases do not, in general, merit repetition here. An exception, however, was an action brought in 1974 against Tenby Borough Council by a man who suffered quadraplegia on 2 September 1968 as a result of diving into the sea from a diving board provided by the council on Goscar rock on the north beach at Tenby. It was a bank holiday and the plaintiff, a 37-year-old coalminer, arranged an outing in two buses and a minibus for himself, his family and a group of friends and neighbours from Capel Henry, his Carmarthenshire village. The intended destination was Pendine Sands but they decided at the last minute to go to Tenby instead.

The plaintiff spent what was left of the morning on the north beach with his wife and numerous children but then repaired to a public house with the men of the group, returning to the beach at about 3 p.m., having drunk (according to his own evidence) only three pints of beer. About half an hour later he decided to have a swim, entering the water about an hour after high tide, and he swam to Goscar rock in order to dive from the higher of two diving boards first installed by the council in 1946 to discourage bathers from diving from the rock itself. The plaintiff alleged that he then made two conventional dives successfully but, on his third dive, he went into the water more steeply. From this dive he did not return to the surface: he was dragged from the water unconscious by a young man and it was later found that he had broken his neck.

The plaintiff's action against the council for damages was heard in April 1973 at Carmarthen Crown Court before Mr Justice Ackner and I represented the council, leading an outstanding Swansea junior counsel, Lawrence Griffiths, while John Davies QC led the future Attorney-General and Leader of the House of Lords, Gareth Williams, for the plaintiff. The trial judge was a keen swimmer who swam daily wherever he was, if it was practicable to do so, and it became obvious very early in the hearing that he had made his own inspection of the accident site before we assembled. It became clear also that his sympathy was entirely with the unfortunate plaintiff, who was indeed a pathetic figure.

I had confirmed in writing my junior's advice that the council was likely to be held liable because of the absence of any appropriate warnings on the rock and any depth gauge to show the depth of water there as it varied with the tide. However, we expected a finding of substantial contributory negligence on the basis that the plaintiff had dived into a depth of about 3 feet 8 inches of water from a board at a height of 11 feet 9 inches above the sand when his judgement was probably affected by the beer that he had consumed. On this footing, I advised that the council would be unlucky if the plaintiff was to be held less than one-third to blame for his injuries.

At the trial this proved to be an unduly optimistic view because it did not take into account the emotional response of the judge to the case. He had been a formidable advocate at the Bar and the hearing proved to be a battle for me because he was determined to acquit the plaintiff of blame. The way in which he did this was vividly illustrated by the judgments subsequently given by Lord Denning, the Master of the Rolls, and Lords Justices Megaw and Scarman, as reported in the Lloyds Law Reports for 1974, on the council's appeal. He held, for example, that the depth of water into which the plaintiff dived was 6 feet and, further, in order to explain the tragic consequences of the third dive, that he probably dived some two or three feet from the end of the board and to the right with the intention of joining a friend on a raft, doing so more steeply because he slipped and/or because of movement of the board caused by its loose mountings.

The interesting point about these findings was that neither the plaintiff nor anyone else had given evidence to that effect. He had been cross-examined in detail about the dive and had said that he had intended to dive in the same way as in the previous dives and then to swim out to the raft. The board was wet but he had no recollection of slipping: he was standing right at the end of the board and could not tell if he slipped. His feet went out from under him and he had said earlier that he thought the board moved a bit from side to side. He had felt himself going to the right and deeper: he might have intended to dive to the right but he did not turn to the right and he did not think that he had turned to dive diagonally.

The result of the judge's findings, based on his own theorising, was that he held the council to be fully liable, rejecting the allegations of contributory negligence on the part of the plaintiff, and awarded him £41,411 damages plus nearly £6,000 interest. The council's appeal was heard in February 1974 and the three judges there found the trial judge's findings of fact both puzzling and troublesome in the light of the evidence before him, as they explained in their judgments. Reluctantly, they felt unable to disturb the judge's finding that the water was 6 feet deep because of the long-recognised disinclination of an appellate court to interfere with findings of fact by a trial judge but all three of them rejected his finding that the plaintiff had dived to the right because it was contrary to the evidence. The court rejected also the judge's acquittal of the plaintiff of blame and found that he was guilty of 25 per cent contributory negligence.

I have not narrated the facts of this case in some detail in order to try to prove any forensic skill on my part but rather to underline the perils of judicial emotion, however well intended. I was fortunate to practise at the Bar mainly after the most difficult and tiresome High Court judges, exemplified by Mr Justice Hallett, had retired; but my contemporaries and I still had to contend with problems when appearing before judges guided by their emotions instead of strict impartiality and other judges, albeit of good intellect generally, who had too high an opinion of themselves to try cases at a conventional pace with the needs of the litigants in mind. Mr Justice Ackner was always most courteous and conscientious, rising eventually to the House of Lords, but he did allow his emotional view of the personalities in a case to affect his findings of fact, and the delightful and stimulating Mr Justice Brabin, one of the outstanding advocates of my time, tended to fall into the same trap. As for the too clever judges, arch offenders were Mr Justice Brandon, who also rose to the Lords, and Mr Justice Ormrod (not Ormerod), who packed the court list with too many cases whenever he was able to have a say in the matter and who seemed at times oblivious of the feelings of litigants before him, even though he proved later to be an able member of the Court of Appeal. For me, the exemplar was Mr Justice (later Lord Justice) Patrick Browne, who always listened courteously and found the facts as they probably were 'without affection, favour or ill will', however complicated or inconvenient the consequences might be.

As an advocate, I did not find the House of Lords a comfortable venue in which to appear after the immaculate Lord Reid retired as the senior Lord of Appeal. Lord Wilberforce and Lord Diplock had worldwide reputations as jurists and possessed considerable charm out of court (both were loyal benchers of the Middle Temple) but I found them to be intimidating and haughty in the course of my infrequent appearances before them. This was particularly so in October 1976 when I resisted successfully two consolidated appeals, argued by John Mortimer QC, leading Geoffrey Robertson. The appeals were against the convictions of a newsagent and a bookseller under the Obscene Publications Acts 1959 and 1964. The Northampton newsagent and the Swansea bookseller had been convicted of possessing many obscene articles for gain, such as films, magazines and books of a hard pornographic character, but had sought to avail themselves of a defence provided by section 4(1) of the Act of 1959, namely, that publication of the article in question was justified as being for the public good on the ground that it was in the interests of science, literature, art or learning or 'of other objects of general concern'. In short, without disrespect to Mortimer and Robertson, who both addressed the appellate committee, they argued that the pornographic articles were of therapeutic benefit for men in dirty raincoats as a relief for their fantasies and that this was an object of general concern because the articles were likely to disincline them from committing actual sexual offences.

It is not surprising that this argument was rejected by the Circuit judges who tried the cases and on appeal; applications to call expert evidence in support of the defence were rightly rejected. I cannot suggest that my task in rebutting the argument in the Lords was particularly onerous or that their Lordships were likely to be swayed on such a stark issue by anything that I said but I shall not forget the lofty disdain with which my references to the 'eiusdem generis' rule of statutory interpretation and its ramifications when there is no definable 'genus' were received.

The nature of my work at the Bar was obviously not such as to take me before arbitrators or into the commercial court except on rare occasions, but it was in an arbitration, conducted in the basement of opulent city offices, that I found myself against Derry Irvine for the first and last time. This was in May 1974 and the case involved engineering construction rather than commercial law. The claimant in negligence, for whom I acted with Michael

Gibbon, was Bridgend Urban District Council and the defendant was a Danish civil engineer who had designed, and supervised the installation of, the central heating system for one of the council's new housing developments known as the Wildmill Estate. The system had proved to be a disaster but it was not entirely clear how much this was due to the design or the choice of materials and how much to the shortcomings of the contractors who had carried out the work.

I found Derry to be quite an acrimonious opponent and we had daily tussles, which must have been quite tiresome for the arbitrator to listen to, but eventually we agreed a settlement after 10 days' struggle, which began four days after the birth of my daughter Laura. The settlement itself was memorable because the defendant was anxious to express his admiration for British justice. Derry and I agreed therefore to host a lunch there and then on the premises (Winchester House, now the British headquarters of Deutsche Bank) at which the defendant made a speech to that effect and from which we all tottered at about 6 p.m. Derry and his charming wife Alison have been close friends of ours ever since.

A result of this encounter was that Derry subsequently recommended that I should lead him in several cases and he became my junior, on my own recommendation, in the Slater and Tarling case, as I have described earlier. His goodwill led to an appearance in the commercial court, where we were fortunate to find ourselves before Mr Justice Goff (later the senior Lord of Appeal). Our client, an Old Etonian and former royal page, had been the managing director and main shareholder of Mitfords Advertising Limited, a financial advertising agency of which Lord Redesdale was chairman. The agency had been sold to an investment company, which then claimed damages for alleged failures to disclose relevant information and misrepresentations, but (to our considerable relief) Mr Justice Goff found in the defendant's favour after a 12-day trial.

This civil work was, of course, interspersed with appearances for the prosecution and rather less frequently for the defence in criminal cases, nearly all of which were heard on my own circuit. An onerous task in my early years in silk was the prosecution (with two excellent juniors, Michael Gibbon and Crispin Masterman) of a conspiracy based on Ebbw Vale steelworks. The essence of this conspiracy was to falsify the weighings of scrap metal delivered to the works to the great financial benefit of local dealers and the weighbridgemen involved in the plot. The conspiracy was on a large scale, with 24 defendants alleged to be implicated, so that there had to be seven different indictments and the trials at Newport Crown Court lasted, with appropriate breaks, for a year from October 1972.

Unhappily, a popular local police sergeant was alleged to have been a party to the conspiracy but successive juries in a trial and a retrial failed to agree on a verdict, so he was acquitted on the direction of the judge when we (the prosecution) opted against a further trial. Altogether, the trial lasted 134 days and thus occupied a large slice of my life at the time. One of the more entertaining moments in those trials occurred when one defendant insisted that it was necessary for the jury to have a view of one of the loads alleged to have been false. The trial judge, Judge Pitchford, reluctantly agreed to this but the exercise proved to be conclusive against the defendant, whose wagon appeared to be about to collapse under the grossly excessive load, to the amusement of the jury. All the defendants, except the police officer, were convicted and I fear that the economy of Ebbw Vale must have been significantly depressed for a time as a result of the convictions.

I enjoyed particularly visits to Swansea Crown Court, especially during the summer. I had joined the Bristol Channel Yacht Club at Mumbles and it was very pleasant to escape from court to the relaxed atmosphere of the club, where I stayed with other London members of the Bar and dined well. Breakfasting there while looking across the expanse of Swansea Bay was also an uplifting start to the day. It was there that one would meet some of the characters depicted by Kingsley Amis in *The Old Devils*, particularly Kingsley's close friend and fellow literary trustee of Dylan Thomas, the redoubtable solicitor Stuart Thomas. He was not an easy man to get to know and he had rather more enemies than friends but he was a very able and witty man, with a charming and extrovert wife, and I still laugh at some of their witticisms.

Almost the only period when I did not stay at the yacht club was when I appeared throughout May until mid-June 1976 for the prosecution against five defendants who had been involved in the construction of the DVLA's headquarters at Morriston in 1972 and 1973. One of the defendants had been the architect, three were senior employees of the main contractor and the fifth described himself as a high-level contact man. Thus, the case was another bonanza for lawyers, with four silks involved for the defendants and 15 counts (charges) in the indictment. There were five counts of false accounting, four of obtaining or attempting to obtain money by deception and six of corruption relating to alleged gifts to the architect between 1969 and 1972, so the prosecution was of considerable gravity.

As the trial was certain to last a long time, I arranged to rent the seaside cottage of a commercial silk and friend, Anthony (later Lord Justice) Evans, who was also a member of the circuit, at Port Eynon on Gower peninsula. There I was joined by my two juniors, Nigel Fricker and Anthony Seys-

Llewellyn, both of whom subsequently took silk and became Circuit judges. Our stay almost had the flavour of a holiday because the weather was fine and, at the close of the prosecution case, following rulings by the trial judge, Judge Bruce Griffiths QC, four of the defendants pleaded guilty to a variety of counts. The fifth defendant, a quantity surveyor, maintained his pleas of not guilty and was discharged but his superior pleaded guilty to several of the joint charges involving that surveyor. These pleas were orchestrated by Sir Alun Talfan Davies QC, a master of such arrangements, and the prosecution felt bound to accept them, not least because there were pleas of guilty to all six corruption charges, although it was not an outcome that we would have sought. The judge then imposed substantial fines and suspended sentences of imprisonment ranging from 18 months to three months; it was the architect who received the longest sentence and he was also fined a total of £4,500 and ordered to contribute £10,000 towards the costs of the prosecution. Nevertheless, some at least of the defendants were lucky, in my view, to escape without imprisonment.

One other popular circuit venue for me was Caernarfon. My last visit there as a barrister is worth mentioning because it involved a very unusual indictment. The judge sitting at Caernarfon in November 1975 was Mr Justice Cobb, who was on his first trip outside London as a newly appointed Queen's Bench judge. I was instructed to appear for the Director of Public Prosecutions in a case in which the defendant was alleged to have tried to influence a member of a jury improperly. The charge laid against him was of the antique common law offence of embracery. I describe it as antique but it was still recognised by the criminal lawyer's 'bible', *Archbold: Criminal Pleading*, as an offence against public justice in the following terms:

> indictable at common law, punishable by fine and imprisonment, and consists in any attempt to corrupt or influence or instruct a jury, or any attempt to incline them to be more favourable to one side than the other, by money, promises, threats or persuasions, whether the jurors on whom such an attempt is made give any verdict or not, or whether the verdict given be true or false.

In support of this proposition four decided cases were cited and the great legal text, Hawkins' *Pleas of the Crown*.

What had happened was that, in the course of a trial at Caernarfon Crown Court before Mr Justice Mars-Jones and a jury, of a man charged with wounding with intent to cause grievous bodily harm, a member of the victim's family had followed some members of the jury near the court during a luncheon break and had said very audibly, 'He's bloody guilty. He's knifed someone before.' This was reported to the judge by a jurywoman and he referred the matter to the DPP. I do not think that I was asked to advise about the charge: my recollection is that the defendant, Norman Owen, had already been committed for trial for embracery by the time that I was instructed. Before Mr Justice Cobb and a jury the defendant was represented by my friend Peter Weitzman QC, who did not (and could not) submit that the charge was invalid: there was no dispute that the words complained of had been uttered by the defendant and heard by the jurywoman so the issues were whether he had done so knowingly in the hearing of someone he knew to be a member of the jury and intending to influence her in her service as such. Owen was convicted after a very short retirement by the new jury and sentenced to nine months' imprisonment.

The case was tried by Mr Justice Cobb impeccably but the surprising outcome was that the conviction was quashed on appeal; I am at a loss to try to explain how this was achieved. My own records show that an appeal by Owen was withdrawn in April 1976, presumably because he had by then served his sentence or very nearly so, and I was paid on that footing. Later that year, however, the Court of Appeal, with Lord Justice Lawton in the chair, ruled that the offence of embracery was 'obsolescent', whatever that may mean in the context of the criminal law; and I was not given the opportunity to argue the contrary. In the judgment of the court Lord Justice Lawton said that, if more than one person was involved in the relevant misconduct, the charge was likely to be one of conspiracy and, if only one person, the charge was likely to be contempt (see (1976) 3 All ER 239). I have no particular affection for the offence of conspiracy, which was invented by the Court of Star Chamber, and more relevantly I should like to have had the opportunity to draw the court's attention to some of the many difficulties that can arise in a prosecution for contempt of court, including issues as to the appropriate court of trial and the procedure by which the facts are to be decided. In contrast, trial by a jury of the charge of embracery most appropriately fitted the circumstances of Owen's case. Moreover, at what point is the Court of Appeal, rather than Parliament, justified in declaring that a known criminal offence has, in effect, ceased to exist?

As I said earlier, I was appearing in Cardiff in December 1977 when I was told that the Lord Chancellor wanted to see me. Having been forewarned of the reason by his permanent secretary, Sir Wilfrid Bourne, and given the opportunity to consider it overnight, I had no hesitation in accepting the appointment when I saw the Lord Chancellor. He passed me on to Bourne, who expressed surprise when I told him that I had accepted, commenting that he himself would be very uneasy about exercising the wide discretion conferred upon Family Division judges, in contrast to the more precisely defined limits within which Queen's Bench judges had to make their decisions. His view was expressed, however, before judicial review litigation expanded dramatically and the European Declaration of Human Rights became part of our law.

I had not appeared in a divorce or family case since I had taken silk in 1969, and the Family Division itself had only existed from January 1972 as successor to the Probate Divorce and Admiralty Division but these facts did not deter me from accepting my new role. At the age of 51 I felt ready for change and I could not expect to continue earning high fees at the Bar indefinitely. Lord Elwyn-Jones apologised when I saw him for the fact that he could not do anything about the judicial salary in the prevailing economic climate; but the certainties of a substantial pension after 15 years' service and employment for longer than that if I wished were compelling factors in favour of acceptance. It must be remembered also that income tax was still 83 per cent for high earners and the surtax on investment income an additional 15 per cent, so the prospect of building up a substantial financial reserve at the Bar seemed to be highly doubtful. It had not yet become fashionable to refuse a judicial appointment and competition for the bench was intense so that it would have been unwise of me to refuse without any certainty that the offer would be renewed later.

The one major disadvantage was my substantial liability for income tax as a result of changes introduced by Roy Jenkins as Chancellor of the Exchequer in 1968. Before then, a barrister was entitled, on retiring from practice, to receive post-cessational payments of his outstanding fees free of tax, having paid tax on his actual receipts rather than his earnings while in practice. The latter method of assessment continued after 1968 but post-cessational receipts were made liable to income tax (on top, of course, of any salary being earned after retirement from the Bar). Thus, judges appointed prior to the Finance Act 1968 were able to receive a substantial 'nest egg' after retirement from the Bar. One of the last to benefit from this was Sir Henry Fisher, who then left the bench for the City after only two years. The difficulties of the new rules did not end there, however, because a further change provided that the Inland Revenue would reassess one's income tax liability for the last three years of practice on the basis of fees earned rather than fees received. This seems to me to be an unfair form of double taxation, and its impact on most judicial appointees is and was severe because the earnings of a very high proportion of them increased substantially in that three-year period. The result of this was that I had to pay income tax at

83 per cent on my post-cessational receipts, which continued to come in for two or three years, and additional tax at the same rate on the increase in my income assessments for my last three years at the Bar. With my wife's help, I was able to survive this crisis, and steeply rising property prices provided some financial comfort in the end but some newly appointed judges in the era of very high income tax found themselves in serious financial straits.

The public announcement of my appointment was made in *The Times* on 22 December and I made my last appearance in court as an advocate, leading Derry Irvine, before Mr Justice Phillips in the Employment Appeal Tribunal in St James's Square three days earlier. It was quite a frenetic time and Sarah and I hosted the chambers' Christmas party at our home in Cavendish Avenue the evening of the announcement day. Two other High Court appointments were announced at the same time: James Comyn QC to the Family Division, succeeding Mr Justice Rees, and my Cambridge contemporary, Tony Lloyd QC (now Lord Lloyd of Berwick), to the Queen's Bench Division, replacing Mr Justice Crichton, while I was to replace Mr Justice Faulks.

Sarah and I had a celebration dinner party at home for 44 of our close friends at seven round tables. True to form, Robin Day insisted that there should be speeches and Geoffrey Howe rose to the challenge, doing so charmingly and wittily as he always did. I was relieved and surprised that the general response to my appointment was remarkably warm and friendly: the camaraderie of the Bar was then still very evident and I received some 300 generous letters of congratulation (not, I think, a very unusual number). I was particularly gratified also that Auberon Waugh welcomed the promotion of James Comyn and me in his diary in *Private Eye* on 20 January, saying, 'Both these blameless Queen's Counsel have defended Lord Gnome against various piratical forays on his Lordship's most excellent Purse (buckram 8vo slightly foxed).'

I left the Bar at just about the right time before I had grown stale but when I was ready for a new role and glad to be relieved of the stress of always arguing someone else's case. I had enjoyed my years at the Bar more than I could have reasonably hoped when I started and I was to miss the great friendships and gossip but it was not a moment for regrets: the major loss, as I have said before, was of the element of surprise about what lay ahead and the exciting trips to Singapore from time to time. I was sad also to miss serving as leader of my circuit, to which office I had been elected unopposed in succession to Philip Owen QC from January 1978, but a safe seat on the consolidated fund was not to be spurned.

18

JUDICIAL SPRINGTIME

The Lord Chancellor had quite a busy afternoon on 9 January 1978 because, apart from anything else, he had to swear in separately three new High Court judges, freshly robed in ermine and red, and Judge Gabriel Hutton. As you would expect, it was a very pleasing informal ceremony before Lord Elwyn-Jones and I was very grateful that my wife and all three children were allowed to attend, with my 81-year-old mother as well, in his room overlooking the river Thames. The following day I took possession of room 30 in the West Green building of the Royal Courts of Justice and attended a sentencing conference in the Lord Chief Justice's court; but there was no time to familiarise myself with judicial life in London because I was off on 11 January to the Western Circuit at Bristol, driving myself down the M4 motorway in a full-blooded gale.

By then, I had acquired a clerk, having taken on the droll and very Irish Stanley Boyle, who had most recently been clerk to Mr Justice Faulks and before that to Mr Justice Waller (senior) until he became a presiding judge. Stanley was popular with his colleagues, not least because he was a great storyteller. He was a loyal Liverpudlian and bachelor who shared a house there with his sister. He had been a lowly member of the Northern Circuit administrative team until the Assize system ended, having worked initially in a solicitor's office. He remained with me for nearly 10 years, until July 1987, when he retired, and to minimise his cost of living when I was sitting in London he slept very discreetly on a camp bed in my room at the law courts, as he had done previously, removing all traces before I appeared. He was by no means unique in this practice and he was only found out by administrators in the building on the eve of his retirement, a fact that may well have helped to reconcile him to leaving. For some judges' clerks, especially those who were unmarried, life on circuit was a great luxury: they were looked after very well by the lodgings staff, who were usually agreeable, and their duties were not onerous unless their judge was particularly demanding. Moreover, they would save a great deal in living expenses while their food and accommodation were paid for by the government.

I was particularly lucky to be assigned to Bristol for my first sittings on circuit because the two other judges sitting there at the same time were Mr Justice Park and Mr Justice (later Lord Justice) Dunn. Both were highly experienced and excellent judges who were willing to explain to me gently how to behave and I ended my visit there with much greater confidence than I had begun. Hugh Park had been a member of the Special Operations Executive (SOE) during the war and still looked like a comparatively young man when he died in his late eighties. He was a former presiding judge of the Western Circuit; Robin Dunn, who won the Military Cross as a regular soldier, was one of the two presiding judges in office in 1978: he is still going strong at the age of 92 as I write, having just published his history of stag hunting on Exmoor since 1940. The atmosphere in lodgings was very relaxed and I enjoyed daily walks on Clifton Green with Hugh, who was a neighbour in St John's Wood and became a lifelong friend.

My visit to Bristol and my subsequent tour of duty at Newcastle with Mr Justice Boreham passed without untoward incident. I did have the rather daunting task at Bristol of trying a 'running-down' action in which the injured plaintiff was Benjamin Mancroft, the son and heir of the well-known Conservative politician, who became the second Lord Mancroft. The plaintiff had been returning to Cirencester after acting as whipper-in for the day for the Portman Hunt in November 1975 when he collided with another motor car, the driver of which was killed instantly. The plaintiff himself sustained head injuries, with the result that he could not remember what had happened at the moment of collision and there was no independent witness. Thus, the issue of liability depended on reconstruction from the positions of the vehicles afterwards and marks on the road with the assistance of expert evidence. Lord Mancroft showed proper parental concern by attending throughout the trial but his rather fierce stare at me could have been quite intimidating. Fortunately, the realistic inference from the evidence was that it was the deceased driver who was wholly to blame and I was able to find in the plaintiff's favour with a clear conscience. I did not see him again until over 20 years later when I found that he was presiding for me when I addressed a group of peers about the first private member's anti-hunting bill, which was about to be considered in the House of Lords, and I was glad to see that he seemed to be very fit.

These visits to circuit gave me my first experience since marshalling of the remarkably generous hospitality that successive high sheriffs give to visiting High Court judges. Shrieval duties used to be much more onerous than they are now and included attending every hanging within their county until capital punishment was rightly abolished in 1965, except for treason and some associated archaic offences. One was always invited to dinner by the high sheriff and his hospitality was, of course, returned at the lodgings so that gradually one built up a range of friends in counties that were regularly visited. My early experience of this was particularly favourable because the High Sheriff of Avon in January 1978 was Malcolm Anson, then a director of Imperial Tobacco Limited and later chairman of the group, who took Sarah and me some months later to *The Magic Flute* at Glyndebourne in the David Hockney setting, with Felicity Lott and Benjamin Luxon. Then in Northumberland the Borehams and I were very well looked after by the public-spirited Michael Straker, especially when we were snowbound there one weekend.

Back in London I sat in the Family Division for the first time, with encouragement from Sir George Baker, the genial and popular president. I had asked him earlier, when I was appointed, what I should read to prepare myself in view of my lack of recent experience in family disputes but he had assured me that common sense was the key, of which two guidelines were examples: the first was that the custody of young children should be committed to their mother, unless there were really compelling reasons for not doing so; the second was that one should never split brothers and sisters up if that could possibly be avoided. Thinking has changed to some extent since then and joint custody has become a favoured option when practicable but, if one substitutes care and control for the word custody, Sir George's guidance is still sound as a general approach. Like other judges trying family cases, I found that intractable problems usually arose when embittered mothers used children in their custody to vent their anger against their former husbands by denying them reasonable access for a variety of reasons, which were often spurious. In those cases the available penalties for contempt of court rarely provided an adequate and appropriate sanction.

In the Family Division most of the cases listed for hearing before a judge sitting alone were heard privately in chambers so that one dressed in a suit without any formal trappings. Divorce cases were heard in open court, when one wore a black silk gown and judge's wig with wing collar and white bands, but High Court judges only dealt with defended cases and these had become comparatively rare (only about 50 cases each year throughout the country fought to the end at the time when I was appointed). All ancillary matters, including the financial arrangements and the fate of the children, were dealt with in private, as they continued to be until very recently. I agree that some changes were needed to ensure that the public is properly informed about what is happening in the Family Courts but I remain convinced that privacy is a necessary protection for children who are the victims of broken marriages or whose care and control have to be decided by a court for other reasons. Furthermore, I do not consider that publicity about domestic family disputes needs to be enlarged beyond what has been allowed in recent cases.

I remained in the Family Division for 10 years. Throughout that time my own room was on the first floor of the West Green building and my court was number 31, from the bench of which I could look out across the car park to the Strand and St Clement Dane's Church, the central church of the RAF. At first I was in the rather narrow end room, later beautified by Mrs Justice Butler-Sloss, but I soon graduated to the larger room, giving direct access to the bench of court 31 because Mr Justice Comyn chose to move elsewhere. I remained there quite happily until I was transferred to the Queen's Bench Division. The one disadvantage was that, on leaving the judges' corridor, one had to pass through the litigants who had been before one in order to leave the building. It was wise, therefore, to exercise some restraint when speaking during the hearing! Fortunately I did not provoke any attack on me, although feelings inevitably ran high from time to time.

One's early days as a judge were preoccupied with learning the ropes and assembling the necessary judicial equipment. The first priority was to acquire judicial robes because, although they were not required for family work as such, one needed them for work on circuit and formal occasions, including Anglican 'red letter days' in London. On circuit Family Division judges spent much of their time trying Queen's Bench civil actions in formal winter or summer robes and, on occasions, they would try criminal cases, if they were willing to do so, wearing scarlet robes lined with ermine in winter and a lighter version with silk facings in summer. When I was appointed one was granted a once-for-all allowance of £6,000 to cover the cost of robes and a judge's wig and this amount was just about adequate. Sometimes one could acquire a robe second-hand from a departing judge to mitigate the expense and Mr Justice Ackner had been very astute, as the judges' shop steward, in finding a way of defeating the monopoly of Ede and Ravenscroft.

One of the great privileges of appointment to the High Court is the grant of a knighthood by HM the Queen. Some judges will deny vehemently that this influenced their acceptance of the appointment but, rightly or wrongly, I question whether all of them are sincere in doing so. In my case I accepted gratefully and my wife shared my pleasure when I received a letter from the prime minister's secretary two or three weeks after being sworn in as a judge. There followed a private audience with the Queen at Buckingham Palace lasting 15 to 20 minutes on 3 March, immediately after James Comyn, and we then met our wives, who were not allowed to be with us when we were dubbed, at the Connaught Hotel for a celebratory lunch.

There was, of course, the customary round of congratulatory dinners for a newly appointed judge, including a chambers dinner at the Reform Club in June and a circuit dinner at Gray's Inn in September, at both of which my old friend and colleague Esyr Lewis QC, who later became an official referee, presided. It was a special pleasure that the Lord Chancellor and Lord Edmund-Davies headed the judges at the circuit dinner and that both Peter Thomas and Geoffrey Howe were also able to attend. Another less usual, but very welcome, event was a dinner in April at the Shire Hall in Mold given in my honour by the chairman of Clwyd County Council, which was attended by many old North Wales friends.

The Family Division proved to be a very agreeable division in which to sit as a judge. An important factor was that there were only 16 judges under the president so that one had a real sense of belonging to a team; successive presidents fostered this feeling by holding regular informal meetings at which we were able to exchange views on current issues. The work was much more varied than I had expected and included quite frequent three-week stints in both the civil and criminal divisions of the Court of Appeal. I enjoyed particularly sitting in the divisional court with the president to hear appeals from magistrates, and Sir George Baker gave me an early opportunity to make a small mark by giving the leading judgment in a reported case about the power of a local authority to assume parental rights over a child (*Wheatley v. London Borough of Waltham Forest*), which received a kindly comment from Lord Salmon in the House of Lords.

Other opportunities to spread one's wings arose from time to time and added considerably to the interest of one's work. After only about 18 months Sir George invited me to succeed Mr Justice Arnold as one of the judges of the Employment Appeal Tribunal (EAT). The appointment ran for four years from 1 October 1979 and involved sitting for three weeks each term with two lay representatives to hear appeals from industrial tribunals all over England and Wales. We sat rather grandly at 4 St James's Square, which had been the home of the Astors and then the wartime residence of General de Gaulle.

The work was varied and interesting and most cases were completed within a day so that the lay composition of the tribunal often changed daily. There was usually remarkable harmony in our decision-making, despite the fact that there was always one employers' representative and one trade union member sitting. There were usually two or three appeal tribunals sitting on any one day and the president of the EAT would normally preside over one of them. In October 1979 the president was Mr Justice Slynn and he was succeeded by Mr Justice Browne-Wilkinson when he accepted appointment as a judge advocate of the European Court of Justice. Both were exceptionally able and ended up as Lords of Appeal so that one did not have to look far for expert advice when it was needed. There was always a useful exchange of information and views because the judicial and lay members would all lunch together when sitting.

The other important new feature of my life on the bench was the requirement to read applications by persons who had been convicted and sentenced in the High Court for leave to appeal. Dealing with these 'section 31s', as we called them, was probably the least known of the activities of a High Court judge but it was certainly onerous and became increasingly so for about 60 judges of the Queen's Bench and Family Divisions who undertook the work. The annual number of applications varied between 6,500 and 7,500 and my own contribution was usually above average, but not spectacularly so. One had to give reasons for one's decision for the benefit of the applicant and for the Court of Appeal whether or not one granted leave to appeal because an aggrieved applicant had the right to renew his application to the full court. Section 31s provided regular homework for judges, mainly at weekends, and I was glad to say goodbye to them when I retired. One judge who contributed to the work prodigiously and disproportionately until his retirement in 1983 is said to have achieved his target of dealing with 1,000 applications a year by 1982 (he reached 963 in 1981) but my admiration for this is muted because I believe that his threshold for granting leave was too low: it facilitated his speed of turn around but added unnecessarily to the work of the Court of Appeal.

Having had some experience of sitting judicially at Quarter Sessions and then as a Crown Court recorder, I expected that I would enjoy working as a full-time judge for a limited period of about two years, until the novelty of a new vocation wore off. I am glad to say, however, that this rather pessimistic view proved to be wrong. I agree with Lord Templeman that ideally one should change one's role every 10 years in order to avoid growing stale and I do not think that I quite achieved that, but important changes did occur during the 18 years in which I served as a full-time judge. The most significant of these were my appointment as a presiding judge of my old circuit from 1980 to 1984, with which I will deal in the next chapter, and my later transfer in 1988 to the Queen's Bench Division. These changes, combined with the variety of work that was assigned to me, including sittings in both divisions of the Court of Appeal for short periods, kept me focused throughout and prevented me from looking back with unrealistic nostalgia to my days at the Bar.

A particular advantage of becoming a judge was that one had more leisure time, especially during vacations once one had carried out the compulsory vacation duty functions imposed on recently appointed judges. The length of the law vacations is frequently the subject of sniping by some politicians and journalists but the reality is that the work of judges increased throughout my time on the bench and has continued to do so ever since; the work of most members of the Court of Appeal has grown considerably also, alleviated only by a weekly reading day. At least one distinguished judge known to me accepted appointment only because of the prospect of long summer vacations and I believe that recruitment to the High Court bench of the best legal practitioners would be rendered even more difficult than it is now if the vacations were to be reduced significantly.

Accepting appointment as a full-time judge meant that I had to give up most of my other public work, particularly the chairmanship of the Local Government Boundary Commission for Wales, but I was able to continue as a member of the council of London Zoo, with a year's break every three or four years, until the end of 1992. I enjoyed my association with the zoo very much, especially whilst Lord Zuckerman remained at the centre of its operations: he continued as secretary until 1977 and then became president himself until the beginning of 1984, shortly before his eightieth birthday. During this period I served on the finance committee from 1974 and continued until it was replaced in 1983 by a management committee. I was also a member of the executive committee for the latter part of this period.

Another main non-judicial activity during my early years on the bench was much more closely involved with the law. I mentioned earlier that I had joined the management committee of the Greater London Citizens' Advice Bureau Service (GLCABS) in March 1976. My purpose in doing so was to help the development of Citizens' Advice Bureau-linked legal services in London and, in that connection, I met regularly with their legal advisers, including Richard Thomas, who later became director of public policy at Clifford Chance and has been the information commissioner since December 2002. This led to my close involvement in establishing a citizens' advice bureau in the Royal Courts of Justice, which first opened with one full-time staff member on 13 February 1978 and was financed for 18 months by the Nuffield Foundation and then by the Department of Trade.

The Lord Chancellor's department had approached GLCABS in 1975 with a view to setting up the bureau, and it operated on an experimental basis for the first two years. The need for it was underlined by a research report by Leonie Kelleher published in December 1980. A full-time organiser, Catherine Clarke, was appointed from October 1980 and the Department of Trade agreed to fund the bureau for five years from April 1980. The Lord Chamberlain's Department later agreed to contribute to this support and provided the bureau with its accommodation and essential services, including some books and stationery, free of charge.

I served as chairman of the bureau's management committee for 12 years from April 1980 and then as president for six years after Mr Justice Cazalet had generously agreed to take over as chairman. It was a rewarding venture and it proved to be very successful because of the dedication of its staff led by Catharine Clarke, who sadly died soon after qualifying as a barrister, and her successor from 1986, Pamela Lloyd-Hart. The work of the bureau grew from 1,370 clients in 1979/80 to nearly 9,500 in 1985/86 but various restraints prevented us from reaching our target of 10,000 until 1992/93, when some staffing problems had been overcome. The main role was to provide help for litigants in person. Increasing limitations on the availability of legal aid have underlined the importance of this work and comparatively few people are aware that a substantial proportion of applications for leave to appeal to the Court of Appeal are made by litigants who are not represented by counsel.

Returning to my apprenticeship in the Family Division, there were further circuit visits successively to Liverpool twice in 1978 and then to Cardiff, Lincoln, Birmingham, Leeds, Sheffield and Nottingham in 1979. It cannot be said meaningfully that judges in the Queen's Bench and Family Divisions lead isolated lives in an ivory tower, or even a succession of ivory towers, because they spend long periods in widely varying areas, unlike many other professionals, dealing with cases arising from the everyday lives of so-called ordinary people. Moreover, they have the opportunity to meet a range of persons in those areas whom they would be unlikely to encounter in a different career.

My two fellow judges in lodgings on my first visit to Liverpool as a judge in April 1978 were Bill Mars-Jones, my former pupil master, and Derek Hodgson, who had been a law commissioner before being appointed to the bench in October 1977. Derek Hodgson's first task as a judge had been to try several Liverpool councillors on charges arising from their activities as such and the trials had already lasted almost six months when Mars-Jones and I arrived. There was understandable consternation in the closing stages when it was discovered that the jury had been supplied, inadvertently, early in the trial with copies of the official report on the case by the senior police officer in charge. This was, of course, a gross and potentially very prejudicial error and I remember that Mars-Jones and I had some difficulty in convincing Hodgson that he should nevertheless proceed to verdicts rather than discharge the jury and order a retrial with all the unavoidable expense that would involve. Fortunately, he did proceed to verdicts and the jury acquitted all the defendants so that a very large sum of public money was saved and the Court of Appeal Criminal Division did not have to adjudicate on the matter.

One of the burdens of sitting on circuit as a High Court judge was the requirement that one should attend and speak at large formal dinners. I refer to this as a burden because, contrary to the general impression, barristers (including ex-barristers) do not rise to their feet automatically when asked and then launch into a series of jokes and amusing anecdotes. After-dinner speaking is an art form on its own and it has some excellent exponents in the law, of whom Gilbert (Gillie) Gray QC was the outstanding example in my time, but for most of us (including ex-presidents of the Union Society) a great deal of preparation was needed. Lord Lane, for instance, always spoke wittily and pleasingly on such occasions but I know that he was invariably restless for 48 hours before the event. For the judge on circuit the most frequent invitation was to address the local solicitors' annual dinner and one's record on such occasions was likely to be at best patchy. The most daunting were dinners in the biggest local venue, to which members of the local law society would invite their most important clients and supporters, such as bankers, building society representatives and insurance claims managers. One might be a complete stranger in a previously unknown town addressing a large disparate audience without a common theme and expected to perform as skilfully as a professional comedian.

Perhaps I exaggerate a little, and small formal dinners were often very agreeable, particularly if one was not asked to speak. My initiation into the ritual was at Grimsby and Cleethorpes Law Society's dinner when I was sitting at Lincoln, and my most intimidating experience occurred on my first visit to Nottingham, when I had to respond to the toast to the bench and the Bar. The first of these was in the Masonic hall at Grimsby, many miles north of Lincoln, on a very wet Friday evening when I would otherwise have been travelling home. I had never before visited Grimsby and have not since, so we remain almost totally ignorant of each other and I am sure that my inadequate words were soon forgotten. My performance at Nottingham was fortunately rather better because the occasion was the annual dinner of the

Nottinghamshire Law Students' Society, apparently the largest social event in Nottingham's legal calendar. As I had only arrived in the city 48 hours previously, I was rather short of local anecdotage and was quite unknown to the very large assembly but I managed to survive with appropriate ingratiating remarks.

I will not weary the reader with a further catalogue of early circuit recollections but I must mention a very unusual criminal case that I had to try at Sheffield in October 1979. The defendant, represented by the impressive Wilfred Steer QC, was a 13-year-old boy who had pushed an old television set, weighing 33 pounds, off the wall of a walkway in a huge block of council flats 70 feet above the ground. The set had fallen onto the head of an eight-year-old girl, who had emerged from under the flats at the critical moment and who died subsequently from her massive head injuries, with the result that the boy was charged with manslaughter. The block of flats was close to the centre of Sheffield so that it was practicable to agree to a view of the scene by the jury at the beginning of the trial. It seems that the flats had been the subject of an European award soon after the Second World War but they were fashioned out of brutal concrete and presented a very unattractive face to the world by 1979. As we toured the buildings we were assailed by the raucous comments of the tenants on their accommodation and were left in no doubt about the inadequacies of post-war urban planning.

The trial was, of course, exceptionally distressing for the victim's family and for the defendant's too and it raised unusual and difficult questions of law about the criminal culpability of a child in relation to gross carelessness and disregard of risk. At common law a child between the age of 10 and 14 years was presumed not to know the difference between right and wrong, and therefore to be incapable of committing a crime because of the absence of a guilty mind (*mens rea*) but the presumption could be rebutted by appropriate evidence, which would depend to some extent on the nature of the alleged crime. A child might know that an act was wrong but might still not be sufficiently mature to appreciate the natural and probable consequences of his act. In the event, the prosecution was unable to produce any persuasive evidence to rebut the presumption in the case before me and I directed the jury to acquit the defendant. The presumption itself was subsequently abolished by statute in 1998.

In London professional life proceeded at a very acceptable pace without many of the strains and demands of life as a senior barrister. I missed the comradeship and informality of the Bar but there were compensations, including some new social experiences. It is, for example, the practice to invite a small number of judges to attend the state opening of Parliament each year as a relic of the tradition that High Court judges received (and continue to receive) a writ requiring them to attend Parliament to advise legislators, if their advice is sought. This means that a Family Division judge is likely to attend the state opening at least once during his period of service and I was fortunate to do so as early as November 1978 and again in November 1982. Similarly, one is likely to be invited at least once to the Lord Mayor's banquet on his taking office in November, at which it is customary for the prime minister, the Archbishop of Canterbury and the Lord Chancellor to speak. The small group of judges, led by the Lord Chief Justice and the other heads of division, are the last to arrive on this grand occasion: they are fully robed and are required to remain bewigged (in full-bottomed wigs) until after the soup course!

Other more frequent invitations that High Court judges may expect to receive are an annual invitation to a royal garden party in July and the Lord Mayor's dinner in the same month for the higher judiciary. This last event was not invariably annual during my early years on the bench but became so, possibly because of the influence of Dame Mary Donaldson, who was Lord Mayor in 1983/84 when her husband was Master of the Rolls.

In 1978 we took advantage of our first extended long vacation with another chateau venture, this time renting most of the first floor of the Château de la Vienne at le Grand-Pressigny in the Indre-et-Loire. It was well placed for visits to the Loire chateaux, the lakes and forests of Sologne and the valley of the Creuse. Not far away, Derry and Alison Irvine had rented a farmhouse at Semblançay, north of Tours, so that we were able to exchange visits with them and witness together 'son et lumière' at Chenonceaux. It was delightful also to spend time with the family at Compton with Sarah's mother, in the grounds of Frank Cundell's stables and to play golf at the Streatley and Goring club.

Our holiday in 1979 was quite different but also unusual because we rented half of Garden Cottage at Gregynog in Montgomeryshire for four weeks. Gregynog is a large house within a 750-acre estate between Welshpool and Newtown and was the home of the famous Davies sisters, Gwenllian and Margaret, whose spectacular collection of pictures is now a significant part of Wales' art heritage. The survivor of the sisters bequeathed Gregynog to the University of Wales, which succeeded to it in 1960, and its warden for many years was my Cambridge Liberal friend Dr Glyn Tegai Hughes. I first stayed at Gregynog, in the main house, for a weekend course in September 1978 organised by a member of my circuit, Professor Hywel Moseley, who later became the Chancery Circuit judge at Cardiff and Bristol. It was then that I realised that one of the cottages on the estate would provide an ideal base for a family holiday in the loveliest of the Welsh counties, with both Emlyn Hooson and Philip Owen within striking distance. Sarah's mother joined us for 10 days and all of us revelled in our rural freedom. The other half of the cottage was rented by Graham Whettam, a composer, who was the artist in residence at Gregynog that year, and he proved to be a very helpful neighbour when we had plumbing difficulties.

A major change occurred in the Family Division 18 months after my appointment when Sir George Baker, the very well liked president, was succeeded by Mr Justice Arnold, although Mr Justice Dunn had been thought to be the likely successor. John Arnold was a very different personality from either Baker or Dunn: he was a Chancery lawyer who had earlier been chairman of the Bar Council and was of quite a combative temperament, but he presided over the Family Division successfully for nine years while defending its interests aggressively, and my personal relationship with him was excellent. Unlike many common lawyers, he was quite a keen draftsman, always ready to consider improvements to practice rules and he did much to foster the team spirit of the judges with regular meetings to discuss common problems. In retirement he said goodbye to the law completely and lived to a great age in Italy.

The most unusual case that I tried in the Family Division came before me first at the end of June 1978 but its facts were such that I had to ask the Queen's Proctor to intervene (to use legal phraseology) by briefing counsel to assist the court, and the Attorney-General instructed for this purpose Tony Ewbank QC, who was soon to become a judge of the Family Division himself. In the end the full hearing did not take place until March 1979 and I spent most of the Easter vacation preparing my judgment, which I was unable to deliver in London until 8 May, my fifty-third birthday, after sitting for nearly a fortnight at Lincoln.

The petitioner in the case, listed as *Vervaeke v. Smith (Messina intervening)*, was a Belgian former prostitute who had married 'Mr Smith' at Paddington Register Office in August 1954 in order to enable her to stay in England and work as a prostitute without fear of deportation. There was no cohabitation with Mr Smith and he played no part in the petitioner's life after the wedding day. The following month she was registered as a citizen of the UK and her colonies but in November 1963 she went to live in San Remo with a notorious Belgian criminal and organiser of prostitutes, Eugenio Messina, who owned a number of valuable freehold and leasehold properties in London, some (at least) of which were conducted as brothels. Eventually, on 12 March 1970 the petitioner went through a ceremony of marriage with Messina in San Remo but the excitement proved too much for him and he died that very evening. Letters of administration in respect of his estate were granted to members of his family but caveats were entered on behalf of the petitioner and she then sought to establish that she was Messina's lawful widow.

The petitioner's first step was to seek a decree of nullity in the UK in respect of her Smith marriage and she was successful in doing so in an undefended suit heard in Sussex. By chance, however, a barrister in court had some knowledge of the circumstances and, before the decree was made absolute, a member of the Messina family intervened, as did the Queen's Proctor. Without going into unnecessary detail, the upshot was that in May 1971 Mr Justice Ormrod refused the renewed application by the petitioner for a decree of nullity, despite the addition of further grounds for it (see the report of judgment at (1971) P 322). She then turned her attention more successfully to the Belgian courts and obtained a pronouncement in June 1972 that the Smith marriage had been 'absolutely void *ab initio*' because it was a sham marriage, a finding which was upheld by a Court of Appeal in Ghent in April 1974. This latter judgment was then declared to be valid in Italy by a Court of Appeal in Genoa over three years later. The scene was set, therefore, for an application to the English court for a declaration that the 1972 Belgian decree was to be recognised here, despite the adverse earlier decision of Mr Justice Ormrod, thus entitling the petitioner as lawful widow to Messina's English estate. There was an application also for a declaration that her marriage to Messina had been valid and subsisting when he died.

The case obviously raised numerous interesting and quite difficult questions of private international law, which were fully and ably argued before me by the three leading silks of the Family Division in the case, including Joseph Jackson QC for the petitioner. A rather chilling aspect of the hearing was that the petitioner's new husband was at her side, apparently unmoved, throughout. One of the questions that arose was whether the convention between Belgium and Great Britain and Northern Ireland for the reciprocal enforcement of judgments in civil and commercial matters, dated 2 May 1934, applied to the case, but all three counsel agreed that it did so that the hearing proceeded on that basis. In the end this view was not crucial to the outcome of the case but I will say more about it later. My reserved judgment on the many issues ultimately filled 51 quarto pages and I rejected both petitions. Part of my reasoning in relation to the petitioner's application for recognition of the Belgian declaration of nullity was procedural but I refused to declare her Messina marriage valid on the ground that the decision of Mr

Justice Ormrod refusing a decree of nullity in respect of the Smith marriage was recognised as final and conclusive under English law.

There was a further issue as to whether the petitioner's applications should be rejected on the ground of public policy. An underlying basis of the argument was the different attitude of the Belgian courts to that of the English courts in relation to the validity of marriages in which there was no intention to cohabit; but reliance was placed also by the petitioner's opponents and by the Queen's Proctor on her conduct and intentions from 1954 onwards as a bar to both her applications. It was unnecessary for me to decide this further issue, although I doubted whether the application of public policy could be decided by reference to the petitioner's conduct as a prostitute or the avoidance of deportation and the later conduct of the nullity proceedings.

In view of the value of the Messina estate it was inevitable that there would be an appeal against my judgment and the case ultimately went via the Court of Appeal to the House of Lords, where Lord Hailsham was waiting eagerly to preside over the hearing as Lord Chancellor. Before it reached the Court of Appeal I met by chance at the Temple Church my old friend and Cambridge law supervisor, Professor Kurt Lipstein, who upbraided me for applying the Anglo-Belgian convention, presenting me with formidable arguments that it did not apply to matrimonial cases. As I had failed to deal with the question because of the agreement by counsel, I felt compelled, most unusually, to write to them explaining Professor Lipstein's opinion and requesting them to raise the matter in the Court of Appeal to avoid any perpetuation of the error, if error it was. In the event, however, neither the Court of Appeal nor the appellate committee of the House of Lords thought it necessary to deal with the issue and the petitioner's appeals were duly rejected (see the law reports in 1981 Fam Div and 1983 AC for all the judgments).

My close involvement in Family Division matters was greatly diluted for a substantial period after two years on the bench for two reasons. The first was my appointment as a judge of the Employment Appeal Tribunal from 1 October 1979, in succession to Mr Justice Arnold, at the suggestion of Sir George Baker, as I mentioned earlier. This meant that for four years about half of my sittings in London were with that tribunal, and quite often the other half was spent sitting in one or other division of the Court of Appeal. More demandingly, I was telephoned early on 2 April 1980 by Lord Lane, who was about to be sworn in as Lord Chief Justice in succession to Lord Widgery, and invited to succeed Tasker Watkins, who was being promoted to the Court of Appeal, as a presiding judge of the Wales and

Chester Circuit. Needless to say, I accepted the invitation with alacrity and the following period of nearly five years proved to be the most fulfilling of my 18 years on the bench. It meant that my circuit visits would always be to my old circuit during that period and would occupy half of every term. It meant also that my work on circuit would be almost wholly that of the Queen's Bench Division, both civil and criminal. Thus, there would be some terms in which I would deal only rarely with Family Division cases.

19

PRESIDING JUDGE FOR WALES AND CHESHIRE

The appointment of presiding judges for each of the six surviving barristers' circuits was a recommendation of the Beeching Report on Assizes and Quarter Sessions, and the first appointees took office in a 'shadow' capacity in 1971, a year before taking on the fully operational role. The idea was that they should act as delegates of the Lord Chief Justice, dealing with a range of administrative and judicial functions that he would otherwise have to attend to unnecessarily. The need for such delegation had become increasingly obvious from the time of Lord Goddard onwards and it was welcomed by the legal profession as a whole.

In my case I could not match the prestige of some of my predecessors, particularly the unique Tasker Watkins, but I did have the very good fortune to serve initially with Raymond Phillips until his untimely retirement and death shortly afterwards on 2 August 1982 from leukaemia. After very successful service as the first president of the Employment Appeal Tribunal, he had succeeded Phillip Wien, who also died much too young, as a presiding judge with Tasker and I found him to be witty and wise invariably in all our many discussions; it was a great comfort to have a substantial running-in period as his junior before becoming the senior presiding judge for the circuit. His successor as a presiding judge was John Leonard, who had been Common Serjeant of the City of London, sitting at the Central Criminal Court, before he was promoted to the High Court bench in 1981. He was not a member of the circuit when practising at the Bar but there is much to be said for having an 'outsider' as one of the presiding judges to ensure that an independent view is expressed and that a too-cosy atmosphere does not prejudice the career of anyone who is thought to be outside the favoured circle. In the event I cannot recollect that John Leonard and I ever disagreed on any major circuit issue and he became a valued and helpful colleague.

Rightly or wrongly, I believe that the presiding judge system was working at its best in the 1980s, at the time when I was fortunate to be part of it. One advantage was that there was a very able permanent secretary to the Lord Chancellor from 1980 to 1989, Sir Derek Oulton, who had been secretary to the Beeching Commission and who was already deputy to the permanent secretary when I was appointed to the bench. In my period as a presiding judge the demarcation line between the jurisdiction of the judges and that of the administrators was still being worked out, and I remember with special pleasure a working weekend at Pembroke College, Cambridge, when Lord Lowry, then Lord Chief Justice of Northern Ireland, and I had to conduct an exercise, largely devised by Michael Blair, which was designed to probe the uncertain grey areas on the boundary of the rival jurisdictions. On the whole, however, most important issues had already been settled and a considerable degree of harmony achieved. It is sad that much bitterness developed later and, with hindsight, I think that it is a pity that, after Lord Havers' very brief tenure following Lord Hailsham's retirement in June 1987, an English practitioner was not appointed as Lord Chancellor. Despite his great ability and natural charm, Lord Mackay of Clashfern could not match Lord Hailsham as a defender of the legal profession and the judiciary, and himself became the object of considerable antagonism by some lawyers in the following 10 years: it may be that this was due, in part at least, to his lack of familiarity with the traditions and practice of the law in England and Wales.

When I was appointed as a presiding judge it was made clear to me that Raymond Phillips and I would be consulted about all judicial appointments on circuit, other than lay magistrates, and about appointments to silk of junior members. I was told also that our recommendations would be implemented unless, unusually, there was some special reason for not doing so. Like most, if not all, of the presiding judges, I regarded this as my most important function and I am glad to say that during my period as a presiding judge all our recommendations were accepted. More importantly, I am convinced that those recommendations were right and proved to be fully justified.

The scrutiny of practising members of the Bar was not limited to occasions when an appointment had to be made, because the permanent secretary, and from about 1983 his deputy, conducted an annual review of the progress of barristers in consultation with the presiding judges. Thus, in my case, Derek Oulton (later Tom Legg) would visit me and we would discuss all the members of the circuit of about 10 years or more in seniority. He would then send me a summary of the views that I had expressed to enable me to correct or amend any comment that I wished. He would have a similar discussion with my fellow presiding judge and with a sample of the Circuit judges sitting on our circuit. Thus, he accumulated a broad picture from a variety of sources of the practising Bar as essential background to decisions on a wide range of appointments: these included stipendiary magistrates, assistant recorders, recorders and Circuit judges and some other judicial appointments such as chairmen of various tribunals as well as Queen's Counsel. The scrutiny also embraced solicitors because they were eligible for nearly all these appointments: there were, for example, a number of solicitors who were already recorders or assistant recorders and others whose applications for such appointments or as district registrars, now called district judges, were being considered.

There are, of course, many critics of this system on the ground that it savoured of nepotism and exclusivity but I make no apology for it. Much of the criticism came from failed applicants whose applications had been rightly rejected or from special interest groups. The recurring complaints about the low percentage of women appointees, for example, were quite unjustified because, throughout my time as a judge, the proportion of eligible women appointed to the bench was high and increasing: the pace of increase in the numbers reflected the rate at which women barristers were achieving appropriate seniority rather than any past discrimination in making the appointments. At one point there was scarcely a senior woman barrister left on the Northern Circuit because they had all been appointed to the High Court or Circuit bench (and three of the latter were subsequently promoted to the High Court). I accept that an able barrister who was truculent or whose 'face did not fit' for some other reason might find him or herself rejected but the breadth of consultation by the Lord Chancellor's department was intended to minimise this risk; and it was extended, for example, to the elected leader of each circuit to ensure that the views of the practising Bar were heard.

I cannot accept that the new appointments commission will achieve any better results and the risk of inappropriate selection is now significantly higher. Performance at interview can be misleading, and question papers addressed to potential judges are both demeaning and rather ridiculous. What I have said applies with even greater force to the appointment of High Court judges. In my time there was no requirement or opportunity to apply for such an appointment. The range of consultation about potential appointees was very wide indeed, including the presiding judges and many other judges, and the ultimate decisions were made by the Lord Chancellor in close final consultation with the heads of division. I am not aware that this process resulted in any important error in an appointment: there were, inevitably, some injustices for a variety of reasons but no appointments system can eliminate these entirely and a commission certainly will not do so.

Other duties of the presiding judges were, in my opinion, less important, and, writing now as an ill-informed outsider, their present role seems to me to be much diminished, despite (or perhaps partly because of) the ill-considered 'de facto' abolition of the Lord Chancellor's department and the transfer of some administrative responsibilities to the Lord Chief Justice. There are still, however, decisions to be made about the trial of the more important or lengthy cases, liaison must also be maintained with the circuit's full-time and part-time judiciary, and seminars must be arranged to keep them abreast of current developments, all of which is worthwhile work. The continuous contact with members of a circuit for several years is also very rewarding; and I found the regular meetings every term with the Lord Chief Justice and his deputy, Lord Justice Watkins, who was at first appointed as the senior presiding judge for England and Wales, very stimulating because they kept us up to date with many administrative developments and sometimes ahead of them.

My first visit as a presiding judge to circuit occurred straightaway and was to Cardiff in April 1980, where I was greeted by the most attractive of high sheriffs, Henry Gethin Lewis, who became a firm, but all too short-lived, friend. He was immensely convivial as well as highly intelligent and it is recorded that, as a young man, he cleared a five-barred gate in his MG sports car. He was complemented by his popular and public-spirited wife, Bridget or Bud. It was a tremendous sadness when he died early in 1997 and I still miss him greatly. The 1980/81 roll for Glamorgan as a whole was notable because the High Sheriff of Mid Glamorgan was Robert Knight (of Cooke and Arkwright) and of West Glamorgan, Michael Llewellyn, soon to succeed his father as the second baronet. Moreover the Lord Lieutenant for the whole of Glamorgan was still Sir Cennydd Traherne, later a Knight of the Garter, at whose wedding my mother-in-law had been a bridesmaid. They were all the most generous of hosts and I confess that Sarah and I basked in their kindness and hospitality.

The downside of that moment was that our son Thomas, who had just started his last term at Uppingham and was about to sit his A levels, went down with measles as soon as the term began. It was very worrying and disappointing for all of us, not least because he had to spend some time in a darkened room to avoid injury to his sight. Quite apart from the damage to his academic prospects, he had been looking forward to opening the batting for Uppingham first XI and that was no longer a practical possibility. He had previously been opening batsman for the second XI with the brother of Jonathan Agnew the cricket commentator and another contemporary member of that XI, James Whittaker, went on to captain Leicestershire from 1996 to 1999. Not surprisingly, Thomas' A level results were disappointing but Davies' College in London proved to be very helpful in preparing him to resit and he gained a place at the University College of Wales, Aberystwyth, in 1981 to read law and politics, emerging with a respectable 2(1) honours degree in 1984.

In the second half of the Michaelmas term 1980 I managed to sit at Swansea, Chester, Mold and Caernarfon so that I had an almost full nostalgic tour of my old circuit. The most intriguing case before me during that circuit visit was a civil action for negligence heard at Caernarfon in which the subject was a devastating fire at Moriah Chapel there, which destroyed the large building and its fine organ. The properties board of the Calvinistic Methodist Church of Wales understandably sued the local firm of building contractors who had been carrying out repairs and refurbishment of the chapel at the time, on the grounds that a blow lamp, which the contractors admitted using on a relevant wall, had started the blaze. Liability was strongly denied by the builders' insurers and a fierce battle was joined before me. Various experts were called by either side and one of the theories canvassed was that a bird had picked up a cigarette stub that was still alight and had flown with it to the seat of the fire. One of the counsel in the case, who included Emlyn Hooson and David (later Mr Justice) Clarke, drew a sketch to illustrate this line of defence, which I still have, but I was compelled to find in the plaintiff's favour.

The judges' lodgings for Caernarvonshire were particularly interesting because they were at the joint country home of the Earl of Snowdon and his aunt, Lady Buckley, the wife of Lord Justice Buckley, in the village of Bontnewydd; it was the Snowdon part of the house that was let for visits by High Court judges. The whole house, standing in 15 acres, is now a country house hotel and the village has Bryn Terfel as its most famous resident. The lodgings were thus more elegant than the functional and modern Mold lodgings on the top floor of the Crown Court building but I have always had a special feeling for the latter, so conveniently placed above the court and with quite spectacular views, because my father was chairman of the county finance committee when the estate was bought.

The High Sheriff of Clwyd that year was a member of one of North Wales' oldest families as heir to the Myddleltons of Chirk Castle. David Myddelton was not at all grand, however; on the contrary, he and his wife were devout Christians, living quite simply on a farm at Chirk, where we greatly enjoyed visiting them. My most troublesome case when sitting at Mold that autumn centred on a campaign of arson attacks on English holiday homes in North Wales that had started in December 1979. The main defendant called himself Eurig ap Gwilym and had established a small 'private army' named Cadwyr Cymru (Keepers of Wales) but he and his three co-defendants were largely ineffective in their own contributions to the campaign, unlike some others, four of whom had already been convicted and sentenced. There were strong grounds of mitigation in respect of the co-defendants so that it was appropriate to impose moderate sentences of imprisonment, and the campaign led by Meibion Glyndwr, a much larger organisation, petered out eventually by the mid-1980s.

The most memorable social event for me in the autumn of 1980 was a dinner at the BBC's Television Centre on 15 October to celebrate the twenty-fifth anniversary of Robin Day's debut in television with Independent Television News. The director-general, Ian Trethowan, presided and there was a constellation of guests, including Christopher Chataway and Ludovic Kennedy, Robin's first colleagues. Ted Heath and Denis Healey made the speeches and I was recognised above my station by sitting between Ian and Shirley Williams because of my minor role in Robin's introduction to newscasting. At the request of Dick Taverne I had to sing for my supper at a large British Oxygen Company dinner in Lincoln's Inn for their executives worldwide later the same month and the previous weekend I climbed Moel Famau (a modest 1,880 feet) in the Clwydian range on a glorious autumn day with grouse rising at my feet.

The following year began very auspiciously with the announcement of a knighthood for Robin Day, and Sarah and I attended a celebratory lunch at the Garrick Club in February on the day of his investiture. At the next table Kingsley Amis was hosting a similar celebration of his CBE, without rancour, but I was glad when he received the same recognition as Robin in 1990. Another notable event for Sarah and me early in the year was dinner with Geoffrey and Elspeth Howe at 11 Downing Street, where Geoffrey had been installed as Chancellor of the Exchequer from May 1979. Among our fellow guests on this occasion were Hugh and Margaret Casson (of Portmadoc lineage, he was then president of the Royal Academy), Peter and Elizabeth Emery and the Staffords. As I said earlier, the Howes were both very loyal friends and generous hosts, so we enjoyed their hospitality on several occasions at 11 Downing Street, Chevening and Dorneywood. Most important of all, however, we celebrated the seventieth birthday of Sarah's mother Diana with champagne and dinner on 15 February.

The pattern of my judicial work for the following four years to the end of 1984 had been set by my appointments as a presiding judge and to the Employment Appeals Tribunal (the latter to October 1983) and remained very similar to that of 1980. The high point of my sittings in 1981 was the unexpected chance to sit for a week in the Court of Appeal Civil Division under the presidency of the already legendary Lord Denning, the Master of the Rolls. When I reported for work on 15 June 1981, I could not help reflecting that Lord Denning, then 82 years old, had been promoted to the Court of Appeal as long ago as 1948, the year in which I had returned to Cambridge to study law; and that he had already by then delivered his famous High Trees judgment (in *Central London Property Trust Ltd v. High Trees House Ltd* (1947) KB 130), which was one of the major talking points for law students of my generation. Fortunately, the other member of the court was Lord Justice Griffiths, a fellow Johnian against whom I had appeared at the Bar, so I did not feel totally isolated; but the two cases that we heard, selected by Lord Denning as of appropriate importance and interest, were both challenging and raised some quite difficult questions of law.

The second of these was of wide public interest and was brought by the Commission for Racial Equality, for whom Michael Beloff QC appeared, against a ruling by Mr Justice Woolf. The background to the hearing was that the London Borough of Hillingdon had been faced with the problem of providing accommodation for many families of Asian origin who were fleeing from persecution in Kenya and some other East African countries. It was the policy of the Labour government in office until 1979 to grant asylum to the refugees but the political control of Hillingdon, which was particularly affected by the policy, changed from Labour to Conservative in May 1978. There was then an incident in November 1978 when an immigrant Kenyan family arrived at Heathrow airport from Malawi and were sent by taxi to the Foreign Office on the instructions of the leader of Hillingdon Council.

This provocative action received much publicity in the national press, with the result that the commission wrote to the council seeking an explanation for its actions. The commission was dissatisfied with the council's reply and decided to carry out a formal investigation into the latter's policy and performance under the Housing (Homeless Persons) Act 1977, the purpose being to ascertain whether or not the belief that the council discriminated against Asian families was justified. The council had challenged the notice of this investigation on the ground that it was outside the commission's powers and Mr Justice Woolf had accepted that the terms of reference of the investigation had been more widely drawn than could be justified by the material before the commission on which its decision to proceed had been based. He had indicated, however, that an investigation could proceed on narrower terms of reference.

The hearing before us lasted three full days and in the end we were agreed that the council's case, put by Lionel Read QC, should prevail and that the appeal should be dismissed. Lord Denning, who was (as always) very busy, asked Lord Justice Griffiths to prepare the leading judgment and I went off to Swansea the following Monday, happy in the expectation that I would only need to say 'I concur' or words to that effect in due course. Lord Justice Griffiths duly sent me a copy of his proposed judgment, with which I agreed fully but, rather to my dismay, Lord Denning decided to deliver a judgment of his own, agreeing with the result but describing the housing problem faced by Hillingdon in characteristic purple prose. I was forced, therefore, to prepare a short judgment agreeing that the appeal should be dismissed for the reasons stated by Lord Justice Griffiths; my embarrassment was complete when the judgments were delivered because my own words had to be read out by Lord Denning in my absence on circuit. The story does not quite end there because the commission appealed unsuccessfully to the House of Lords and the Appellate Committee dismissed the appeal 'for the reasons stated by Lord Justice Griffiths, with whom Mr Justice Waterhouse agreed'.

I have recounted the history of that particular appeal without any vainglorious motive. My role was quite trivial in the greater scheme of things but the story does illustrate that even a 'consenting adult' who acts as the third member of the court (often referred to derisorily as a 'book end') can find himself or herself in embarrassing situations, however much he or she may wish to maintain a low profile. Permanent members of the Court of Appeal face similar problems, of course, routinely. In my time on the bench at least one senior member of that court was known on occasions to deliver his unreserved judgment without having felt able to tell his colleagues which way he intended to find before doing so: the anxiety that this caused can readily be imagined but he obstinately opposed reserving his judgment if he could avoid doing so.

The most unusual case that I had to try in 1981 was the prosecution at Swansea of about 11 antique dealers for taking part in a mock auction at Carmarthen, contrary to the provisions of the Mock Auctions Act 1961. I was told that it was the first successful prosecution under that Act and it was presumably the last because the Act has since been repealed and replaced by a statutory instrument. The background was that a number of antique dealers had been observed by police attending sales at a well-known auction house in Carmarthen at which they did not bid against each other but later conducted further auction sales amongst themselves at other locations, including a beach and a well-known Carmarthen hotel (the Ivy Bush). The police therefore prepared in advance to video an auction in a room at the hotel favoured by the conspirators and enlisted the help of the hotel cleaning staff to ensure that the participants remained within range of the various discreet cameras by deft use of their hoovers and brushes.

For once, this rather elaborate plan worked well and a good film of the proceedings was recorded so that the lines of defence available to the defendants were rather limited and Gareth Williams QC had ample scope for his ready wit in conducting the prosecution. All the defendants, except for two rather charming Italians seated nearest to the jury, were duly convicted and I fined each of them £500, ordered them to pay the costs of the prosecution and banned them from attending auction sales for six months.

One of the lesser known tasks of the presiding judges, particularly if they are in office on their native circuit, is addressing large gatherings of magistrates, solicitors and others involved in the administration of justice, usually at weekends. Looking back now, I see that I was asked to do this over and over again, especially in the middle years of my period as a presiding judge, during which I seem to have visited every corner of the circuit. There were seminars for judges and recorders, law society dinners, annual conferences (for example) of the British Legal Association at Llandudno and of prosecuting solicitors at Swansea, magistrates' conferences in all the Welsh counties and even a senior police officers' mess in Gwent.

The most enjoyable of all these was a weekend conference in October 1982 for our Circuit judges and recorders at Gregynog. This had been arranged by Raymond Phillips and me following a previous initiative by Hywel Moseley QC, which I mentioned earlier. Raymond died two months before it came to fruition but Mr Justice Leonard took over from him enthusiastically and I had the pleasure of driving Lord Justice Lawton to and from Gregynog, where he gave the leading lecture. We also had lectures by J.E. Hall Williams of the London School of Economics and by the chief constable of Gwent. Altogether, the event was a great success and provided an opportunity for wide-ranging talks with the Circuit judges as well as our formal annual meeting. The estimated cost beforehand to the

Lord Chancellor's department was only £1,510 and it was a disappointing mistake by the department to refuse subsequently to repeat the event on the ground of cost, except in 1988 when I was fortunate to be asked to take part. Instead, we reverted to the more formal and less enlightening annual meeting at Cardiff followed by dinner.

That year (1982) I heard one case in the Employment Appeal Tribunal that was of special interest to me because of my Nonconformist upbringing. This was the *President of the Methodist Conference v. Warton Parfitt*, in which the Church appealed against the majority decision of an industrial tribunal that there had been a contract of employment between the Church and the respondent, who had been a minister on the Jersey (Channel Islands) Circuit until the synod of the district had ordered, on disciplinary grounds, that he should no longer be allowed to act as a minister. The Church's case was that Parfitt had been the holder of an office and not an employee under a contract with the Church.

The industrial tribunal had been unanimous in holding that Parfitt was not an office holder but the chairman, Lady French, the wife of Mr Justice French, had not accepted that he was an employee either: it was the lay members who had accepted that he was an employee and whose view had prevailed. On the hearing of the appeal there was a similar division of opinion because I agreed with Lady French whereas the two lay members were for dismissing the appeal. Explaining my dissent from them, I said that the nature of the control exercised over a minister by the Methodist Church was not that of a master over a servant and that the spiritual nature of his work was not such that it was susceptible to a master's control. It seemed to me that the concept of a minister as a man called by God, a servant of God and the pastor of his local church members, was central to the relationship and I was unable to accept that either party intended it to be contractual.

This decision and another at about the same time by the EAT provoked a silly leading article in *The Times* of 18 November 1982 headed 'Anti-employment Tribunal'. However, the Methodist Church, no doubt emboldened by Lady French's dissent and my own, appealed and at last won its case by a unanimous decision of the Court of Appeal in October 1983. From my point of view, it was a very satisfactory outcome and I was fortunate to have the Court of Appeal on my side seven months earlier in similar circumstances in the only other case in which I was in a minority (*Martin v. Glynwed Distribution Limited*). The status of ministers of religion in relation to employment law continues to be argued in the appellate courts, including the House of Lords, and the issue may well be resolved, at least for some denominations, by legislation.

An unexpected bonus resulting from my appointment to the EAT was an invitation to take part in an Anglo-American judicial exchange in September 1982. The English part of it was at the Dormey House Hotel at Willersey Hill, near Broadway in Worcestershire, and its purpose was to exchange information about equal opportunity law and procedures in the USA and the UK. There was a strong delegation from the USA led by a Circuit Court of Appeal judge and the British representatives included Lord Lowry, then Lord Chief Justice of Northern Ireland, as well as Mr Justice Browne-Wilkinson, the president of the EAT, and a very wide range of judges and chairmen of industrial tribunals. In my case this led to a most welcome invitation to my wife and me to take part in a return exchange in Philadelphia and Washington in April 1985. The first exchange here, however, was itself very useful and enjoyable: a lasting memory is of Lord Lowry and Lord Justice O'Donnell (a Roman Catholic member of the Northern Ireland Court of Appeal) dancing to and singing together the Protestant marching songs after dinner on Saturday evening to the astonishment of our American guests; it was Lord Justice O'Donnell who knew all the words! The weekend concluded with drinks at 11 Downing Street as the guests of Geoffrey Howe, who had played a leading role in establishing the National Industrial Relations Court in 1971.

The years between 1982 and 1984 were saddened for us greatly by the slowly developing illness of Sarah's mother, who had a melanoma removed from her leg in November 1982. The prognosis seemed to be favourable at first but cancer reappeared in 1984, with the result that she had to undergo further surgery at the Wellington Hospital in the spring of that year, followed by radiotherapy. She relapsed after a last holiday with us and died at our home on 7 October 1984. A requiem mass was held for her at St John's Wood Church five days later. Her death was an immense blow for us because she had been an integral part of our married life for 24 years and a joyful and much-loved granny to our three children.

I had to try a particularly gruesome murder case at Caernarfon in February 1983 in the Welsh language with the aid of instantaneous translation facilities, which had been installed there and also at Mold, Carmarthen, Swansea and Cardiff. The application for trial in Welsh was perfectly genuine because the defendant came from a rural village and his first language was undoubtedly Welsh. But, when the time came for him to give evidence himself, he decided that he preferred to do so in English because he had been in custody at Risley remand centre, near Warrington, for so long that he had become accustomed to speaking English rather than Welsh. In the event neither language availed him: he was rightly convicted of murder and sentenced to life imprisonment. Each of the courts where translation facilities had been installed had access to specially trained interpreters, often Nonconformist ministers, who provided an excellent service in relays from a soundproof box linked by microphone to the earphones that were supplied to everyone who had to hear the translation; parties had a right under the Welsh Language Act 1967 to require proceedings to be conducted in Welsh (under the later Act of 1992 Welsh has equal status with English in public life).

A special pleasure for the circuit in 1983 was a visit by the Lord Chief Justice, Lord Lane, and his wife to Cardiff, where he sat as a trial judge for a week at the end of June. I was not due to be on circuit then but John Leonard was committed to sittings in the north so Sarah and I went to Cardiff for the week to accompany the Lanes, together with Mr Justice and Lady Stocker, who were already in residence there. Circuit visits of this kind by the Lord Chief Justice were greatly welcomed by the Bar and by civic dignitaries and Lord Lane enjoyed renewed contact with actual trials as a change of diet from appeals. But the visits were always strenuous for him because of the social obligations that he had to fulfil and every evening of his Cardiff visit was thus occupied, including a dinner given by the Lord Mayor at Cardiff Castle. As a holder himself of the Air Force Cross, he was particularly impressed by Lady (Rowena) Traherne, the Lord Lieutenant's wife, who (as a member of the Air Transport Auxiliary) had piloted Spitfires and many other types of aeroplane during the war when delivering them to RAF squadrons.

My own most interesting case that year was heard at Swansea and Carmarthen in May, a month before the general election in which Mrs Thatcher won her second great victory. There were two civil actions, one brought by the Welsh Office against 43 defendants and the other by seven local authorities, led by Dyfed County Council, against 36 defendants, all of whom were defendants also in the first action. The complaint of the plaintiffs was that the defendants were 'travellers' who had established themselves unlawfully on various sites, including a lay-by on the A40 main road, over a period of nine years. The plaintiffs' case was that they had responsibilities under a range of statutes relating to planning, public health and highways to prevent persistent breaches of the law that had been committed by the defendants but that enforcement procedures available under the legislation had proved to be ineffective. The plaintiffs therefore sought from the court injunctions against the defendants to prevent repetitions of the unlawful conduct.

Against these submissions, the defendants denied that they were nomads: they said that they wished to settle in Pembrokeshire permanently and for their children to be educated there. At the heart of their case was the argument that there had always been practicable alternatives open to the local councils under the Caravan Sites Act 1968 and, in particular, the provision of a site for the defendants. They submitted that they had been the victims of unjust harassment and discrimination. I was satisfied, however, that the defendants had deliberately and flagrantly flouted the law and would continue to do so unless they were restrained. There were viable lawful alternatives open to them in conformity with their own wishes, and I granted injunctions, limited in application to the area of Dyfed, to begin at the end of the current school term.

My last year as a presiding judge was very much one of ups and downs domestically. On the plus side, Thomas graduated in July 1984 and Sarah and I were able to attend his graduation ceremony, staying the night before with Philip Owen at his home in Llanbrynmair. Then when we were on holiday in Scotland, we heard that Sophie had gained three As in her A levels and an S level 1, which led to acceptance by my Cambridge college, St John's, for entry in 1985 to read philosophy. In contrast, a blow for Thomas especially was his rejection by the Regular Commissions Board (RCB) in November after he had successfully completed the demanding brigade squad course at Pirbright under Welsh Guards sponsorship and had visited the Welsh Guards in Germany. He had struck a particularly difficult time when the RCB was accepting only about one in 10 of those who were tested and we learnt later that his apparent weakness had been in practical decision-making on the hop. There followed several dark months for him but his failure proved to be in his best long-term interest because he would have emerged from a short service commission at a very difficult time. As it was, through the good offices of my ex-Singapore friend, Graham Starforth Hill, he obtained a good banking appointment with American Express Bank, which led several years later to even more fruitful employment with the Sumitomo Bank, now Sumitomo Mitsui Banking Corporation Europe Limited, of which he is a joint general manager.

In London I no longer sat in the Employment Appeal Tribunal, where Mr Justice Balcombe had succeeded me, and my most memorable sittings were short stints in both divisions of the Court of Appeal. In the Criminal Division I spent two weeks with Lord Justice Watkins and a week with Lord Justice Ackner. The other member of the court was Mr Justice Bristow, an Old Etonian, who had been Treasurer of the Middle Temple when I became a bencher of the Inn. He gave me an excellent teasing lesson when approving a draft judgment that I had been asked to give. He wrote: 'Your draft is masterly. I was particularly impressed with your Latinity at line 3 of p.23 [my use of the word *lacunae*] where some ignorant Middle Temple benchers might have put "holes".'

On circuit I managed to sit for the last time as a presiding judge in the second half of the Michaelmas term 1984 at all the main crown courts, apart from Carmarthen, and ended up at Chester, where the high sheriff, Richard Roundell, now deputy chairman of Christie's, arranged a very pleasing dinner party at Dorfold Hall, Nantwich, attended by all the Cheshire high sheriffs of my period as a presiding judge and their wives. At Swansea a notable event was a recital of French songs by the soprano Deborah Rees, daughter of my former barrister friend Breuan, who died in 1966, and in November I spoke with Lord Kenyon at the annual dinner for old students of Ruthin school on the occasion of its seventh centenary. Much of my time on circuit, as usual, was taken up with murder trials but Chester provided a welcome final diet of civil actions, none of which were noteworthy.

My most constructive activity in the criminal field in 1984 was to prepare, on behalf of the Family Division judges, a memorandum to a committee presided over by Lord Roskill in which we recommended that juries should be dispensed with in the more complicated fraud trials. Having had over 40 years' experience of jury trials, I am a strong supporter of this recommendation and I am glad to say that it had the unanimous support of the Family Division judges. One aspect of the matter that is not fully understood by laymen is that a judge hearing a case without a jury would have to deliver a detailed judgment justifying his conclusions, against which it could well be easier to appeal than against a jury's verdict, which does not require any reasons to be given. The recommendation was duly made in 1986 by the Roskill Committee and I remain hopeful that a strong government will implement it some day.

It was fortunate that I was due to spend the first half of the Michaelmas term 1984 in London because it meant that I was at home in the immediate aftermath of my mother-in-law's death on 7 October. We attended very few social events, of course, but Geoffrey Howe had become foreign secretary immediately after the 1983 general election and I made the first of three visits to his official country residence at Chevening, near Sevenoaks, with Sophie deputising for Sarah on this occasion, to attend a large luncheon party. The only social events in 1984 to rival it for me were Lady Donaldson's summer banquet for the judges as Lord Mayor of London and the last of the great London Zoo dinners that I attended, in May in the presence of the Duke of

Edinburgh to salute Lord Zuckerman's 29 years at the helm, the last seven as president.

When my period as a presiding judge came to an end I was sad to sever my close connection with the Wales and Chester Circuit, although the blow was softened later by my election as an honorary member. As I have explained in chapter 8, the circuit as I knew it lasted for only 62 years; and even that is not strictly correct because Monmouthshire did not become part of it until 1972. I was pleased to disregard such pedantry, however, when I became Treasurer of the Middle Temple in 1995 because we organised a very well-attended circuit dinner to celebrate its golden jubilee.

I cannot leave this subject without expressing my deep regret that the circuit has now been reduced in size by the exclusion of Cheshire, including the city of Chester, and its transfer to the Northern Circuit, which did not actively seek such a change. It was difficult to resist after the devolution legislation, even though administration of justice is not a devolved matter; and circuit resistance to the proposal was undermined by at least two successive presiding judges in recent times. The concept of a separate Welsh system of justice, as in Scotland, with Welsh-speaking judges and barristers, is, in my judgement, unreal and would result in a disastrous decline in both the quality of advocacy available and the standing of the judges. Moreover, Chester has been the natural focus for North Wales for centuries, and its strong local Bar has provided an excellent and expanding service for the whole of North Wales as well as Cheshire, most notably since 1945. But it is unlikely that this expansion will continue and I cannot predict what quality of service will be available to North Wales litigants in the medium- and long-term future.

20

SOLDIERING ON IN THE FAMILY DIVISION

When my term as a presiding judge was near its end, Tasker Watkins asked me if I would like to be transferred to the Queen's Bench Division. I had by then served seven years in the Family Division and would normally have been keen to accept this offer but I did not do so for a particular reason. It was not generally known that John Arnold's second wife had left him and I think that she had returned to her native Canada. It seems that he thought that the press would soon get hold of the story and that he would then feel obliged to resign because of the nature of his position as head of the Family Division. Whatever the reason, he began to make it clear to me quite unambiguously, without stating so expressly, that he expected me to succeed him; he even said on one occasion as he faced my wife and me that his rather long robe would fit his successor much better. At roughly the same time it was reported to me by reliable friends that both the Lord Chief Justice and the new Master of the Rolls, Sir John Donaldson, had spoken of me as suitable to be the next president, and some months later, Lord Edmund-Davies mentioned the matter when he sat with me at the end of October 1985 at Cardiff for a nostalgic morning. I felt that it would be disloyal, therefore, to John Arnold and the division generally to accept Tasker's kind offer and I do not think that I made the wrong decision, even though I was looking at a mirage.

In the event the press miraculously failed to pursue John Arnold and he was able to continue as president until he decided to retire at the end of 1987 without any external pressure to do so. By then much water had flowed under the bridge and I believe that at least three members of the

Court of Appeal declared their interest in the presidency. In the past, when the division was known as the Probate, Divorce and Admiralty Division, the practice had been for the Solicitor-General at the time to be offered the post, and the last law officer to accept was Sir Jocelyn Simon, later a distinguished Lord of Appeal during my last six years at the Bar. He was succeeded by Sir George Baker, followed by Sir John Arnold, neither of whom was a Lord Justice of Appeal at the time of his appointment, but it is understandable that the pattern changed again in 1987 in the light of the different attitude to the post of members of the Court of Appeal, and it is unlikely that a puisne judge (an ordinary judge of the High Court) will be appointed as president in the future.

John Arnold, who had earlier suggested that I might become president of the EAT at a time when I was needed as a presiding judge, remained loyal to his preference for me but was outvoted by the other heads of division and I have no complaint about that. The appointment went to Lord Justice Stephen Brown, who proved to be a very capable president, and I suspect that he was happier in the post than I would have been over a substantial period.

It will be apparent from what I have said earlier that, in my view, the judicial appointments system worked reasonably well throughout my time as a judge, although some injustices could have been avoided. I was aware of two major causes for general concern. The first was the failure from time to time after the retirement of Lord Edmund-Davies to ensure that one of the Lords of Appeal was steeped in the practice of criminal law in England and Wales. It is true that fewer and fewer criminal appeals now seem to reach that level but the gap in expertise has been glaring on occasions and it is not appropriate to rely wholly on the representatives of Scotland and Northern Ireland because there are significant differences in procedures and ways of thought. The second failure, which is not now apparent, was in the representation of the Family Division in the Court of Appeal, despite the excellent general contribution made by a succession of appointees from that division. A major cause of difficulty was the opinion of Sir John Donaldson that only 'common sense' was needed for decision-making in family appeals of all kinds without the benefit of specialist knowledge or experience (rather similarly, he thought that almost all employment appeals involved questions of fact rather than law). John Balcombe was so incensed about this in April 1984 in relation to the Family Division that he pressed me to attend with him upon Mr Justice Latey, the highly respected and influential senior judge of the division (without appellate ambitions of his own), in order to urge him to write in protest. He did so and John Balcombe was promoted the following year.

My personal priority in 1985 was to move house in two directions. Sarah was keen to acquire a home in the country and 12 Cavendish Avenue had become too big for our London needs because Thomas and Sophie were about to leave home. They had been left very generous provision for their future accommodation needs by Diana (as had Laura, but she was only 10 years old). We had in mind a house in Somerset or Dorset possibly but Bernard Thorpe included particulars of a house on the Herefordshire/ Monmouthshire border, and we fell in love with its spectacular view when we first saw it on 8 June 1985. We bought it that summer and it has been our main home since I retired in 1996.

Our search in London was more time consuming but reached a climax at about the same time because our offer on 11 Abbey Gardens was accepted on 12 June 1985. Completion of Sarah's purchase of our country home in Herefordshire took place in mid-August and we completed the sale of 12 Cavendish Avenue and the purchase of 11 Abbey Gardens in late October. Thus, the year was one of domestic upheaval and all of us felt great regrets on leaving our elegant house in Cavendish Avenue after 15 years. Another mourner was our much-loved cocker spaniel, Orlando, who had been with us since Christmas 1973. One dreadful evening, when we thought that he was lost, we eventually found him sitting outside the front door of 12 Cavendish Avenue; but he was compensated in the end by spending most of his last years in the country, where he is buried.

We were able to take possession of our new home in Herefordshire in August and slept there for the first time on 29 August. This was after I had sat as a vacation judge for over a fortnight, so there was no time for a summer holiday abroad. There was much to do in Herefordshire and London but we were rewarded by a prolonged and beautiful autumn lasting beyond the end of November.

There was compensation also in two official trips abroad. The first of these was to Washington and Philadelphia as a return exchange following our weekend at the Dormey House Hotel in 1982. Sarah and I enjoyed our 10 days in the USA in April 1985 and learnt a great deal about their legislation and procedure in dealing with racial and sexual discrimination. In Washington we met Supreme Court Justice Sandra O'Connor and Judges Ruth Ginsberg and Antonin Scalia, both of whom were later promoted to the Supreme Court. One afternoon we heard a particularly interesting appeal by a Florida judge who had, in effect, been barred from sitting following his trial and acquittal on a charge of being corrupted by his co-accused, a New York lawyer, who was himself convicted at the same time of corrupting the judge. The latter had continued subsequently to draw his judicial salary but the president of the court had ordered that no cases were to be listed for trial by him. The District of Columbia Court of Appeals for the hearing included Judge Robert Bork, whose nomination for the Supreme Court by President Reagan in 1988 was rejected acrimoniously by the Senate.

Very memorable also were visits to the National Gallery of Art in Washington and the Phillips Collection in Philadelphia. In the latter city we were introduced to the distinguished Judge Louis H. Pollak, watched him preside over an asbestosis case and attended a seminar at the University of Pennsylvania. Our introduction to the American 'class action' was particularly instructive.

The other official visit, to the European Court of Justice in Luxembourg in September 1985, was more conventional because such visits were arranged at least annually. Again, Sarah was able to come with me and we went in the company of Bill Mars-Jones from the Queen's Bench Division and Mr Justice Scott (later Lord Scott of Foscote) from the Chancery Division and their wives. Our immediate hosts were the president, Lord Mackenzie Stuart, and Sir Gordon Slynn, the British Advocate General, with whom I had previously worked closely at the EAT. Other notable participants in the British delegation were Lord Elwyn-Jones and Lord and Lady Mackay of Clashfern. We were entertained very generously and our schedule was not very taxing. I do remember, however, that the Italians were extraordinarily voluble whenever we had a general discussion.

Thomas recovered from his gloom following his rejection by the army and learnt early in April 1985 that his application to American Express Bank had been successful. He started work 10 days later and spent his first weekend travelling to Paris to deliver some documents to HH the Aga Khan. His later tasks were less exotic but much of his time with American Express was spent dealing with the financing of aircraft leasing, involving large sums of money and intricate legal arrangements.

This was also a time of great change for Laura because in the summer she left St Mary's Convent and started at the much larger Francis Holland School in September, at the age of 11, where she stayed for the next two years. We all decided then that she would do better at a boarding school and she moved on to Ellerslie School at Malvern, which was conveniently placed for school exeats and holidays in Herefordshire.

My judicial work between 1985 and the summer of 1988, both in London and on circuit, consisted mainly of family cases. In London, the only diversion was provided by three-week sittings in the Court of Appeal, two of them in the Civil Division and two in the Criminal Division. The diet was more varied on circuit because it was usual for the Family Division judge to take a mixed list of civil actions and family cases; but, during this period, the family work grew steadily and I seem to have tried only a couple of criminal cases at first instance.

I continued to enjoy these circuit visits, which were no longer restricted to the Wales and Chester Circuit, as they had been during my period as a presiding judge. In the three and a half years before I transferred to the Queen's Bench Division I made 22 visits to circuit and sat at 14 of the court centres. Only one of these was on the South-Eastern Circuit because most of the family work from that region was heard in London and only Norwich and Lewes were visited by Family Division judges; but the rest of my visits were fairly evenly divided among the other circuits, although Newcastle and Cardiff figured most prominently as a result of the luck of the draw when we made our choice a term in advance.

One is not permitted to write of the family cases that one heard in camera and my main recollection now is of a galaxy of high sheriffs who looked after me during these visits and agreeable judicial companions in lodgings, too many of whom are now dead, most particularly Peter Taylor, who was to become Lord Chief Justice in 1992. I sat with him in February 1985 at Newcastle, which had been his principal home and main centre of practice until he became a judge, and we enjoyed pre-breakfast swims at Consett Baths, when we had the swimming pool to ourselves and followed each other down the excellent slide. Swimming was a much-needed form of exercise on circuit and a small group of us sought out pre-breakfast arrangements at several other towns, including Manchester, Winchester, Lewes (Newhaven) and Cardiff (Radyr).

My last circuit visit as a Family Division judge was to Stafford in June and July 1988 in the company of Mr Justice Tucker; it was an added pleasure to have my daughter Sophie as my marshal immediately after she graduated. She had read philosophy for Part I of the Tripos and then switched to history for Part II, emerging with a 2(1) degree, but she did not show any inclination to follow me into the law and instead was accepted by the National Film School at Beaconsfield to train as a film producer from September 1988. Mr Justice (Richard) Tucker, the son of a former County Court judge and himself a presiding judge of the Midland Circuit, was well known in the region and, as usual, we were very well looked after. I remember particularly delightful evenings with the Heber-Percys (he is now Lord Lieutenant for Shropshire) after touring their lovely garden and with Douglas and Sara Graham (of the *Express and Star* newspapers), with whom I shared a mutual friend in Robin Jenks.

The new Crown Court at Stafford had not been opened by then and we still sat in the old Assize Court in the Shire Hall, immediately behind which were (and probably still are) the judges' lodgings. The dining room gave direct access to one of the courts and I have never been so close to 'living on the job' again. When I returned to Stafford later the new Crown Court was open and within walking distance of the lodgings so that it was refreshing to walk there, rather than to travel by judicial car, before the day's work.

A very pleasant surprise resulting from my roots in Wales was the award of an honorary degree of doctor of laws by the University of Wales in July 1986. The ceremony, conducted by the Prince of Wales as chancellor, took place at Swansea; among my fellow honorary graduands were Sir Harry Secombe, Sir Ronald Mason, Bernard Ashley and Magdi Yacoub (the last two named were both later knighted). It was a very pleasing event, following an excellent dinner at the university the previous evening, at which I was grateful not to have to speak, and I was allowed to take my family to the ceremony in the Brangwyn Hall.

In London nearly all my judicial work in the Family Division was in chambers, that is, in a court hearing to which only the parties and their legal representatives were admitted; not even the judgment could be reported in the press, unless the judge gave a special dispensation for an appropriate reason. There were, however, enjoyable sittings in the Court of Appeal from time to time during which one was exposed, at least potentially, to the full glare of publicity.

In the Court of Appeal Criminal Division probably the most significant judgment that I had to give was in an appeal about the meaning of the word 'new' in section 1(1) of the Trade Descriptions Act 1968, on which I sat with Lord Justice Woolf and Mr Justice French. The appellant defendant was the managing director of a large-scale dealership in Nissan motor cars and the short point was whether cars purchased and registered by his company from Nissan and then later resold to customers were properly described as 'new' when thus resold. The point arose because the manufacturers were, by agreement with the British government, restricted to a specific percentage of the British market; if Nissan did not sell its full quota in a particular year, a percentage equivalent to the shortfall would be allocated in the following year to one or more of the other Japanese manufacturers. Accordingly, it was the practice of Nissan to require its main dealers to register a certain number of cars in each dealer's name before any retail sale took place, in return for which service they received bonus payments.

The trial judge had rejected a submission that there was no case for the defence to answer and had, in effect, left the jury to decide the meaning of the word 'new'; there was quite powerful evidence for the prosecution from purchasers both that they had been misled into believing that they would be the first registered keeper and that they were concerned about the potential impact of the first registration in the dealer's name on the ultimate re-sale value of the car. We were persuaded, therefore, that the judge had been right to leave the matter to the jury and we dismissed the appeal. In the Criminal Division it is the practice for only one judgment, the judgment of the court as a whole, to be delivered and it fell to me in that case to draft it and then to deliver it after it had been read and agreed by the other two judges.

The work in the Civil Division was more varied and I was fortunate to sit there in two separate periods, first with Lord Justice Fox and then with Lord Justice (John) May in July 1987. The most contentious appeal that we dealt with during the latter period raised the familiar question of whether a former wife who began to cohabit with another man on a permanent basis after her divorce was entitled to continuing maintenance from her ex-husband. The marriage had lasted almost 22 years and the wife had obtained a decree on the ground of her husband's behaviour when their two daughters were grown up and financially independent. The trial judge had been satisfied that the decision of the wife and her cohabitee not to marry was 'financially motivated to a very large extent' because to marry would involve the loss by the wife of periodical payments by the husband of £6,000 per annum, an increased amount that had been agreed almost a year after the couple had separated finally.

The case had been heard at first instance by a very experienced retired Circuit judge, who said in his judgment that, if he had not been constrained by higher authority, he would have made an order reducing the payments progressively over a period of two or three years to nil. In the light of the reported cases, however, he decided to reduce the payments to £4,500 per annum from a year hence on the ground that the wife's cohabitee should be able to obtain more remunerative employment by then, reducing the wife's needs by about £1,500 per annum.

These basic facts enabled counsel to deploy the full range of arguments about the basis of maintenance for an ex-wife and to consider a wide sweep of earlier decisions on the application of the relevant provisions of the Matrimonial Causes Act 1973. I concluded:

It follows that I would dismiss the husband's appeal because, on a review of the financial and other circumstances outlined earlier in this judgment, a reduction in the periodical payments order beyond that ordered by the trial judge would not be justified. Any greater decrease would reduce her virtually to poverty level and I do not understand counsel for the husband to argue that there should be a further variation unless the wife's cohabitation is regarded as decisive without detailed consideration of the figures.

I would add finally that I am not impressed by the argument that the result of all this is to make the law appear to be an 'ass'. It may be that, if the bald question were put to a man, rather than a woman, in the street the immediate response would be that maintenance should cease on an ex-wife's cohabitation. What is more important is that, in my view he would be at best nonplussed if presented with the succinct and forceful arguments that have been addressed to us by counsel on both sides on the hearing of this appeal.

See (1987) 3 All ER 849: leave to appeal to the House of Lords was later refused.

A major sadness for our family occurred during this period of my life with the wholly unexpected death of my brother Neil on 31 October 1986 at the age of only 63. He had had some heart trouble but, ironically, had been signed off by his hospital consultant the day before he collapsed and died immediately while driving his motor car. Apparently, an aneurysm burst and it was fortunate that he was driving slowly, after delivering a talk at a business conference in Leeds, and no one else was injured. Neil had faced the ups and downs of life with great courage and optimism and he deserved a kinder fate.

It was earlier in the year of Neil's death that I had my most unusual holiday, flying (without Sarah on this occasion) to Mexico City to stay for nine days in the British ambassador's residence with Kenneth and Teresa James. It was the year of the soccer world cup in Mexico City but more relevant to me was the fact that there had been an earthquake of 8.1 magnitude on 19 September 1985, causing the deaths of about 10,000 people; the later of two serious aftershocks occurred on 30 April 1986. Fortunately for me, nothing untoward occurred while I was there and remarkable progress had already been made in repairing the devastation. The residence was in a very attractive modern building and I enjoyed greatly my one and only experience of diplomatic life at close quarters. Kenneth had been our ambassador to Mexico since 1983, succeeding Sir Crispin Tickell, and was due to retire in April 1986 on reaching the compulsory civil service retirement age of 60, so this was my last opportunity to be with him in post.

We spent a busy week travelling around and visiting Puebla, among other places. One evening there was a medieval and renaissance performance in aid of the British earthquake fund and on another a dinner party for 20 followed by a showing of the film *The Shooting Party*. I remember even more clearly a luncheon party attended by Loel Guinness, then rising 80, who had flown up from Acapulco en route to Houston to give his servants a short rest, the United States ambassador (an actor friend of President Reagan) and both a former Miss Universe and a former Miss Argentina. I did also manage, however, to see an impressive display of Diego Rivera's frescoes in the National Palace.

There was one quite onerous long vacation commitment for me because I had been elected chairman of the Middle Temple's Scholarships and Prizes Committee in succession to Gordon (Lord) Borrie in February 1986, after serving as a member from 1982, and I held that office for four years. The Middle Temple had had a generous range of scholarships to bestow throughout the period during which I had been a member and it had adopted the attractive practice of interviewing every applicant for an award. The interviewing process was carried out by sub-committees, usually during vacations, and taking part was quite demanding, particularly in late September, when the main awards were made. In my last year as chairman, for example, there were 106 applicants that month for Queen Mother's Fund scholarships, 19 of whom had achieved first-class honours degrees and a further 35 had been classed as 2(1).

The leading position of the Middle Temple in the scholarships field has been eroded gradually and there was even some pressure in the late 1980s to centralise the scholarship-awarding processes of the four Inns of Court but, not surprisingly, the idea proved to be unacceptable. It was agreed that the Council of Legal Education (CLE), which was responsible then for the Bar examinations, should award 10 studentships each year from October 1986 and Mr Justice Bingham, as he then was, played a leading role in this. The studentships were tenable for two years and the number was soon increased to 24 but the scheme petered out in the early 1990s and the CLE itself ceased to exist in 1997, when its functions were taken over by other bodies. I enjoyed taking part in the selection process, however, while the scheme lasted.

Recruitment to the Bar has been an unresolved problem throughout my period in the law and most acutely for the past 30 years. It has been difficult for barristers, who are essentially a collection of individuals, even though they amalgamate for limited purposes in sets of chambers, to compete with large and successful firms of solicitors in funding beginners in the law. The earnings of articled clerks employed by the larger firms had risen sharply to more than £25,000 per annum while the scholarship funds of the Inns of

Court and awards by chambers to barrister pupils had not kept pace. Forty years after my student days, when Bar scholarships were only £200 a year, Inns of Court studentships were at the annual rate of £6,000 but were still insufficient to cover the cost of living. Yet the number of applicants for the Bar each year continues to exceed the places available many times over and no one has been able to devise a fair and reliable means of selecting who should survive the entry process.

It was in the summer of 1987 that it became known generally that John Arnold had decided to retire at the age of 72 and speculation about the identity of his successor lasted for five months until it was announced in December that Lord Justice Stephen Brown was to be the new president of the Family Division. Lord Havers had succeeded Lord Hailsham as Lord Chancellor in June of that year and there was some conjecture as early as July in the *Evening Standard* that his sister, Dame Elizabeth Butler-Sloss, might be the new president, but she had to wait several years for Sir Stephen to retire and, meanwhile, was promoted to the Court of Appeal, becoming the first woman to achieve this distinction. These appointments rested, in fact, upon the recommendation of the Prime Minister (still then Margaret Thatcher) rather than the Lord Chancellor. Lord Havers had to retire in October 1987 because of ill health, giving way to Lord Mackay of Clashfern, who held the office for nearly 10 years. Unhelpfully for my own prospects, my name was mentioned as a candidate for the presidency in each of the short newspaper articles on the subject that I saw and *The Times* diary even suggested as late as 4 December that I looked set to follow Sir John as president, by which time Sir Stephen must already have been informed of his appointment.

In July 1987 I had said goodbye to my long-serving clerk, Stanley Boyle, who had been with me since my appointment. Stanley had never encumbered himself with a wife, although he enjoyed female company; he favoured circuit life with all three judges whom he served successively. He retired to live with his sister in Liverpool and I saw him occasionally when I sat there or at Chester. In his place I appointed Ronald Kidd, an ex-detective chief inspector of the Metropolitan Police and a very different personality, who served me well until shortly before my own retirement. He was a capable secretary and both his son and his daughter achieved excellent professional positions, the former as a partner in a major firm of London solicitors and the latter as an accountant here and in Australia.

The new president of the Family Division took office from the beginning of the term in January 1988 and I decided by Easter that it would be sensible for me to 'test the water' about a possible transfer to the Queen's Bench

Division in view of Tasker Watkins' offer to me three years earlier. I had been happy in the Family Division but I thought that, after 10 years, a change was likely to be refreshing for me. A further consideration was that I did not expect any advancement or particularly interesting opportunities under Stephen Brown. While we were friendly enough, we were very different in temperament and outlook and there were other judges with whom he was more in tune. I also looked forward to working more closely with Lord Lane, the Lord Chief Justice, for whom I had considerable affection and admiration, if he were to agree to my transfer.

I raised the possibility with Tasker soon after Easter and, to my relief, he welcomed the idea. Soon afterwards he told me that Geoffrey Lane approved and I learnt at Stafford on 1 July that the transfer was going through. The Lord Chancellor signed the necessary order 10 days later, providing that it took effect on 1 August. I must emphasise that I left the Family Division with some regrets because I had enjoyed my time as a judge of that division and my sense of satisfaction with its work lasted much longer than I had expected. The comparatively small number of judges in the division encouraged a sense of fellowship, and both George Baker and John Arnold gave me opportunities to vary my range of work. It was a great benefit to serve both on the Employment Appeal Tribunal and as a presiding judge and there were two other fields in which I was particularly active. The first was law reform because I became a member of the trio of judges of the division forming a sub-committee to advise on this from 1979. Our chairman at first was Mr Justice Dunn, until he was elevated, when Mr Justice Balcombe took over, and then I was chairman from 1985 to 1988 after he went to the Court of Appeal. The other subject was the newly fashionable procedure of conciliation, in relation to which John Arnold asked me to act as his representative and to report to him. In the past this had not developed at all in the field of divorce, not least because any form of collusion between the parties could be a bar to obtaining a decree. By the 1980s, however, much of the old law on that subject had been swept aside and conciliation was being encouraged in the interests of the children of broken marriages and in the hope of minimising bitterness as far as possible.

This is not the place to discuss the work done in these areas during my decade in the Family Division but I am glad to say that the judges, including many senior and experienced Circuit judges, were ready to play a full part in these developments, including the establishment of the Family Court. It was undoubtedly a stimulating time and the legal issues that had to be dealt with were much wider ranging than outsiders realised. The only tiresome repetitive work tended to be disputes about access to children, founded upon the bitterness of the marital breakdown, especially those in which the former wife sought to deny access on the grounds of trumped-up allegations against the ex-husband (and sometimes his girlfriend).

My major legal regret, shared with most of the other Family Division judges of my period, was the imposition of unnecessary and inappropriate restrictions on their jurisdiction in wardship by Parliament in 1989, a subject on which I disagreed profoundly with Baroness Hale of Richmond, who (as Brenda Hoggett) was the relevant law commissioner at the time. The changes, which greatly fettered judicial supervision of local authorities in relation to looked-after children and children at risk were already being canvassed when I left the division, and it appeared to me that the proposals were being made in the interests of financial economy rather than the best interests of the child, although I do not suggest that this was Mrs Hoggett's own reasoning. The views of the judges on the subject were set out in a memorandum that I drafted, which the president sent to the Law Commission on 22 July 1987 in response to its working paper number 101.

21

QUEEN'S BENCH JUDGE

My last eight years as a judge in the Queen's Bench Division culminated in a year in office as Treasurer of the Middle Temple in 1995. Substantial changes occurred during that period and the workload seemed always to be increasing. For half of it Lord Lane remained Lord Chief Justice but he retired in 1992 and was succeeded by Lord Taylor of Gosforth. Very sadly, Lord Taylor developed cancer and had to retire in 1996, when Lord Bingham of Cornhill, who had succeeded Lord Donaldson as Master of the Rolls in 1992, was appointed Lord Chief Justice and Lord Woolf then became the new Master of the Rolls. As for the work of the Queen's Bench Division, immigration had not then become a major cause of litigation as it now is, but judicial review was developing very rapidly, with troubling political problems about the jurisdiction of the judges coming to the surface, and the concept of an administrative court had already taken shape.

I was not assigned to this embryonic administrative court and was not sufficiently enthusiastic about much of its work to volunteer for it. Instead, in London, where I sat usually for half of each term, my normal diet was three weeks in the Court of Appeal Criminal Division and three weeks trying civil actions or occasionally sitting with a Lord Justice for three weeks as a Queen's Bench Divisional Court to hear mainly appeals on points of law from magistrates' courts. The nature of the civil work dealt with in London, apart from that in the commercial court, had also changed quite radically as the result of a series of procedural changes made before Lord Woolf's own recommendations on access to justice in 1995 and 1996. An effect of these earlier changes was that an increasing proportion of personal-injury claims arising from road and industrial accidents were being settled by insurers by agreement before trial. In contrast, the volume of contested litigation based on alleged professional negligence, particularly medical negligence, seemed to be expanding rapidly. Cases in this category necessarily involved substantial expert evidence and the facts on which they were based were often quite complex so that one's three-week slot of civil work could be filled with a single professional negligence action.

My initiation into the Queen's Bench Division was a baptism of fire because I was required immediately to try long and difficult civil actions, the first at Newcastle and the second in London. In both cases, although the plaintiffs had suffered serious physical damage without fault on their part, I was compelled to find in favour of the defendants.

The first case was unusual, although later it proved not to be unique. The plaintiff was a widower whose wife had died in January 1986 of mesothelioma and the essence of his claims was that the disease had been caused by the inhalation of asbestos dust by his wife from his own working clothes during that period of his marriage when he was exposed to heavy concentrations of the dust as a plater employed by shipbuilders at Wallsend between 1948 and 1965. I was familiar with the link between asbestos and mesothelioma because, as a junior barrister, I had attended one of the first inquests at which it had been established, and asbestos-related litigation had become rife in my last years at the Bar. This was the first time, however, that I had heard of the transmission of asbestos dust from a workman's clothes to an outsider.

A great deal of expert evidence was given during the trial and I was persuaded that the plaintiff had proved his case on the physical cause of his wife's death. Unfortunately, however, knowledge of the risks associated with exposure to asbestos had progressed very slowly and it was not until the publication of a medical paper in 1965 that the incidence of mesothelioma among the immediate family of asbestos workers became publicly known. I could not therefore hold conscientiously that the employers in my case ought to have foreseen the risk of injury to the plaintiff's wife before the end of his relevant period of employment. Since my decision one or two other judges have found for the plaintiffs in cases involving similar exposure to asbestos-affected clothing over different periods and on the basis of different expert evidence but, on the evidence before me, I could not find likewise and there was no appeal from my decision.

The second case involved two civil actions that I tried together and which lasted nearly a month in November and December 1988. Both plaintiffs had suffered severe burns in separate accidents in March 1968 (when the first plaintiff was three and a half years old) and August 1969 (when the second plaintiff was just under nine months old); both had had their burns sprayed while they were in hospital, one in Carshalton and the other in Merton, with neuromycin powder, following which they had become profoundly deaf. The complexity of the issues arising in the trial is underlined by the fact that my judgment, delivered after the Christmas vacation, extended to 100 pages. But the basic problem of the foreseeability of injury was similar to that in the Newcastle case.

The first aerosol spray for administering neomycin powder with two other drugs in powder form had been produced by a Cheshire company in 1956; it was used at first in surgery because the drugs were used to kill bacteria. It was called polybactrin, and a substantial trade in it developed rapidly, its use being extended later to the treatment of burns. This led to the development of a cheaper alternative spray, referred to as a generic spray, and my finding was that it was strongly probable that the latter had been used in the treatment of both plaintiffs. Moreover, on the balance of probabilities, neomycin alone could be blamed for the plaintiffs' disability. It is an antibiotic that was developed in 1949 but was of limited use because of its toxic side effects, including permanent deafness, when injected. It was not thought, however, to cause such side effects when administered orally or topically (to the body surface) and that was the state of knowledge when the polybactrin aerosol was first produced.

There was no satisfactory evidence as to when neomycin first came to be used in the treatment of burns but in about late 1960 clinical tests of polybactrin were instituted by one of the leading burns units in the UK and a report about them was published in the *Lancet* in November 1962. The report did not reveal any toxic effects of the treatment and showed that the spray was effective in countering infection. The result of this report was that polybactrin became widely used in the treatment of burns and there was no warning in this country that neomycin might cause deafness as a result of topical application until a leading article entitled 'Deafness after Topical Neomycin' appeared in the *British Medical Journal* after, but not because of, the treatment of both plaintiffs. The *British Medical Journal* article referred to a case in Columbus, Ohio, reported in the *New England Journal of Medicine* in June 1969.

These basic facts are sufficient to indicate the scope of the arguments before me. I was not persuaded that the defendants could be held liable on the basis of what lawyers call 'strict liability' for supplying a substance akin to poison; and, in my judgment, the plaintiffs could only succeed if they could show that the health authorities should, in 1968/69, have foreseen that there was a risk of injury to a patient by the topical application of neomycin to burns.

The plaintiffs relied on four expert witnesses and argued that there had been pointers from 1962 onwards that should have made the health authorities aware that neomycin might be absorbed from the surface of burns and should have prompted appropriate trials. The defendants, however, were able to counter that trials had demonstrated the efficacy of polybactrin in combating infection and that it was still being administered in significant quantities worldwide without any relevant warning until October 1969. This argument proved to be decisive: all the relevant medical literature had been combed through; there was no other persuasive basis on which the plaintiffs' case could be put. As I said at the end of my judgment, I reached my conclusions with some dissatisfaction. It was alarming that the possibility that neomycin might be absorbed to a significant extent had not been foreseen and that the causal link between neomycin and deafness in individual cases was still a matter of conjecture. I felt also that it was regrettable that no compensation could be awarded to the plaintiffs, who were medical casualties through no fault of their own. The *News of the World* echoed this and it provoked critical comment from my friend Lord Ashley.

For Sarah and me, the most intriguing social event in the autumn of 1988 was a weekend at Chevening as guests of Geoffrey and Elspeth Howe, when our fellow guests were the president of the European Economic Community, Jacques Delors, and his wife Marie, the Pallisers (he a former permanent under-secretary of state at the Foreign Office), Lady Elizabeth Cavendish, the long-standing friend of John Betjeman, and Anthony Hobson, the historian. The following day there was a large luncheon party for the Japanese ambassador and his wife and at least 10 other additional guests, including my Cambridge friend Lord Thomas of Swynnerton; the house party visited Chartwell before lunch.

That year ended with a family Christmas again in Herefordshire but already our children were beginning to disperse. Thomas had been posted to New York by American Express at the end of August 1988 and worked (essentially trained) there for just over a year at its new headquarters in the 51-storey Three World Financial Center, which was damaged 13 years later in the terrorist attack on the World Trade Center directly opposite. He was, however, able to return to the UK briefly for a Christmas holiday. Sophie had visited India, Nepal and Tibet during the summer holiday but had then embarked on a postgraduate training as a film producer at the National Film and Television School at Beaconsfield.

The general pattern of my judicial life remained much the same from October 1988 to December 1994. In that period I spent about 121 weeks in lodgings on circuit, equivalent to about three working years in London, where I sat for about the same number of weeks; about 46 weeks were spent in the Court of Appeal Criminal Division; just under 10 weeks in the Queen's Bench Divisional Court and six weeks in the autumn of 1989 at the Old Bailey. Only about 10 weeks a year were left for the civil work that had been my staple fare at the Bar. In that period of six years and three months I sat in 18 different crown courts, all of them only once or twice, except for Swansea, which I visited three times. The result was that, in the course of my 18 years and three months as a judge, I sat in most of the main court centres in England and Wales; my only regret was that I missed out some of the attractive smaller centres such as Truro and Carlisle.

These rather dry statistics do underline the considerable demands made upon Queen's Bench and Family judges in terms of absence from home and general competence in dealing with a wide range of criminal and civil work. They are too easily forgotten when glib suggestions are made about dispensing with judges' lodgings and compelling judges to stay in local hotels. It is very doubtful whether any significant savings in costs could be achieved, bearing in mind staff requirements, the work to be done outside court hours and the need for security in relation to the judges' working papers and so on. But what is more important is that few top practitioners would be willing to sacrifice living at home for long periods of hotel existence; I believe that recruitment for the High Court bench is already increasingly difficult without that obvious additional disincentive.

My own circuit visits as a Queen's Bench judge were dominated by a small number of very different criminal trials which attracted widespread newspaper coverage. The first of these was the trial of the comedian Kenneth Dodd in June and July 1989 at Liverpool for alleged tax evasion. Then there were three specific murder trials worth mentioning at Liverpool, Newport and Leeds in 1992, 1993 and 1994, and lastly (but not in sequence) the trial of Derek Hatton and six others early in 1993 at Mold for alleged conspiracies to defraud.

Of these, the trial of Ken Dodd was easily the most notorious and still attracts interest, not least because Dodd himself refers to it quite frequently. Lord Lane asked me to try the case and it was the main reason for my sitting at Liverpool on that occasion. Altogether the hearing lasted five weeks but it was delayed for nearly a fortnight at the outset by a surprise application made by Dodd's counsel, George Carman QC, with virtually no notice beforehand.

I had appeared against Carman more than once as a junior barrister and was on quite friendly terms with him. However, I had not had any experience of him as a QC and had been warned by another judge, who was a mutual friend, to be watchful when dealing with him. This warning seemed to me to be justified when Carman applied for the case to be adjourned indefinitely on the ground that his client was unfit to stand trial. He produced a medical report to the effect that Dodd was suffering from emphysema and a heart condition that could be life threatening, particularly if he was subjected to the prolonged stress of a trial. The prosecution had not had any opportunity to obtain another medical opinion. My own lay view, which I stated in court, was that a similar report could probably be written about many men in their sixties but obviously the case had to be adjourned for a fortnight to enable the prosecution to obtain a second opinion. In the event, when we reassembled there was no request for a further adjournment and Dodd has pursued his career with great success for the past 20 years.

It would be inappropriate to rake again over all the issues that arose during the trial but it was unusual for many reasons. One was the fact that the trial took place in Liverpool itself, where Dodd lived and was so well known, apparently because the prosecution thought that it would seem to be an admission of weakness if an application were to be made to have it tried elsewhere. Secondly, Dodd was to a substantial extent the author of his own misfortune because he had over the years retained very large sums of money in cash, which he had then transported to banks in Jersey and the Isle of Man, subsequently denying or at least failing to acknowledge the existence of those bank deposits when questioned by tax inspectors, who had seen letters from Dodd to his accountant that had alerted them to the possibility that he had undisclosed assets.

The prosecution case against Dodd involved an attempted reconstruction of his income throughout his career in order to show that he had evaded income tax; there were also some specific counts in the indictment alleging that he had been paid more than he had declared for a series of individual 'gigs'. His answer to these latter counts was straightforward: the difference between the amount that he had declared for each 'gig' and the amount that he had received from the promoter was represented by the cash paid to him on top of his personal fee to enable him to pay his numerous assistants, including the band at the performance, all of whom required to be paid in cash straightaway. As for the more general charge, Dodd said that he had relied on his accountant to present correct returns, emphasising the chaotic state of his affairs administratively; he said that he had believed advertisements and advice from bank managers to the effect that he was not liable for income tax on any interest etc. earned in the Channel Islands or the Isle of Man.

This, in very brief summary, was the battle fought out before the jury and me over several weeks. There is no doubt that Dodd was defended brilliantly by Carman and I was amazed to read years later, in Carman's biography by his son, that he spent most nights during the trial gambling until the early hours in casinos. It must be said also that there were major weaknesses in the prosecution case. Dodd's accountant was serving a sentence of imprisonment for dishonesty wholly unconnected with Dodd, and the prosecution did not call him as a witness. As for the bank managers, they were outside the jurisdiction of the Crown Court and could not be compelled to give evidence for either side. Moreover, reconstruction of a person's lifetime earnings on limited factual material inevitably involves a substantial degree of speculation rather than proof and Dodd was able to show that he was a man of excellent character and charitable disposition, who had the support in evidence of such popular members of his profession as Eric Sykes and Roy Hudd. Perhaps equally importantly, it was common ground between the prosecution and defence (and, indeed, notorious) that Dodd had been almost eccentrically thrifty, not to say miserly, in his personal expenditure throughout his life, enabling him to save an unusually high proportion of his income.

The jury retired for just over a day, staying at a hotel overnight, and then acquitted Dodd of all the charges amid scenes of great jubilation. There were so many assembled outside the court on the final Friday of the hearing that I had some difficulty in reaching the court door from the judicial motor car. The overall financial cost to Dodd, however, was very severe in payments of tax, penalties and legal costs. I was told that, despite the failure of the prosecution, the Inland Revenue was satisfied with the outcome because so many tax defaulters had communicated with them during the trial, offering to make full disclosure of their financial affairs. This was the result of the publicity given during the trial to an Inland Revenue practice, following a wartime decision by Sir John Anderson as Chancellor of the Exchequer, of waiving the threat of prosecution if truthful information was provided after a solemn warning invoking the rule had been given by a tax inspector.

Between the beginning of 1989 and the end of 1994 I tried, to the best of my recollection, about 22 cases of alleged murder and three of attempted murder, involving in all some 29 defendants. About a quarter of these defendants were found guilty of the lesser offence of manslaughter but only three were acquitted altogether. One of those acquitted was tried by me at Leeds in February and March 1994 and the case attracted national attention because I had to rule as inadmissible an unambiguous confession by the defendant that he had killed his wife. The prosecution's difficulty was that a woman detective had extracted the confession after several meetings with the defendant following his response to a 'lonely hearts' advertisement by another woman. That woman had sought advice from the police as to whether it would be safe for her to reply and the police had arranged that the detective would take her place in order to meet the defendant. The detective subsequently responded to the defendant's amorous advances (including talk of marriage) by insisting that she needed to know what had happened to the defendant's wife, who had apparently disappeared without warning. He was obviously under suspicion for murder and it was a clear case of entrapment by fraud so that I could not permit the confession to be put before the jury.

Various 'media' organisations then instructed Gilbert Gray QC to apply for permission to report the argument about the confession and its admissibility once the verdict had been given and he was able to demonstrate that there was no lawful basis on which I could refuse the application. Thus, the details of the confession were published widely despite their inadmissibility as evidence in the trial (there was no possibility then of a second trial following an acquittal, even if fresh evidence came to light). The result was that the case became front-page news in all the major newspapers that weekend and provoked first leading articles in the *Daily Telegraph* and the *Sunday Times*. While some representatives of the police criticised my decision to exclude evidence of the defendant's confession, I was relieved that the majority of comment from other sources, particularly from those familiar with the relevant rules, was supportive.

A strange coincidence was that Mr Justice Ognall was presented with a very similar problem at the Old Bailey later that year when trying Colin Stagg on a charge of murdering Rachel Nickel two years earlier on Wimbledon Common. That judge had been sitting at Leeds and sharing the lodgings with me when I was trying the case that I have just summarised and he was obviously aware of my ruling. In the Stagg case he rightly ruled that the defendant's alleged confession was inadmissible and the prosecution case collapsed (in any event the 'confession' was not truly an admission of the charge). Now, well over a decade after that trial, another man has pleaded guilty to the manslaughter of that tragic victim.

One of the men convicted of murder before me appealed successfully against his conviction. The Court of Appeal ordered a retrial on the ground that his able leading counsel, now a High Court judge, had uncharacteristically misunderstood a correct evidential ruling that I had given and had consequentially failed to pursue cross-examination of a witness who might have proved favourable to the defendant. The latter was a cold, calculating man who had murdered his wife and had then taken careful steps to try to establish an alibi, apparently following a pattern derived from an earlier notorious Liverpool case.

The trial before me at Liverpool early in 1992 lasted almost a month and I was mortified that an expensive retrial had been ordered by the Court of Appeal. In the event the witness I have referred to was not called by the prosecution or the defence at the retrial before Mr Justice McCullough: the defendant was convicted again and the judge made the same recommendation for the minimum period of detention of the defendant as I had done, without knowing what my recommendation had been. If you detect a certain edge in my account of this, you will be correct. My ruling, in accordance with well-established law, had been that a witness cannot be cross-examined by putting to her a previous written statement by her unless and until she has given some oral evidence inconsistent with that written statement (she had merely been called to the witness box by counsel for the prosecution, who had chosen not to ask her any questions).

A substantial proportion of these murder trials were sad domestic cases in which the victim was usually a wife, whether or not she had done anything to provoke the fatal attack. But others were quite horrifying for different reasons. They ranged from a case at Nottingham in which a father procured the murder of his mistress by his own son to the murder in Hastings by a member of a Hells Angels group known as the London Road Rats of the leader of a rival group from Birmingham known as the Cycle Tramps. Security for this latter trial at Lewes in March and April 1990 was extremely strict because the two opposing 'chapters' were encamped nearby for the occasion and police snipers were even posted on the roof of the court. There was no untoward incident, however, and the defendant was duly convicted by a unanimous verdict.

The longest of these murder trials took place in Newport in 1993 and lasted seven weeks. The defendant was a 31-year-old habitual gambler who entered a Newport betting office just before it closed at 6 p.m. and stabbed the young manageress nine times in the back before strangling her with a telephone flex and then leaving with the day's takings of £440. Having committed this offence, he resumed a holiday with his wife and young daughter at Weymouth. There was quite abundant evidence to identify the defendant as the offender, including a thumbprint and a shoe mark, but it was one of the early cases in which the prosecution was able to rely upon DNA evidence in relation to various bloodspots found in an inner office and on the defendant's black jacket, which was recovered from his home. Leading counsel for the defendant, John Charles Rees QC, launched a wholesale attack on the forensic evidence, particularly that based on DNA, making the ingenious (or perhaps ingenuous) suggestion that conventional statistics about the reliability of such evidence could not be regarded as applicable in South Wales because of the extent of the interbreeding that had occurred there over the centuries.

This surprising suggestion led the prosecution to call additional evidence from a University of Wales professor of economic history about population movements in South Wales during and since the Industrial Revolution. He was able to say that, for well over a century, there had been a tremendous inflow of workers, including Italians, into the valleys in pursuit of employment in the numerous coalmines and iron and steel works. Thus, a misunderstanding of history and a slur on the population of South Wales were avoided and the defendant was rightly convicted.

Probably the most dangerous man who appeared before me was not charged with murder but with attempted murder. He was Peter Tobin, who came before me at Winchester on 16 May 1994, when he pleaded guilty to raping two 14-year-old girls who were babysitting for his son at Havant. He had held the girls at knifepoint and forced them to drink strong cider and vodka; he had gone on the run after committing the offences. The prosecution rightly accepted his pleas of not guilty to attempted murder, which is always difficult to prove because an actual intention to kill has to be proved, in contrast to murder, in which an intent to cause very serious physical injury is sufficient. The case was so grave, however, that I sentenced him to concurrent terms of 14 years' imprisonment, from which he was not released until 2004. Since then, he has been convicted of murdering three young women: one was a Polish student murdered in Glasgow in September 2006 after his release from my sentences but the other two had been killed before I dealt with him.

The trial of Derek Hatton and four co-defendants at Mold Crown Court lasted eight weeks from January to March 1993 and attracted almost as much attention as the Dodd trial nearly two years earlier. Although the relevant events had all taken place in Liverpool, the venue of the trial had wisely been changed to Mold to avoid any prejudice either way. Hatton was by then a notorious figure and had been a leading member of the controversial dominant group on Liverpool City Council, dubbed by the press as socialist militants. Two of the other defendants had been fellow city councillors. The other two defendants were Liverpool businessmen alleged to have been the beneficiaries of certain land transactions in which the council had been involved. The relevant pieces of land were two valuable car parking lots and a 20-acre building site in respect of which an option to purchase had been granted.

While the case for the prosecution was reasonably clear, there were serious weaknesses in the evidence available to establish the three counts of conspiracy to defraud on which the trial proceeded. The prosecution was ably conducted by Alan Rawley QC but there was no direct evidence to support any of the adverse inferences that the jury was asked to draw. The result was that, when the prosecution evidence closed after six weeks, I heard strong submissions on behalf of each of the defendants, lasting four days in all, to the effect that there was no case to answer; I upheld those submissions in relation to the third count, which referred to the building site and was laid against Hatton, a woman councillor and one of the businessmen. The latter was charged only in that count so he walked free but I ruled, with some hesitation, that the case should proceed against the remaining four defendants on the two other counts.

A major problem was that, in the end, much of the case rested upon a couple of documents found in a desk at Hatton's office premises and various diary entries that he had made. All the entries were terse and rather ambiguous, however, and the more important referred to persons by their initials only, if they were references to individuals. There was a great deal of speculation involved in the inferences against the defendants that the prosecution relied upon and little other evidence to support them. There was also the serious evidential difficulty that Hatton's own jottings could only be regarded as evidence against the others if they had been made in furtherance of the alleged conspiracies rather than merely for his own benefit; such a distinction is a very fine one even for a trained lawyer to apply, let alone a lay jury.

It was not surprising in these circumstances that none of the remaining defendants elected to give evidence. Rodney Klevan QC, who was the leader of the Northern Circuit and later a High Court judge, made a particularly witty speech on behalf of Hatton, referring to the contribution made by the huge amount of paper in the case to the destruction of the Brazilian jungle, and all the defendants were acquitted after the jury had retired for just over a day. Hatton was touchingly grateful to his leading counsel, describing him to the press as the best in the world. Jonathan Foster commented in the *Independent*, 'Even if all three charges had been successful, the sums involved in the two car park licenses were so small in terms of land value and alleged bribes and the evidence so ambiguous that prosecution was scarcely justified.'

My first experience of trying a civil jury action in London was another northern case attracting blanket newspaper coverage. This was William Roache (*Coronation Street*'s Ken Barlow) against the *Sun* newspaper, which I

tried in the autumn of 1991. He was the only actor who had remained with
the soap opera from its beginning, a period of 30 years by the date when the
Sun's article about him appeared in November 1990. The article alleged that
he had been nicknamed 'boring Ken Barlow' universally and that it was a
reputation that 'the poor bloke' had earned both on and off the TV screen.
There were other wounding assertions but the nub of his complaint was that
he had been untruly and unfairly dubbed 'boring' and it was this word that
was echoed in all the press comment as the hearing proceeded. Needless to
say, the press enjoyed several field days as the plaintiff's case unfolded and a
series of stars from the show gave evidence on his behalf. The newspaper did
not have much evidential basis for its defences of truth and fair comment
and the jury duly found in the plaintiff's favour, awarding him £50,000
damages.

This was a most unfortunate assessment from the plaintiff's point of view
because, unknown to the jury and to me, that amount precisely had been
paid into court by the defendant a very short time before the trial began.
It meant that the defendant's leading counsel, Charles (later Mr Justice)
Gray QC, was able to submit forcefully that the plaintiff had gained nothing
by pursuing his action after the payment had been made: counsel asked
therefore that the plaintiff should be ordered to pay both sides costs from
the date of the payment in, which was the normal order prescribed by the
rules of court in such circumstances.

It was then that I made what I regard as my worst mistake as a judge.
The hour was late and I should have adjourned my decision overnight but I
was persuaded by the plaintiff's leading counsel, David (also later, and still,
Mr Justice) Eady QC to grant the plaintiff an injunction restraining the
defendant from repeating the libel and consequentially to grant the plaintiff
his costs of the action to be paid by the defendant, despite the payment into
court. It was proper to grant the injunction, bearing in mind the way in
which the defence had been conducted, but that was not a sufficient reason
for denying the defendant the usual costs order in its favour. I confess that
I was led into this error by sympathy for the plaintiff, who was faced with
a financial disaster and who was represented by a strong-minded solicitor
whose judgement in the matter I doubted.

In the end justice prevailed because the Court of Appeal allowed the
defendant's appeal against my costs order and made the normal order in its
favour. I did note with concern, however, that the Court of Appeal discovered
that the plaintiff's solicitor had responded to the offer or payment into court
of £50,000 by demanding £200,000, to include £60,000 in respect of the
plaintiff's legal costs.

The other libel action worth mentioning, which attracted much less public attention, was brought by Wafic Said, a Syrian-born multi-millionaire arms dealer and philanthropist who established the Said Business School at Oxford University in 1996. Said's background was that he had moved to Saudi Arabia in 1969 and had become close to Prince Khalid bin Sultan, a member of the Saudi Arabian royal family and a leading military and business figure. A result was that Said played an important role in various substantial arms deals between Saudi Arabia and Britain involving billions of dollars and including what was called the Al-Yamamah arms deal in 1985.

The defendant in the libel action was an Arab of very small means called Misbah Baki, who was a former college friend of Said and happened to be a distant relation through marriage. It seems that Baki had got himself into substantial financial difficulties in 1986 to the tune of more than £200,000 by stock exchange speculation and had gone to Said for help. Said had responded by giving him £100,000. Nevertheless, Baki considered that he had been let down badly by Said because, in his view, Said had promised to give him sufficient to pay off his debts fully. He manifested his bitterness by publishing scandalous gossip about Said in an Arab magazine but the subject of the libel action against him was a letter that he had written to Prince Khalid accusing Said of breaking his word. Said's case was that this allegation was particularly damaging to him because in the Middle East many deals involving millions were sealed with a handshake: a man's word was his bond, so Bakim's accusation to Said's business friend was highly defamatory.

The defendant represented himself at the hearing and sought to establish that what he had said in the letter was true. A particular problem was that Baki wanted to widen the issues by calling evidence from the ex-chairman of another arms firm about the Al-Yamamah agreement signed by Mrs Thatcher. This man had given widely publicised evidence to a House of Commons select committee, in which he had alleged that there had been inappropriate links between Mrs Thatcher, her son Mark and Said, but there was no basis on which such evidence could be regarded as relevant to the action before me, even if it was within the witness' own direct knowledge. I ruled therefore that it was inadmissible and the public were denied the pleasure of hearing further irrelevant gossip.

Said won his action, almost inevitably, but I was shocked by the jury's assessment of the damages at £400,000. Said had said in his evidence that he intended to give any sum that he recovered to charity and it was reasonably clear that Baki would be unable to pay any substantial sum on top of the plaintiff's legal costs for a nine-day trial. In a sense, therefore, the jury's verdict was simply a gesture, fully vindicating Said, but, in my summing up, I had counselled moderation in the assessment, bearing in mind the very limited publication of the libel, even though the recipient was both royal and highly influential. I have never been told what happened about the damages and costs but I am sure that the plaintiff suffered a substantial net financial loss as a result of the litigation.

The rest of my time sitting in London as a Queen's Bench judge was mainly spent, as I have said, trying civil cases without a jury and hearing criminal appeals. Some of these cases were of particular interest including a specially complex civil action and a very unusual criminal appeal.

The civil action involved two paintings sold by Sotheby's in November 1989 and June 1990 to an international establishment for £2.4 million. These paintings were by the Catalan impressionist Joaquin Sorolla y Bastida (1863–1923). The plaintiff in the action was a New York charitable foundation that claimed title to the two pictures under the self-made will of its founder and subsequent transactions entered into by the Cuban 'executor'. Sotheby's and the purchaser from them, on the other hand, contended as defendants that the will and the executor's transactions had been void and that the sales by Sotheby's had been valid on the basis of title acquired by the state of Cuba through prescription ('*usucapio*' or long undisputed possession) and subsequently passed to valid intermediate purchasers before being sent by the last of these to Sotheby's for sale.

The two paintings were part of a notable collection made by Oscar Cintas, a former Cuban ambassador to the United States who died in May 1957, very shortly after setting up his foundation and just over 18 months before the Cuban revolution. The collection was deposited on loan to the National Museum of Havana in September 1959 by the judicial administrator for one of the beneficiaries of the Cuban estate; that loan was made permanent, as far as the museum was concerned, a year later.

In order to succeed in its action to recover the paintings, the plaintiff had to win on about eight difficult issues involving the interpretation of the Cuban will and another New York will as well as Cuban testamentary law and procedure, which had to be proved by expert witnesses on either side, and various decrees made by the revolutionary government. In the end I was persuaded that both wills were valid and that there had been a valid disposition of the residuary estate for the benefit of the poor of Havana. I held also that the state of Cuba had not acquired title to the collection by nationalisation or by adverse possession but that the evidence did establish that the plaintiff's action was statute barred, albeit only by a couple of months, in accordance with a new Cuban code that came into force in April 1988.

The most bizarre appeal that I sat on came before the court in October 1994, when Lord Taylor was presiding and the third member was Mr Justice Bell. The appellant had been convicted at Hove Crown Court of murdering by shooting a married couple at their cottage home and there was no suggestion of any error in the trial before the jury retired to consider their verdicts. However, the jury were unable to reach a decision that day and were put up at a local hotel overnight before delivering unanimous verdicts of guilty the following day. The problem was that the court became aware subsequently of an allegation by a juror that, at the hotel, some members of the jury had purported to make contact with the deceased man by means of a Ouija board and to have received certain information from him.

This appeal raised quite difficult questions about the extent to which, if at all, it was permissible for the Court of Appeal to inquire into a jury's activities when it retired to consider a verdict and how any such inquiry could be carried out properly. Our conclusion was that we were entitled to inquire into what had happened in the hotel (when the jury were not supposed to be considering their verdicts) but not into what happened in the jury room later. The upshot was that we received affidavits sworn by each of the 12 jurors and the two jury bailiffs. From these it was clear that, despite strong injunctions to the contrary from the bailiffs, four jurors had assembled in the bedroom of one of them and that a form of seance had taken place in which the appellant was named as the murderer and his motive was stated to be money. Moreover, what had occurred had been discussed with the other jurors at breakfast the following morning. On this evidence we had little hesitation in concluding that there had been a material irregularity and that there was a real danger that what had happened in the Ouija session might have influenced some jurors. We therefore allowed the appeal and ordered a retrial. The whole episode had the flavour of a television play rather than a real-life (and very grave) criminal trial.

As 1995 approached, I became increasingly preoccupied with the affairs of the Middle Temple. However, because I would be based in London throughout my year of office as Treasurer and I expected to retire in that year, I was allowed to visit my old circuit in the autumn of 1994. This was a very nostalgic trip for me in the first half of the Michaelmas term and, in the course of it, I sat at Chester and Swansea, each for three weeks. There were, of course, parties for the Bar, and my visit ended with a very well-attended Bar mess at the Marriott Hotel in Swansea for which my pupil master Bill Mars-Jones, by then retired, made a special journey from London. I was also touched by the presence of Tasker Watkins, Alun Talfan Davies and Philip Owen, all stalwarts of the circuit who travelled far to be there. My election as Treasurer by the Middle Temple parliament followed in December, eight days after our family dinner for benchers at which I had the honour of sitting on the right of our royal bencher HM the Queen Mother, who was then 94 years old and still in vigorous form.

22

FAMILY EVENTS AND MORE EXTRA-JUDICIAL ACTIVITY

The major family events for us between 1988 and 1994 were the marriage of our son Thomas, and the death of my mother the following year. My mother died peacefully on 17 December 1993, when I was fortunate to be with her. She was 97 years old and had managed to live in a ground-floor flat in Fernshaw Road, Chelsea, near to my sister, until 1989, albeit with nursing care from August 1988, but after a fall in November 1989 and admission to hospital she agreed that she should move to the comfortable Meadbank nursing home in Park Gate Road, Battersea, on 30 January 1990; it was there that she died. I was particularly glad that we had mustered a large family party at the nursing home for her ninety-fifth birthday, which she was able to enjoy with all her wits about her. But she was beginning to fail at the time of our lunch party for her two years later. She was buried in the same grave as my father and brother Tom at Calcoed Chapel on Brynford Common just before Christmas after a funeral service at our former church in Holywell.

Like many other women of her generation, my mother led what now seems to have been an almost saintly life as a married woman and then had to endure very many years of lonely widowhood, in her case 32 years. She worked exceptionally hard looking after my father, who was quite demanding, and four children with only a small amount of domestic help, particularly in the later years. My father was not expected to help with any of the domestic chores. Despite this imbalance, my mother always seemed to be cheerful and she found time to play an important role in a variety of public activities, including the Women's Liberal Federation, the

Women's Institute, of which she was county chairman, and demanding work as the local representative of the Soldiers, Sailors, Airmen and Families Association (SSAFA) throughout the war. Above all, she was always spoken of with great affection because of her charm and modesty. My father was indeed a lucky man to have found such a partner and to be provided with such a secure basis for his own life and work.

The year 1992 was momentous for Thomas because he married a Danish girl, whom he had met at American Express, and also left that bank, after very nearly eight years there, in order to move to another city bank. This was the Japanese bank Sumitomo (then the second largest in the world), now Sumitomo Mitsui Banking Corporation Europe Ltd or SMBC Europe Division, where he joined the project finance team and has remained ever since, currently as head of energy and natural resources and a joint general manager. Our first grandson David was born on 5 December 1993. Then Thomas was posted to Hong Kong in October 1996, 18 months after moving from Emperor's Gate to a house in Edenbridge, Kent. A second son, James, was born on 1 June 1996 shortly before the move to Hong Kong, and Mark was born on 15 September 1998 while they were still out there. They stayed in Hong Kong for nearly two and a half years before returning to Kent at the end of February 1999.

Sophie completed her course at the National Film and Television School in the summer of 1993 and graduated as a film producer. She had, however, become disillusioned with the atmosphere of Wardour Street and moved to Rhodes in August 1993. She lived at first in the lovely town of Lindos, then at Pefkos and finally at Kattavia. She learnt to speak modern Greek, worked as the cashier of a restaurant and became quite a good potter while beginning to explore the challenges of writing novels.

Laura left Ellerslie School at Malvern in the summer of 1992. Her sixth form studies had been at and with Malvern College, which was a benefit for her, despite the distraction of boys, and the two schools amalgamated from September 1992. She read history, English and classical civilisation and was accepted by London University's School of Oriental and African Studies to read history with special reference to Africa from October 1992, graduating in 1995 with a 2(2) degree.

I said earlier that my close association with the council of London Zoo continued until the end of 1992; its history during the latter part of that period was quite turbulent. After Solly Zuckerman's retirement early in 1984 there was persistent anxiety about its financial future in the absence of assured government funding. Eventually, in May 1988 the government agreed to make a single endowment payment of £10 million coupled with an annual payment of about £1.3 million to provide core funding for the Institute of Zoology. But the following years were very anxious and the financial crises reached a climax in 1991 and 1992, coinciding with my last period on the council. Field Marshal Sir John Chapple, the retiring Chief of the General Staff, agreed to become the president from March 1992. In the meantime, I was asked to preside at a difficult general meeting of the society on 6 January that year at London University following a decision by the council the previous July that London Zoo would have to close in September 1992 unless substantial funding was found by March.

The result of that meeting was that the decision to close was revoked by the council and a modernisation plan was approved, but the fellows present at the meeting carried a motion of no confidence in the council, which was only negatived by a postal ballot. To make matters worse, the decision to close had to be reinstated in June, leading to further adverse votes at special general meetings in July, which I was unable to attend. A gift from the Emir of Kuwait and increased numbers of visitors in the summer alleviated the situation temporarily but I was again asked to preside, this time at a council meeting in September 1992 in the absence of the field marshal, when four of the council members, including me, indicated that we wished to retire as soon as it was practicable for us to do so; and that ended my active participation in the management of the society.

Solly Zuckerman died on 1 April 1993 at the age of 88 and I was glad to be asked to write an appreciation of him for the society's annual report for 1992/93. At his memorial service Roy Jenkins, William Waldegrave and Rabbi John Rayner paid tribute to him and William Walton's *Roaring Fanfare*, dedicated to Solly, was played. After that my continuing work for the society was as chairman of the trustees of its pension fund until July 2001. The fund, a generous and far-sighted initiative, had been started by Solly in July 1958 and it grew from about £7 million in value to about £17.5 million during the period of my chairmanship. It was not without its dramas, most notably the repercussions from Robert Maxwell's activities elsewhere, but I was lucky that the misfortunes of pension funds generally did not occur until after I ceased to be a trustee.

More closely related to my judicial work was my continuing involvement with the citizens' advice bureau in the Royal Courts of Justice. The funding of the bureau was a persistent worry, partly because of successive changes in the organisation and financing of London local government. After the abolition of the Greater London Council in 1986 we had to rely upon subventions under the London boroughs grants scheme and some indirect funding by the Department of Trade and Industry. It became clear, however, that substantial additional funds were needed and Mrs Justice Booth agreed to chair an appeal with a target of £250,000, which had a degree of success, although it did not reach its target. The outstanding event was a concert in Middle Temple Hall on 10 November 1992 at which Lord Taylor of Gosforth, the new Lord Chief Justice, as pianist, and Maureen Smith, the violinist wife of Judge Rivlin, played Beethoven and Mozart sonatas and John (second Viscount) Dilhorne, a junior barrister and fine bass, sang some operatic arias and Russian songs most memorably. The profit from the concert was over £12,000 and by the end of April 1997, when Mrs Justice (now Lady Justice) Arden had taken over as chairman of the appeal, a trust fund balance of over £170,000 had been achieved.

After I had retired from the bench, substantial changes were made in the working arrangements and financing of the bureau, and very praiseworthy developments were made possible by 22 leading London firms of solicitors who volunteered to provide free expert advice and assistance. I must add that litigants in person who make use of the bureau's service owe a great debt of gratitude to Mr Justice Cazalet (now retired), who worked extremely hard for several years to bring about these improvements, with the benevolent interest of a new Lord Chancellor, Derry Irvine.

For our holidays we remained loyal to France and Italy, except when our children called us elsewhere. Sarah and I paid a visit to Venice in April 1992, where we saw a great deal of Sir Derek Hodgson, who had just retired from the High Court bench and who was writing a book on the paintings in Venice's churches (which, sadly, was never published). We stayed at the very conveniently placed Hotel Flora close to St Mark's Square and were fortunate to hear Felicity Lott and Ann Murray, accompanied by Graham Johnson, at the Gran Teatro la Fenice, which was celebrating its bicentenary before the disastrous fire of 29 January 1996. Under Derek's guidance we visited many churches and I remember particularly the Carpaccios in the Scuola di San Giorgio degli Schiavoni as well as a feast of Tintorettos. Derek also introduced us to Philip and Jane Rylands, joint custodians of the spectacular Peggy Guggenheim Collection, with the result that we dined with them and later had a private view of the collection, ending with a drink on the roof and an unforgettable view of Venice at dusk.

Apart from work and holidays, my Queen's Bench years seem to have been as busy as ever socially for Sarah and me. The year 1990 was rather special because of developments in Geoffrey Howe's career. He had been the foreign secretary very successfully for six years when Margaret Thatcher foolishly demoted him to the roles of Lord President of the Council and deputy prime minister in July 1989, just three months before Nigel Lawson resigned as Chancellor of the Exchequer. Geoffrey's demotion meant that Chevening ceased to be his country retreat, although he was allocated the less attractive Dorneywood in partial compensation. He and Elspeth continued to be the most generous host and hostess and we were part of a large luncheon party there in July 1990, just over three months before he too resigned from the Cabinet and made his historic statement in the House of Commons on doing so. But it was at Chevening that they truly flourished, and earlier in 1990 I decided to take up a suggestion previously made to me by a mutual friend, Judge Bruce Griffiths QC, that the many friends of the Howes who had enjoyed their hospitality in office should entertain them to dinner and make a presentation to them as a small expression of our gratitude.

In the end 87 of us (out of a maximum possible 100) assembled at the Garrick Club to dine Geoffrey and Elspeth on Sunday 20 May 1990. It was a very wide-ranging and distinguished gathering led by the Speaker of the House of Commons, Bernard Weatherill. Our Cambridge contemporary, Lord Jenkin of Roding, presided, and the toast to the Howes was proposed very wittily by another Union Society contemporary, Alistair Sampson. We presented Geoffrey with a camcorder and Elspeth chose a suitable domestic machine to ease her labours.

I was given great help in organising this affair by an old friend from Cambridge days, Peter Cooper, who had spent his post-university years as personal assistant to Sir Edward Hulton and then Tim (Lord) Beaumont at *Time and Tide* before joining Sir Bernard Audley, who attended the Howe dinner with his wife. I mention this particularly because shortly before that dinner Sir Bernard's market research company AGB Research plc, which he had founded in 1962, had been acquired by the appalling Robert Maxwell. At that time Peter Jay was still Maxwell's chief of staff but he left in 1990, whereupon Maxwell, having consulted others, singled out Peter Cooper and told him that he was to be the 'new Peter Jay'. Maxwell then departed for 10 weeks or so without leaving Peter Cooper any instructions about what he should do; and, on his return, he dismissed Peter peremptorily, at the age of 62 without a pension, presumably for alleged inactivity. AGB was used by Maxwell subsequently as the vehicle for a number of mysterious financial transactions.

One unusual event that occurred in 1991 was an interview for television by Hugh Dehn, an independent producer and son of the prominent leading counsel, Conrad Dehn. Hugh's idea was to make a programme illustrating the lives of a few contemporary judges outside court coupled with discursive interviews about their work and leisure activities. Five judges, namely, Lord

Hoffmann, Lord Justice Brooke, Mrs Justice Booth, Judge Medd QC and I agreed to participate. Before doing so, I sought permission from Lord Lane, who disliked press or other media intrusion and who replied, very reasonably, 'Be it on your own head!' In the event Hugh Dehn visited me in Herefordshire in June 1991 with a charming camerawoman with the famous surname Cunningham-Reid: a film was made of my various weekend activities and I still have a transcript of the friendly and wide-ranging interview. Subsequently, Hugh sent me a video of the whole programme, which seemed to me to be entertaining and quite revealing but it was swiftly rejected by both the BBC and ITV, no doubt on the ground that it presented a friendly picture of judges and was insufficiently 'edgy', to use that hideously fashionable and meaningless description (unless it means obscene).

On 9 January 1993 I completed 15 years on the bench and became entitled to a full pension of half my salary at the time of my retirement. I was then 66 years and 8 months old but I had the right to continue sitting until the age of 75 because I had been appointed before the compulsory retirement age was reduced to 70. However, it was becoming unfashionable for judges (except, perhaps, Lords of Appeal) to linger on and my initial intention was to retire some time in 1995, when I was due to be Treasurer of the Middle Temple. In the end, I found that I could cope with the duties of Treasurer whilst continuing to sit as a judge because I did not have to go on circuit during my year of office and I postponed my retirement until the end of the Easter vacation in 1996, very shortly before my seventieth birthday.

I was duly elected Deputy Treasurer of my Inn of Court in December 1993 and it was inevitable that I would be mainly occupied with Middle Temple business outside court for the following two years. I was persuaded, however, to take part in some other extramural work in that period. The most public work that I took on was the presidency of the International Musical Eisteddfod at Llangollen in succession to Emlyn Hooson. This eisteddfod, founded in 1947, is held annually in the second week of July and attracts about 2,000 competitors from over 50 countries. After a 'training run' in 1993 I was president for the following four years, including the golden anniversary year of 1997. It was an exciting time, notable particularly for the return of Luciano Pavarotti in 1995, 40 years after his first appearance there with the Modena choir and accompanied by his father and the choir on both occasions. Other famous virtuosi and opera stars who performed at the evening concerts were Igor Oistrakh, Emma Johnson, Anne Evans, Bryn Terfel, Tasmin Little, Montserrat Caballe, James Galway and Marisa Robles, to name but a few. We were also honoured by a visit from our patron, HRH the Prince of Wales, on 10 July 1996. It was a great pleasure for me to work during these years with the very able chairman, Gethin Davies, and his talented wife Eulanwy, the music administrator, as well as Roy Bohana, the veteran music director of the eisteddfod. It is amusing to record that one of our distinguished guests, Montserrat Caballe, proved to be ahead of the time in her distrust of banks because she insisted on payment of her substantial fee (£20,000) in cash before departing by privately chartered aeroplane for her next engagement in Hamburg: this necessitated the opening of a local bank on a Sunday by its manager, who happened to be our treasurer!

The other presidency that I undertook was of the St John's Wood Society, in succession to Brian Johnston, the very popular BBC cricket commentator. I took over in 1994, when he resigned at the age of 82, but I myself resigned two years later because Sarah and I sold our house in Abbey Gardens after 26 years of residence in St John's Wood. The live wire of the society was the chairman, Michael Salmon, so that my own duties were light but it was certainly worthwhile to be involved in the very necessary and persistent interventions of the society in planning and road traffic matters. The only lasting mementos of our presence in this attractive and famously artistic 'village' are two catalpa trees planted by Sarah on 1 October 1995 to mark the renovation of the almshouses in St John's Wood Terrace founded by Count Woronzow in the nineteenth century.

23

MIDDLE TEMPLE TREASURER

The Temple is a very attractive quarter of London, between Fleet Street and the Embankment, which is little known apart from its ancient round church and famous choir. Lawyers have practised there in 'chambers' since the fourteenth century and their tenure of the land was formalised in 1608 by a grant for 400 years made by the Crown by letters patent and recently renewed. By 1608 the Temple's lawyers were divided into two collegiate institutions, the Inner Temple and the Middle Temple, two of the four Inns of Court that now survive. The business of these Inns was and is conducted by elected senior members known as benchers, broadly equivalent to fellows of a college, and the principal officer for the past 500 years or so has been the Treasurer who, since the seventeenth century, has held office for one year only. The second senior officer is the reader, whose duties are mainly concerned with student members; practice in relation to this office varies between the Inns but in the Middle Temple in most recent times there have been two readers each year, who serve separately for six months each and are elected from senior benchers who will not serve as Treasurer. In my year of office as Treasurer the first reader was Lord Justice (later Lord) Nolan and the second Ben Hytner QC, a very well-known silk who was a Cambridge contemporary of mine and incidentally the father of the theatre and film director Sir Nicholas, now of the National Theatre and an honorary bencher of the Middle Temple.

It is a much-prized honour to be elected Treasurer of one's Inn and the duties associated with the office have become more onerous as the membership of the Bar has increased (by over 500 per cent in my time in the law, and now 600 per cent) and the desire of governments to regulate every profession seems to have grown similarly, irrespective of party allegiances.

When I was elected Treasurer for the year 1995 there were about 250 benchers of the Middle Temple, including two royal and 48 honorary, but the voting benchers were restricted to a maximum of 150, whereas the most recent list that I have seen (November 2010) shows a total of 494, of whom 345 have been elected since 1 January 1996 and about the same number are voting members. Thus, the possibility of becoming Treasurer has diminished significantly although only a small proportion of the voting members play a really active role in the business of the Inn. Since 1980 the field of potential candidates for the Treasurership has also been restricted by an age rule that the Treasurer must be under the age of 70 on completing his year of office, an innovation that had the unhappy consequence of excluding Judge King-Hamilton QC, an assiduous and witty bencher, from selection.

The interests of the four Inns of Court and of the Bar Council, the profession's elected body, are obviously closely interlocked so that there are many meetings at Treasurer and senior officer level in the course of the year to discuss matters of common concern and to try to achieve a degree of uniformity of approach. My fellow Treasurers were Lord Justice Hirst at the Inner Temple, Lord Justice Glidewell at Gray's Inn and Oliver Lodge, a chairman of industrial tribunals, at Lincoln's Inn. Fortunately I knew and liked both Lord Justices already and all four of us were able to work together very harmoniously with Peter (now Lord) Goldsmith QC, the future Attorney-General, who was then chairman of the Bar Council. The practice was for the five of us to dine together informally at regular intervals, each Treasurer acting as host in turn in his own Inn, and these paved the way for more formal discussions subsequently.

Our common interests had long been recognised by the establishment in 1974 of what was called the Senate of the Inns of Court and Bar, which eventually gave away to the Council of the Inns of Court (COIC) under the presidency of a Lord Justice of Appeal. Each Inn had three representatives on this body (normally the Treasurer, Deputy Treasurer and another senior bencher, in our case Lord Justice, now Lord, Saville) and the Bar Council was similarly represented. We met every four to six weeks in term time with our chief executives in attendance, and our discussions covered a wide range of topics affecting the future of the Bar in the light of indications by the government of its future regulatory intentions. I was already familiar with these subjects before I began to attend as Deputy Treasurer because I had chaired the future planning committee of the Middle Temple for a couple of years and because COIC's discussions and decisions were reported regularly to our parliament.

The smooth running of each Inn depends to a great extent on its chief executive, who is the Under Treasurer in the Middle Temple. I was particularly lucky to have Brigadier Charles Wright as my Under Treasurer. He is a former officer of the Royal Dragoon Guards, who became Under Treasurer late in 1993 in succession to Rear-Admiral Richard Hill, an excellent administrator as well as a distinguished naval historian. Charles Wright had exactly the right combination of ability and temperament for the job and he and his wife Jeanie quickly became very popular with all members of the Inn and its staff. He also became secretary of COIC and his service to the Inns of Court over a decade was extremely valuable.

The year began happily for me with a well-deserved knighthood for my old friend and professional sparring partner in Cheshire and North Wales, Judge Robin David QC, and the wedding of my nephew Piers Thompson in Winchester Cathedral. However, an unpleasant shock followed soon afterwards when the Under Treasurer reported that a Middle Temple cheque for £180,189.89 dated 4 January 1995 in favour of Sun Alliance Insurance Co. Limited to pay the premiums required by the Inn's insurance policies had ended up in Bulgaria and had been collected by our bankers on 20 January for a Turkish bank despite the fact that the cheque was crossed and endorsed with the words 'Not negotiable Account payee only'. There followed some acrimonious correspondence with our bankers but the Inn had able members specialising in banking to advise it, particularly Antonio Bueno, and the matter ended with a successful action by Sun Alliance, taking over the Inn's rights, against the bank.

Troubles rarely come singly and a second, more serious, financial blow followed very soon afterwards with the collapse of Barings plc in late February 1995. The Middle Temple was affected because, on the advice of our investment consultants, our charities fund had purchased 100,000 Barings preference shares at a cost of nearly £116,000. As preference shareholders, we ranked behind three other main tiers of creditors and, despite joining the Barings preference shareholders' action group, we were unable to recover anything from our investment.

Happily, the other financial affairs of the Inn ran quite smoothly throughout the year and we achieved an acceptable surplus, despite some necessary spending in excess of our budget. The Treasurer's preoccupations were much less with financial matters than with the general political concerns of the Bar. At the forefront of these were the questions of appropriate selection and training for the profession, bearing in mind the need for a coherent equal opportunities code and the limited ability of the Bar to absorb new members in contrast to the ever-increasing demand for places.

Despite the immense effort that has been put into tackling these problems throughout more than two decades, I cannot pretend that any satisfactory long-term solutions have yet been found. My years as an active lawyer were essentially years of natural expansion in response to increasing demand and the willingness of successive governments to fund generous and widespread legal aid. Thus, the central problems to which I have referred were to some extent masked, but they were already recognised by the profession's leaders by 1995 and they have intensified ever since.

In one field at least, that of advocacy training, Middle Temple was and remains a leader. We were exceptionally fortunate that Michael Sherrard QC, who was to succeed me as Treasurer and was therefore my Deputy Treasurer in 1995, had retired from the Bar the previous year and had volunteered to become the Inn's first director of advocacy. For some years it had been thought that the Bar final course was too academic and failed to provide adequate training in the art and practice of advocacy. Two senior members of the Bar, Michael Hill QC of Gray's Inn and our Michael Sherrard, had been impressed by the advocacy training that they had witnessed on a visit to Australia and they had returned to persuade their Inns to follow suit. The training is now an essential part of a barrister's education before and after call to the Bar, and the programme of training provided by senior members of the Inn who volunteer is highly organised. Michael Sherrard's vast unpaid work for the profession continued for 10 years and was rightly recognised in the honours list by the award of the CBE. His excellent portrait by Israel Zohar now hangs prominently in the benchers' quarters as a mark of the Inn's gratitude to him (and I was so impressed by it that I arranged for Zohar to paint Sarah, with an equally satisfactory result).

The future of Bar training generally was in the melting pot when I became Treasurer. Until then it had been the responsibility of the Council of Legal Education, most recently under the chairmanship of Lord Justice Phillips, later Lord Chief Justice. It had been decided, however, to make the training available more widely by franchising the law departments of a small number of provincial universities, as well as the Inns of Court School of Law (ICSL) located in Gray's Inn, to provide both an academic course and a vocational course to qualify students for call to the Bar. The process of enfranchisement, which was referred to as validation, raised many issues but these were close to resolution by early 1995. It had been agreed that responsibility for the regulation of education and training for the Bar would pass from the CLE to the Bar Council on 1 January 1996, although there was considerable dispute about the fate of the CLE reserves of the order of £6 million. The ICSL was to remain the sole provider of the Bar vocational course (BVC) for the time being and an interim admissions policy requiring candidates to have at least a second-class degree had been authorised for a limited period. It was intended, however, that the ICSL's monopoly should end by September 1997 and that a small number of university law departments should be authorised to provide the course, 10 having already expressed an interest in doing so.

The background to these developments was that a working party had assessed the requirement of the profession at 750 to 800 candidates each year whereas the number of applications for the BVC was far in excess of this (2,300 for the 1994/95 course). It was thought, therefore, that the ICSL could provide places for 500 to 700 students in the future but that it would be prudent to limit the other validated institutions to about 120 students each.

Validation was a solution to only a part of the Bar's overall training and admission problems. In the course of 1995 an equality code for barristers was adopted and a working group under Mr Justice (later Lord Justice) Hooper considered the content, regulation and supervision of pupillages for barristers. At the same time proposals for deferring call to the Bar until after pupillage were under discussion, as were the status and role of employed, in contrast to self-employed, barristers; the funding of students and pupil barristers during training in order to ensure that the profession was accessible to every worthy candidate was the subject of almost continuous debate. My recollection is that it was thought at the time that the profession could absorb about 500 new practising barristers annually, despite the recent innovation of granting some solicitors defined rights to practise in the higher courts. Nevertheless, in 1994 nearly 2,000 new students were admitted to the Inns of Court and in the Middle Temple alone I called 486 to the Bar during my year of office. It is not surprising in these circumstances that fair selection for the Bar was and remains an intractable problem, even in times of recession. Admission as a student has been limited for some years to candidates who have obtained at least a 2(1) class in their degree examination but it would be folly to make this requirement more stringent because academic excellence has never been a necessary quality for success at the Bar; I do not believe that academic elitism is more tolerable than any other form of elitism.

The social side of the Treasurership is demanding but very enjoyable, particularly in retrospect. Its peak is Grand Night, or more accurately dinner on Grand Day, when the Treasurer chooses 20 or so distinguished guests to dine with the benchers and other members of the Inn in hall. In the past there was a Grand Day each legal term in all the Inns but the practice varies now and Middle Temple sensibly limits itself to one per year. It is usual for full evening dress and decorations to be worn, and Middle Temple Hall provides an unforgettable setting for the occasion. In my year Grand Night was held on 18 May 1995. I was delighted that Lady Joan Zuckerman, Solly's widow, was able to be a principal guest: her grandfather was the famous Rufus Isaacs, a former Lord Chief Justice and then Viceroy of India, and her father, the second Marquess of Reading QC, had been Treasurer of the Middle Temple in 1958. She herself was a talented artist and I was especially pleased to be able to use one of her paintings to decorate the menu. Other guests included Lords Cledwyn, Peyton, Wyatt and Taylor (Lord Chief Justice) and Baroness Warnock, Sir Percy Cradock (my Johnian contemporary), Sir Thomas Bingham (then Master of the Rolls) and, from the stage, Sir Donald Sinden. My major regrets were that my former pupil master, Lord Brightman, and the Master of St John's College were unable to be there, but my other pupil master, Sir William Mars-Jones (by then retired) was present, as was my own former pupil, Gerard Elias QC, then leader of the Wales and Chester Circuit.

One of the many pleasant tasks of the Treasurer is calling to the bench newly elected benchers of the Inn. The custom in the Middle Temple is for the ceremony to be performed in hall immediately before dinner and then after dinner the new bencher is required to deliver a short biographical, but light-hearted speech. In 1995 we elected nine new ordinary benchers but a significant increase was already being envisaged because we agreed at the end of the year to increase the permitted core establishment from 150 to 170 and to elect 12 new benchers the following year. In addition we elected two Chief Justices as honorary benchers, namely, Lord Taylor and the Chief Justice of India, Mr Justice A.N. Armadi, although the latter was not called to the bench until November 1996. His election was prompted by another honorary bencher, the popular and very learned High Commissioner for India in London from 1991 to 1997, Dr R.M. Singhvi, whom I had first met when he was a day president at Llangollen International Musical Eisteddfod and who subsequently proved to be a generous and active member of the Inn. He planted a tree in memory of Sir William Jones, a notable Middle Templar and Orientalist of the eighteenth century who originated a compilation of Hindu and Islamic law and became a judge of the Supreme Court of Bengal in Calcutta.

It also fell to my lot to call another new honorary bencher, the Honourable William H. Rehnquist, the Chief Justice of the Supreme Court of the USA, in July 1995. He had been elected as long ago as November 1986 but there had not been any earlier opportunity for him to take his place. A reason for his election was the long association of the Middle Temple with the USA: five members of the Inn signed the Declaration of Independence and at least three other Middle Templars were prominent in the foundation of the republic. Successive ambassadors of the United States to this country are always elected honorary benchers of the Inn; and it was fitting that the Pilgrims' Society entertained Chief Justice Rehnquist to dinner in Middle Temple Hall the previous evening.

For me, the most poignant of these occasions was the call of Peter Taylor on 14 December 1995. He was a very dear and much-admired friend who had taken part in memorable recitals as a pianist in Middle Temple Hall, the last as recently as 16 October with Fanny Waterman, his charming wife of many years had died earlier that year. Peter himself was to die, aged only 66, within less than 18 months of his call to our bench and to retire within six months, because of a brain tumour of which he had first become aware when he found one evening that he could not play the piano. It was a great privilege for me to sponsor his call to the bench before it became too late.

Another notable event for me personally was a dinner in Middle Temple Hall on 29 September to celebrate the golden jubilee of the Wales and Chester Circuit. As I explained earlier, the two previous halves of the circuit did not amalgamate formally until 1945, so that there was good cause for celebration in 1995; we did not know then that we were to lose Cheshire soon after our diamond jubilee. Although there had been several Treasurers of Gray's Inn who had been members of the circuit, I was the first and last to be Treasurer of the Middle Temple, so our hall was a suitable venue. It had been intended that Tasker Watkins should be Treasurer earlier but he had had to withdraw on the eve of his election because of his wife's indisposition at the time. The previous Treasurer from the former South Wales Circuit had been Viscount Sankey, who was Lord Chancellor for six years from 1929 and then Treasurer in 1936. The dinner was very well attended and it was a delight that the distinguished doyen of the circuit, His Honour David Pennant, then aged 83, was there to propose the toast to the circuit, to which Tasker Watkins and I replied.

There were, of course, many other memorable events during the year, but one's moments of glory as Treasurer soon pass, although they do not fade away in one's memory, and one returns to more pedestrian routine. It is probably unwise to harbour any ambition to leave a permanent mark on one's Inn because all four have managed to exist for centuries without a revolution. This advice is particularly appropriate at times when others are casting their eyes upon the law and lawyers with ill will and an urge to cut them down to size. In my time the Inns were also subject to the covetous desires of the Bar Council, or at least of many of its officers, who wished to take over the responsibilities and property of the Inns as far as possible under the cloak of democratic progress. However, the reality of the matter is that the elected leaders of the Bar change frequently whereas the benchers of the Inns provide continuity and considerable experience in administering the profession and its property. I was content, therefore, to have as my main ambition the preservation intact and in good order of the Middle Temple and its functions throughout my term of office. I hope that I achieved this and the only mark that I left behind, apart from my newly acquired coat of arms, was the replacement of the rather uncomfortable ancient wooden benches on which members had to sit in hall with comfortable and attractive chairs designed by Luke Hughes, a popular member of the Garrick Club and son of a former judge.

This was the only year in which I sat in the Royal Courts of Justice throughout and there was no let up in the flow of work but I was inevitably less able to put in much overtime. My main activities were almost equally divided between trying civil cases and sitting in the Court of Appeal Criminal Division or the Queen's Bench divisional court. Some of the civil actions were likely to be long drawn out, particularly an action arising out of the collapse of the Eagle Star insurance company against its auditors, but it was eventually disposed of in July by agreement after numerous preliminary hearings before me in the preceding six months.

The year ended with the retirement of my clerk, Ronald Kidd, who had been with me throughout my time in the Queen's Bench Division. He has spent his time well since then playing golf in Alderney and cruising the world as frequently as possible with his wife. In his place I appointed a 40-year-old Yorkshireman, Trevor Galtress, with 20 years' service in the army, ending as an administrative manager in the Royal Logistic Corps at Grantham. He proved to be very competent, possessing all the necessary modern skills, and he has continued successfully as a judge's clerk after my own retirement.

24

WINDING UP TO THE NORTH WALES TRIBUNAL

I had written to the Lord Chancellor on 8 November 1995 forewarning him of my intention to retire on 15 April 1996, the last day of the Easter vacation, but this meant that my last sitting would be on 3 April, the Wednesday before Easter. My delay in implementing my original intention to retire in 1995 meant that I was able to pay another last visit to my old circuit, despite having said farewell in November 1994; and the result was that I enjoyed further stays in Mold and Chester in January and February, for part of which I had the agreeable company of the newly appointed Mr Justice (now Lord Justice) Wilson of the Family Division.

The work in court during this period was not very demanding but the social life certainly was. The Bromley-Davenports were especially kind and gave a large dinner party at Capesthorne Hall, into which they were about to move from The Kennels. There was also a very generous dinner party for Nicholas Wilson and me given by the High Sheriff of Cheshire, John Pickering, at the Swan Hotel, Tarporley, attended by Lord Leverhulme, five Circuit judges and other old friends. In court, I was rather less successful because a jury managed to return inconsistent verdicts in a case in which a North Wales headmaster had struck an intrusive press photographer at the school entrance and had damaged his camera. The headmaster's defence of reasonable self-defence applied equally to both charges against him but the jury decided to convict him of criminal damage and acquit him of common assault. The Court of Appeal had no difficulty later in quashing the conviction. My visit ended with a trip to Cardiff Arms Park as a guest of the charming Henry Lewis to witness the regrettable narrow defeat of Wales by Scotland.

My last seven weeks' sitting in London were spent mainly in the Court of Appeal and the Divisional Court, dealing with criminal appeals, but I did have two weeks in my familiar court 14, opposite my retiring room, trying a medical negligence action from Newcastle. It had recently become the custom to have a valedictory gathering in court when a Queen's Bench judge retired and my turn came on 2 April, the penultimate day of that term, when I was sitting with Lord Justice Roch and Mr Justice Bennett. It was a very touching occasion for me with short speeches from Lord Justice Roch, Lord Williams of Mostyn QC, the head of my former chambers, John Griffith Williams QC, the leader of my circuit and now a High Court judge himself, and Eleanor Lawson QC, for the Family Law Bar Association. Sir Stephen Brown, the president of the Family Division, also very kindly attended. My reply reflected the generosity and warmth with which I had always been treated as a judge.

The immediate prospect for Sarah and me was an early summer holiday in term time after celebrating my seventieth birthday on 8 May. On my last day of sitting as a judge I dined with Sarah, Sophie and Laura at the Savoy Grill and on my birthday I was yet again at the Savoy Hotel for the High Sheriff of Greater London's breakfast; but my own party was arranged by our son Thomas at Brooks' Club. It was a very happy occasion at which Robin Day proposed my health (he later included his speech in his published collection *Speaking for Myself*), and Peter Taylor was good enough to attend, five days after the announcement of his impending retirement.

Our holiday destination once more was Provence and we again rented a house on the river at L'Isle-sur-la-Sorgue, where we had stayed the previous September. We drove the 885 miles from Cherbourg in a leisurely way, staying overnight at favourite hotels in Avranches and le Grand Pressigny. Our second grandson, James, was born on 1 June, the day that we started back, and we celebrated unknowingly by dining at the outstanding Paul Bocuse restaurant, near Lyons, en route home.

Our stay in France was shorter than it might otherwise have been because I had agreed to sit for three weeks from mid-June in place of a recently appointed judge, Mr Justice Poole, who had become seriously ill unexpectedly. At Liverpool I found myself sharing lodgings unusually with two women judges, Heather Steel, the daughter of a popular former Circuit judge and Brenda (now Baroness) Hale, who had been a professor of law and then a law commissioner before becoming a Family Division judge. My Liverpool stint ended just in time for me to attend a family wedding in Savernake Forest on 6 July, when my niece Eliza Thompson married Valentine Low, a journalist then working for the *Evening Standard* but now of *The Times*. I do not usually enjoy weddings very much these days but this was very well organised in lovely sunshine for the reception at the Thompsons' home at Bedwyn Common. A high spot of the service was the reading of Shakespeare's sonnet no 116 by Eliza's great friend Natasha Richardson, now sadly mourned, the daughter of Tony Richardson and Vanessa Redgrave, who was there with her husband Liam Neeson.

A surprising development while I was sitting in Liverpool was an invitation from the secretary of state for Wales, William Hague, to preside over a tribunal of inquiry into the abuse since 1974 of children in care in the former county council areas of Gwynedd and Clwyd. My own first knowledge of my involvement came with a telephone call from the secretary to the Lord Chief Justice, seeking permission to give my telephone number to the Welsh Office to enable them to speak to me about 'the inquiry that you are going to conduct'! There was not much scope for refusal, therefore, without great embarrassment but I was treated with great courtesy by William Hague, who spoke to me from a Conservative conference in South Wales, and I dined with him at the House of Commons a month later. It was clear that the wide-ranging inquiry covering almost half the area of Wales over a period of 22 years would take a very long time but I did not foresee that I was about to postpone my retirement, in effect, for three and a half years.

There was a great deal of work to do before the tribunal could begin to hear evidence. We were formally appointed as a tribunal of three on 30 August 1996 and we had the advantage of an expert adviser on police matters, Sir Ronald Hadfield, the recently retired chief constable of the West Midlands. Sitting with me on the tribunal itself were Morris le Fleming, a former chief executive of Hertfordshire County Council, who had already sat on a similar (but non-statutory) inquiry in Leicestershire, and Margaret Clough, a highly experienced former social services inspector with roots in Cheshire.

The complexity of the preparatory work can readily be imagined but some bare statistics are worth mentioning. The inquiry involved about 85 children's homes and the preliminary work required examination of 9,500 unsorted children's files and 3,500 statements to the police as well as other records of the former county councils. A result was that 12,000 documents had to be scanned into the tribunal's database. All this work had to be carried out by a team of 30 paralegals under the supervision of senior solicitors. There was also the parallel problem of interviewing the complainants and other residents in care to obtain their statements and this highly sensitive work had to be carried out in accordance with a strict protocol by persons with appropriate experience, principally by former police officers from forces outside North Wales. In the event they interviewed 400 potential witnesses and travelled 80,000 miles. Supervising and guiding this work overall was the tribunal's own team of counsel briefed by the Treasury solicitor on the nomination of the Attorney-General. We were fortunate to have three very able barristers acting for us, namely, Gerard Elias QC, a former pupil of mine, Gregory Treverton-Jones (now a QC himself) and Ernest Ryder of the Manchester Bar, who took silk as early as April 1997 and is now Mr Justice Ryder of the Family Division.

Considerable administrative back-up was needed and we occupied half of the former, but new, headquarters of Alyn and Deeside District Council at St David's Park, Ewloe, near Hawarden, for about 21 months from September 1996. There our counsel were installed with the solicitor to the tribunal, Brian McHenry, a member of the Treasury solicitor's staff, who stayed with us until he moved at the end of 1997 to a similar role with the BSE inquiry. Administrative responsibility was shouldered by a chief administrative officer but the members of the tribunal relied heavily upon the clerk to the tribunal, Fiona Walkingshaw, who was a young solicitor with some European Commission experience and who remained with us until the publication of our report, ensuring that we had all the necessary material before us throughout.

Although it was pleasant for me to be in my native county again for a substantial period, I had not envisaged that I would again be leading a circuit life in my retirement. However, the impact of this was mitigated for me by an arrangement that I should stay in the judges' lodgings at Mold for the duration of our hearings. The staff there could not be expected to take on cooking for me except for breakfast but we managed to make adequate arrangements locally so that I was housed in reasonable comfort and able to work in the evenings undisturbed. It was also agreed that we should sit four full days each week, from Monday afternoon to Friday lunchtime, in order to lessen as far as possible the disruption of everyone's lives. Sarah and I had decided to sell our London house when I retired and to downsize to a flat in the Temple so that, once our daily hearings began, I commuted at weekends usually to our Herefordshire home but occasionally to the Temple.

Through the summer of 1996 I had numerous meetings with the able solicitor and legal adviser to the Welsh Office, David Lambert, and other meetings with the Attorney-General and Solicitor-General, the Treasury solicitor and the new permanent under-secretary at the Welsh Office, Rachel Lomax, to iron out personnel and procedural matters and the need for a legal indemnity from action for the members of the tribunal. At the same time I was preparing to move in London to the flat at 3 Essex Court in the Temple, of which we had been granted the tenancy from the September quarter day. There was also the Llangollen International Musical Eisteddfod to attend in the second week of July, at which we had the honour of a visit by our patron, HRH the Prince of Wales, on Wednesday and outstanding concerts at the weekend by Anne Evans and Bryn Terfel.

Once the tribunal team had established themselves in St David's Park at Ewloe I arranged several preliminary meetings in public to deal mainly with the legal representation of all the interested parties, totalling over 300. Our object was to ensure fair and proper representation but to avoid unnecessary duplication where, for example, there was no conflict of interest between relevant complainants. Some criticism of the arrangements was inevitable initially but we made good progress in arranging joint representation as far as possible. Apart from the counsel to the tribunal, nine silks and 25 junior barristers appeared before us, including three women barristers who took silk in April 1998, and there were also five solicitor advocates.

It was clear that our hearings would be in public and that daily transcripts of the evidence would be made available for the parties and the press but there was a thorny problem as to whether (and, if so, to what extent) anonymity should be accorded to the witnesses who gave evidence. The easier part of this related to the complainants because there was obviously the strongest case for their anonymity in the light of the established practice of the courts and the need to encourage them to come forward to give their evidence about what had occurred, despite the very substantial lapse of time in most cases since the events had occurred. We were dealing mainly with mature complainants, many of whom had settled down with partners who were unaware of the relevant part of their history. Much more difficult was the question of whether anonymity should be granted during the hearings to persons against whom allegations of sexual or other physical abuse had been made. It was, of course, open to us to rule that we should follow the practice in rape trials, for example, and grant anonymity until we had made our findings but, as always, there was strong pressure from newspapers for freedom to 'name names' and this pressure was said to be based upon support from at least some of the more prominent complainants who had campaigned for an inquiry.

Having heard the arguments, we reached the firm conclusion at our first preliminary hearing that the names of alleged abusers should not be published. As we said in our report, we considered that the course of justice in our proceedings would be seriously prejudiced or impeded in the event of publication of the names because potential witnesses might be deterred from testifying or testifying fully to the tribunal. The guidance was particularly necessary because it was impracticable for us to grant anonymity in the actual hearings to witnesses, whether as complainants or alleged abusers, having regard to the number of persons involved on either side. Any form of index by letter or number would have been both intolerably time consuming and potentially confusing. It was important also that the Attorney-General authorised the tribunal to say that anything said by a witness would not be used in evidence in any criminal proceedings, except in relation to perjury or perverting the course of justice.

At a later stage, after our full hearings had begun, an application was made on behalf of the BBC, the *Liverpool Daily Post* and the *Western Mail* that the tribunal should revoke its directions on anonymity. The application was rejected for the reasons that I gave on 12 February 1997, which are reproduced in our full published report. We reserved, however, our decision as to the naming of alleged abusers in our report. This subject was dealt with in chapter 6 of the report and needs brief mention here.

What is not understood by the general public, including some prominent critics of the tribunal's findings, is that the substantial majority of the acts of sexual and other physical abuse detailed in our report had already been the subject of trial and conviction by juries in criminal proceedings or of pleas of guilty. We had to decide at the outset, therefore, what our approach to these decisions by juries, including acquittals, ought to be. It would obviously have been inappropriate for us to sit, in effect, as a court of appeal from jury decisions that had not been appealed in the courts unless evidence was produced compelling us to question the validity or safeness of the verdicts. As for the allegations against alleged abusers that had not been the subject of criminal proceedings, we had to have in mind that, although the proceedings before us were not strictly criminal in category, allegations of sexual abuse and serious physical abuse were particularly grave and required a proportionate standard of proof in accordance with the highest appellate authority in this country. Moreover, similar considerations applied to the much-publicised allegations against a former police superintendent of the North Wales Constabulary, Gordon Anglesea, who had been the plaintiff in a successful libel action heard in November and December 1994, in which he had recovered £375,000 damages.

When it came to writing our report it was obviously necessary that we should maintain the cloak of anonymity for the complainants because that was part of the understanding on the basis of which they had given evidence. This understanding did not extend to the alleged abusers but we considered that we should exercise what we called a 'restrictive discretion' in naming them. We had been able to give assurances in advance to a substantial number of them because of the comparative triviality of the allegations against them or the very limited number of minor allegations made against them over a long period; there were some others to whom no assurance had been given but in respect of whom the evidence, in our judgement, did not warrant naming them. Nevertheless, we considered it necessary to name a substantial number of alleged abusers, many of whom had already been convicted, for reasons that we set out in detail in paragraph 6.16 of our report. Such identification was essential, in our view, to enable us to report coherently and fully upon the evidence that we had heard and as a basis for our recommendations. Our freedom to do so, however, was subject to the caveat that we were unable to report at all upon some allegations because they were the subject of current police investigations or proceedings.

We were able to start our full hearings about six months after our appointment, which was itself a considerable achievement by everyone involved in the preparatory work. There was a great deal of national publicity at that time and I found myself giving interviews to a wide range of broadcasters and newspapers, including, for example, the BBC's *Newsnight*, French TF1, *Le Monde* and even the *Baltimore Sun*. After opening statements in the third week of January we began hearing oral evidence on 4 February and, in all, we sat on 207 days. We heard the evidence of 575 witnesses, of whom 264 gave oral evidence, between then and 12 March 1998. There were then final submissions and a concluding seminar on 6 and 7 May 1998, in which we canvassed in public some potential recommendations with the assistance of a small group of experts. Despite the fact that the hearings took much longer than we had expected because of the number of witnesses to be heard, the total cost of the exercise was kept within bounds as much as possible.

There followed the most onerous task of all, the drafting of our report; there was no escape from this for me. There were so many matters of fact and opinion to be covered that delegation of even parts of this work was quite impracticable. From our continuous discussions during the period of the hearings I was aware of my fellow tribunal members' views on most of the issues so that the only way forward was for me to prepare a first draft, chapter by chapter, and then to discuss the draft with them at convenient intervals in order to incorporate agreed amendments. For the purpose of this work the Welsh Office rented a suite of offices at Ley Court, just off the Gloucester ring road, and the tribunal and a small secretariat, led by Fiona Walkingshaw, occupied this with all the documents and transcripts for about 20 months from April 1998. Thus, I was able to commute 20 miles or so from Herefordshire each working day while compiling our 857-page report with its 74 pages of appendices.

While it was possible to map out tentatively the structure of the report earlier, I could not sensibly begin to draft it until late April 1998 and it took about 19 months to complete even though I worked at it daily, including August and September in two successive years, apart from a short vacation. I had finished 24 chapters by Christmas 1998 and we handed over the first agreed 650 pages to the Welsh Office on 12 February 1999. By that time the secretary of state, Ron Davies, had resigned and had been succeeded by Paul Murphy, who was still in office when we presented the completed version on 30 September 1999, by which time it had grown to 56 chapters with 11 appendices. To describe the work as painstaking is an understatement: it was undoubtedly the most arduous task that I had ever undertaken and my estimates of how long it would take, which were inevitably sought by others from time to time, were always over-optimistic, as have been those by the chairmen of virtually every other similar inquiry before and since.

Those with experience in these matters will realise that this was by no means the end of my work. There were, of course, numerous matters to attend to in relation to the printing and publication of the report, including translation of the whole into Welsh. More perturbingly, I was asked to prepare a summary for distribution at the same time as the full report. This was yet another major undertaking: it could not be brief because few potential readers would be prepared to read the full report and the summary had to be sufficiently wide to give an adequate picture of our findings and the basis of our 72 detailed recommendations. It was certain that we would be judged mainly by the summary rather than the report itself. The kind description of the report by Lord Laming, now the doyen of reporters on child abuse, in the House of Lords debate about it was 'voluminous'; but he was much less experienced in reporting then.

I embarked upon this further phase of work with a rather heavy heart but at least it did not require further consultation and I was able to work at it partly at home. In the end the document extended to 227 pages but it was ready to accompany presentation of the report to Parliament, again with a full Welsh translation, on 15 February 2000. The secretary of state was very generous in his comments and I joined him at a press conference that day, which seemed to be quite successful.

The response to the report was predictably mixed. The supporters and critics of anonymity joined battle again without troubling to examine our detailed explanation of it. Sections of the press yearned to be able to name rumoured abusers about whom we had not heard any concrete evidence and there was disappointment about our acquittal of Freemasonry for the same reason. On the other hand, some supporters of former staff in the children's homes apparently thought that we had been hoodwinked and that we should have rejected all the allegations, particularly those in relation to the home known as Bryn Estyn, despite jury verdicts and, in some cases, pleas of guilty. In general, however, I was satisfied with the response of the press and the public. The scale of the abuse and the widespread failings of the care system in North Wales were recognised, as was the urgent need for remedial action.

I will not attempt here to summarise our conclusions or comment in detail on our hearings but I will explain why I chose to entitle the report *Lost in Care*. The evidence of sexual and other physical abuse was, of course, appalling but we were steeled in advance to expect that. What I had not foreseen was the catalogue of other failings with which we were presented by the overwhelming majority of the complainants who gave evidence. We analysed these basic failings in the quality of care provided in the two former counties in chapters 31 and 46 of our report and there were striking similarities between them. Over and over again we had been told by the former children in care of the frequent changes of placement to which they had been subjected with consequent disruption of their educational opportunities, but this was only one of many common denominators in their experiences. We found that there had been a lack of adequate planning for each child and an absence of any strategic framework for placements. These failings were coupled with ineffective reviewing processes and lack of consultation with the children themselves, of which inadequate surveillance by field social workers was an important aspect. Perhaps most important of all, there was an almost complete failure to prepare residents for their discharge from care. It is not surprising that a high percentage of children were leaving care without any qualification and that many of them became young criminal offenders. As we said in paragraph 31.31, 'The overall effect was to leave many of the former residents with a lifelong resentment that precious years had been wasted and that they had emerged from care as damaged (if not worse) as they had been when they were admitted.'

It is not a function of members of a tribunal of inquiry to remain involved once their report has been presented but I have continued to be to a limited extent, partly because I have been accessible in Herefordshire. I was invited by one of the organisations represented at the inquiry, Voices from Care (Cymru), to be their patron and I have been kept in touch with major events by their energetic chief executive, Deborah Jones. It has also been my lot to address numerous conferences, particularly in the two or three years immediately following the publication of our report. Looked-after children are a devolved responsibility of the Welsh Assembly, which has been active in issuing guidance on the subject and in making statutory regulations such as the Children's Homes (Wales) regulations 2002 and the Placement of Children (Wales) regulations 2007. Moreover, Wales led the way in securing the appointment of a children's commissioner by an Act of Parliament that received the Queen's approval in May 2001, but much remains to be done.

It was unhelpful, in my view, of the prime minister, Tony Blair, to respond to our report by suggesting that the remedy would be greater resort to adoption for looked-after children and some relaxation of the restrictive guidelines used when assessing the suitability of prospective adoptive parents. I have no objection at all to the encouragement of adoption but it cannot sensibly be regarded as an answer to the problems that our inquiry disclosed. There are very many children for whom adoption is not a practicable proposition for a variety of obvious reasons that do not require elaboration. Moreover, the swing from care in residential community homes to fostering had probably reached beyond its appropriate limits before our hearings began, and this was reflected in the frequency of the breakdown of foster placements. What was needed was real strengthening of the provision of residential care for those children who needed the kind of security and skilled care that it could provide; but councillors in both England and Wales seem to have been unwilling to face up to this conclusion because they wished to avoid responsibility for potential failure of the kind that we described and the financial consequences of providing appropriate residential care themselves.

The result of this was that most councils in Wales and a large number in England (for which I do not have the details) ceased to provide children's homes, as did some charities such as the NSPCC. Instead, councils have delegated the responsibility to organisations such as the National Children's Home (now renamed Action for Children) that were willing to assume it. I was astounded to discover in October 2001, for example, when I addressed a training seminar in Kent, that there were more children in residential care homes in that county than in any other county in England or Wales, but that none of the homes was provided by Kent County Council. I was told that the seminar would provide 'an important (indeed unique) opportunity for senior managers and proprietors of private and voluntary children's homes to spend a structured/focused day together with senior representatives from the "key" agencies concerned with the safety, protection and welfare of children in public care'. More recently, when preparing an address to a Barnardo's national conference in April 2007, I learnt that on 31 March

2006 only about 4.5 per cent (203) of the 4,529 looked-after children in Wales were in children's homes and that in England the number of children's home places had fallen from 28,205 in 1971 to 5,700 (11 per cent) but that there were 16,000 children waiting for long-term fostering. Surprising additional facts are that only about half of the 203 looked-after children that were placed by Welsh local authorities in children's homes as at 31 March 2006 were placed in their own local authority area. Yet, at that time, there were 126 children's homes in Wales able to provide 516 places (but only 27 per cent of these homes were provided by local authorities).

I remain hopeful, though certainly not confident, that there will be a reappraisal of the allocation of financial resources to vital children's services and re-emphasis on the importance of residential care for looked-after children by professionally trained staff but the need is urgent. There is also a pressing need for the provision of readily accessible independent advocacy services for looked-after children. Ten years since the North Wales tribunal reported, arguments about this rumble on. The obvious fact that local authorities appear to be unwilling to concede is that, unless the appointed advocates are seen to be fully independent of the providers of children's services and pledged to confidentiality when it is required by the children, the latter will be unwilling to rely upon the advocates' guidance and help. I believe that local authorities still seek to insist upon a too close relationship with the advocates and upon immediate disclosure of any complaints of abuse, regardless of the wishes of the child. Much further progress also needs to be made, particularly in this time of recession, in the development of services for young persons on their discharge from care. The enactment of the Children (Leaving Care) Act 2000 represented a major step forward but the most recent statistics I have seen confirm that young persons who have left care remain at the heart of the problem of social exclusion. In the words of the central government green paper entitled 'Care Matters', published on 9 October 2006:

> We want an approach which continues to support them as long as they need it, which ceases to talk about 'leaving care' and instead ensures that young people move on in a gradual, phased and above all prepared way.

25

WINDING DOWN

Whilst my tribunal commitment meant that my full retirement had to be postponed, I was determined to make the most of any additional leisure that I could find; one objective that Sarah and I had was to change the focus of our lives to our country home to a much greater extent. As I explained earlier, this involved moving our London home from 11 Abbey Gardens, NW8, to a Middle Temple flat at 3 Essex Court. This was on the third floor and we were granted the tenancy from September 1996. There was much redecoration to be carried out, however, and we did not sleep there until 7 December. It proved to be a most convenient and comfortable home for us until September 2005; the only disadvantage was that we had to negotiate 66 steps to it without the alternative of a lift; but I do not attribute my later heart attack at the end of January 2004 to that. On the contrary, the exercise probably postponed it.

Meanwhile, in the autumn of 1996 we had to set about selling 11 Abbey Gardens. This proved to be reasonably straightforward because the property boom was in full swing and we were able to agree the sale in November, after carrying out some necessary redecoration. The sale was completed on 11 December, which was a busy month for us as we downsized and prepared for Christmas. Thomas had been posted to Hong Kong in October 1996 but was able to get home for Christmas and we attended the christening of our second grandson on 21 December in the Temple Church, before repairing to Herefordshire for Christmas with Sophie and Laura. That December was also notable for a reception at the Garrick Club, attended by HM the Queen and our patron, the Duke of Edinburgh, to mark the completion of its picture catalogue.

At Christmas it was a great pleasure for us to be joined by Robin Day for a week and, as always, he was the life and soul of the party. How greatly he is missed now by those of his many friends who survive! We could not know then that he had less than four years to live but he had had heart problems in recent years, culminating in an extensive bypass and later a valve replacement, and he insisted that he was in the departure lounge of life. Despite his natural exuberance and excess of energy, he was also an excellent and responsive guest who did not overtax our own strength.

In pursuit of Thomas we went to Hong Kong at the end of March 1997. I was glad to have the chance to visit Hong Kong before the end of the British lease because my Far Eastern visits at the Bar in the 1970s had all been to Singapore. We were astounded to be met at the airport, then still in the heart of the city, by Thomas driving a Rolls-Royce. He had bought it second-hand, of course, but he and his wife had a splendid Bentley as their second car, which they retained for some years after their return to the UK. This was par for the course because the Hong Kong Chinese were very competitive in keeping their expensive vehicles up to date, which created a buyers' market in top-class second-hand cars.

Thomas and Bente were very comfortably housed with their sons David and James in a flat in Southside Villas on the hill and we spent an enjoyable fortnight with them. We were fortunate to be given a tour of Government House, ending with tea with the Governor, Christopher Patten, and his wife Lavender, through the kind intervention of Derry Irvine and Alastair Goodlad. Altogether, it was a very satisfying break from the grim disclosures that I was hearing daily in the course of the tribunal's inquiry.

When the hearings were over Sarah and I set off for our last visit to Rhodes, at least for the time being. Laura was in the Far East (in Kathmandu after a partial ascent of Everest) because she had left for what turned out to be several gap years in April 1997, travelling to Indonesia at first, and remaining abroad until December 2002, apart from brief visits home. Rhodes in June was less comfortable than we would have wished because of the intense heat in the middle of the day. This time we stayed in Lachania, close to where Sophie was now living in Kattavia.

That was to be our last holiday abroad for 21 months because I had to concentrate on writing the tribunal's report and the summary. But it was not all doom and gloom. Our third grandson, Mark, was born in Hong Kong on 15 September 1998 and he was baptised in the Temple Church on 19 December, followed by lunch at the Savoy. Thomas and his family returned finally to Edenbridge on 27 February 1999. Meanwhile, Laura was wandering around the world: she was in Bangkok in September 1997, where she was robbed, in Hong Kong with Sophie two months later, then in Thailand, India and Nepal for much of 1998 and Australia followed by

Vietnam in 1999, where she was in Hanoi from 24 July. As for Sophie, she left Rhodes for California, taking her dog and cat with her, on 23 July 1998 and found accommodation in an apartment in Berkeley. She had enrolled for a three-year MA degree in counselling psychology with expressive arts therapy at an institute in San Francisco starting from September.

Once I was free of the shackles of the inquiry hearings and writing the report, Sarah and I set off on a round-the-world trip to see our daughters, Sophie in San Francisco and Laura in Hanoi, where she was staying and working with her friend Andrew Shakeshaft, whom she was later to marry on 17 May 2003. We flew first to San Francisco on 15 March 2000 and stayed for 11 nights at the pleasant Rose Garden Inn on Telegraph Avenue in Berkeley, broken by two nights with Sophie and her dog Izzie at the friendly Carmel Country Inn, during Clint Eastwood's mayoralty. We ate very well at a wide variety of places, including the Mission Ranch at Carmel and Scoma's at Sausalito, and Sophie took us on a series of tours in her venerable Cadillac. The cultural high point was a Sunday evening concert in the Davies Symphony Hall by the Czech Philharmonic Orchestra conducted by Vladimir Ashkenazy.

From San Francisco we flew to Singapore, with a three-hour stop at the new Hong Kong airport en route, to stay at the Shangri-La Hotel, my first nostalgic return visit for 24 years. It was a delight to be back there, albeit too briefly, and to dine with Tan Boon Teik, the former Attorney-General, and his clever lawyer wife Soukyee at the Shang Palace. Then it was off to Hanoi, where we were met by Laura after our three-and-a-half-hour flight. North Vietnam was very much a new and strange world for us but still showed many lingering traces of its long occupation by the French. We stayed for 10 days, mainly in Hanoi in the house Laura and Andy had rented, but visited Halong Bay for two nights with Laura, where we had our most spectacular lunch on a small boat in the course of a six-hour trip on the bay.

At this point my seventy-fourth birthday was looming, which meant that I was eligible to sit as a deputy High Court judge for one further year. I was uncertain whether to take advantage of this when, to my surprise, I was asked to sit in the Civil Division of the Court of Appeal when I could because they were short-handed while various Lords Justices were fulfilling special commitments elsewhere or were off sick. It was quite usual for retired judges to sit in the Criminal Division, as one did before retirement, but I welcomed the chance to sit in the Civil Division, which had not come my way after leaving the Family Division. The result was that, between January 2000 and March 2001, I sat in the Court of Appeal Civil Division for just over 14 weeks with a total of 14 different Lord Justices so that I was able to savour nearly half the membership of the Court of Appeal as it then was. In addition, I sat for a week in the Criminal Division in February 2000 and for a week as a deputy High Court judge at Cardiff in June the same year. Overall, I think that my stint was about par for the course at my age then and I do not envy those of my predecessors who sat on into their eighties before a compulsory retirement age was imposed.

A major sadness during the period of my Court of Appeal sittings was the unexpected death of Robin Day on 6 August 2000, just 50 years after I had first met him on the river Cam at that farcical inter-university union boat race. He had been a steadfast friend throughout the intervening years and a great stimulus in my life in so many ways. Robin left a direction in his will that his memorial service should be in the Temple Church, a privilege to which he was entitled as an honorary bencher of the Middle Temple, and a request that I should organise it. He also wrote that he did not wish the service to be at a 'BBC Church'. His instructions were clear and easy to follow but I do not think that he had foreseen that many of his admirers would have wished the service to be in Westminster Abbey. The result was that there was public argument about the venue but, in the end, I decided that Robin's affection for the law was such that I must obey his expressed wishes and I was sure that he would prefer a church packed by his friends to an abbey with a less intimate atmosphere.

The preparation involved more work than I had expected but I received a great deal of help from Robin's friends and not least from both the BBC and ITN, who contributed generously to the cost. Over 700 tickets were issued in response to the many applications and the Temple Church was filled to, and almost beyond, its capacity. Addresses were given by Dick Taverne and Paul Fox, and there were readings by William Rees-Mogg, Ludovic Kennedy, Keith Kyle and Donald Sinden. Immediately after the service we played the Flannagan and Allen recording of 'Underneath the Arches' at the special request of Robin's sons. I am sure that he would have been well pleased with the affection for him that was so evident and by the host of distinguished admirers from every aspect of his life who attended.

I had envisaged later retirement to be a slow descent into torpor and had been warned that life in one's seventies was inescapably a journey downhill but I was saved from excessive inertia by a request from Ann (Baroness) Mallalieu to me to chair a hunting authority. She was the very effective president of the Countryside Alliance and the supervisory board which that organisation had in mind to sponsor was part of its defence to the anti-hunting campaign. Such a board had been recommended by the Phelps Review of Hunting with Hounds published in 1997 and my understanding was that Lord Nolan had been approached initially as the prospective chairman but had been unable to accept because of his other commitments. Following a series of meetings with prominent members of the alliance and of the Masters of Fox Hounds Association, in the course of which I was vetted, detailed plans were made for the incorporation of the Independent Supervisory Authority for Hunting (ISAH Ltd), a company limited by guarantee, which was duly effected on 30 December 1999.

A major aim was to ensure as far as possible that the seven commissioners forming the authority were transparently independent of hunting organisations except for the one ex officio commissioner, namely, the chairman of the Council of Hunting Associations, who would provide practical experience of hunting to help us in our deliberations. My own appointment was by the original members of the authority, and the other five commissioners were appointed by an appointments panel, the members of which were themselves nominated by organisations such as the National Farmers' Union and the CLA (now the Country and Business Association), apart from one nominated by me. The result was that we ended up with a strong body of commissioners, including two distinguished academic veterinary surgeons, my former pupil Gerard Elias QC, who was chairman of the England and Wales Cricket Board's disciplinary committee, a prominent farmer in Cumbria and a leading Shropshire and Herefordshire landowner. Our ex officio member was Sam Butler, an MFH and grandson of Rab Butler.

Looking back now, I am surprised at the amount that we achieved during the five years of our existence, despite the efforts of organisations such as the League against Cruel Sports to sabotage hunting and the determination of most Labour and Liberal MPs to ban it. A great deal of the credit for what we did must go to Brian Fanshawe, the wise and energetic secretary of the Council of Hunting Associations, as he became in 2002, Professor John Webster of Bristol University, one of our two academic commissioners, and our secretary, David Manley, of an old Herefordshire family, who came to our rescue on retiring to the country after a busy life in the City of London. They proved to be most congenial colleagues, as did the other commissioners, and I made many new friends in the hunting world so that the whole experience was a very stimulating accompaniment to retirement.

There were 10 member organisations of the authority led by the MFHA, with 185 recognised packs, and the Association of Masters of Harriers and Beagles with 92 packs. They also included the National Coursing Club and the Association of Lurcher Clubs. All these organisations submitted voluntarily to our jurisdiction and our expenses were met by a levy on them by the Council of Hunting Associations, which was itself part of the

Countryside Alliance. From our inception we reviewed the annual reports of these organisations and their separate codes of conduct, which we revised where we could in the interest of uniformity. Most importantly, we required reports to be submitted to us on all incidents in the hunting field that led to disciplinary proceedings by a member organisation or were the subject of significant complaint. These reports and minutes of disciplinary proceedings were reviewed by the commissioners, who had appropriate powers to intervene if they were dissatisfied with the outcome.

Quite apart from this more or less routine disciplinary work, ISAH took the initiative in setting up a system of monitoring the MFHA hunts by appointed inspectors who were required to report in standard form, and their valuable work provided the basis for a protocol for the supervision and regulation of hunting with dogs, which was in an advanced stage of preparation at the time when hunting was 'banned'. There were also separate field visits to hunts by individual ISAH commissioners.

All this work was very time consuming and it must be remembered that contemporaneously we had to deal with a series of government initiatives in relation to hunting, including a temporary ban between February and December 2001 because of the very serious outbreak of foot and mouth disease. The minister for rural affairs from 2001 onwards was Alun Michael, who had been Tony Blair's choice as the initial first minister of Wales to lead the Welsh Assembly but who had, in effect, been ousted from that position; it was with him that we had to deal mainly in the following four years. However, before that, when the first government hunting bill received its first reading on 8 December 2000, it was a Home Office responsibility, and David Manley and I met the junior minister handling it, Mike O'Brien, two days earlier. There followed persistent representations by ISAH that hunting should be permitted to continue under the supervision of ISAH or a similar body.

It would be tedious to refer in detail to the long drawn-out public debate that culminated in the enactment of the Hunting Act 2004 but there were major events from ISAH's point of view in the course of that debate. The first bill presented three options for selection on a free vote, namely, an outright ban or a form of licensing advocated by an ad hoc organisation calling itself the Middle Way Group or self-regulation on the ISAH model. It passed the House of Commons with a substantial majority in favour of an outright ban (399 to 185 on the second reading). Before the second reading in the House of Lords in March 2000 I wrote to every peer and peeress with a vote explaining the role of ISAH and the progress we had made thus far, and I addressed a meeting of interested peers on 6 March, at which Lord

Mancroft presided. The general response to us was very favourable and a majority of 141 voted in favour of self-regulation (the majority against an outright ban was 249).

There was much discussion as to whether the government would seek to steamroller the bill through by invoking the Parliament Acts 1911 and 1949 but a general election was looming so that there was a major timing difficulty. In the event the general election took place on 7 June 2001 and it was stated in the Labour manifesto that the House of Commons would be given an early opportunity to express its views, after which Parliament would be enabled to reach a conclusion on the issue. The result was that both Houses again debated the three options in March 2002 and again I wrote to the members of the Lords updating information about our drafting of a protocol for hunting. As before, the Commons voted for a complete ban but this time the Lords chose the Middle Way Group option.

Before these votes in 2001 and 2002 took place a report by a committee chaired by Lord Burns had been published in June 2000. As the committee itself said, 'that report might appear long on analysis and short on solutions.' But the committee believed that it would help to inform the debate and, in the penultimate chapter, there was detailed discussion of the 'concerns' about practical aspects of hunting. In view of the continuing rift between the Commons and Lords, Alun Michael decided to hold a public consultation to assist him in framing legislation and he indicated that two key principles to be addressed were the prevention of cruelty and the concept of utility. The consultation was to be by written submission initially but culminated in hearings at Portcullis House, Westminster, from 9 to 11 November 2002, over which the minister himself presided. Hunting had been banned in Scotland by then with effect from 1 August 2002.

ISAH played a full part in this consultation and Professor Webster and I were called to give oral evidence at the hearings to supplement our written submissions but ultimately to no avail, despite the extraordinarily successful Liberty and Livelihood march in London, said to have been attended by 400,000 supporters, which took place shortly afterwards. The opposition to hunting at the hearings was dominated by a relatively obscure Bristol professor of environmental sciences, Stephen Harris, who purported to be an expert on most aspects of the inquiry. My main regret was that the then chairman of the Countryside Alliance, whose experience of the type of advocacy needed was (at best) remote in time, chose to present the alliance's case instead of relying upon the excellent silk, Richard Lissack, who was near at hand throughout the hearings.

An attempt to pre-empt government action was made by Lord Donoghue, who promoted a bill to amend the Wild Mammals (Protection) Act 1996. This reached the report stage in the House of Lords in November 2003 but then ran out of time, as did the government's own hunting bill, which was introduced in the Commons in December 2002. The intention of the latter bill as drafted was to prohibit the hunting of wild mammals with dogs except when the hunting was registered (on satisfying tests of utility, least suffering or exempt). Deer hunting and hare coursing were to be prohibited. By the time that the bill had passed through the Commons, however, it had been amended to provide a complete ban on hunting with dogs and it was in this amended form that it went before the Lords. In September 2003 I wrote to all the peers and peeresses again and received very helpful responses from a large number of them; we held a further meeting in the Lords before the second reading there on 21 October, when the Lords voted to reject an outright ban and agreed to reinstate the proposals for registered hunting by 261 votes to 49.

The result of all this was that the Hunting Bill 2002 was finally enacted on 18 November 2004 and came into force on 18 February 2005. This was achieved by reintroducing the bill in September 2004 in the form in which it had left the Commons the previous year; and it passed through all its remaining stages there on 15 September. The Lords stuck to their guns and restored the original registration provisions, subject to some amendments, and rejected the ban. A short game of ping-pong between the Commons and the Lords then ensued, ending on 18 November, when the Commons decided not to give the bill any further consideration and the speaker certified that it had complied with the Parliament Acts 1911 and 1949, whereupon it received the royal assent.

Despite the parliamentary distractions, ISAH had managed to carry out some excellent work in the short period of its existence. The system of inspection of hunts had been instituted successfully by the MFHA; there was also regular reporting by the hunts, which provided valuable information about wildlife that had not previously been available, and this was being developed and refined in discussion with the Wildlife Conservation Research Unit at Oxford University, whose director, Professor David Macdonald, was one of our commissioners until 2004. The commissioners met as a body on 17 occasions and I personally benefited greatly from field visits to a number of hunts, including the Devon and Somerset Staghounds in their lovely country, where Sarah and I stayed with the legendary Tom Yandle. It was also a special pleasure to visit the Wynnstay with Lord Daresbury and the Beaufort with Captain Ian Farquhar; Sarah and I enjoyed two memorable luncheons at Badminton House on puppy show days at the kind invitation of the Duke and Duchess of Beaufort. Thus, I was able to glimpse a world that would otherwise have been wholly unknown to me.

Apart from these quasi-hunting activities, my life in retirement from 2001 was reasonably normal. My remuneration as chairman of ISAH enabled me to afford the rent of our Temple flat but it was not practicable to continue the tenancy once ISAH was put to sleep, and our house in Herefordshire became our sole residence from September 2005. Fortunately, by that time the Garrick Club had taken advantage of a large windfall from its share of the estate of A.A. Milne to provide excellent bedroom accommodation for members, which their wives are allowed to share, at reasonable rates. The Garrick has, therefore, become our London home in a very real sense.

My pleasantest personal surprise in the new century was the award of the GBE (Knight Grand Cross of the Order of the British Empire) in the New Year's honours list for 2002. This is a comparatively rare honour (I was the thirty-third living holder at that time in the civil division, of whom 15 were former Lord Mayors of London, and there were 20 in the military division), and I felt more than amply rewarded for such public service as I had performed.

Domestically, the most important event was Laura's wedding. She and Andy had left Hanoi in May 2000 and had established themselves in Seoul later that year, after visits to Thailand and the UK. They were with us just after Christmas 2002 and we announced their engagement on 17 February 2003. By that time she and Andy had joined with his parents in buying quite a large house in Lincolnshire, and the wedding was fixed for 17 May in a pretty church nearby. Most unhappily, Andy's father died shortly before that date but the wedding went ahead, as he wished, and he was very present in our minds on the day. The reception for just under 100 guests was at Laura and Andrew's house, where we had erected a marquee in the large garden, and the weather was kind to us, despite threatening to be otherwise.

Laura and Andy have remained there ever since and have been the sole occupants since Andy's mother remarried. They have established themselves as Ayurveda practitioners, having previously acquired a franchise for a range of Ayurvedic products when they were in India. They also provide retreats of varying length with treatments, demonstrations of Ayurvedic cooking and daily sessions of yoga, meditation and relaxation techniques.

A very pleasant surprise shortly before the wedding was an invitation from Geoffrey and Elspeth Howe to share a holiday with them and some fellow guests in Tuscany at the end of May 2003. We had broken our Provençal habit the previous year by spending a week in Sicily, at Taormina, at the end of April and had greatly enjoyed our stay there so that the chance to explore Tuscany and relax after our wedding labours was very welcome. The Howes' friends David and Anne Skeggs, he a distinguished oncologist, had rented a former monastery, Santa Maria Novella, near Radda in Chianti, which slept 11, and our fellow guests were Peter and Susan (née Chataway) Hordern, Leon and Diana Brittan and David Hopkinson.

Sarah and I flew to Pisa two days in advance, where we hired a car and drove to the delightful Villa de Barone at Panzano, where (to our surprise and amusement) we met up with the Howes, Horderns and Skeggs. We liked the hotel and the Chianti countryside so much that Sarah and I returned for a 10-day holiday at the Villa de Barone in May the following year; we have an engrossing account of the hotel's former role in *A Farm in Chianti* by Maria Bianca Vivani Della Robbia. Our holiday in 2003 proved to be very lively and harmonious and I managed to finish reading Patrick Marnham's excellent biography of Georges Simenon with great pleasure. The weather was all that we could have asked for and we returned to Pisa via Arezzo, where we saw the frescoes by Piero della Francesca, and La Verna, where Sarah climbed to the sanctuary in which St Francis of Assisi received the stigmata.

A temporary setback for me early the following year was a heart attack late at night on 26 January. Fortunately, I accepted the advice by telephone of an emergency doctor to call an ambulance because I experienced a cardiac arrest the next afternoon in Hereford County Hospital. No doubt my smoking habit of 65 years was largely to blame and I have not smoked since but I have been let off lightly as the result of a successful quadruple heart bypass operation by Mr Ian Wilson on 9 February at the (old) Queen Elizabeth hospital in Birmingham. I was home again nine days later and enjoyed recuperating in Tuscany subsequently.

The Garrick Club and the Middle Temple have remained centres of attention for me in London in the new century. The club held a great celebration at Armoury House, the home of the Honourable Artillery Company, on 10 June 2001 to mark the successful sale of the A.A. Milne literary estate to Disney. There was a huge turnout and Sarah and I dined in the very amusing company of the Onslows, Michael and Christine Mates, Jeremy and Verna Hanley and my sister Sylvia and her husband, John Thompson. Part of the excellent entertainment was provided by Kit and the Widow, ex-Cambridge Footlights, whom we had not heard before. Another milestone that we celebrated on 7 May 2004 at the Garrick was the seventy-fifth birthday of the witty Alistair Sampson, which he called a celebration of longevity and at which Geoffrey Howe proposed his toast; but Alistair was to die of cancer only 20 months later.

There were more celebrations at the Middle Temple. The Queen Mother again graced our family dinner on 5 December 2001, although it was to be for the last time, and in July HM the Queen and HRH the Duke of Edinburgh attended a service in the Temple Church to celebrate her golden jubilee. In February 2002 we marked the four hundredth anniversary of the first performance of *Twelfth Night*, which was in Middle Temple Hall, by repeat performances by the Globe Theatre Company. A particularly happy occasion on 5 November 2003 was a reception to mark Michael Sherrard's CBE and the completion of his excellent portrait for the Inn, and a year later there was a unique celebration dinner for the forthcoming hundredth birthday of His Honour King-Hamilton QC, coupled with a farewell to our popular Under Treasurer, Brigadier Charles Wright.

By 2005 my connections with London and the law were weakening significantly. It was already 10 years since I had been Treasurer of the Middle Temple and very many new benchers had been elected in that period so that I belonged very much to the past. Hunting was being banned, and I was about to give up our Temple flat, at which we spent our last night on 25 September. Moreover, our children were still rather scattered. Thomas was travelling a great deal, although based in London with his home in Kent. Sophie had moved from San Francisco to Los Angeles in August 2001 and had found work with an independent film producer and manager, Lou Pitt. His office was in Beverly Hills and she rented an apartment near Venice and Santa Monica. It seems that she made herself useful because she progressed to director of development for the Pitt Group and then became a vice-president from June 2005. As for Laura, she and her husband were busy establishing their Ayurveda practice. It is not surprising, therefore, that Sarah and I were increasingly content to spend most of our time, especially during the summer months, in our Herefordshire home.

Faced by an ocean of leisure when I gave up the chairmanship of ISAH in June 2005, I acquired a computer and set about educating myself in its mysteries with the aid of one of the many published tutors. To my surprise, I made reasonable progress and eventually persuaded myself to embark on these memoirs. It has certainly proved to be a useful daily companion and most of the information that I have Googled from it has proved to be fairly accurate.

Sophie decided to forsake Los Angeles for London in 2006 and arrived back in the UK just in time to take part in June in a joint family celebration of her fortieth birthday, Sarah's seventieth and my eightieth. Most of our surviving friends and family were able to make it and we were blessed with a glorious summer's day at our Herefordshire home. Altogether, it was a joyous occasion, graced by many distinguished friends and, most notably, by Tasker Watkins, who was to die just over a year later, aged 88.

It is sensible to end this record here because nothing much happens in one's eighties. Like many soldiers and even more lawyers I am gently fading away now and trying not to be too much of a nuisance. Our friends and family diminish in number but it is still good to be alive and I have enjoyed reliving my life through the medium of writing about it.

INDEX

Aberconway, Lord, 95
Aberfan inquiry (1966–67), 130–4
Abse, Leo, 117, 145, 161–2, 170–1
Abse, Marjorie, 170–1
Ackner, Mr Justice (Desmond), 132, 133–4, 192, 194, 195, 206, 230
after-dinner speaking, 211–12
Ainslie, Katherine, 122
Air Training Corps (ATC), 23–4
Alan, Hervey, 111–12
Albany Trust, 117
Alport, Lord, 185
Anns, Bryan, 153–4, 156
Anson, Malcolm, 205
appeals: problems for judges, 224–5
Arden, Lady Justice, 264
Arnold, Lord Justice (John), 214, 233–4, 242, 243
ARP service, 23
Arran, Earl of, 117
asbestos, 246
Ashley, Jack, 51, 52, 55, 56–7, 81, 89, 248
Asquith, Herbert, 7, 11
Assizes, 62–3, 80
Associated Leisure Limited, 153–61, 166
Astor, David, 145
Atkinson, Mr Justice (Fenton), 128
Audley, Sir Bernard, 265
Ayer, James, 8–9
Bacon, Grania, 111

Bacon, Sir Ranulph, 155
Bailey, Stanley, 46, 47
Bailey, Trevor, 46
Baillie, Isobel, 25
Baker, Sir George, 205, 207, 214, 234
Baki, Misbah, 257–8
Balcombe, John, 169, 230, 234–5, 243
Bally Manufacturing Corporation, 154, 155, 157
Balon, Norman, 117
Bankes, Wynne, 65
Barlow, Captain Sir Thomas, 146
Barraclough, K.J.P., 173
Barrowclough, Anthony, 72
Bateson, Andrew, 176
Baxter, H.J., 72
Beale, Doone, 81
Beauclerk, Sidney de Vere, 9–10
Beecham, Sir Thomas, 41
Beeching Report on Assizes and Quarter Sessions, 218, 219
Bell, Mary Hayley, 128
Bell, Mr Justice, 259
Beloff, Michael, 224
Benenson, Peter, 126
Benn, Tony, 52, 89
Bennett, Mr Justice, 277
Bernardino, José, 125–6
Besch, Anthony, 81
Bevan, Aneurin, 88, 105
Beveridge, Sir William, 35, 36
Bingham of Cornhill, Lord, 241, 245

Birch, Nigel, 36, 55, 104
Birkett, Lord Justice, 51
Bivett, Brian, 87
Blair, Michael, 219
Blair, Tony, 175, 285
Blaker, Peter, 190
Bohana, Roy, 267
Booker, Christopher, 116
Booth, Mrs Justice, 175, 264, 266
Boothby, Bob, 54–5
Bork, Judge Robert, 236
Borrie, Lord (Gordon), 241
Bourne, Sir Wilfred, 200–1
Bowen, Roderic, 77, 100, 114
Bowsher, Peter, 162
Boyle, Stanley, 203–4, 242
Brabin, Mr Justice (Daniel), 94
Braddock, Bessie, 105
Brady, Ian, 128–30
Braithwaite, Bernard, 152
Brandon, Mr Justice, 195
Breasley, Scobie, 113
Bridge of Harwich, Lord, 134
Bridgend Urban District Council,
    196–7
Brightman, John, 61, 65
Bristow, Mr Justice, 127, 230–1
Brittan, Diana, 296
Brittan, Leon, 162, 164, 165, 296
Brogan, Denis, 54
Bromley-Davenport family, 276
Brook, Eric, 23, 37–8
Brookes, George, 91–2
Brown, Lord Justice (Stephen), 234,
    242, 243, 277
Brown, William, 2
Browne, Mr Justice, 162, 196
Browne-Wilkinson, Lord Justice, 208,
    228
Bruno, Angelo, 158
Bryn Estyn children's home, 284
Bueno, Antonio, 270
Bullard, Julian and Margaret, 190
Burton, Michael, 176, 179
Butler, Sam, 291
Butler-Sloss, Dame Elizabeth, 242
Butlins Limited, 154
Byrne, John, 118
Caballe, Montserrat, 267

Cadwyr Cymru (Keepers of Wales), 223
Caernarfon: Moriah Chapel fire, 221
Callaghan, Jim, 54
Cambridge Union Society, 34, 48, 50–6
Cambridge University Air Squadron
    (CUAS), 33
Cambridge University Liberal Club, 48,
    49, 50
Cameron inquiry (1963), 124–5
Campaign for Democratic Socialism
    (CDS), 120
Carlile of Berriew, Lord, 79
Carman, George, 249–51
Casals, Pablo, 41
Casson, Ann, 24
Casson, Hugh, 223
Casson, Lewis, 24
Casson, Margaret, 223
Castle, Barbara, 105
Cavendish, Lady Elizabeth, 248
Cazalet, Mr Justice, 264
celebrity concerts, 24
Cellini, Dino, 154, 159
Chamberlayne-Macdonald, Nigel, 117
Chapple, Field Marshal Sir John, 263
Chapple, Frank, 90, 118
Charles, Prince of Wales, 136, 139, 238,
    266
Chataway, Christopher, 86, 89, 102, 223
Christie, Stuart, 116
Church of Scientology, 151–3
Churchill, Randolph, 88
CIA, 157, 161
Cintas, Oscar, 258
circuit courts: procedures, 182; presiding
    judge system, 218–21
Clarke, Catherine, 210
Clarke, Mr Justice (David), 222
Clement Davies, Stanley, 34
Clough, Margaret, 278
Cobb, Mr Justice, 199, 200
Cobon, Sheila, 67
Coleman, Bill, 184
Colony Club, 154, 155, 159
Comyn, James, 202
conciliation, marital, 243
Connah's Quay power station, 148–50
Conway, Michael David, 143–4
Cooke, Sarah Grace, 10, 21, 22

Cooper, Peter, 265
Cooper, Raymond, 136
Coote-Robinson, R.A.R., 39, 40
Corrallo, Antonio Dux, 157, 158
Corrie, Hugh, 62
Coslett, Dennis, 137, 138–9
Council for Freedom in Portugal and her
  Colonies, 125–6
Countryside Alliance, 290, 292, 293
Courtaulds Limited, 8
Cox, Sir Geoffrey, 122
Cradock, Percy, 47–8, 51, 72
Crane, Frank, 71
Crawley, Aidan, 86
Crespi, James, 153
cricket, 15, 27, 117
Cripps, Stafford, 14, 60
Crisp, Clement, 123
Croom-Johnson, Sir Reginald, 62, 66,
  122
Crosland, Tony, 86, 87, 120
Crossman, Dick, 54–5
Crown Prosecution Service:
  establishment, 189
Cumming-Bruce, Mr Justice, 144

Dai Bomber, 137, 138
Daily Mail, 153, 154
Daniel, Alan, 170, 171
Danvers, John, 89, 101
Daresbury, Lord, 294
Daube, David, 47
David, Sir Robin, 79, 126, 134, 143,
  270
Davies, Sir Alun Talfan, 78, 114, 128,
  133, 199, 260
Davies, Clement, 30, 79, 95
Davies, D.T.M., 184
Davies, Edmund, 64, 76–7, 84, 85, 91,
  92, 94, 96, 100
Davies, Dr Elwyn, 184
Davies, Gethin and Eulanwy, 267
Davies, John, 138, 194
Davies, Rhys T., 20–1
Davies, Ron, 283
Davies, Sir Walford, 24, 111
Davies, William Arthian, 64, 68, 70, 77,
  100
Davies of Llandinam, Lord, 29

Dawson, Beatrice Maud (née
  Waterhouse; RW's aunt), 3–4
Dawson, Christopher, 3–4
Day, Alexander, 122–3
Day, Kathy, 171
Day, Robin, 53, 59, 60, 61, 72, 74, 81,
  86, 101, 102, 107–8, 109, 122, 151,
  171, 190, 202, 223, 277, 287–8, 290
Dehn, Hugh, 265–6
Delors, Jacques and Marie, 248
Denning, Lord, 93, 153, 155, 194, 224,
  225
Devlin, Mr Justice, 51
Dilhorne, Viscount, 117
Dilhorne, John, second Viscount, 264
Dillon, Michael, 59
Diplock, Lord, 196
Dobie, Laurence, 123
Dobry, George, 68–9
Dodd, Ken, 249–51
Donaldson, Sir John, 62, 233, 234
Donaldson, Lady Mary, 213, 231
Donoghue, Lord, 294
Duff, P.W., 47
Duke, Dick, 158
Dunn, Lord Justice, 204, 243
Dwell Construction Ltd, 141–3
Dymes, Albert, 158

Eady, Mr Justice (Charles), 256
Eagle Star insurance company, 275
Ebbw Vale steelworks, 197–8
Edmund-Davies, Lord Justice, 131, 133,
  135, 156–7, 180, 193, 233, 234
Edwards, Jimmy, 53
eisteddfodau, 16, 107, 266–7, 280
Electrical Trades Union (ETU), 117–19
Elias, Gerard, 72, 273, 279, 291
Ellis, T.I., 21
Ellis, Tom, 121
Elwyn-Jones, Lord, Frederick Elwyn
  Jones Jones, Elwyn, 77, 84, 100, 114,
  124, 125, 128–9, 131, 132, 134, 153,
  154, 156–7, 179, 201, 236
embracery, 199–200
Emery, Elizabeth, 223
Emery, Peter, 33, 87, 223
Employment Appeal Tribunal, 207–8,
  216, 227, 230

Ennals, Martin, 120
Eurig ap Gwilym, 223
European Court of Justice, 236
Evans, Anthony, 198
Evans, Cayo, 137, 138–9
Evans, Meurig, 78
Everiss, S.F., 33
Ewbank, Tony, 214

Fairgrieve, Russell, 98
Fanshawe, Brian, 291
Fantoni, Barry, 116, 117
Farquhar, Ian, 294
Farrar's Building, 66, 70–2
Faulkner, Charles, 111
Fay, Charles, 149
FBI, 157, 161
Ferrier, Kathleen, 65, 82
Field, Mr Justice, 179
Fine, Max, 153, 156, 158
Fisher, Sir Henry, 201
Fitzgerald, Michael, 149
Flannery, Martin, 163
Foot, Dingle, 30, 50, 51, 105
Foot, Paul, 116, 117, 186, 191–3
Fort Development Limited, 169–70
Forum (TV series), 120
Foster, Sir John, 152, 160
Foster, Jonathan, 255
Foulkes, Frank, 90, 118
Fox, Lord Justice, 239
Fox, Paul, 290
Francis, Judge Norman, 78, 79, 132
Franck, Betty, 123
Fraser and Company, 166–9
fraud trials, and juries, 231
Free Wales Army, 135–9
Freeth, Denzil, 50
French, Lady, 227
French, Mr Justice, 238
Fricker, Nigel, 198

Galtress, Trevor, 275
Gardiner, Gerald, 106, 118, 126–7, 137
Garrick Club, 122, 295
Gatehouse, Robert, 106
Gaventa, Joseph (Chummy), 164–5
General Strike (1926), 1
George, William, 90, 115

Ghows, Wahab, 166
Gibbins, Peter, 72
Gibbon, Michael, 137–8, 183, 184, 196, 197
Gibson and Weldon, 59, 60
Ginsberg, Judge Ruth, 235
Glanville, Brian, 127–8, 151
Glidewell, Lord Justice, 269
Glynne, Walter, 25
Goddard, Lord, 93, 95
Goff, Mr Justice, 197
Goldman, Peter, 34
Goldsmith, James, 175–6, 180
Goldsmith, Lord (Peter), 269
Goodbody, Patrick, 173
Goodhart, Philip, 50, 51, 81
Goodlad, Alastair, 288
Goodman-Roberts, Sir Ernest, 65–6
Gorman, Mr Justice, 106, 107
Gough, Ellen (née Sylvester; RW's maternal grandmother), 5, 6, 69
Gough, Harold (RW's uncle), 6, 113
Gough, May (née Dixon), 6, 113
Gough, Muriel, 6–7
Gough, William (RW's maternal grandfather), 5–6
Gower, John, 138
Graham, Douglas, 120, 237–8
Graham, Sara, 237–8
Gratey, Meg, 81
Gray, Anthony, 117
Gray, Gilbert (Gillie), 211, 252
Gray, Mr Justice (Charles), 156
Greater London Citizens' Advice Bureau Service, 209–10
Green, Roger Lancelyn, 135
Gregynog, 213–14
Gregynog judges' conference (1982), 226–7
Grenfell, Julian, 120
Gresford Colliery disaster, 14
Griffith Williams, John, 277
Griffiths, Judge Bruce, 199, 265
Griffiths, John, 105
Griffiths, Lawrence, 194
Griffiths, Mr Justice (later Lord), 164, 224, 225
Grundy, P.G., 173
Guinness, Loel, 241

Hadfield, Sir Ronald, 278
Hague, William, 278
Hailsham, Viscount, 91–2, 116
Hale, Brenda, 244, 277
Hales, George, 117
Hall Williams, J.E., 226
Hallett, Mr Justice, 195
Hanratty, James, 186–7
Harding, Rowe, 78
Harries, Ronald, 84–5
Harrington, Patrick, 72
Harris, Professor Stephen, 293
Hatton, Derek, 249, 254–5
Havers, Lord, 242
Haw Par Bothers International Limited, 172–80
Hawser, Judge Lewis, 187
Head, Anthony, 54
Healey, Denis, 223
Heath, Ted, 223
Heber-Percy family, 237
Heilbron, Rose, 64
Heilpern, Godfrey, 130
Hertford, Marquess of, 117
Hess, Myra, 34
Hetherington, Tony, 189
Hilbery, Mr Justice, 111
Hill, Charles, 89
Hill, Graham Starforth, 230
Hill, Michael, 271
Hill, Rear-Admiral Richard, 270
Hillingdon Council, 224–5
Hinchcliffe, Mr Justice, 127
Hindley, Myra, 128
Hirst, Lord Justice (David), 51, 127–8, 155, 156, 158, 159, 269
Hobhouse, Sir Arthur, 12
Hobson, Anthony, 248
Hodgson, Sir Derek, 210–11, 264
Hogben, Lancelot, 26
Hollond, H.A., 46
Holywell, 1, 8–13
Hooberman, Ben, 90, 118
Hoolahan, Tony, 155
Hooson, Emlyn, 48, 79, 101, 102, 105, 111, 114, 214, 222, 266
Hopkin Morris, Rhys, 11
Hopkinson, David, 296
Hordern, Peter, 151, 152, 296

Hordern, Susan, 296
Horne, Alistair, 190
Howard, Elizabeth Jane, 170
Howe, Elspeth, 223–4, 248, 265, 295–6
Howe, Geoffrey, 51, 54, 55, 81, 87, 88, 114, 120, 190, 202, 207, 223–4, 228, 231, 248, 264–5, 295–6, 297
Howell, Denis, 120
Hubbard, L. Ron, 152, 153
Hughes, Cledwyn, 36
Hughes, Glyn Tegai, 48, 49, 213
Hughes-Parry, Sir David, 41
Hurd, Douglas, 55
Hutt, John, 113
Huxley, Harry, 64
Hytner, Ben, 268

Independent Supervisory Authority for Hunting (ISAH Ltd), 291
Ingram, Diana, 102, 110, 113, 119, 187, 213, 214, 228, 231, 235
Ingrams, Richard, 115, 116, 117
Inns of Court: scholarships, 241–2; administration, 269; see also Middle Temple
Irvine, Alexander (Derry), 175, 177–8, 179, 196–7, 202, 213, 264, 288
Irvine, Alison, 197, 213
Itkin, Herbert, 156, 157–9, 160–1

Jackson, Joseph, 215
Jackson, R.M., 46
James, Kenneth, 81, 188, 190, 240
James, Teresa, 188, 190, 240
Jarred, Mary, 25
Jarrett, Professor William, 146
Jay, Peter, 117
Jenkin, Patrick, 72, 87
Jenkin of Roding, Lord, 265
Jenkins, Roy, 117, 120, 123, 171, 184–5, 186, 263
Jenks, Robin, 120, 238
Jessel, Lord, 155, 156
Joad, C.E.M., 34
Johnson, Pamela Hansford, 128
Johnson, Paul, 88
Johnson-Hill (Slater Walker employee), 174
Johnson Smith, Geoffrey, 151–3

Jolowicz, Poppy (formerly Stanley), 47, 190
Jolowicz, Tony, 47
Jones, Sir Austin, 65, 66
Jones, Barry, 121, 121–2
Jones, Cyril, 90, 115
Jones, Deborah, 284
Jones, Glyn, 64, 76, 100
Jones, Janie, 191–2
Jones, Tom, 121
Jones, Wyn Brynford, 14
Joseph, Maxwell, 154
Jowitt, Earl, 62
judges: robes, 206; workload, 209, 248–9; duties, 216; appointment system, 219–21, 234–5
judiciary, expansion of, 75
Juliana, Queen of the Netherlands, 56
Jupp, Kenneth, 188

Kelleher, Leonie, 210
Kempster, Michael, 162
Kennedy, Ludovic, 86, 109, 186, 223, 290
Kenyon, Lord, 231
Kerfoot-Roberts, J., 68, 90, 101
Kerfoot-Roberts, Lilian, 23
Kettle, Arnold, 4
Keynes, John Maynard, 32
Kidd, Ronald, 242, 275
King-Hamilton, Judge, 191, 192, 297
Kinnersley, David, 33
Klevan, Rodney, 255
Knight, Robert, 221
Kossoff, David, 127
Kyle, Keith, 52, 81, 87, 88, 107–8, 290

Lambert, David, 279
Laming, Lord, 283
Lancaster, Osbert, 117
Lane, Lord, 211, 229, 243, 245, 249, 266
Lang, Gordon, 16
Lannigan, Dennis, 33
Lansky, Meyer, 159
Las Vegas Coin Company, 155, 156
Latey, Mr Justice, 234–5
Lauterpacht, Sir Hersch, 47
law reform, 243
Lawson, Eleanor, 277

Lawton, Mr Justice, 140, 155, 157, 158, 160–1, 200, 226
le Fleming, Morris, 278
Lee Kuan Yew, 168, 181
Legg, Tom, 220
Lennox-Boyd, Mark and Arabella, 145
Leonard, Mr Justice, 218–19, 226, 229
Leverhulme, Viscount, 135
Levi, Thomas, 11, 40
Levin, Bernard, 89, 193
Lewis, Bridget, 221
Lewis, Esyr, 68, 69, 85
Lewis, Henry Gethin, 221, 276
Lewis, Michael, 192
Lim Cher Keng, 169, 170
Lind-Smith, Gerry, 79
Lipstein, Kurt, 46–7, 216, 218
Lissack, Richard, 293
Llangollen International Musical Eisteddfod, 107, 266–7, 280
Llewellyn, Michael, 221
Lloyd, David, 24–5, 106–7
Lloyd of Berwick, Tony 202
Lloyd George, David, 11–12, 16–17, 35
Lloyd-Hart, Pamela, 210
Lloyd Jones, Mr Justice, 175, 179
Lloyd-Jones, Vincent, 64, 77, 84, 100, 114
Local Government Boundary Commission for Wales, 183–4, 209
Lodge, Oliver, 269
Lomax, Rachel, 279
London Road Rats, 253
London Zoo, 182–3, 209, 231–2, 262–3
Lord Mayor's banquet, 213
Lost in Care, 284
Low, Valentine, 277
Lowry, Lord, 219, 228

M53 inquiry, 134–5
McCartney, Paul and Linda, 145
McCormack, Martin, 48
Macdonald, Professor David, 294
McHenry, Brian, 279
McIntyre, Ian, 82
Mackay of Clashfern, Lord, 219, 236, 242
Mackenzie Stuart, Lord, 236

McLaren, Hon. John, 64–5
Macmillan, Donald, 50, 56
Macmillan, Harold, 89
McNair, Sir Arnold, 47
McNeill, Mr Justice, 135
Macrae, Duncan, 51
Mafia, 154–5, 157–8, 159
maintenance, post-divorce, 239–40
Mallalieu, Baroness (Ann), 290
Mancroft, Lord (Benjamin), 204, 292–3
Manley, David, 291, 292
Marks, Gordon, 153–4, 158
Marnan, John, 68
Marnham, Patrick, 116
Marnham, Sir Ralph, 134
Mars-Jones, Adam, 67
Mars-Jones, Sir William, 25, 64, 66–7,
    68, 72, 77, 80, 81, 84, 96, 99, 100, 106,
    114, 126–7, 128, 129, 135, 210–11,
    236, 259, 273
Marshall, Louis, 33, 35, 38, 45
Martin v. Glynwed Distribution Limited,
    227
Masterman, Crispin, 197
Mathur, Gautam, 52
Matthew, John, 176
Matthias, Winifred, 184
Maxwell, Hamish, 33, 38, 42
Maxwell, Robert, 265
Maxwell Fyfe, Sir David, 91
May, Lord Justice (John), 239
Measor, Tony, 166–8
Megarry, Sir Robert, 165
Megarry, Ted, 92
Megaw, Lord Justice, 194
Meibion Glyndwr, 223
Melbourne Unit Trust, 175, 177
Melly, George, 38, 40
Merriman, Lord, 71, 93
mesothelioma, 246
Methodist Church: status of ministers,
    227
Mexico City, 240–1
Michael, Alun, 292, 293
Middle Temple: history and workings,
    268–75
Milmo, Mr Justice, 192
Moiseiwitsch, Benno, 41
Molony, Sir Joseph, 116, 134–5

Monckton, Sir Walter, 69, 87–8
Monro Davies, W.L., 72
Montgomery, Viscount, 117
Moors murders, 128–30
Morgan, John, 116
Morland, Lord Justice, 135
Morris, Gwyn, 116
Morris, John, 183
Morris, Malcolm, 111, 122, 134, 165
Morris of Borth-y-Gest, Lord, 71, 94
Mortimer, John, 138, 196
Moseley, Professor Hywel, 213, 226
Motor and General Underwriters
    Investment Holdings Limited,
    169–70, 175
Mulcahy, James, 138
Munro, Sir Alan, 111
Murphy, Paul, 283
Myddelton, David, 223
Myerson, Aubrey, 138

National Coal Board, 132
National Union of Bank Employees
    (NVBE), 124–5
National Union of Mineworkers
    (NUM), 162–4
Neale, Guy, 38
Neale, Paul, 27
Neeson, Liam, 278
neomycin, 246–8
Nicholls, Clive, 176
Nickel, Rachel, 252
Nield, Sir Basil, 63
Nield, Mr Justice, 126
Nissan, 238–9
Nolan, Lord, 268
North Wales child abuse inquiry,
    278–86

O'Brien, Mike, 292
O'Connor, Sandra, 235
O'Donnell, Lord Justice, 228
Ogden, Minnie (née Waterhouse; RW's
    aunt), 3, 4, 5
Ogden, Richard (RW's cousin), 3
Ogden, William (Billy), 3, 4, 5
Ogilvy Watson, Donald, 173–4
Ognall, Mr Justice, 252
Ormerod, Mr Justice, 63, 65, 66

Ormrod, Mr Justice, 195
Oulton, Sir Derek, 219, 220
Owen, Norman, 200
Owen, Philip, 96, 114, 138, 202, 214, 230, 260

Pain, Peter, 118
Palliser family, 248
Parfitt, Warton, 227
Park, Mr Justice, 204
Parker, Lord, 94, 126–7
Parkinson, Michael, 117
Parliament, state opening of, 213
Parsons, Miss, 38
Patten, Christopher and Lavender, 288
Peace Pledge Union, 16
Pennant, David, 9, 78, 274
Perrick, Eve, 81
personal-injury claims, 245
Philip, Prince, Duke of Edinburgh, 182, 183, 231–2
Phillips, Lord Chief Justice, 202, 271
Phillips, Raymond, 134, 218, 219, 226
Pickering, John, 276
Pickthorn, Charles, 52
Pinder, Dennis, 171–2
Pitchford, Judge Charles, 43, 76, 77, 198
Plant, Sir Arnold, 22
Platt-Mills, John, 135
Pollak, Judge Louis H., 236
Poole, Mr Justice, 277
Potter, Harold, 40–1
President of the Methodist Conference v. Warton Parfitt, 227
Private Eye, 115–17, 151, 180, 202
professional negligence, 245–6

Queensberry, Marquess of, 117

rabies, 145–8
Raft, George, 154, 155–6
Rajendran, S., 172
Ramanujan, 170
Rankin, Andrew, 135, 138
Rawley, Alan, 255
Rawlinson, Sir Peter, 152, 153, 154
Read, Lionel, 225
Reading, Marquess of, 51
Rees, Breuan, 78, 131, 133, 231

Rees, Deborah, 231
Rees, Geraint, 77
Rees, Haydn, 91, 92
Rees, John Charles, 253–4
Rees-Mogg, William, 290
refugee asylum, 224–5
Rehnquist, the Hon. William H., 273–4
Reid, Lord, 196
Rhys-Roberts, Tommy, 78
Richards, Bertrand, 141, 182
Richards, Sir Gordon, 113
Richards, Norman, 77, 78, 100, 114
Richardson, Kenneth, 176
Richardson, Natasha, 278
Rimmer, Thomas, 143–4
Roache, William, 255–6
Robens, Lord, 132
Roberts, Eifion, 149
Roberts, John, 90
Robertson, Geoffrey, 196
Robinson, Kenneth, 152
Roch, Lord Justice, 72, 132, 277
Rodgers, Bill, 87, 120, 170–1
Rodgers, Silvia, 170–1
Rolfe, Frederick, 9–10
Ronson, Gerald Israel, 141, 142
Ronson, Howard, 142
Rosenthal, Ellen, 90
Roskill Committee, 231
Rothermere, Viscount, 158
Rothschild, Leo de, 190
Roundell, Richard, 231
Routledge, Graham, 59
Royal Air Force Volunteer Reserves (RAFVR), 27
Royal Courts of Justice Citizens' Advice Bureau, 209–10, 263–4
Rushton, Willie, 116
Russell, Brian, 57
Rutter, John, 78
Ryder, Ernest, 279
Rylands, Philip and Jane, 264

Said, Wafic, 257–8
St John-Stevas, Norman, 47, 50, 51, 53, 72, 81, 120
St John's College, Cambridge, 24, 27, 31, 32, 45

St John's Wood Society, 267
St Winifred's Well, 1, 9
Salkin, Alfred, 154, 159
Salmon, Michael, 267
Salmon, Mr Justice, 105–6
Sampson, Alistair, 119, 265, 296–7
Samuel, Herbert (later Viscount
    Samuel), 16, 17, 49
Sandys, Edwina, 171
Scalia, Judge Antonin, 235
Scargill, Arthur, 162–4
Scarman, Lord Justice, 194
Scott, Kenneth, 46
Scott, Peter, 183
Scott of Foscote, Lord, 236
Seaborne Davies, Dewi, 40, 43
section 31s, 208
Sedley, Stephen, 192
Seldon, Arthur, 22
Sellers, Mr Justice, 96–7
Semple, Professor Andrew, 146
settlement negotiation, 128
Seys-Llewellyn, Anthony, 198–9
Seys-Llewellyn, John, 79
Shack, Cyril, 153–4, 155, 156, 157, 158,
    159–61
Shackleton Report, 186
Shakeshaft, Andrew, 289, 295
Shaw, Lord Justice (Sebag), 178
Shawcross, Lord (Hartley), 14, 178
Shen Yuen Pai, 166–7, 168
Sherrard, Michael, 271, 297
Short, Renee, 120
Shove, Gerald, 32
Shulman, Milton, 164
Shulman, Ronald, 153
Sieghart, Paul, 59
silk, applications for, 99–100
Silkin, Sam, 189, 191
Sime Darby Group, 171–2
Simon, Sir Jocelyn, 234
Simon, Sir John, 1
Sinden, Donald, 273, 290
Singapore, 166–81; Glass Tower, 169–70
Singapore Traction Company (1964)
    Limited, 166–8
Singhivi, Dr R.M., 273
Sinnathuray, Judge T.S. (Sam), 168, 172
Skeggs, David and Anne, 296

Slater, James, 173–8
Slater Walker group, 169, 172–80
Sloman, Bob, 31, 34, 123
Slynn, Lord Justice, 191, 208, 236
Smee, Joseph, 71
Smith, Godfrey, 33, 50, 55, 56
Smith, Dr Gordon, 146
Smith, Professor J.C., 177
Smith, Maureen, 264
Soames, Sir Christopher, 147
Socialist Worker, 191
Sofer, Jonathan, 118
Sorolla y Bastida, Joaquin, 258
Sparrow, Charles, 149
Sparrow, Gerald, 128, 129, 130
Spydar Securities Limited, 173–80
Stable, Owen, 168, 172
Stagg, Colin, 252
Stanley, Poppy *see* Jolowicz, Poppy
Steare, J.C., 141
Steel, Heather, 277
Steer, Wilfred, 212
Stocker, Mr Justice and Lady, 229
Stokes, R.R., 54
Storey, Jim, 91
Straker, Michael, 205
Stratton, Dick, 190
Streatfield, Mr Justice, 68
Stuart-Smith, Murray, 111
Summerskill, Edith, 88
Summerskill, Michael, 72, 87
Sunday observance, 15–16
Supperstone, Mr Justice, 179
Sutton, Ralph, 76
Swift, Lionel, 161

Tamblyn, Ian, 169, 173
Tan Ah Tah, Mr Justice, 170
Tan Boon Teik, 169, 170, 178, 289
Tarling, Richard, 173–80
Tattersalls, 164–5
Taverne, Dick, 87, 88, 89, 120, 150, 223,
    290
Taylor, Lord Justice (Peter), 237, 245,
    259, 264, 274, 277
Templeman, Sydney, 46, 61, 118
Tenby Borough Council, 193
Teresa, Vincent, 159
Terraine, John, 89

terrorism: detainees' rights, 184–6
Thalben-Ball, George, 111
Thatcher, Margaret, 61, 257, 264
Thatcher, Mark, 257
Thesiger, Gerald, 70–1
Thomas, Dylan, 82
Thomas, H.R., 101
Thomas, Huw, 33, 65
Thomas, Peter (later Lord), 77, 114,
    140–1, 182, 183
Thomas, Richard, 209
Thomas, Stuart, 198
Thomas of Gresford, Lord, 79
Thomas of Swynnerton, Lord, 248
Thompson, Eliza, 277
Thompson, John, 85, 89
Thompson, Mr Justice (John), 106, 107,
    137
Thompson, Piers, 270
Thorneycroft, Peter, 54, 105
Thorpe, Jeremy, 49–50, 72
Tickell, Crispin and Chloe, 190
Tobin, Peter, 254
Tomorrow's Citizens' conference, 29
Traherne, Sir Cennydd, 221
Traherne, Lady, 229
Trapnell, John, 141
travellers' rights, 229–30
Trethowan, Ian, 223
Treverton-Jones, Gregory, 279
Tucker, Mr Justice (Richard), 237
Tudor Price, David, 176
Twenty-Four Hours (TV programme),
    152
Tynan, Kenneth, 53–4

Union of University Liberal Societies
    (UULS), 49
USA, 56–8, 228, 235–6

van der Gucht, Jan, 25
Vervaeke v. Smith (Messina intervening),
    214–16
Voices from Care (Cymru), 284

Wade, E.C.S., 47
Wait, John, 33
Wales: Free Wales Army, 135–9; attacks
    on English holiday homes, 223

Wales and Chester Circuit, 75–80;
    changes, 232; golden jubilee, 274
Walkingshaw, Fiona, 279, 282
Waller, Mr Justice, 162, 163–4
Wallis-Jones, Ewan, 77
Walsh, Dennis, 156
wardship, 244
Waterhouse, David (RW's grandson),
    262
Waterhouse, Doris Helena (née Gough;
    RW's mother), 5, 7, 34, 62, 113,
    261–2
Waterhouse, Ethel (RW's aunt), 4, 42
Waterhouse, Horace (RW's uncle), 4–5,
    16, 42, 113
Waterhouse, James (RW's grandson),
    262
Waterhouse, Laura (RW's daughter),
    67, 183, 188, 235, 236, 262, 277, 288,
    289, 295, 297
Waterhouse, Margaret (née Owen;
    RW's sister-in-law), 82
Waterhouse, Mark (RW's grandson),
    262
Waterhouse, Michael (RW's nephew),
    82
Waterhouse, Neil (RW's brother), 7, 17,
    23, 40, 98, 240
Waterhouse, Ronald
    GENERAL: birth, 1, 7; early life
    and education, 14–28; and wartime,
    22–4; early experience of the law, 26;
    enlists in RAFVR, 27; early public
    speaking, 29; RAF short course at
    Cambridge, 31–5; in RAF, 35–6,
    36–44; and 1945 general election,
    36; at India Office, 39–40, 43–4; Bar
    examinations, 41, 42, 59–61; visits
    Switzerland, 42; joins Middle Temple,
    42–3; at St John's College, Cambridge,
    45–58; Liberal Party activities,
    48–50; and Cambridge Union
    Society, 48, 50–6; debating tour of
    USA, 56–8; pupillage, 61; called to
    the Bar, 61–2; marshal to Croom-
    Johnson, 62–3; pupil to Mars-Jones,
    64, 66–9; joins Farrar's Building
    chambers, 70–2; fees commanded
    in early career, 72–4, 80–1, 85,

90, 100, 109, 113; and Wales and
Chester Circuit, 75–80; Ronald
Harries case, 84–5; suggests ITN job
to Robin Day, 86; and 'The Group',
87; and Suez crisis, 87–8; work
for BBC, 89; George Brookes case,
91–2; receives red bag, 92; and Lord
Goddard, 93; drink-driving cases,
95–6; and 'verbals', 96–7; licensing
cases, 100–1; holidays in Europe,
101–2; meets future wife, 102,
104; as Labour candidate for West
Flintshire, 104–5, 108–9; Flintshire
rape case, 105–6; David Lloyd case,
106–7; wedding and honeymoon,
110–12; judicial appointments, 114;
appendicitis, 114, 134; and *Private
Eye*, 115–17, 151; and Earl of Arran's
bill, 117; ETU election-rigging case,
117–19; birth of children, 119–20,
188; and *Forum* (TV series), 120;
and Labour Party politics, 120–2;
and Garrick Club, 122; NVBE
case, 124–5; Williams case, 126–7;
Glanville case, 127–8; Moors murders
case, 128–30; Aberfan inquiry,
130–4; M53 inquiry, 134–5;
takes silk, 135; Free Wales Army
case, 135–9; sheep-stealing case,
140–1; investigation into building
and development companies, 141–3;
Rimmer case, 143–4; rabies inquiry,
145–8; Connah's Quay nuclear
power station inquiry, 148–50;
Church of Scientology case, 151–3;
Associated Leisure case, 153–61, 166;
Meyer Lansky case, 159; Leo Abse
case, 160–1; Sheffield Newspapers
case, 162–4; Joseph Gaventa case,
164–5; cases in Singapore, 166–81;
Fraser and Company case, 166–9;
Fort Development case, 169–70;
Sime Darby Group case, 171–2;
Slater Walker case, 172–80; joins
council of London Zoo, 182–3, 209;
chairs Local Government Boundary
Commission for Wales, 183–4, 209;
acts as adviser to Home Secretary on
terrorist detainees, 184–6; becomes

head of chambers, 188; Paul Foot case,
191–3; Tenby Borough Council case,
193–5; obscene publications case,
196; Bridgend Urban District Council
case, 196–7; Ebbw Vale steelworks
case, 197–8; DVLA case, 198–9;
embracery case, 199–200; increased
income tax, 201–2; appointed judge
of Family Division of High Court,
179, 200, 203–7, 210–16; sits on
Employment Appeal Tribunal, 207–8,
216; helps establish citizens' advice
bureau in Royal Courts of Justice,
209–10; appointed presiding judge
of the Wales and Chester Circuit,
216–17; exchange visit to USA, 228,
235–6; mother-in-law's death, 228,
231; returns to Family Division after
term as presiding circuit judge, 233–4;
moves to Abbey Gardens and buys
Herefordshire home, 235; official
visit to European Court of Justice,
236; awarded honorary doctorate by
University of Wales, 238; brother's
death, 240; fails to be appointed
president of Family Division, 233–4,
242; transfers to Queen's Bench,
242–3; Ken Dodd trial, 249–51;
murder trials, 251–4; Hatton trial,
254–5; Roache libel trial, 255–6; Said
libel case, 257–8; Sorolla y Bastida
paintings case, 258–9; retirement
circuit tour, 259–60; mother's death,
261–2; more work for London Zoo
and Royal Courts of Justice Citizens'
Advice Bureau, 262–4; TV interview
filmed but never broadcast, 265–6;
elected Middle Temple treasurer, 260,
268–75; retirement from bench, 277;
North Wales child abuse inquiry,
278–86; moves into Middle Temple
flat, 279, 287; visits abroad, 288–9,
295–6; sits in Court of Appeal Civil
Division, 224–5, 289–90; chairman
of ISAH Ltd, 290–5, 297; moves to
Garrick Club, 295; awarded GBE,
295; heart attack, 296; Middle
Temple events, 297; eightieth birthday
celebrations, 297–8

Waterhouse, Ronald (*continued*)
    INTERESTS: music, 25, 111–12;
    sport, 27, 117; theatre, 41, 42, 81–2,
    97, 123
        OPINIONS: grammar schools,
    20; competitive sport, 24; length
    of modern cases, 124; company
    investigation procedures, 143; judges,
    195–6, 219–21, 234–5, 248–9;
    wardship, 244; children in care,
    285–6
Waterhouse, Sarah (née Ingram; RW's
    wife), 102–4, 107, 108, 110–12,
    113, 119, 125, 134, 138, 141, 150,
    166, 168, 170–1, 185, 202, 223, 229,
    230, 235–6, 248, 264, 267, 271, 277,
    295–6
Waterhouse, Sidney (RW's uncle), 2–3
Waterhouse, Sophie (RW's daughter),
    119, 123, 130, 141, 148, 159, 171,
    187, 230, 231, 235, 237, 248, 262,
    277, 288–9, 297
Waterhouse, Stuart (RW's brother), 7,
    17, 22, 22–3, 40, 48, 61, 82, 98, 105
Waterhouse, Sylvia (RW's sister), 7,
    59–60, 61, 81, 85, 86
Waterhouse, Thomas (RW's brother), 7
Waterhouse, Thomas (RW's father), 2,
    3, 4, 7, 11–13, 16, 26, 35, 36, 41, 61,
    98, 111, 112
Waterhouse, Thomas (RW's paternal
    great-grandfather), 12
Waterhouse, Thomas (RW's son), 18,
    119, 123, 138, 141, 144, 171, 187,
    189, 221–2, 230, 235, 236, 248, 261,
    262, 277, 287, 288, 297
Waterhouse, Thomas Holmes (RW's
    paternal grandfather), 2
Watkins, Tasker, 78, 114, 131, 133, 135,
    137–8, 166, 216, 221, 230, 233, 260,
    274, 298
Waugh, Auberon, 202
Weatherill, Bernard, 265
Webster, Professor John, 291, 293
Weitzman, Peter, 200
Welsh: court translation facilities,
    228–9
Welsh Schoolboys' Camp, 21–2
West, Richard, 116

*Wheatley v. London Borough of Waltham
    Forest*, 207
Wheeler, Gerald, 161
Whettam, Graham, 214
Whitby, Charles, 33
White, Eirene, 105, 109, 121
Widdicombe, David, 149
Widdup, Walter, 25
Widgery, Lord Justice, 135, 192, 193
Wien, Philip, 78, 114, 126, 128, 132
Wilberforce, Lord, 196
Williams, Emlyn, 10–11, 21, 82, 128,
    129
Williams, Francis, 79, 114
Williams, Gareth, 194, 226
Williams, Glanville, 41, 46
Williams, Gwyndaf, 90
Williams, Ian and Shirley, 223
Williams, Reverend J. Ellis, 112
Williams, J. Gwynn, 28–9, 35, 40,
    112–13
Williams, Julian, 52, 56
Williams, Norman, 126–7
Williams, Philip, 87
Williams, Stanley, 121
Williams of Mostyn, Lord, 72, 277
Wilson, Harold, 120, 121, 180
Wilson, Mr Ian, 296
Wilson, Nicholas, 276
Winn, Mr Justice, 118
Woolf, Lord Justice, 224, 225, 238, 245
Worsthorne, Peregrine, 171
Wright, Brigadier Charles, 270, 297
Wright, Jeanie, 270
Wyatt, Verushka, 170, 189–90
Wyatt, Woodrow, 118, 170, 183,
    189–90

Al-Yamamah arms deal, 257
Yandle, Tom, 294
Yates, Ivan, 55, 81, 82, 86, 87, 88, 89,
    90, 111
Yorks and Lancs Construction Co. Ltd,
    141–3

Zohar, Israel, 271
Zuckerman, Lady Joan, 146, 273
Zuckerman, Lord, 146, 147, 182–3,
    209, 231–2, 263